# The Darkest Year

ALSO BY WILLIAM K. KLINGAMAN

—

*The Year Without Summer: 1816 and the Volcano That
Darkened the World and Changed History*
(with Nicholas P. Klingaman)

*1919: The Year Our World Began*

*1929: The Year of the Great Crash*

*1941: Our Lives in a World on the Edge*

*Abraham Lincoln and the Road to Emancipation*

*Encyclopedia of the McCarthy Era*

*The First Century: Emperors, Gods, and Everyman*

# *The*
# Darkest Year

## THE AMERICAN HOME FRONT

## 1941–1942

### William K. Klingaman

ST. MARTIN'S PRESS ❧ NEW YORK

www.stmartins.com

Library of Congress Cataloging-in-Publication Data

Names: Klingaman, William K., author.
Title: The darkest year : the American home front 1941–1942 / William K.
    Klingaman.
Description: First edition. | New York : St. Martin's Press, [2019] |
    Includes bibliographical references and index.
Identifiers: LCCN 2018045704| ISBN 9781250133175 (hardcover) |
    ISBN 9781250133182 (ebook)
Subjects: LCSH: World War, 1939–1945—United States. | World War,
    1939–1945—United States—Psychological aspects. | World War,
    1939–1945—United States—Economic aspects. | World War,
    1939–1945—United States—Social aspects. | United States—
    History—1933–1945. | United States—Economic conditions—
    1918–1945. | United States—Social conditions—1933–1945. |
    United States—Social life and customs—1918–1945.
Classification: LCC D769.K55 2019 | DDC 940.53/73—dc23
LC record available at https://lccn.loc.gov/2018045704

Our books may be purchased in bulk for promotional, educational, or business use. Please contact your local bookseller or the Macmillan Corporate and Premium Sales Department at 1-800-221-7945, extension 5442, or by email at MacmillanSpecialMarkets@macmillan.com.

First Edition: February 2019

10  9  8  7  6  5  4  3  2  1

*For Noah, Richard, Henry, and Sophie*

# Contents

# Author's Note

When Americans retired for the evening on December 6, 1941, they were looking forward to a glittering holiday season, with their pockets full of cash and department stores filled with a wealth of material comforts. Although they could see the war drifting toward them from a distance, it seemed to still be a long way off. A day later, they were thrust into a conflict for which the nation was painfully unprepared.

The twelve months that followed would be, by any measure, "one of the toughest years in American history." In the Pacific theater, American military forces suffered a string of setbacks that included the loss of Wake Island, Corregidor, and the Bataan Peninsula, and a devastating naval defeat in the Java Sea. Off the Atlantic coast, German U-boats sank hundreds of American and Allied merchant ships, sometimes in full view of onlookers on eastern beaches. By the autumn of 1942, both civilian and military officials were openly acknowledging the possibility that the United States might lose the war.

On the home front, Americans did not lay aside their differences and join together in the war effort, cheerfully making whatever sacrifices the government requested. Instead, a society that was already deeply divided before the Japanese attack on Pearl Harbor splintered further as numerous interest groups sought to turn the wartime emergency to their own advantage. Blunders and repeated displays of ineptitude by the Roosevelt administration—at a time when the federal government was exercising unprecedented power over its citizens—added to the sense of anxiety and uncertainty that hung over the nation.

Goods vanished from their familiar places in American life: gasoline, rubber, sugar, coffee, and nearly anything made of metal. Heavy-handed censorship hid discouraging war news from the people, or deliberately misled them into believing the military situation was less desperate than it was. Civilian defense drills demonstrated that neither federal, state, nor local governments could protect their people; fears of sabotage led to the wholesale internment of American Japanese. Perhaps most disturbing was the disappearance of people, especially sons and husbands who entered military service—whose families could never be certain, at any given time, whether they were still alive.

This book attempts to study the psychological effects of total war on the American people, focusing on the public's state of mind as revealed not only in what Americans said, but in the day-to-day details of their behavior. It is based almost exclusively on contemporary sources, especially newspapers, magazines, diaries, letters, journals, and essays. Given the well-demonstrated unreliability of human memory, particularly regarding events which occurred years or even decades earlier, I have treated oral histories and memoirs with caution. There are, however, a number of excellent secondary sources which proved invaluable in providing both a sense of perspective and exemplary analyses of the period. In particular, I should like to acknowledge David Kennedy's *The American People in World War II*; Richard Polenberg's study *War and Society: The United States, 1941–1945*; Lynne Olson's narrative of the election of 1940, *Those Angry Days*; and Richard Reeves (*Infamy*) and Greg Robinson (*By Order of the President*) on the Roosevelt administration's decision to intern Japanese Americans. If I have shortchanged specific aspects of the home front experience—I am well aware, for instance, that I could have written far more on race relations during this period—it is because those topics more properly belong in a study of the American home front in the later years of the war.

# The Darkest Year

# Prologue

*We were slipping swiftly down the*
*shelf of time into another era in*
*the soft fall days of 1941, but we*
*had little or no awareness of it.*

—MARQUIS CHILDS

Christmas 1941 was shaping up to be the most delightful holiday season
Americans had enjoyed in a long time. After more than a decade, the
economy was finally emerging from the Great Depression, a recovery
fueled by the Roosevelt administration's rapid expansion of defense
spending over the past eighteen months. Hard times vanished in munitions factories, shipyards, and aircraft plants. Americans had never had so
much money to spend in their lives.

In the first week of December, department store owners expected "the
biggest Christmas rush in United States history," and so they greeted customers with display windows filled with a dazzling array of gift ideas. Fur
coats seemed to be everywhere: Russian ermine, Japanese mink, blended
sable capes, and silver fox jackets. ("A good long-term investment, no
matter how you look at it," chirped one ad. "She'll love it!") There were
silk dinner pajamas, and waist-length ostrich capes with crepe linings;
women's blouses covered with sequins, and nightgowns with tiny embroi-
dered rabbits riding bicycles down the front. Masses of glitter were stuck
to everything from V-neck jackets to black crepe evening dresses.

Wise men purchased at least several pairs of hosiery for their wives and
girlfriends—a sudden war scare with Japan over the summer had provoked panic buying of stockings, and merchants warned that they were

facing "the vanishing last few yards of silk." Jewelry with oversize semi-precious stones was in fashion, along with watches of red gold and, for those on a budget, silver bangle bracelets with animal charms. Chanel announced it was still possible to buy its famous perfume, although stocks were starting to run low now that the German army had occupied Paris. Another option came from Russia—a new perfume that came in a bottle shaped like a tank, with turrets and all. To ease the anxieties of gentlemen whose knees buckled at the prospect of buying gifts of intimate apparel for women, one store on Fifth Avenue in Manhattan hosted a "stag party," where two dozen young models demonstrated how negligees, lingerie, furs, and jewels might look (more or less) on their customers' sweethearts; more than a thousand appreciative men attended.

Perhaps it was time to replace the family radio with a new set capable of receiving one of the new frequency-modulation stations that provided high-fidelity, static-free programs. A year earlier, there had been no FM radio stations in the United States; by December 1941 there were twenty-two. RCA Victor offered a combination radio-phonograph with a "Magic Brain" that automatically played records on both sides without turning them over, a useful feature if one was listening to the recently released three-disc performance of Ronald Colman as Ebenezer Scrooge in Dickens's *A Christmas Carol*. ("Though one might think Colman was miscast," reported *Newsweek*, "he performs nobly.") RCA apologized to its customers, however, for the shortage of new sets on store shelves; as the government increasingly allocated raw materials for defense needs, the company was forced to cut back production of civilian goods.

Those who wished to listen directly to the latest war news from Europe could purchase radios with overseas dials or international bands. And a fortunate few in select markets (primarily in New York City) enjoyed the option of "the modern magic of television." Combination radio-television receivers started at $159.95 and went up to $550; or one could simply buy a "picture receiver" and plug it into a compatible radio with a special adapter. In Manhattan, the NBC and Columbia networks each broadcast several hours of programming most days from their studios—the transmissions were available within a fifty-mile radius of the city—along with occasional sporting events such as baseball, boxing, basketball, or professional football, although there seem to have been no plans to televise the upcoming showdown between the New York Giants and Brooklyn Dodgers in the final week of NFL regular season games, scheduled for Sunday, December 7.

One week into the Christmas shopping season, consumers were buying gifts at a record pace. "Furious local counter attacks are now raging," declared the *Chicago Tribune*, as customers battled in stores for prized merchandise. In Washington, authorities assigned seventy-two additional policemen and -women to the shopping district to handle the crowds. The U.S. Department of Commerce predicted that Christmas retail sales nationwide would reach $5.5 billion, 15 percent higher than the previous mark set in the last pre-Depression year of 1929. For the entire year of 1941, retail sales were expected to surpass $54 billion, nearly 20 percent more than 1940, and 11 percent greater than 1929.

"Enhanced income and the prospects immediately ahead are the major factors influencing the expansion in consumer purchasing this year," declared a Commerce Department report, and few could blame American consumers for feeling bullish about the future. Nearly every economic indicator inspired optimism. More than 3 million new workers had been added to business payrolls over the previous year, sending the total number of trade and industrial wage earners over the 42 million mark for the first time in the nation's history. Federal unemployment benefit payments declined every month, and by October 1941, fewer Americans were receiving jobless benefits than at any time since the program began. Driven by higher wage rates and lots of overtime hours in defense plants, national income was approaching $100 billion, more than $20 billion above the 1929 record.

Agricultural prices were rising, and farmers' income was up by $2 billion over 1940, finally returning to pre-Depression levels. At long last "farm people," as the *Baltimore Sun* noted, "are able to join in the Christmas buying on a generous scale." Add the nearly 2 million men serving in the armed forces, who received a steady if not particularly generous income from Uncle Sam, and undoubtedly, concluded the *Sun*, "there are more people in position to do Christmas shopping . . . than ever before in our history."

Returning prosperity lifted corporate profits in virtually every corner of the American business world. United States Steel reported earnings for the first three quarters of the year more than 30 percent higher than 1940, and steel industry payrolls set new records. Railroads carried more freight in November 1941 than in any month since the Depression began; railway executives estimated their net income for the year would top $400 million, the highest in a decade. Oil production boomed as industrial and consumer demand for gasoline soared. Cotton textile production from January through October had already surpassed the total of any previous year. *Time* magazine claimed that 1941 represented the biggest year ever for phonograph record sales, "in spite of the present low grade of popular tunes."

More new homes were built in the United States from January through October than in any year since 1929. Restaurants nationwide enjoyed their thirty-first consecutive month of increased business. Racetracks took in $517.4 million in parimutuel wagers, an increase of more than $100 million over 1940 (thereby earning state governments an additional $5 million for their share of the take). Domestic airline travel in the first ten months of 1941 surged 30 percent above the previous year. Department store sales in Los Angeles were up sharply; Sears, Roebuck and Company declared its profits were at the highest level in its history; and Pepsi-Cola basked in profits nearly 50 percent above 1941.

Looking back over the first eleven months of the year, one observer noted that "the country lived better in 1941 than it ever had before." As a result, more Americans decided that they could afford to get married. Applications for marriage licenses ran at a record pace in Chicago and its suburbs in the first nine months of 1941, and Washington, D.C., easily surpassed its previous annual mark. At one point in June, New York State nearly ran out of blank marriage license forms. "The consistent increase of marriages is due mainly to the defense program," explained a spokesman for New York's Marriage Record Bureau. "We find the rate fluctuates pretty much with economic conditions." Unfortunately, so did the divorce rate. "Prosperity has an unhappy effect upon many marriages," lamented a state official in New Jersey, where the number of divorces approached an all-time annual high. Americans' consumption of alcoholic beverages also rose as the economy recovered, an effect experts attributed to higher wages, the need to relax after working longer hours, and "the psychological effects of the war" in Europe. But the nation's prison population was dwindling. The rising standard of living produced a drop in crimes against property, and the growing need for labor encouraged parole boards to release their less dangerous prisoners; Chicago authorities paroled twice as many prisoners in 1941 as they had in the previous year.

"Insofar as trade is concerned, the Christmas outlook is rosy," concluded a *Baltimore Sun* editorial, "and if trade is any indication the holiday season itself will be rosy too. This may be a small benefit, but at a time when there are so many problems and so many dangers, it is something to the good." Those dangers—the threat that the United States would be pulled into the war in Europe, or forced to brake Japanese aggression in East Asia—lent an almost wistful quality to Americans' preparations for Christmas in 1941. "This will be a Christmas full of compassion for the unfortunates of the world," wrote one hopeful midwesterner, "mixed with Thanksgiving that we have been spared the sufferings of Europe." But anyone who could read a headline knew that this might be the last peacetime Christmas the nation would know for a long time. "Now we see the distant fire rolling toward us," warned newspaper columnist Raymond Clapper. "It is not being put out. It is still some distance away, but the evil wind blows it towards us."

Hence President Franklin D. Roosevelt's decision to move the annual national Christmas tree lighting ceremony from the spacious but sterile Washington Mall to his backyard, formally known as the White House South Lawn. Christmas trees held a special place in Roosevelt's heart—the president still maintained a profitable tree farm on his property in Hyde Park, New York, and gave away evergreens to his friends each December—and a year earlier he and his wife, Eleanor, had decided to move the 1941 lighting ceremony inside the White House gates, to give it a more "homey" feel and encourage a spirit of neighborliness among the thousands of ordinary Americans expected to attend. The Roosevelts planned to lead the gathering in singing four well-known Christmas carols as part of the hour-long proceedings (previously, the public had not been invited to sing along), and the *Washington Post* agreed to print a leaflet with the lyrics ahead of time. In fact, the *Post* desired to make this holiday "a caroling Christmas," to use traditional music to promote "that feeling of camaraderie which is only too acutely needed now."

Somehow it all seemed to blend with the nation's preparedness program, which by early December had made military images and slogans a part of Americans' everyday lives. "I am astonished," reported one observer, "at the frequency with which the word 'defense' is used in reading matter and even in advertisements." Some of the commercial messages actually made sense. "A strong automobile industry is the backbone of defense," argued Plymouth. "Buick Builds for Defense," claimed General Motors, which added that its trucks were "Partners in Power for the Nation's Defense." B. F. Goodrich touted its research into synthetic rubber; the Chesapeake and Ohio Railroad boasted that its trains rushed goods to Army bases; Bendix promoted the brakes, carburetors, and starters it built for military vehicles. Dodge perhaps stepped over the line when it claimed that "when you decide to buy a new Dodge motor car or truck, you actually assist in the maintenance of this vast and essential production system for National Defense." Other advertisements seemed shamelessly opportunistic: "In cigarettes, as in dive bombers, it's modern design that counts!" (Pall Mall); "A *new* defense weapon [against] the bomb of vitamin deficiency" (Fleischmann's yeast); "Marines Beat Tough Scrapes—with COOL SHAVES" (Ingram shave cream); "WAR on red rough hands" (Barrington hand cream); "ACTION NOW—While Time Is On Our Side" (Dixie Cups); and "National Unity is the Gift We Want *This* Christmas" (Parker fountain pens).

Anne Morrow Lindbergh, wife of famed aviator Charles Lindbergh (who had become a leading spokesman for the isolationist cause), found the spectacle disgraceful. "All the billboards have gone 'Defense' mad, with pictures of soldiers and sailors on them," she wrote in her diary after a trip to New York. "*Vogue* photographs its models in front of Bundles for Britain planes. Longchamps [an upscale restaurant chain] has V's done in vegetables in the windows. Elizabeth Arden gets out a V for Victory lipstick." To Anne Lindbergh, the shops along Fifth Avenue in early December were "nauseating with the richness of material attractions. What appalled me was not so much the unawareness of people skating about on the thin surface of materialism as the insincere attempt to gild the materialism with patriotic motives, especially in advertising. 'Be brave with Diamonds,' 'Defense of good taste—Buy So-and-so's Ale.' 'For the service of America . . .'"

Military motifs also invaded the $30 million Christmas card industry, most notably in the introduction of cards that included an album for defense stamps (essentially inexpensive versions of defense bonds). The cards themselves featured familiar American images on the front—Uncle Sam, a bald eagle, or a Minuteman—and bore inscriptions such as "A Patriotic Gift with Best Christmas Wishes," or "A Tip From Uncle Sam with Christmas Greetings." The sender could then purchase (separately) and paste in as many ten-cent defense stamps as desired as gifts. There were also cards designed especially for servicemen ("Hope You 'Fall In' for a Merry Christmas, Sailor!"), and others that replaced Santa's sleigh with Army planes. And for those who objected to the cost of the administration's preparedness program, one card complained that "We pay a tax on holly, / We pay a tax on 'cheer,' / We pay a tax on 'livin' / All through the dog-gone year! / We pay a tax on workin' / We pay a tax on playin' / But anyway I'm thankful / There ain't no tax on sayin' / Merry Christmas!"

But nowhere were the effects of the nation's military preoccupation more visible than in the stores' displays of children's toys, particularly for boys. (Girls retained their traditional preference for dolls, especially the new "Magic Skin" dolls—"Touch it, and it warms under your startled hand . . . expose it to the sun, and, by golly, it tans!"—although dolls with Red Cross nurses' outfits were more popular than in previous years.) Kids could use a combination toy searchlight and antiaircraft gun to hunt for enemy planes in the sky, or slow advancing imaginary tanks with child-size howitzers that used a spring mechanism to fire real projectiles. Toy tommy guns that formerly battled gangsters morphed into home-defense guns to fend off invading troops. Miniature battleships and submarines that really dove underwater kept bathtubs free of foreign foes. Buck Rogers outfits and American Indian costumes disappeared as younger boys, especially, chose to dress up as soldiers. One firm promoted its "Boys' Complete Military Playsuits" for ages four to fourteen, complete with khaki jacket, trousers, and cap, along with a Sam Browne belt, holster, and gun. And toy soldiers appeared in every conceivable guise: parachute troops, pilots, infantrymen, antiaircraft gunners, and stretcher bearers carrying tiny stretchers; there were even miniature sandbags and wire barricades in case of air raids.

# 1: Before Pearl

## SEPTEMBER 1939–DECEMBER 1941

*There has probably never been a time of such
confused prophecy, no time when the nation
has been led so frantically in so many
directions at once.*

— *THE NEW YORKER*, JUNE 1940

When the war in Europe began in September 1939, it seemed unlikely
that the conflict would provoke dramatic changes in American society.
Americans were united in their desire to avoid involvement in the fighting; public opinion polls revealed that more than 80 percent of the nation's
voters opposed entry into the war—a number that would remain remark-
ably stable over the following two years.

In fact, many Americans had spent the past two decades resolutely
ignoring the rest of the world. "Throughout most of my childhood there
had always been war," recalled Russell Baker, then a teenager growing up
in Baltimore. "Dimly, I had been aware through all those years that worlds
were burning, but they seemed far away. It wasn't my world that was on
fire, nor was it ever likely to be, or so I thought. Sheltered by two great
oceans, America seemed impregnable. I was like a person on a summer
night seeing heat lightning far out on the horizon and murmuring, 'Must
be a bad storm way over there someplace.' It was not my storm."

Americans' views of the European conflict also were colored by memories of the nation's participation in the First World War. Anyone over
thirty years old could remember when the United States declared war on

Germany in 1917, an experience that most Americans came to regard as a mistake. Widely publicized congressional hearings in the mid-1930s strengthened the popular perception that the Wilson administration had entered the war at the behest of bankers and arms merchants eager to protect their loans and profits; accordingly, between 1935 and 1937 Congress passed a series of measures known collectively as the Neutrality Acts, which prohibited American citizens from selling "arms, ammunition, or implements of war" to belligerent nations, or making loans to their governments, or traveling on ships of nations at war.

In the autumn of 1939, the embargo on American arms sales clearly favored Nazi Germany, which possessed an impressive advantage in military hardware over France and Britain. Most Americans, however, favored the Allied cause, partly because they believed that a victorious Hitler would sooner or later launch a war against the United States, but also because they had no illusions about the brutal nature of the Nazi regime. "There are few save propagandists and crackpots," observed the *Baltimore Sun*, "who regard the ethics of Herr Hitler and his entourage with anything but a contempt which frequently becomes loathing."

To redress the balance, Roosevelt asked Congress to repeal the ban on arms sales. The president had promised the American people that there would be "no blackout of peace" in the United States, and strengthening Britain and France seemed to provide the best chance of keeping the United States out of the war. In mid-September 1939, more than 60 percent of Americans supported arms sales to the Allies—on a cash-and-carry basis, to avoid endangering American lives, ships, and investments— largely because they hoped the increased production of war material would give a boost to the American economy, still plagued by high unemployment and sluggish economic growth despite six years of New Deal initiatives.

Nevertheless, Roosevelt's proposal to repeal the arms ban ran into the determined opposition of a vocal minority of congressmen (primarily from the Midwest), who warned that selling weapons to the Allies would drag the nation into the war by provoking retaliation by Germany. "I frankly question," said Republican senator Arthur Vandenberg of Michigan, "whether we can become an arsenal for one belligerent without being the target for the other." They were backed by a well-organized lobbying campaign that flooded legislative offices with letters, petitions, and telegrams, including a single-day record of 487,000 pieces of mail (mostly from women and clergymen) on September 19. Protests on Capitol Hill grew so impassioned that the Department of Justice dispatched a half dozen FBI agents to protect pro-repeal congressmen against demonstrators.

While Congress debated cash-and-carry, news of the war brought the world suddenly very close at hand to Americans. Newspapers carried page after page of the latest dispatches from Europe. Radio, which had been in its infancy in 1917, became a constant companion—"the box we live in," wrote one observer—and reports of the Wehrmacht's crushing victories in Poland gave rise to a new and disturbing form of entertainment known as a radio sandwich: "two bars of music with an ominous voice in between." Even programs of Muzak in elevators interrupted the usual soothing selections from Victor Herbert with bulletins on the war.

As Americans grew increasingly aware that events abroad could become the determining factor in their immediate destinies, a brief moment of panic ensued. Housewives began to hoard food, especially sugar. Towns up and down the East Coast reported sightings of submarines, and one group of fishermen two hundred miles off the coast of Massachusetts swore that "a big, gray plane with swastikas on its wings had circled their fleet twice before putting back for Europe." In department stores, mothers snatched toy pistols and soldiers out of their children's hands, and substituted footballs or a Wizard of Oz doll instead.

"We try to reconcile the cheerful and familiar details of our life with news that may well mean the end of all of them, but it is too soon," noted the *New Yorker.* "The ten million men who will die are still an arbitrary figure, an estimate from another war; the children who will be starved or bombed belong to people we can never know, the bombs themselves will fall only on strange names on a map." In fact, a Rand McNally spokesman reported that in the first twenty-four hours of the war, the company sold more maps in the United States than it had since 1918; Macy's book department in downtown Manhattan sold more maps than in any week in the store's history.

On Wall Street, investment firms encouraged their customers to buy shares of steel companies. "The machines of war are being continually destroyed," one financier observed, "and replacements use up tremendous additional quantities of steel." Others predicted similar opportunities amid the wartime dislocations of trade. "Unquestionably, war is going to require a lot of imports into England and France," noted one New York businessman, "and that's going to mean business here and all over the United States. Factories are going to boom and smoke's going to come out of stacks. That is, if we're allowed to ship."

And they were. In early October, three weeks of congressional debate ended with both houses approving repeal of the arms embargo by margins of nearly two to one. By that time, any sense of urgency had vanished as the fighting in Europe slowed to a standstill. For the next six months, military operations paused while the German high command completed its preparations for the invasion of western Europe. Americans relaxed. "The fatalistic feeling that if a great war came we would inevitably be drawn into it has subsided," reported columnist Ernest Lindley.

Then the Wehrmacht's blitzkrieg tore through Europe. Norway and Denmark fell in April. In May, German troops slashed through the Netherlands and Belgium. ("The terrible geography lesson goes on," murmured one American journal.) Day after day in that nightmare month, radio networks in the United States delivered "the brisk, cultivated voices of studio announcers giving us a few hints of the end of the world between dance tunes," until weary listeners came to believe that "the only good radio is a dead radio."

"It was like a newsreel of history which should have marched at a sober pace so that men everywhere would know what was happening," recalled journalist Marquis Childs, "and instead it whirred crazily through the cosmic projector. . . . It was like standing in a familiar house that has had one side blasted away. Everything is normal, or almost normal. Life goes on. . . . But nothing is the same nor ever can be again. The light falls in the familiar rooms in a new harsh way so that what has been safe and comfortable now looks naked and unprotected." The almost contemptuous ease with which German forces rolled over, around, and through the British and French armies surprised everyone—in both Europe and the United States—and forced Americans to confront the possibility that they might have to face the Nazi war machine alone if the Allies collapsed. "Only a miracle," wrote columnist Walter Lippmann, "can now prevent the European war from becoming a world war. . . . Our security is gravely jeopardized."

Suddenly the condition of American defenses became the most vital topic in the nation. "Congress and the country," reported *Time* magazine, "had no eyes nor ears for anything but Defense." Bipartisan majorities in both houses hastily passed or even increased every emergency defense spending bill Roosevelt lay before them. In the space of a few weeks, Congress approved over $3 billion in additional military appropriations, far surpassing defense expenditures in any fiscal year in the nation's history. At one point, the House gave the Roosevelt administration a virtual blank check, voting 391–1 in favor of "an unlimited expansion of Army warplane strength and unlimited funds for speeding production of munitions and supplies."

Public opinion overwhelmingly supported the accelerated defense program. A survey by *Fortune* magazine revealed that 93.6 percent of Americans favored spending "whatever is necessary to build up as quickly as possible our Army, Navy, and Air Force." But the consensus broke down over whether the United States should continue to sell arms to Britain and France—in hopes of keeping the anti-German coalition afloat and the war three thousand miles away—or hoard all its weapons at home to construct a (hopefully) invulnerable Fortress America. The debate was no less bitter for the fact that most of the armaments in question were entirely imaginary, since the actual output of American defense plants was still "largely in the blueprint stage."

Leading Republicans almost unanimously opposed shipping any more arms abroad. New York City district attorney Thomas E. Dewey, the frontrunner for the Republican presidential nomination, demanded that the United States concentrate on building up its military forces "to levels which will make this country impregnable to attack." Former president Herbert Hoover, who was making his own belated bid for the Republican nomination, agreed that "what America must have is such defenses that no European nation will even think about crossing this 3,000 miles of ocean at all. . . . We want a sign of 'keep off the grass' with a fierce dog plainly in sight." For his part, famed aviator Charles Lindbergh—the second most famous man in America, behind only Roosevelt—told a nationwide radio audience that "we need not fear a foreign invasion unless

American peoples bring it on through their own quarreling and meddling with affairs abroad. . . . No one wishes to attack us, and no one is in a position to do so." (Listening to Lindbergh's speech, Roosevelt decided it might as easily have come from Nazi propaganda minister Joseph Goebbels. "I am absolutely convinced," the president told Secretary of the Treasury Henry Morgenthau, "that Lindbergh is a Nazi.")

Roosevelt had no intention of abandoning the Allies, although the surrender of the French armies on June 17 left him to rely entirely upon what one veteran diplomat called "the slow-grinding will power of the British people." To marshal public support for the president's policy, publisher Henry Luce used his magazines to illustrate in a graphic way the horrors of Hitler's bloody march across Europe, and veteran Kansas newspaper editor William Allen White—a lifelong Republican—helped organize the Committee to Defend America by Aiding the Allies. Among the ten thousand Americans who joined the committee in the first few months were columnist Joseph Alsop, former heavyweight champion Gene Tunney, diplomat Dean Acheson, novelist Rex Stout, Wall Street attorney Allen Dulles, and playwright Robert Sherwood, who predicted that unless the rest of the world united against the fascist aggressors, "we are all headed back to the Dark Ages in a hand basket."

By late June, the ongoing debate and the continual stream of bad news from Europe was taking its toll on the well-being of the American public. Contemporary observers reported a mood of "bleak despair," of "gloom and terror" among "a nation not sure of its way." The fall of France struck a particularly heavy blow. "We looked at the faces in the street today," wrote a reporter in the *New Yorker,* "and war is at last real." At a time when most Americans went to the movies at least twice a week, the latest newsreels in theaters displayed in graphic detail "all the horrors of this 'total war,'" including Nazi bombings of civilian targets such as maternity hospitals. ("SEE the 'Panzer' Armored Divisions striking swiftly," boasted one advertisement. "SEE the helpless refugees fleeing for their lives.")

Patients whose nerves had been "blitzkrieged by the war" crowded doctors' offices. Psychiatrists in New York City treated a significant number of new patients who complained of "a general state of 'jittery' nerves," as if awaiting some type of apocalyptic reckoning. At the annual convention of the American Medical Association in June, physicians from all parts of the country reported a surge in cases of "headaches of unexplained origin, digestive disturbances, insomnia, loss of appetite, respiratory ills and aggravation of chronic ailments." The most likely cause, the doctors agreed, was a "repeated shock to the nervous system from a succession of bad news over the radio and in the newspapers."

A majority of Americans expected Britain to collapse or surrender; many braced for a German attack on the United States. Pennsylvania officials established a special legislative committee to bolster protection of the state's factories, mines, and naval yards against enemy air raids. In Chicago, members of the American Police Revolver League joined with several hundred skeet shooters to form the Sportsmen's Defense Reserve, a model for a prospective nationwide "civilian army of modern minute men." Middle-aged patriots on the Pacific coast launched a special defense unit composed entirely of men over the age of forty-five, whose official slogan was "Death Before Surrender." Not to be outdone, the Manhattan chapter of the National Legion of Mothers of America founded the Molly Pitcher Rifle Legion (target practice held once a week) and called for the establishment of women's rifle corps in every state to pick off German paratroopers. "Enemy parachutists in America," declared a National Legion official, "will rue the day they first drew breath."

Reports that "fifth columnists"—Nazi supporters or sympathizers amid the populations of the defeated western European nations—had helped prepare the way for the German blitzkrieg convinced many Americans that they needed to keep a closer watch on the nearly 4 million aliens living in the United States. To help uncover potential saboteurs, Congress voted to require all resident aliens to be registered and fingerprinted. When Attorney General Robert Jackson asked the public to report "acts, threats, or evidences of sabotage [or] espionage" to the FBI's newly created "national defense investigation" unit, the Bureau's switchboards were flooded with several thousand tips a day. Throngs of enthusiastic patriots volunteered to spy on their neighbors on a regular basis. Local governments assigned special guards to protect bridges, tunnels, and highways near defense plants, and dropped aliens from their unemployment relief rolls. The Federal Communications Commission forbade amateur radio operators in the United States from maintaining communication with any foreign stations. George Britt's recently published book, *The Fifth Column*

*Is Here*—which claimed there were more than a million fifth columnists in the United States, including native-born fascists and members of the German American Bund—soared to the top of the bestseller list, and the meeting places of several German fraternal organizations were bombed (Chicago) or burned down (St. Louis). "America isn't going to be any too comfortable a place to live in during the immediate future," wrote Secretary of the Interior Harold Ickes in his diary. "Some of our super-patriots are simply going crazy."

Revelations of the woeful condition of U.S. military forces did not ease Americans' anxieties. Two decades of budgetary neglect by both political parties had left the nation with an infantry that one critic dismissed as "a muleback army hardly large enough for an Indian campaign." In an extensive critique published in late 1938, *Life* magazine had concluded that "among the armies of the major powers, America's is not only the smallest but the worst equipped; most of its arms are outmoded World War [One] leftovers; some of its post-War weapons are already, in the military sense, obsolete; it has developed up-to-date weapons, but has far too few of them for modern war; if America should be attacked, it would be eight months before the nation's peacetime industry could be converted to production of the war supplies which the Army would need; whether there would be any Army left to supply at the end of those months is disputable."

Germany's springtime blitzkrieg made it perfectly clear just how far behind the United States really was. "The coordination between air and ground, tanks and motorized infantry, exceeded anything we had ever dreamed of in the U.S. Army," recalled Omar Bradley, then an officer serving under Army chief of staff General George Catlett Marshall. "We were amazed, shocked, dumbfounded, shaking our heads in disbelief. . . . To match such a performance, let alone exceed it, the U.S. Army had years of catching up and little time in which to do it." General Henry "Hap" Arnold, chief of the Army Air Corps, made a similarly glum assessment about American air power during a briefing to a Senate committee. "The German planes have opened the eyes of the War Department," reported one senator after hearing Arnold's testimony. "In the purely combat field, we do not have planes that could stand up against the German fighters."

Thus far Army officials had focused on acquiring new and better weapons, but the fall of France also fueled the movement for conscription, to provide a reservoir of trained manpower the nation could call upon in an emergency. Marshall estimated that the Army would need at least 1.2 million men to defend the continental United States from a direct attack, and several million more to protect the Western Hemisphere. In the summer of 1940, however, there were fewer than 250,000 regular soldiers in the U.S. Army. With enlistments running about 20,000 per month—and a pay scale that began at twenty-one dollars a month (plus food, housing, and health care)—the president's military advisers concluded that there was no way to reach their goal anytime soon without a draft.

Yet the United States had never resorted to compulsory military service in peacetime. The notion struck many Americans—who shared an inherent suspicion of the military—as undemocratic, a violation of individual liberties, the sort of thing oppressive European governments imposed on their citizens. Even the worldly *Washington Post*, a strong supporter of aid to Britain, expressed reservations about "the un-American principle of compulsion."

Opposing conscription was a disparate coalition of groups that *Time* magazine called "as weird a hash as was ever dumped on Washington": isolationists, labor union leaders, clergymen, college students, civil libertarians, communists, and pacifists. Most dismissed the prospect of an imminent German invasion as fantasy; "the only emergency," declared Senator Burton Wheeler of Montana, "is the one created by propagandists who are trying to frighten Congress and the country." To opponents of the draft, peacetime conscription represented "the use of totalitarian methods to safeguard us from totalitarianism," and "the opening wedge to pure and unadulterated fascism." In the Senate, Nebraska Republican-turned-independent George Norris predicted that conscription and an expanded Army would lead to an American dictatorship with a population of men trained in "how to fight and how to kill," and "women working in the fields to support a huge military machine." Burton Wheeler foresaw an even more lurid future for the United States once a broad swath of the population had completed military training. "You will have a country of Al Capones. You will have a country where robbery and murder will run riot," he declared. "Hushed whispers will replace free speech—secret meetings in dark places will supplant free assemblage."

Congressional mail ran heavily against the draft; anticonscription zealots packed the legislative galleries; women dressed in black veils kept a silent vigil each day outside the Senate chamber; and a group that called itself the Congress of American Mothers hanged a coconut-headed effigy of Senator Claude Pepper of Florida—an outspoken critic of Hitler, Lindbergh, and isolationism in general—on the Capitol lawn. In a less violent protest, an attractive twenty-year-old college sophomore who called herself "Pauline Revere" set out to ride a white horse from her home in Seattle, Washington, to the nation's capital, bearing a petition against conscription on behalf of the Emergency Peace Mobilizing Committee to Defend America by Keeping Out of War. (The young lady actually traveled most of the way by automobile, disembarking in cities along the way for photo opportunities with local equines.)

But flamboyant theatrics could not overcome the public's desire for security. Polls indicated a rapidly increasing majority of Americans in favor of conscription—from 39 percent in October 1939 to 66 percent in late July 1940—and on September 15, Congress approved the Selective Service Act, requiring all American men between the ages of twenty-one and thirty-five to register for the draft. The measure included an amendment, however, that prohibited the 800,000 draftees who would be called in the first year from serving outside the Western Hemisphere, except in territories of the United States.

The past year's battles over cash-and-carry, conscription, and aid to the Allies had left Americans sharply divided, with a substantial minority fearful that the nation was on the brink of being pulled into the European war. Many of the same citizens were convinced that Franklin Roosevelt—having vastly enlarged the powers of the federal government, and particularly the executive branch during the New Deal—planned to overthrow democracy in the United States and establish a dictatorship by appointing enough judges and hiring enough bureaucrats to quash any threats to his imperial whims. The president's decision in the summer of 1940 to run for an unprecedented third term only deepened their anxiety.

Although Roosevelt possessed the largest and most devoted following of any American politician of his generation, he also had engendered the enmity of the wealthy classes and a significant portion of the business community. The president had spent much of the past eight years—and particularly his second term—excoriating businessmen publicly ("privileged princes of new economic dynasties"), as well as investigating them, regulating them, taxing them, stripping them of political power, and throwing the weight of the White House behind organized labor's efforts to unionize American industry. "To many of his own class he was the figure of evil personified," recalled Marquis Childs, "a personal devil symbolizing the forces that were stirring deeply in American life." As a result, there existed "in a large and powerful class of our citizens, an almost universal suspicion as to the ulterior purposes of the government." No wonder that the business community desired "above everything else in the world that some person other than 'F.D.R.' were president."

To challenge Roosevelt in November, Republicans nominated the forty-eight-year-old Wendell Willkie, a former Wall Street attorney and utility company executive who had never run for public office, much less held one. Articulate, charismatic (in a rumpled midwestern sort of way), and exceptionally well-read, Willkie supported much of the New Deal—although he wished to reduce the federal government's role in the economy—and favored further aid to Britain, particularly since the immediate threat of a German invasion across the Channel had passed by the autumn of 1940. Unable to separate himself substantially from Roosevelt on either domestic or foreign policy, Willkie hammered repeatedly on the third-term issue, hoping to attract Democrats who felt uneasy about the president's ambitions. Democratic spokesmen responded by pointing to the recent revival of the American economy (unemployment had dropped to 9 percent by October), and reminding voters of the value of Roosevelt's experience while the nation faced a dangerously combustible situation abroad.

It seemed a rather tame affair until Willkie began to portray Roosevelt as a warmonger who "manufactured emergencies" to scare American voters into reelecting him. "This administration is rapidly pushing us toward war," Willkie charged in a radio address in early October, "and also is pushing us toward a totalitarian state." (With his Indiana accent, it came out "totalitairrn.") Alf Landon, who had lost to Roosevelt in 1936, warned voters that if they returned the president to the White House for a third term, "the bells throughout the country should toll for a people who have lost their liberties of their own free choice." Labor leader John L. Lewis, president of the Congress of Industrial Organizations (CIO) and a former Roosevelt ally, warned American mothers that the president—"a man who plays with the lives of human beings for a pastime"—intended to "make cannon fodder of your sons."

Democrats accordingly lowered their own punches, accusing Willkie of planning to impose "an American brand of fascism" in alliance with Big Business. At every turn, they strove to associate Willkie, whose parents had emigrated from Germany, with Hitler and the Nazi regime. They spoke of Willkie's "blitzkrieg tactics," whispered that the Republican candidate was "practically a German," and assured voters that "Nazi agents in this country have been ordered to work for his election." A Willkie victory, claimed Democratic vice-presidential nominee Henry Wallace, "would cause Hitler to rejoice."

As election day neared, the *New York Times* reported that "American opinion is today moving 'away' from the war. . . . The public demand that this country stay out of the war . . . is becoming louder and louder." Willkie responded with a promise "not to send your husbands and sons and brothers to death on a European or Asiatic battlefield." On October 30, Roosevelt made a similar pledge—one he surely knew he could not keep— when he told an audience in Boston that "your boys are not going to be sent into any foreign wars."

In the end, more voters trusted than feared Roosevelt, although the president's share of the popular vote was the smallest of any winning candidate since 1916, and at least one post-election poll suggested that voters actually would have preferred Willkie had there been no war in Europe. To columnist Raymond Clapper, it seemed "a return to power voted by many with reluctance and with strong inner doubts."

"There was a sense of relief that a bitter election was over," reported *Time*, although some observers feared the hardening divisions among Americans would prevent the public from uniting behind the president. "Men have been wondering," noted one writer, "whether campaign eggs would turn into bricks and bricks into bombs." To speed the process of reconciliation, William Allen White suggested that partisans on both sides dump all of their campaign literature and buttons into huge piles and set them alight, turning them into giant bonfires to exorcise the passions of the election. (At least one town—Salina, Kansas—took him up on the suggestion.) On every print of new motion pictures, Hollywood studios appended a plea for Americans to transcend partisan animosities and come together. And in New York, a bipartisan group calling itself the Council for Democracy held an "America United" rally at a sold-out Carnegie Hall, with politicians, columnists, labor leaders, and entertainers delivering speeches broadcast over a nationwide radio network. "We have all had our say," concluded novelist Booth Tarkington, but "when the strangers with guns begin to surround a house it is time for the family inside to stop arguing."

And for a brief moment they did. Britain's stubborn survival permitted Americans to breathe a sigh of relief in the final months of 1940. They relegated war scares to the back burner for the holiday season, replacing them with more measured talk of defense and preparedness, and sought comfort in patriotic symbols. Christmas gifts promoting "Americanism" dominated the department store shelves: jewelry with red, white, and blue stones; children's balls, kites, and drums decorated with eagles, American flags, or the Liberty Bell; and scenes of American landmarks everywhere. Crowds thronged Bedloe's Island in New York Bay to see the Statue of Liberty in person; attendance in November 1940 was up 42 percent over the previous year. "They keep hearing 'God Bless America,'" explained a guard at the site. "That sends them over here." Unlike ordinary times, however, many of the visitors were native New Yorkers. Instead of asking how to get to Sing Sing, or whether the Hudson River runs into Hudson Bay, they gazed at the Manhattan skyline and talked about harbor defenses and bomb shelters.

Hostesses eschewed previously popular entertainments such as "headline parties"—where guests dressed up as world leaders—or war games with elaborate military costumes. "Older folk are rather fed up with playing at war," reported a New England newspaper. Instead, they wanted "something that could insure a few hours off . . . to shut out the great conflicts in the world." Sales of hobby kits soared; others preferred to relax reading the latest adventures of Superman, the comic book character who had taken the nation by storm in 1938. The widespread desire to escape, concluded one cultural critic, represented "a determination to cling to sanity":

"It is next to impossible to be entirely aloof from the war in such a time as this. It is, however, very necessary to have some sort of bomb shelter for the mind."

And yet reminders of war—and the growing military presence in American life—appeared with increasing frequency. The draft was easily the most visible. More than 16 million men (including Henry Ford II, Winthrop Rockefeller, actors Jimmy Stewart and Henry Fonda, heavy-weight champion Joe Louis, and three Philadelphians named Rudolph Valentino) had registered for the draft in October without protest, an accomplishment that demonstrated just how far the nation had traveled during the past year. "Had some forecaster of say June, 1939, predicted that on October 16, 1940, the United States without going to war would be registering its young manpower for selective military training, he would have been set down by most people as a dreamer," observed the *Boston Globe*. "Such a measure seemed utterly remote from the American way."

By December the first group of draftees was on its way to camp, and a second draft call was set for the end of the month. Men in khaki uniforms began to appear in advertisements, standing on a firing range while comparing the length of their cigarettes. ("Pall Mall is over 20 per cent longer.") Hollywood launched production on a new genre of films that came to be known as "service comedies," beginning with *Buck Privates*, starring Bud Abbott and Lou Costello. Somehow Army life seemed less threatening when a group of inductees was greeted by the Andrews Sisters singing "You're a lucky fellow, Mr. Smith / You really should be shouting with joy" for the privilege of being drafted. (The film went on to become Universal Studio's top-grossing picture in 1941.)

High schools expanded their vocational training offerings, often with assistance from federal officials, to better prepare boys for the Army or defense work. Often their courses proved so popular that schools stayed open on a twenty-four-hour basis, with afternoon and night shifts for adults who wanted to learn how to be aircraft mechanics or sheet metal workers. Colleges and universities established flight-training programs; the University of Chicago doubled the size of its indoor rifle range and offered informal instruction in marksmanship; and Harvard established special "war libraries" across campus with specially selected volumes to deepen students' understanding of the war.

Although American industry's defense production remained sluggish—most disconcertingly, the manufacture of airplanes was running more than 30 percent behind schedule—enough new jobs were created to reduce unemployment to 8 million by the end of the year. Spurred by defense contracts, the steel industry set new records for production in 1940. The construction industry celebrated its best year in a decade, and oil companies reported a substantial increase in earnings. Cosmetics sales also skyrocketed, especially among young women looking toward 1941 with considerable trepidation. With several hundred thousand conscripted American males essentially out of circulation, *Contemporary Modes* magazine predicted that the competition for the remaining men "will be something fierce."

Despite increasing Army purchases and rising civilian demand, food supplies for holiday feasts remained plentiful. "If this isn't the heartiest and altogether most appetizing Christmas you and your friends ever tasted," proclaimed the *New Yorker*, "it won't be the fault of the food shops around town." There were pheasants and grouse and ducks, and Smithfield hams, and cranberry-fed turkeys from Cape Cod, although French wines were growing harder to find—not a single bottle had been shipped to the United States since France surrendered in June. Americans who wished to show their solidarity with England could dispatch food parcels from their local department stores "to brighten London's Christmas." Others preferred to donate money, or knit warm clothing for British soldiers, sailors, and airmen through the "Bundles for Britain" program.

Knit woolen caps were one thing; the weaponry of modern war was quite another. If Britain was to survive another year, it needed American guns and planes, but by December the British Treasury had nearly exhausted its credits and would no longer be able to purchase arms from the United States. Moreover, the British navy desperately needed American ships to help convoy supplies through the U-boat squadrons that infested the Atlantic; in the last three months of 1940 alone, more than 130 merchant vessels and over 700,000 tons of shipping had been lost to German attacks.

Since neutrality legislation still prohibited loans to belligerents, Roosevelt elected to ask Congress for authority to lend ships and planes to England instead of money. Introduced in the House on January 11, 1941, the Lend-Lease bill gave the president virtually unlimited power to sell, trade, transfer, or give outright an initial appropriation of $1 billion worth of defense material (defined so vaguely as to include anything from tanks to corned beef sandwiches) to any foreign government if the president believed the transaction would benefit the national defense. Opponents denounced the measure as yet another Rooseveltian bid for dictatorial power, "a blank check book" that "would bring an end to free government in the United States and would abolish the Congress for all practical purposes." They also warned—again—that shipping still more military supplies to Britain would provoke Germany into attacking the United States.

Two months of congressional hearings featured protests by women who brought miniature coffins to isolationist rallies and hung signs on them that said BUNDLES FROM BRITAIN. Female shock troops of the Paul Revere Sentinels and the Women's Neutrality League paraded in front of the British embassy in Washington, where they hung a grotesque effigy of President Roosevelt upon the gate with placards that read MOVE OVER, UNKNOWN SOLDIER and BENEDICT ARNOLD HELPED ENGLAND, TOO. But when the hearings ended, polls showed that somewhere between 54 and 60 percent of Americans favored the Lend-Lease proposal. Most appeared to agree with a Virginia voter who reasoned that "if another fellow and I have a row, I'd far sooner have the mess in his backyard than in mine." By early March, both houses of Congress had approved the bill by comfortable majorities.

Then a fog seemed to settle over the country. Contemporary accounts described the American public in the spring of 1941 as confused, uncertain, distracted. Numerous observers noted the growing tension between the two primary goals of Americans regarding the war in Europe, both still supported by overwhelming majorities in opinion polls: a resolute determination to stay out of the conflict, and a refusal to allow England to be defeated. "Until we make permanent choice between our two wishes," wrote Mark Sullivan of the *New York Herald Tribune*, "America will be torn with inner conflict between impulses mutually destructive of each other, the result leading to frustration and futility, a soul-sick country."

bibliotheca SelfCheck System
WALNUT CREEK
Contra Costa County Library
1644 N Broadway
Walnut Creek, CA 94596
(925) 977-3340

**Customer ID:** \*\*\*\*\*\*\*\*\*\*\*\*\*\*

**Items that you checked out**

Title: Peril in Paris /
ID: 31901068733478
**Due: Friday, March 17, 2023**
Messages:
Item checked out.

Title: The boys from Biloxi /
ID: 31901068693532
**Due: Friday, March 17, 2023**
Messages:
Item checked out.

Total items: 2
Account balance: $0.00
2/24/2023 1:09 PM
Ready for pickup: 0

_____

Renew online or by phone.
ccclib.org
1-800-984-4636

Have a nice day!

At the same time, Americans increasingly grew resigned to the prospect that the United States would sooner or later be drawn into the European conflict. A year earlier, at the time of the blitzkrieg, polls showed that two-thirds of Americans thought the United States would eventually enter the war. By the end of April 1941, that number had risen to 82 percent, and a month later it reached 85 percent, accompanied by a conviction that the U.S. military would need all the arms the nation could produce.

By any measure, the nation was far from ready for war. Deficiencies in arms production had been obvious for months. At the close of 1940, *Time* magazine had noted that American industry "was still producing more bottlenecks per week than anything else." Several months later, filmmaker Frank Capra journeyed to Washington to offer his services to the defense effort and received a rude awakening. "From what I saw and heard," he wrote later, "we were so woefully unprepared for war that Army chiefs dreaded our possible involvement. They hinted that our troops only slightly out-numbered Washington's Continentals—and were as badly trained and ill-equipped."

Numerous obstacles stood in the way, including the administration itself. Roosevelt and his advisers had not yet decided how to allocate the nation's resources between military and civilian goods. Nor had they approved a coordinated overall plan for defense production, since no one knew precisely whom or when the nation would be fighting; as one critic put it, the United States "was arming to fight Heaven-knows-whom at Heaven-knows-where for Heaven-knows-what."

Roosevelt tangled the situation further by creating war production agencies whose responsibilities overlapped or conflicted with one another and with the military services' own procurement divisions. Logjams inevitably ensued. Columnist Westbrook Pegler envisioned businessmen lost in the labyrinth of the federal bureaucracy, "wandering like bewildered bums in a strange railroad yard, reading meaningless numbers on the glass doors of offices in miles of corridors and wondering just what department had charge of the procurement of woolen drawers."

On the other hand, many American businesses remained reluctant to pursue military contracts, preferring to turn out as many civilian goods as possible until the administration forced them to stop—which it was loath to do, for fear of derailing the economic recovery. Hence the bountiful supply of consumer goods throughout 1941 at the expense of defense production, a situation which Walter Lippmann condemned as "this disgraceful boom." No more reconciled to the administration than ever, businessmen especially did not wish to convert their factories to military production and then entrust their companies' future to the unpredictable whims of New Deal bureaucrats, whom one disgruntled executive denounced as a "pack of semi-communist wolves."

To the American public, however, the main obstacle to full-scale preparedness appeared to be organized labor and the wave of strikes that swept through the defense industry in 1941. Over the past decade, labor leaders had won numerous hard-fought victories—sometimes at the cost of workers' lives—to win recognition of their unions. Yet a number of major corporations remained adamantly opposed to negotiating at all with labor, despite federal mandates to do so. The most notorious holdout was the Ford Motor Company, whose refusal to engage in meaningful collective bargaining had recently earned it a conviction for violating the Wagner Act. "We will bargain with [the CIO] because the law says so," grumbled Ford's personnel director. "We will bargain until Hell freezes over, but they won't get anything."

As the nation's need for skilled labor grew increasingly desperate, unions seized the opportunity to force showdowns with management over long-festering wage and jurisdictional disputes. In late February, there were sixteen major industrial strikes in progress, involving 23,000 workers; more than 468,000 man-days already had been lost on Army contracts. By mid-March, 47,000 workers were out in forty defense industry strikes. In April, 400,000 coal miners walked off their jobs, shutting down the nation's production of bituminous coal. Within weeks American steel plants were forced to reduce operations by nearly 15 percent.

The public's mood turned dark; a Gallup poll revealed that 72 percent of American voters wanted to forbid strikes in defense industries. Congress debated measures to curb union activity, and set out to investigate Communist influence in the American labor movement. Representative Hatton Sumners, chairman of the House Judiciary Committee, announced that if the crisis grew much worse, he would not hesitate "one split second" to recommend the electric chair for "enemies of this nation, in the factory or elsewhere."

African Americans had their own grievances against both labor unions and defense contractors. A federal survey in late 1940 revealed that more than half the companies involved in the preparedness program flatly refused to hire African Americans, especially for skilled jobs. Nor did most of the labor unions representing skilled workers admit African Americans. As a result, fewer than 1 percent of the workers in the nation's aircraft industry were black. In early 1941, civil rights activist A. Philip Randolph announced plans to stage a massive rally in Washington to demand equal employment opportunities in defense industries. Fearful of political embarrassment and further disruptions to the preparedness program, Roosevelt agreed to establish the Fair Employment Practices Committee to investigate cases of discrimination, but the committee possessed little power to remedy the injustices it uncovered.

At a time when the nation needed a unified effort to prepare for war, American society appeared to be splintering further apart. "I can see we haven't got the spirit yet, probably because nobody has dropped a bomb on us," grumbled William Knudsen, the Danish-born former General Motors executive whom Roosevelt had appointed to help lead the Office of Production Management (OPM). Some critics blamed the administration. "The simple truth is that as yet the right kind of spirit does not exist among the people," concluded conservative columnist Frank Kent, "and the reason is that the right kind of spirit does not exist among their leaders—or at least it is not being displayed by them." Several cabinet officials—Harold Ickes, Secretary of War Henry Stimson, Attorney General Jackson, and Secretary of the Navy Frank Knox—expressed their own concerns about Roosevelt's "failure of leadership." "In every direction I find a growing discontent with the President's lack of leadership," wrote the irascible Ickes in his diary. "He still has the country if he will take it and lead it. But he won't have it very much longer unless he does something."

Mounting losses of British ships sunk by U-boats and Nazi planes in the Atlantic rattled Americans' nerves further, raising the question of whether the United States should employ its warships to convoy armaments to Britain. Roosevelt finally responded on the evening of May 27 with a speech that was, in the words of one adviser, "calculated to scare the daylights out of everyone." It was undoubtedly the most eagerly anticipated radio event since the election. At the Polo Grounds, the New York Giants and Brooklyn Dodgers stopped their game for forty-five minutes so fans could hear the speech broadcast over the stadium's loudspeakers. In Manhattan, traffic in Times Square slowed to a standstill; movie patrons left their seats to listen to the president's message in theater lobbies; bartenders turned off jukeboxes.

Speaking from the East Room of the White House, the president—amply fortified with cigarettes and a half dozen glasses of water—told a radio audience estimated at 65 million Americans that "what started as a European war has developed, as the Nazis always intended it should develop, into a war for world domination." As a result, Roosevelt promised to immediately strengthen U.S. naval patrols in the Atlantic with as many ships and planes as necessary to guarantee the safety of American defense shipments to Britain. And in hopes of stirring the public's dedication to the preparedness effort, the president proclaimed that "an unlimited national emergency confronts this country," which required all Americans "to place the nation and its needs first in mind and in action."

Minutes later, newspaper switchboards were flooded with calls from puzzled Americans asking what precisely a "national emergency" meant. The president remained vague when reporters pressed him the following day, and actually backtracked when he admitted that he had no intention of actually using "convoys" to escort British ships across the ocean anytime in the near future. "There was no lack of words," noted one disgruntled journalist. "The deficiencies were all on the practical side."

For the next six months, Americans waited for something to happen. "I wish I knew more than I know," wrote poet Carl Sandburg. "I go on drifting. The nation drifts. It is written for a while we must drift. By drifting I mean guessing as to where the national ship of state is going and what will happen to it in the end. Just now I am willing to throw in everything to save Britain. Beyond that I agree with anyone who has a headache."

Germany's invasion of the Soviet Union on June 22 muddled the situation further. While Hitler's gamble took considerable pressure off Great Britain, and thereby rendered American intervention less likely, the notion of an alliance with a Communist dictatorship gave pause to a substantial segment of the American public which had long demonized

Joseph Stalin. The *Chicago Tribune* denounced the Soviet leader as "the greatest barbarian of modern times," and Charles Lindbergh swore that "I would a hundred times rather see my country ally herself . . . with Germany with all her faults, than with the cruelty, the godlessness, and the barbarism that exist in Soviet Russia." The immediate question for the United States was whether it would divert arms from Britain or the lagging American preparedness effort (or, more likely, both) to equip the Red Army. Roosevelt attempted to finesse the issue in his usual offhand style. "Of course we are going to give all the aid that we possibly can to Russia," he told reporters. Asked to provide specifics, the president replied flippantly, "Oh, socks and shoes, and things like that. What you can get at Garfinckel's [a department store chain] you can probably get at once. . . . When it comes to planes and things that have to be made, we have got orders that will take a long time to fill, of course."

In Tokyo, the Japanese government—taken entirely by surprise—greeted Hitler's invasion of the Soviet Union with dismay. Well on its way to establishing the Greater East Asia Co-Prosperity Sphere, Japan had swallowed Manchuria in 1931 (in the form of the puppet state of Manchukuo), and launched a full-scale, brutal invasion of China six years later. By the summer of 1941, Japanese forces controlled much of China's coastal regions, along with most major Chinese cities. But the Nationalist (Kuomintang) government led by Chiang Kai-shek had not surrendered, retreating instead to Chongqing, in the mountains of southwestern China. Frustrated by its army's inability to subjugate China, and encouraged by the German conquest of France, the Japanese government opted to push southward into defenseless French Indochina, with its valuable resources of rice, minerals, and rubber. Tokyo would then wait for Britain to fall, so it could sweep in and pick up the remnants of the British Empire in East Asia. Germany's attack upon the Soviet Union threatened to delay Britain's collapse; nevertheless, Japan's military and civilian leaders decided at an Imperial Conference on July 2 to proceed with the move into Indochina.

Americans had no trouble choosing sides in this conflict. The American public had long viewed China through a sentimental lens, as the land of *The Good Earth*, populated by simple, earnest peasants suffering under the weight of rapacious landlords, European exploitation, and Japanese atrocities. By contrast, Americans living on the West Coast had long been hostile to—and suspicious of—the Japanese in their midst, and for decades the United States Navy had trained its officers to regard Japan as a potential enemy. Roosevelt viewed Japanese aggression in Asia as part of a single worldwide fascist assault upon vital American interests, a link strengthened in September 1940 when Japan signed the Tripartite Pact, pledging to cooperate with Germany and Italy in establishing a new order in Europe and East Asia. Even isolationists favored a hard line against Japan's military ambitions; as *Life* magazine noted, there was "no fierce emotional resistance to war in the Pacific as there is among many people to war in Europe."

Japan began moving its troops into Indochina in mid-July. Having broken Japan's top-level diplomatic code, American officials knew that the Japanese government intended to use southern Indochina as a springboard for future conquests, most likely the Malay States and the oil-rich Dutch East Indies. For the past year, the Roosevelt administration had tried to forestall such an advance by shipping substantial quantities of oil to Japan, a policy that critics claimed had turned "the arsenal of democracy" into "the filling station of fascism." But events had outpaced American policy.

On July 24, Roosevelt called Japanese ambassador Kichisaburo Nomura to the White House and strongly recommended that Japan withdraw its forces from Indochina. The following day, the president underlined the point by issuing an executive order freezing all Japanese assets in the United States, rendering trade between the two nations more difficult, although not altogether impossible. But when overzealous American officials enforced the freeze more rigorously than the president intended, they effectively cut off *all* trade between the United States and Japan—most importantly, denying Japan the oil and scrap iron upon which its army relied. Since there was no other source from which Japan could obtain such vast stocks of oil on short notice, State Department planners assumed the militarists in Japan would now refrain from further aggression.

In the summer of 1941, it seemed to Marquis Childs that nearly every story from Washington "reflected the uncertainty in the capital. A fog of confusion lay as thick as a blanket over everything. . . . The tempo was incredibly slow; like a slow-motion picture taken in a friendly lunatic asylum."

Weary of the uncertainty of the past two years, many Americans spent the summer searching for escape from talk of national emergencies and preparedness and convoys. "There has never been a summer when it will be so important to relax," declared a popular sporting goods company. "The deluge is coming. . . . Dress up and play." And so Americans put on their white sharkskin tennis dresses or their Bill Tilden–inspired V-neck sweaters and headed to the courts, or to the movies to see Betty Grable in *Moon Over Miami* or Cary Grant in the melodramatic *Penny Serenade*. Looking out from his office in Kansas, William Allen White complained that "two-fifths of our people are more interested in the baseball scores than they are in foreign news," though that probably was a conservative estimate while New York Yankees slugger Joe DiMaggio was compiling his fifty-six-game hitting streak from the middle of May into the middle of July.

"Too many Americans have not yet made up their minds that we have a war to win," declared Roosevelt, "and that it will take a hard fight to win it." Labor troubles continued to bedevil the preparedness program; in September, union leaders launched 435 new strikes—mostly for higher wages, although a significant minority of work stoppages resulted from union demands for a closed shop. "I can't for the life of me understand how in a period of national emergency such foolishness like this can go on," snapped the OPM's Knudsen. "I am quite frank to confess that with our house on fire we can't have a strike in the fire department."

"We grow more like the France that was every day, the France that died fat, unable to walk across the street because she had eaten too much," muttered disgruntled Washington columnist Samuel Grafton. Poet May Sarton concurred. "We are still sitting placid and smug on the edge of a volcano," decided Sarton. "Roosevelt has lost a grip on the country. . . . No one at all will face squarely the fact that we shall someday have to actually fight and send men over to do it. And as long as they don't face that fact everything is half-baked, half-done."

At the close of a hectic summer travel season that far surpassed any previous year for gasoline consumption, Americans fled to the beaches for the Labor Day weekend—Coney Island, Atlantic City, and Asbury Park all were jammed with sun worshippers. Others crowded into buses or railway cars to reach their favorite vacation spots; railroads and bus companies reported that virtually every available seat had been sold. To a *New York Times* reporter, it seemed as if Americans "had put aside their collective worries about the condition of the war-torn world and the rising costs of living and were determined to forget it all in one last fling."

Then they went back to work, increasingly at defense jobs as the engines of defense production at last began to gather momentum. By the end of November, American industry was operating at record production levels, with nearly 25 percent of U.S. productive capacity engaged in defense work. But prosperity engendered its own problems. Prices for a wide range of consumer goods began to rise sharply, driven by material shortages and swollen paychecks. By November the cost of living was climbing at a rate of slightly more than 1 percent per month. Food prices alone had increased by more than 15 percent over the past year; one grocery chain held special classes to coach employees in how to respond to customer complaints.

Shortages in a wide variety of consumer goods loomed on the horizon, as the federal government increasingly allocated raw materials—especially steel, aluminum, copper, and tin—to defense production. For the moment, there were still plenty of goods on the shelves, since manufacturers and retailers had spent much of 1941 building up inventories. But an OPM decree limited automakers to the production of only 205,000 civilian vehicles in the final month of the year, 34 percent below their output of December 1940. Farmers faced a dearth of tractors. Residential housing construction for nondefense workers already had slowed dramatically, since federal agencies allocated most building materials for military encampments, government office buildings, and housing for defense workers.

Public school systems reported a distressing scarcity of trained teachers, as many woefully underpaid educators decided to quit the classroom for lucrative defense jobs. More than half the nation's teachers in 1941 earned less than $2,000 a year; the average annual salary of educators fell somewhere between $1,300 and $1,400. In rural areas, most teachers made less than $900. (The most egregious numbers came from Arkansas, where white teachers averaged about $500 a year, and black educators only $275.) Experts projected a shortfall of fifty thousand teachers for the 1942–43 school year, and an even greater gap in the future, since enrollment in teacher training schools had declined by nearly 20 percent over the past twelve months.

The nation could not afford the loss. Sixty percent of adult Americans (age twenty-five or older) possessed only an eighth-grade education or less; the number of adults without even one year of formal education nearly equaled the number of college graduates. The Census Bureau estimated that about 4 percent of Americans remained illiterate, but the American Association for Adult Education put the total of functional illiterates at three times that number. (In the nation's first draft registration, approximately 340,000 men signed their forms with a cross mark, because they could not write their own name.) While the high school population had skyrocketed in the early twentieth century—there were ten times more high school students in the United States in 1940 than in 1900—educators had repeatedly watered down the curriculum as the student population grew more diverse. Students reportedly spent so much time in English classes reading popular novelists and magazine articles, instead of the classics of British and American literature, that Harvard University found it necessary to introduce a course in reading fundamentals for freshmen. And in late 1941 there were fewer college freshmen and fewer high school students than a year earlier. College enrollment dropped by nearly 10 percent from 1940 as a result of the draft and the attraction of defense jobs, while the number of high school students declined by 3 percent as some of the older boys likewise chose defense work over school.

Women searching for jobs in defense plants faced their own special problems. A congressional investigation discovered that "in most communities there is very real resistance in defense industries to the employment of women." Aircraft companies proved especially reluctant to hire female workers because they preferred skilled mechanics who could perform multiple steps in the complex process of assembling planes, and women traditionally had been shut out from opportunities to obtain the requisite training. Over the past few months, however, local boards of education had begun to establish industrial defense training programs for women, supplemented by classes sponsored by the federal National Youth Administration, and—as the labor shortage began to pinch—by schools operated by the aircraft companies themselves.

Increasingly, male defense workers were being called into the Army, as military officials discovered that they needed to summon far more men for the draft than originally anticipated. They had expected 5 percent of potential recruits to fail their draft physicals, but in the first year of conscription, draft boards rejected between 30 and 50 percent as medically unfit for service. (This despite a recent War Department ruling that men who were "extremely ugly" or who bore "tattooing of an improper nature" would no longer be excluded.) The leading causes of rejection were bad teeth, venereal disease, and tuberculosis. Those who did not suffer from venereal disease before they joined the Army ran the risk of contracting it afterward from the swarms of prostitutes who set up shop near Army camps. The problem mushroomed so rapidly that authorities from twenty-four states asked the federal government for assistance in combating the epidemic.

Most of the men who failed their draft physical had not been under the care of a physician for years, and many had never seen a dentist. "We are physically in a condition of which we should nationally be ashamed," charged General Lewis Hershey, director of Selective Service. The Navy fared no better. Enlistments did not keep pace with the expansion of the fleet; fewer than ten thousand men joined the service each month. On December 6, Navy officials announced that they would relax their physical standards to obtain enough recruits.

War Department authorities were still reeling from the multitude of deficiencies revealed by a series of military exercises in the autumn of 1941. In September, the Army staged the most extensive field maneuvers in its history in Louisiana. Lieutenant General Leslie McNair, director of the maneuvers, acknowledged that the war games proved that the United States Army suffered from poor leadership, a lack of discipline, and incompetent junior officers. Specifically, McNair criticized the practice of "sending masses of troops over roads before ascertaining whether they were safe from enemy fire, disregard of blackout orders, spreading forces too thinly over too large a front, inadequate scouting, and the failure to impress troops with the danger of air attack."

A subsequent series of exercises involving 300,000 troops along the

North Carolina–South Carolina border in late November brought fresh criticisms. "Apparently the men are still seriously handicapped by the lack of materiel," observed the *Washington Post*. Army officials conceded that ammunition was in short supply, its antiaircraft weapons were obsolete, and nearly half of the antitank "guns" were dummies. Competent leadership of platoons and other small units remained elusive—"The process of weeding out inefficient officers," mused the *Post*, "will presumably continue"—and too many soldiers still had not learned how to fight at night. Observers blamed the hidebound Army system of seniority, which had entrenched ineffectual officers in positions of command, and the long-term effects of two decades of "slow starvation" military budgets.

McNair insisted that the Army's capabilities had improved dramatically over the past twelve months, "but the simple fact is you can't perfect units in one year's work and bring them up to the standards of facing anything like the Germans." Asked if American troops were ready for war, McNair replied that "it is my judgment that, given complete equipment, they certainly could fight effectively. But it is to be added with emphasis that the losses would be unduly heavy, and the results of action against an adversary such as the Germans might not be all that could be desired."

From September until December, Congress remained in session, often working around the clock as relations between the United States and Japan continued to deteriorate. China remained the stumbling block. The Roosevelt administration refused to concede Japanese control of the mainland, while Tokyo insisted on preserving four years' worth of hard-won gains. The Japanese government sent one of its most experienced diplomats, Saburo Kurusu (who had an American wife), to Washington to persuade the Roosevelt administration to reopen trade and allow Japan to settle unilaterally what it termed "the China incident," but to no avail. Focused on the danger posed by Nazi Germany, Roosevelt twisted and turned in search of an acceptable compromise that would postpone an outbreak of hostilities in the Pacific, which he feared would be "the wrong war in the wrong ocean at the wrong time." Still he found no solution. Chances for a peaceful settlement were dimmed further by American intercepts of Japanese diplomatic cables, which convinced Roosevelt and Secretary of State Cordell Hull that the government of General Hideki

Tojo, who had assumed the office of premier in October, was using the discussions in Washington to mask preparations for war.

In early November, Roosevelt grimly informed his cabinet that war with Japan appeared inevitable. Shortly thereafter, American cryptographers deciphered a message from Tokyo to Kurusu and Admiral Kichisaburo Nomura, the Japanese ambassador in Washington, advising them that the army would wait only one more week for a diplomatic solution: "After that things are automatically going to happen."

On Friday, November 28, Roosevelt boarded a special train for a belated Thanksgiving celebration at the National Foundation for Infantile Paralysis in Warm Springs, Georgia, where he could swim and relax among the southern pines. The presidential party had planned to stay in Warm Springs for at least three nights. Almost as soon as Roosevelt arrived on Saturday, however, he received a phone call from Hull, who warned that the crisis with Japan was approaching a climax. That afternoon the president listened, distracted, to the Army-Navy football game on the radio (Navy won, 14–6), and then addressed the foundation's polio patients at dinner. "It may be that next Thanksgiving," Roosevelt told his guests, "these boys of the Military Academy and of the Naval Academy will be actually fighting for the defense of these American institutions of ours." Before the evening was over, Hull phoned again and asked the president to return to Washington. As he departed the following morning, Roosevelt paused and told a group of bystanders that "this may be the last time I talk to you for a long time." While the president's train sped to the capital, General Tojo announced in Tokyo that "the United States does not understand the real situation in East Asia."

Roosevelt arrived at the White House shortly before noon on Monday, December 1, and spent the rest of the day closeted with his top military and diplomatic advisers. Over the next several days, newspaper columnists sounded the alarm. "We are close to war with Japan," proclaimed Mark Sullivan on December 3. "The odds, as this is written, are strongly in favor of war in the Far East," agreed Ernest Lindley. Looking back over the long months of diplomatic crises, Walter Lippmann believed that "for the first time the country is now really on the verge of actual all-out war"— not in Europe, as isolationists had long predicted, but in the Pacific. Conventional wisdom still held that Japan would most likely attack Thailand or Burma or the Malay Peninsula, provoking the United States to respond with embargoes and naval blockades.

Despite the furor in the press, most Americans evinced little concern over rising tensions with Tokyo. One journal after another openly questioned Japan's ability to fight a prolonged war against the United States, and no one suggested that Japan might actually win. "Sane strategists would never permit Japan to start such a hopeless war," argued the *New Republic*, while the *Baltimore Sun* insisted that "our island bases are prepared for any emergency. . . . Concerning our ability to hold our position against the use of force by Japan there can be no doubt." A *New York Times* editorial reminded readers that without vital supplies from the United States, "Japan is facing international economic siege and she is very vulnerable." The *Wall Street Journal* concluded that "Japan—economically— is living on borrowed time."

As Washington waited for Tojo's government to make its next move, congressmen began to book their plane tickets for the Christmas holidays; after months of meeting without a recess, legislators looked forward to a two-week break. On December 5, Tokyo assured the Roosevelt administration that recent Japanese military reinforcements in Indochina were merely a response to "threatening movements" of Chinese troops across the border, and not a prelude to further aggression. "A bare chance of peace remained—of a kind of peace very close to war but not quite war," mused *Time* magazine. "This was the last act of the drama."

When Roosevelt held a press conference later that day, reporters found him "polite, mildly affable, and completely uncommunicative." Shortly after four o'clock in the afternoon, the president ducked out of the side door of the White House wearing a light coat and an old gray hat. Accompanied by his Scottish terrier, Fala, he rode around Potomac Park and the quiet outskirts of the city until dark, taking in the scenery. Relaxed and refreshed, the president delegated Eleanor to host a dinner party of over a hundred guests—including Oscar-winning actress Luise Rainer— at the Executive Mansion, while he dined alone off a tray upstairs, working late into the night.

Saturday, December 6: Reports to the State Department indicated that two large Japanese convoys had left Indochina, heading for the Gulf of Siam. Authorities in Singapore ordered all sailors of Britain's Far Eastern fleet to return to their ships, and the government of the Philippines asked nonessential civilians to evacuate Manila and other danger zones.

Maxim Litvinov, the new Soviet ambassador to the Union States, arrived in San Francisco. "I am looking forward to my work with confidence and satisfaction," he told reporters in California, "and rejoice in the thought of future talks in Washington with your great president." Litvinov expected to arrive in Washington shortly before noon on Sunday.

An America First spokesman announced that the isolationist organization would support the election of any congressional candidates who "oppose further steps to involve us in war," regardless of party affiliation. Rallies were scheduled in twenty cities over the rest of the month, including a speech by Lindbergh in Boston on December 12.

"The old way of life has gone, never to return," wrote columnist Elizabeth Gilmer. "Never again will any of us now living see the old, pleasant, easy, secure world in which we once lived. . . . And if this is true of the great world it is equally true of the little private worlds in which each of us lives. . . . Now when the whole world seems a blackout. . . . So many terrible things have happened. So many more terrible things threaten us."

In the Soviet Union, counterattacks by the Red Army continued to force the Wehrmacht back from Moscow, although Russian efforts to break the siege of Leningrad failed. British forces claimed victories in the deserts of North Africa, but Rommel's Afrika Korps quickly reversed the tide. U.S. naval patrols, with "capture or destroy" orders against German submarines, escorted armed merchant ships bearing war matériel for Britain nearly all of the way across the Atlantic.

"I am proud to report that the American people may feel fully confident in their Navy," declared Secretary of the Navy Frank Knox in his annual report to the nation. "The fiscal year 1941 witnessed the virtual transition of the nation from a peacetime to a wartime footing, with tremendous industrial expansion for production of war materiel." As far as Knox was concerned, "the loyalty, morale, and technical ability of the [Navy] personnel are without superior. On any comparable basis, the United States Navy is second to none."

In a lengthy critique of the preparedness program, the *Saturday Evening Post* concluded that the American defense buildup had become "an enterprise beyond anything that has ever been measured. In order to perform it, we shall have to change not only our ways of living but our ways of thinking about many things, especially money. . . . Congress has already ceased to think of billions as money. Just when it did, you cannot say; it could not itself say when. . . . But let us not be deceived. It will hurt. The disturbances already beginning to be complained of are, as yet, nothing."

Issues on the New York Stock Exchange traded slightly higher during the customary two-hour Saturday morning session. It was a welcome respite from the recent series of setbacks for the Dow Jones Industrial Average, which had been sagging due to the uncertain diplomatic situation in East Asia. At the end of the day it rested only slightly above the "panic low" set when France surrendered to Germany in June 1940.

On Saturday evening, jazz lovers in New England could catch Cab Calloway—leader of arguably the most famous swing band in America—and the Cab Jivers at the RKO Boston. "Mister Calloway is in the groove when it comes to jive," noted one critic approvingly. "He's out of this world and his hep-cat swingsters cook with gas." Moviegoers in Washington could choose between the bedroom comedy *Appointment for Love*, starring Margaret Sullavan and Charles Boyer; *Two-Faced Woman*, the Greta Garbo film condemned by the Legion of Decency as "immoral and un-Christian"; and the heroic but highly inaccurate biography of General George Armstrong Custer, *They Died with Their Boots On*. At the Gayety Theater, burlesque dancer Rosita Royce performed her notorious "Dance of the Doves," which employed strategically placed trained birds in what a *Washington Post* critic termed "one of the cleverest acts in show business." On a more intellectual level, the Washington Amateur Astronomers Association met in the National Museum and heard a presentation from a Carnegie Institution physicist on recent efforts to smash the atom: "The Annihilation of Matter."

President Roosevelt spent much of the day working alone with his secretary, catching up on paperwork, and receiving periodic reports of Japanese naval movements off the coast of Indochina. In a last-ditch effort to forestall a showdown, the president composed a personal appeal to Emperor Hirohito, asking him to withdraw Japan's troops from Southeast Asia. Numerous White House staffers took the day off to catch up on Christmas shopping. That afternoon, a strong Canadian cold front swept across the eastern United States. Roosevelt spent a quiet evening at the

White House, dining with a few friends, watching a movie, and looking over his stamp collection. He made vague promises to "take it easy" on Sunday, perhaps allowing himself an afternoon nap and a drive in the Virginia countryside. Before the president retired for the night, a Navy officer handed him a lengthy decoded message from Tokyo that left no doubt that war was imminent.

"So ends our reverie in the twilight," wrote Raymond Clapper, "over the dear, dead days."

# 2: Lights Out

### DECEMBER 7, 1941

*It is the knell of the old world.*

—ANNE MORROW LINDBERGH

News of the Japanese attack on Pearl Harbor reached the White House shortly before two o'clock on the afternoon of December 7. Roosevelt was sitting in his second-floor study with longtime friend and adviser Harry Hopkins, eating an apple. Fala was munching the lunch leftovers from a tray on the president's desk. Though it was a cold, windy afternoon, Roosevelt still hoped to enjoy a ride through the Virginia countryside before nightfall. Then the call came through from Secretary Knox: "Mr. President, it looks like the Japanese have attacked Pearl Harbor."

At Griffith Stadium several miles to the north, a sparse crowd of twenty-seven thousand shivering fans was watching the Washington Redskins battle the Philadelphia Eagles in the last game of the NFL regular season. A few minutes after the game began, the reporter covering the game for the Associated Press received a puzzling message from AP headquarters, instructing him to keep his story short. Then he got another call: "The Japanese have kicked off. War now!" The news made its way through the press box, then spread to the fans sitting nearby. Redskins management chose not to make a general announcement—"We don't want to contribute to any hysteria," the team's general manager later explained—but midway through the first quarter, the public-address system began paging military and diplomatic officials, asking them to return to their stations or contact their offices. By the end of the first half, only one news photographer remained along the sideline.

Alerted by Roosevelt, presidential press secretary Stephen Early telephoned the three major press associations from his home in northwest Washington and gave them the official announcement at 2:22 p.m. "The Japanese have attacked Pearl Harbor from the air, and all naval and military activities on the island of Oahu," he told them. Reporters quickly gathered in the overheated, garishly lighted Executive Office pressroom, which became the de facto news center of the nation. Throughout the afternoon, Early provided updates as the president (who was meeting with a steady stream of advisers in the White House library) passed along the grim reports from Hawaii—as much as military officials were willing to disclose. After each bulletin, dozens of journalists scrambled for one of the few available telephones. Several radio stations and networks set up microphones in the pressroom. High upon one wall, they could see through the clouds of tobacco smoke an old sign perched atop a bookcase: WE AIN'T MAD WITH NOBODY.

It was a cold Sunday in New York, too, but that didn't stop a large, enthusiastic crowd from showing up at the Polo Grounds to watch the Giants-Dodgers football game. Shortly after two o'clock, a message came over the loudspeaker. "Attention, please! Attention! Here is an urgent message. Will Colonel William J. Donovan call Operator nineteen in Washington, D.C." After watching one or two more plays, Donovan (whom Roosevelt had recently appointed as head of American intelligence services) found a telephone and called the capital; he reached the president's eldest son, James, a captain in the Marines, who asked Donovan to return to Washington immediately. He flew back on the same plane as Vice President Henry Wallace and Secretary of Labor Frances Perkins, who had been in New York on administration business.

Those listening to the game on radio heard the news around 2:30, as Brooklyn's relentless running backs pounded the ball into Giant territory. "Japanese bombs have fallen on Hawaii and the Philippine Islands," a voice broke in to announce. "Keep tuned to this station for further details. We now return you to the Polo Grounds."

"It came in slowly—disjointed, fragmentary, contradicting itself now and then," recalled one New Yorker. "The commentators talking rapidly but evasively, not yet knowing what to say about a catastrophe as sudden and preposterous as something contrived by Orson Welles. . . . The difference between being a citizen of a nation even precariously at peace and one of a nation with its outposts already under fire is hard to grasp in the middle of a football game; the old nightmare of the Yellow Peril, a comic bugaboo almost as long as we can remember, is a strange thing to have come true in the early afternoon, with the radio on and the Sunday papers still only partly read. Like practically everybody else, we've been sure for a long time that war was bound to come, but we never thought that it would come like that."

At Rockefeller Center, a small audience sat on folding chairs in the lounge of the Newsreel Theater and stared intently at a compact television monitor that carried NBC news bulletins on the Japanese attack. A correspondent from *Collier's* magazine explained the reasons for the war; then the camera cut to a news ticker too far away to read, followed by another expert who pointed vaguely on a wall map to places he identified only as "here" and "there." After a cartoon advertisement for men's neckties, programming resumed with home movies made by a local couple during their recent trip through Asia. "It was a nice, dreamy way of letting the horrid fact of war seep in," admitted a reporter in the audience. "Except for the eyestrain."

But most Americans received the news from radio or their neighbors as they went about doing the sort of things Americans usually did on a Sunday—"taking it easy," as British journalist Alistair Cooke put it, "taking it easy everywhere." Anne Lindbergh was in her car, driving to Woods Hole, Massachusetts. "Listening to the radio I heard the news. . . . It is the knell of the old world. All army officers all over the United States ordered into uniform. Espionage Act invoked. (If C. speaks again they'll put him in prison, I think immediately.) I listen all afternoon to the radio. I am listening to the Philharmonic, a beautiful concert of Brahms. But it is interrupted every ten minutes with bulletins about the war. This is what life is going to be from now on, I think."

By far the most common reaction was incredulity and then shock, followed frequently by wondering where exactly Pearl Harbor was. In one city after another, contemporary observers saw the startled and stunned looks on Americans' faces. "All that Sunday was a daze," wrote journalist

Ernie Pyle from his home in Albuquerque, New Mexico. "The news seemed too horrible." In Washington, crowds of local residents and Sunday tourists, along with a stray bum or two, had gathered by three o'clock outside the White House and on the steps of the State Department building across West Executive Avenue. They stood close together, some with children on their shoulders, and stared up at the lighted windows of the offices on the second floor of the White House, and wondered what to do. Many of them looked, someone said, "as if they had heard a noise and were not sure where it came from." A few grabbed hold of the iron fence that ran along Pennsylvania Avenue and tried to pull themselves up to see the steady stream of officials entering and leaving. Police kept urging the crowd to "move along, move along," but the people only walked slowly back and forth, still looking to the windows, occasionally asking reporters about casualty lists, and softly but bitterly cursing the Japanese.

Earlier in the day, the streets of the capital had been nearly deserted; by late afternoon they were clogged with government workers heading for their offices (where most of them had nothing really yet to do), and slow-moving cars that drifted past the War Department and the White House, with passengers leaning out of the windows for a better view. Frequently they turned down Massachusetts Avenue toward the Japanese embassy. A smaller crowd congregated in front of that white stone building, perhaps three hundred people at most, including many school-age boys who shouted insults in the general direction of the unseen occupants. The police kept everyone on the far side of the street, although there still were loud boos whenever any Japanese officials arrived or departed, or when a figure appeared in a lighted window. The embassy reportedly had retained a detective agency for additional protection, just in case, but there was no violence, and the police eventually dispersed the crowd.

New Yorkers read the latest headlines on the electronic news ticker in Times Square, mostly in silence. Along Broadway, theaters interrupted their matinee performances to tell patrons the news; after a moment of quiet, some in the audience cheered. Subways were crowded with military men heading to Grand Central Terminal or Pennsylvania Station, and then back to their camps or ships. Mayor Fiorello La Guardia sped downtown from his East Harlem apartment in a police cruiser, convened his emergency board, closed all Japanese clubs and meeting places, and ordered all Japanese nationals in the city—an estimated 2,500—confined to their homes. (Diners in Japanese restaurants were allowed to finish their meals before police ushered the owners and staff back home.) From the Fifth Avenue offices of the *Crisis*, the journal of the National Association for the Advancement of Colored People, editor in chief Roy Wilkins attributed the debacle at Pearl Harbor in part to "the stupid habit of white people of looking down on all non-white nations."

Beginning at 5:15, La Guardia (whose voice had been charitably described as high-pitched and "over-intense" at the best of times) made two speeches on the radio, accusing "the thugs and gangsters who control the Nazi government" of masterminding the Japanese attack, and warning local residents "not to feel entirely secure because they happen to be on the Atlantic coast." Then he asked his listeners to remain calm. That evening, audiences in Broadway theaters were sparse and the city's streets deserted, as New Yorkers listened to the latest bulletins from radios blaring from apartment house windows.

In Chicago, people gathered in small groups on street corners and bars. Hotel guests remained close to newsstands to get the latest reports. Nobody paid much attention to the brightly lit Christmas displays in department stores, or the carols that played over loudspeakers. Here, too, the mayor shut down all the Japanese restaurants in town, but someone smashed the windows of a Japanese gift shop on Madison Street. "Don't it beat hell," remarked baseball commissioner Kenesaw Mountain Landis, in town for the major leagues' annual meetings, "they attacked us without warning as they did the Russians years ago." Railway stations with pinball shooting machines enjoyed a brisk business, especially those that simulated machine-gun attacks on incoming aircraft. In one bar, a Notre Dame student swore that "we'll whip 'em in two weeks." "Don't be silly," replied the guy on the next stool. "They've been fighting; we haven't. We'll whip them, but it'll take a few months to do it."

New York Yankees shortstop Phil Rizzuto heard the news while on a visit to Norfolk, Virginia, where he had played minor-league ball. "Then I get a call from my mother," Rizzuto recalled. She frantically informed him "that Lefty had just called and told her the Japs were right outside Brooklyn and I'd better get right home." John Houseman, the Romanian-born theater director who had worked with Orson Welles on the famed radio broadcast of *War of the Worlds*, was sitting in the club car of a train speeding through western Kansas. He later claimed that he "stayed there for the rest of the day and night drinking and listening to the news with mixed feelings of exhilaration and terror." Ernest Hemingway had no illusions about the immediate future: "Through our (American) laziness, criminal carelessness, and blind arrogance we are fucked in this war as of the first day and we are going to have Christ's own bitter time to win it if, when, and ever. . . . No matter how many countries you see fucked and bitched and ruined you never get to take it easily. Having to watch all the steps and know them all so well."

Sixteen-year-old Russell Baker sat by a small radio in the kitchen of his Baltimore home and followed the bulletins from Washington. "I thought the Japanese attack was ridiculous. A tiny country like that, nothing more than a few specks on the map, a country whose products were synonymous with junk, a pipsqueak country on the far side of the earth. . . . Settling their hash would be as easy as squashing an ant." On a corner not far from Johns Hopkins University, a group of Baltimore boys strung up a crude effigy of a Japanese on a street post and hung on it a placard: "This Jap tried to invade the U.S." An African American barber confirmed that he would fight the Japanese, "but when it comes down to the colored man himself, he has been treated so badly here all along, I don't know how much he will gain. When everything is over, he may be in a worse fix than he is now." In restaurants near Baltimore harbor, people ate their dinners with no visible emotion, and either spoke quietly about the war or said nothing at all; one observer felt they seemed to regard the war as "an unpleasant necessity, a sort of inescapable visitation of fate."

At the University of Illinois in Champaign, over half of the student body joined in a spontaneous procession to the university president's house, chanting "Knock Japan on their can." Louisiana State University students staged a similar march to the home of their school's president, who came out in a dressing gown and said simply, "Study hard." Outside the Japanese consulate in New Orleans, a group of several hundred citizens shouted angrily at two Japanese boys and an African American chauffeur who were burning documents in two large wire baskets inside the building's gates. Moviegoers at the Majestic Theater in Dallas heard the news from Hawaii at the conclusion of the feature film, *Sergeant York*; there was a pause, an audible sigh, and then loud applause and shouted threats against Japan. Farther west, in San Diego, people drifted toward the harbor and stood at the docks, looking out to the Pacific Ocean.

Some Americans claimed to feel a sense of relief that war had finally arrived, bringing two difficult years of anxiety and animosity to an end. As the *New Yorker* noted, "we were safe enough" before the Japanese attack, "but it was an unsatisfactory kind of safety, humiliating to some, foolish to others, clearly temporary to all but a few. It was also a safety strongly mixed with fear. We're sure that a lot of very unpleasant things still lie ahead of us, but we doubt if anything can be much more unpleasant than the uncertainty, frustration, and bitterness that lay between Munich and Manila. On the whole, we'd say we feel much better now."

Troops typically took the news stoically. A civilian visitor to March Field outside of Riverside, California, noticed no particular flurry of activity that afternoon. Some of the soldiers cursed the Japanese; "some just said, 'Well, we're in it'; some said, 'It's a surprise.'" At Fort Leonard Wood in Missouri, a group of recruits who had almost completed their basic training lay on their bunks reading comics or detective stories, or listening to a jazz program on the radio when the announcer interrupted and said that Honolulu had been bombed. "There was silence for a few moments," recalled one private, "and a little tenseness. Then somebody smiled, made a dirty remark, and the tenseness was gone. Nobody got excited—at least not about being in a shooting war. There was some anxiety, but it was for the Christmas furloughs that we feared would be canceled. Somebody said there wasn't any use saving any more for a trip home; he might as well get in a craps game. And so one was started."

Chinese Americans tried to disguise their glee. "Now all doubt is ended, the showdown must come," declared one resident of Chicago's Chinatown. "Everybody is happy," confessed a Chinese businessman in Baltimore, "—not that this country is in the war. Everybody is happy because only victory is ahead." "Japan has signed its death warrant," agreed another. There was also a definite "I told you so" element to their reactions. "That's the way those Japs do," insisted a Chinese American in Arlington, Virginia. "They talk nice to you in front and knife you in the back." But in a preview of things to come, a Chinese journalist on his way home from a White House press briefing was assaulted before he could prove he was not Japanese.

As the reality of war sank in, local and state government officials across the nation called out all available state guards and policemen to provide protection against sabotage to power stations, bridges, public utility buildings, shipyards, tunnels, radio broadcasting stations, and defense plants. Governor Herbert Lehman of New York also instructed his state's mayors to assign special guards "to protect all Japanese nationals residing in your city"; numerous city authorities on both coasts advised local Japanese residents to stay off the streets.

By nightfall the Army and Navy had ordered all officers into uniform. The Civil Aeronautics Board grounded all private planes in the United States, and prohibited commercial airlines from transporting anyone who was a Japanese national or who was suspected of being a Japanese national. State Department officials ordered police along both coasts to stop "all foreign sailings." The Federal Communications Commission suspended all amateur radio operations in the United States, unless authorized by the government for emergencies. The Navy imposed censorship over radio messages and cablegrams to foreign countries; the Army censored military news within the United States. Secretary of the Treasury Morgenthau banned all financial transactions by Japanese aliens. Roosevelt himself authorized the arrest of any Japanese nationals considered "dangerous to the peace and security of the United States." Justice Department officials estimated that fewer than a thousand Japanese would be affected; Attorney General Francis Biddle had declared on repeated occasions that if war came, there would be no mass roundups of enemy aliens as had occurred during World War I.

Troops from Fort Myer in northern Virginia arrived in Washington in the early evening and, armed with bayoneted rifles and gas masks, fanned out to guard strategic locations throughout the capital. (Many Americans had never seen a soldier in uniform in person, much less one with a fixed bayonet.) Soldiers, FBI agents, and plainclothes police barricaded the White House grounds and blocked access to Pennsylvania Avenue and both East and West Executive Avenues. Bystanders who remained in the area were instructed by Secret Service agents to move farther away from the president's home, but the bright red lanterns glowing on the White House lawn helped them identify the cabinet members arriving for an 8:30 meeting. Thirty minutes later, congressional leaders began to appear for a presidential briefing. The meetings adjourned around 11:30, leaving Roosevelt just enough time to relax with a sandwich and beer (off the record) with journalist Edward R. Murrow. Before he retired for the evening, the president sent back the defense production program which administration officials had developed during the past few months, and told his advisers to work up a greatly expanded version. Just before midnight, the dwindling crowd outside the White House suddenly began to sing "God Bless America" as a policeman strolled back and forth in front of the iron gates.

War arrived on the West Coast in a slightly less well-behaved manner.

The initial radio bulletins from Pearl Harbor late Sunday morning were met with the same dazed and disbelieving response, especially from those who were convinced Orson Welles was on the loose again. Man-on-the-street interviews in downtown Los Angeles elicited reactions that might as easily have come from Manhattan: "I can't imagine what the Japanese had in mind." . . . "I guess I had sort of discounted the headlines." . . . "They must be a nation of megalomaniacs over there on that island." . . . "I think the job of beating the Japs won't take long."

But one also heard more frequently the warning that "now we've got to be on the lookout for sabotage," because California was nearly three thousand miles closer to Honolulu (and, of course, Japan) than was New York City, and most of the Japanese nationals on the mainland of the United States lived between Los Angeles and San Francisco. According to the general registration of aliens ordered by Congress a year earlier, approximately 93,000 Japanese nationals resided in the United States: 41,000 in Hawaii, and over 80 percent of the rest in California and Washington State. Nearly half of the nation's 80,000 Nisei—second-generation Japanese Americans—lived in southern California, including 20,000 in Los Angeles County alone. Legal immigration of Japanese had been cut off by the Gentlemen's Agreement of 1908, but white residents of the West Coast had long distrusted and sometimes feared "the yellow peril," partly because of the Japanese Americans' economic success as farmers and fishermen, and partly because of their tight-knit communities and their determination to preserve their native culture.

Evidence of "war hysteria" appeared that first day. After hearing a panicked (and incorrect) rumor that Japanese submarines had been sighted heading toward the California coast, someone in the Los Angeles County sheriff's office issued a radio appeal for 250,000 volunteers for the Civilian Defense Council. Scores of men swarmed into the Hall of Justice to sign up, some wearing .45-caliber pistols on their hips, others brandishing rifles or any of a wide variety of nondescript but lethal weapons. One eager volunteer said that eleven youths in his neighborhood had formed a special defense unit and demanded uniforms. The sheriff finally arrived, straight from a picnic—he was wearing a cowboy suit, which only added to the Wild West atmosphere—and told everyone to go home and await further developments.

Governor Culbert Olson, a liberal and occasionally radical Democrat (with matinee-idol good looks), attempted to calm the public's fears. "I do not believe, even with the sudden and almost unbelievable attack on Hawaii, we may anticipate any immediately similar attack on our coast," Olson assured his radio listeners. That afternoon, there was an uneasy quiet in Little Tokyo, the Los Angeles district that formed the heart of the largest Japanese settlement in the United States. Residents tried to go about their business as usual, despite the steady stream of cars filled with curiosity seekers who drove through the area until police blocked off the streets at 6 p.m. to forestall any incidents.

"There will be no trouble among the Japanese element here," promised H. T. Komai, the editor of the *Los Angeles Japanese Daily News*. "Why should we shoot? We couldn't do anything, anyway." Small groups of Nisei stood on street corners and discussed the news from Hawaii; one suggested that German pilots had actually carried out the attack. A young Japanese American soldier in a U.S. Army uniform told a reporter that "if I have to fight against the Japanese, that's all right with me. I am an American." The Japanese American Citizens League, an anti-Axis organization, declared that "American citizens of Japanese extraction and resident Japanese aliens are deeply stunned," and offered its "fullest cooperation and its facilities to the United States government."

Meanwhile the machinery of military and civilian defense swung into action. Army officials assigned troops from the Ninth Corps to guard strategic points throughout California. The state Highway Patrol ordered numerous roads cleared so antiaircraft batteries could be rushed to the Mare Island Navy Yard in Vallejo. Olson mobilized the State Guard and asked the legislature for authority to add ten thousand volunteers. San Francisco mayor Angelo Rossi (dismissed by one critic as "an elderly florist who can hardly write his own name") declared a state of emergency, and demanded an immediate end to all labor strikes in the strongly pro-union city "in order to present a united front." Los Angeles harbor was officially closed; customs authorities prohibited any boats from leaving Monterey Bay, the home of a substantial Japanese fishing fleet. Civilian air raid wardens reported for duty, machine guns and searchlights were mounted on rooftops in the cities, and antiaircraft crews went on alert at numerous aircraft plants in southern California. Over a hundred military planes from inland airfields in New Mexico, Arizona, and Nevada were dispatched to the coast.

Even before they received instructions from Washington, local authorities began to arrest Japanese aliens—and sometimes Nisei—whom they regarded as suspicious. Leaders of the Japanese community in Santa Barbara were taken into custody and held incommunicado for interrogation by the FBI. Deputy sheriffs and highway patrolmen swept through farmhouses in the Santa Maria Valley, confiscating rifles, revolvers, and shotguns. Federal agents arrested Japanese at religious services, and at weddings. In Hollywood, an amateur baseball team of Paramount Studio employees was playing the L.A. Nippons, an all-Japanese team, when the news about Pearl Harbor came over the radio. FBI agents allowed the game to finish (Paramount won, 6–3), then rounded up the Japanese players.

As the day ended, a crowd of nearly a thousand Los Angelenos in Pershing Square stood at attention as the American flag was lowered and an Army bugler sounded retreat.

# 3: An Anxious Trip

DECEMBER 8–DECEMBER 15, 1941

*The enemy wants you to run into the streets,*
*create a mob, start a panic. Don't do it.*

—OFFICE OF CIVILIAN DEFENSE

"I don't remember at all what I did on Monday," wrote Ernie Pyle. "I only remember that all that day people were talking, talking, talking, and that nobody knew what he was saying or what he was thinking." AT & T, which enjoyed a monopoly on the long-distance telephone business, confirmed that a record-breaking number of Americans attempted to contact their friends and relatives across the country on December 8; since long-distance calls required the assistance of an operator, it often took three or four hours to get through, particularly on calls to and from the West Coast and to military camps in the South.

Working on four hours' sleep and fortified by a breakfast of black coffee, Franklin Roosevelt spent the morning fine-tuning his war message to Congress. Several minutes after noon, his son James helped the president into a black limousine waiting under the White House portico. (Equipped with bulletproof glass in its windows, the vehicle had been supplied on short notice by the Treasury Department, which reportedly had appropriated it years earlier from Al Capone.) With Secret Service agents standing on each running board, flanked by open cars bristling with more Secret Service men armed with sawed-off riot guns, Roosevelt's limousine headed up Pennsylvania Avenue toward Capitol Hill.

At the Capitol, a crowd of more than a thousand people cheered when they caught a glimpse of the president—bundled in his usual old, heavy navy blue cape against the sharp wind—through the blanket of protection afforded by barricades, Marine guards, and several hundred policemen. Spectators inside noticed that Roosevelt's face looked drawn and weary, his pace slower than usual as he made his way into the House chamber on the arm of his son, who was dressed in his Marine Corps uniform. Outside, people hurried back to their cars to listen to the proceedings on the radio. (Off to the side, a group of teenage boys sang a chorus of "You're in the Army Now.") Declaring December 7 "a date which will live in infamy," the president spoke for less than ten minutes, with frequent interruptions for applause. Seated with the rest of the cabinet on the bench in front of Roosevelt, Secretary Hull listened with an expression of deep sadness; Supreme Court justice Hugo Black repeatedly dabbed at his eyes with a handkerchief. The speech concluded with a request for a declaration of war against Japan, followed by "The Star-Spangled Banner." Less than half an hour after he arrived, the president left the Capitol.

Congress wasted no time, either. The Senate unanimously passed a war resolution at one o'clock. In the House, the final tally was 388–1, as only Montana Republican Jeannette Rankin dissented; after the vote, Rankin—the first female member of Congress and a pacifist who also had opposed entry into World War I in 1917—took refuge in a telephone booth as reporters pressed her for an explanation.

Several hours later (after Roosevelt awoke from a much-needed nap), congressional leaders carried the declaration to the White House, where the president signed it at 4:10 p.m. Predictable pledges of unity followed from politicians in both parties. Each of the past three Republican presidential nominees—Wendell Willkie, Alf Landon, and Herbert Hoover—promised his support. Republican Party national chairman Joe Martin, who was also House minority leader, swore that "Republicans will not permit politics to enter into national defense."

Roosevelt's critics outside Congress also fell into line. America First officials canceled a planned rally in Boston, then disbanded altogether three days later and urged their members to support the war effort. Charles Lindbergh—who refused to give out a statement from his estate on Martha's Vineyard on Sunday—grudgingly conceded that the nation must be united "regardless of our attitude in the past toward the policy our Government has followed. Whether or not that policy has been wise, our country has been attacked by force of arms, and by force of arms we must retaliate." Columnist Westbrook Pegler, who rarely had kind words for the president in peacetime, now admitted that he felt Roosevelt was the right man to take on the Axis in a no-holds-barred brawl. "It is well to have a man in the White House who will not bother to break clean or keep his punches up," Pegler wrote. "When our man warms up to a scrap anything goes."

Americans who expected an easy victory faced a rude awakening. "Everyone thinks this is going to be a short picnic," noted Assistant Secretary of State Adolf Berle in his diary. "It is not going to be anything of the kind. It is going to be a long, dirty, painful, bloody business." Walter Lippmann agreed. "The soft talkative times are gone," Lippmann advised his readers, "and the hardest days we have ever known since Valley Forge have begun." For her part, Anne Lindbergh feared that too many Americans had no idea what lay ahead: "I feel as though all I believed was America, all memories of it, all history, all dreams of the future were marching gaily toward a precipice—and unaware, unaware."

In every major city, Army recruiting stations were mobbed. Lines began to form as early as 2:30 Monday morning, with twenty or thirty times the usual number of applicants. Navy recruiters reported twice as many volunteers as on the first day of war in 1917; the Marines, too, were flooded with recruits. Taken by surprise and overwhelmed by the crush of applicants, military authorities reluctantly turned away crowds of men at the end of the afternoon and told them to return another day. That evening, all three military services announced that henceforth their recruiting stations would remain open on a 24/7 basis.

At least for whites. African American men who wished to volunteer found most doors closed to them. Although the number of blacks serving in the United States Army had risen dramatically in the previous decade—increasing from a mere 2,954 in 1934 to nearly 95,000 at the end of November 1941—the military remained very much a segregated institution. Nearly all the commissioned officers in African American units were white; most of their noncoms were black. (Army officials defended their policy by stating that they did not create the problem of racial segregation, and in any case "the Army is no sociological laboratory.") And while the Selective Service Act of 1940 clearly stated that "there shall be no discrimination against any person on account of race or color," Selective Service director General Lewis Hershey routinely advised draft boards to accept blacks for service only when the existing African American units—few of which were slated for combat duty—required replacements. The Navy employed "colored boys" only as messmen, a role one recruit described as nothing more than "a flunky." The Marine Corps refused to accept African Americans at all.

"We colored people are Americans," insisted an editorial in the *Baltimore Afro-American*, "and as Americans who have as much stake in this our land as any other citizens, we will do our share to defend it. . . . But we cannot defend America with a dust brush, a mop and a white apron. We cannot march against enemy planes and tanks, and challenge warships armed with only a whiskbroom and a wide grin."

Far more Americans offered their services to the civilian defense effort, heretofore the object of widespread public ridicule. Roosevelt had created the Office of Civilian Defense in May 1941 to coordinate the efforts of federal, state, and local agencies to protect citizens in case of emergency, including invasion or air attacks. He appointed Mayor La Guardia to head the OCD, assisted by the president's wife, Eleanor. Over the next six months, however, even the hyper-energetic La Guardia failed to persuade many Americans to take seriously the threat of attack from abroad. Prior to Pearl Harbor, much of the nation still viewed civil defense preparations as "a kind of make-believe," as Walter Lippmann put it, "like children playing at war . . . [or] the activities of an excited village improvement society." Apathy had been most profound in the Midwest, but even in towns along the Atlantic coast, residents had shrugged off practice blackouts or rehearsals for evacuations of women and children by sea. "Most people thought these unceasing activities were silly," noted one writer on Cape Cod, "or had the unreality of nightmare."

But on December 8, thousands of Americans signed up for training as air raid wardens. In Arizona, cowboys enlisted as airplane spotters, scouring the desert sky for enemy bombers. Dairy farmers in Puget Sound abandoned their cows and formed beach patrols. Other enthusiastic patriots found these tasks too tame. A group of Texas ranchers organized themselves into "the Guerrillas" in case Japanese paratroopers crossed the Rio Grande; prospective members needed only a high-powered rifle, five hundred rounds of ammunition, and a car with a full tank of gas. In West Virginia, the thousand-member Kanawha Game and Fish Association—the self-described "best shots in West Virginia"—offered their services to state officials in Charleston. (The 1940 census counted three Japanese residents in the Mountain State.) Age proved no barrier, as Georgia's Confederate Veterans—there were about fifty remaining, all over ninety years old—declared war on "those yellow devils" from Japan. On a gentler note, a group of prisoners at San Quentin prison in California asked the warden for knitting lessons, so they could make warm hats, socks, and sweaters for American servicemen.

Women, who had long displayed more enthusiasm for civilian defense jobs than men, volunteered as nurses, airplane plotters, typists, telephone operators, and messengers. Although several towns in New England already had female air raid wardens, the declaration of war convinced some local government officials that such work more properly belonged to men. Boston police commissioner Joseph Timilty boasted proudly that his city had no women air raid wardens, and "we don't want any, either." The police chief of nearby Brookline agreed: "Women," he claimed, "are too bossy and try to run things."

Before leaving for the West Coast on Monday, La Guardia again warned an NBC radio audience that "we who live on the Atlantic coast are just as much in danger as our countrymen who were bombed in Honolulu." So forty thousand volunteer aircraft spotters along the East Coast reported for duty. Over the next several days, the Navy mined harbors up and down the coast. Extra guards were posted at the entrance to the Federal Reserve Bank in New York, and all the building's windows were blacked out with paint. One by one, familiar landmarks were extinguished. Manhattan's giant RCA sign, with its twenty-four-foot-high golden letters seventy stories above Rockefeller Plaza, went dark. In the nation's capital, the Washington Monument and Lincoln Memorial closed at 4 p.m. to protect against sabotage after sunset, and the Army ordered the floodlights illuminating the Capitol turned off for the first time since 1918. (The red beacon lights at the top of the Washington Monument remained on at the request of commercial airlines.) All U.S. mints and the Bureau of

Engraving and Printing were closed to the public, as was the area surrounding Hoover Dam. Workers at the National Archives made plans to ship the Constitution and Declaration of Independence to bombproof shelters in Maryland. Even in Topeka, Kansas, city authorities ordered guards redoubled on bridges, railroads, and radio stations. But Boston traditionalists refused to dim the lights on their annual Christmas tree on the Common; "if they're going to bomb Boston," explained one official, "let 'em bomb the Common."

As if the radio had forecast a hurricane, Americans rushed to grocery stores on Monday to stock up on essentials. A stampede to buy sugar—shoppers bought more than a month's supply in a few days—led the Office of Production Management to freeze sugar stocks and prices to discourage hoarding. Flour came next. Beginning on Monday, stores witnessed "one of the sharpest sales spurts in recent years," despite reassurances by Department of Agriculture officials that the nation's grain reserves were higher than ever. When panic buying of flour subsided, shoppers started in on canned goods.

Automobile owners who feared a shortage of rubber—over 90 percent of America's supply came from East Asian territories either controlled or threatened by Japanese forces—rushed to garages and auto dealerships to buy as many new tires as they could. Caught off guard by this "consumers' buying wave," federal officials announced on December 10 that a temporary ban on new tire sales would go into effect the following day, to conserve the nation's dwindling stocks of rubber for military uses. Drivers took advantage of the twenty-four-hour delay to snatch up enough tires to set new sales records.

No long lines formed at Broadway ticket offices Monday night, but John O'Hara, the theater critic for *Newsweek*, found himself at the opening of a new drama, *Golden Wings*, starring Fay Wray. ("Not one of our great dramatic draws," O'Hara noted sourly.) As the audience filtered in, O'Hara could hear scattered talk of the war until the lights went down. Then from a small orchestra in an upper-tier box there came the opening notes of the national anthem. "That was what I wanted to hear," decided O'Hara. "I don't think I could have stayed in the theater without hearing it. That day we in New York had been warned to expect some 'token' bombings. . . . I don't say that hearing that wonderful, bruised, abused old anthem is going to make a bombing easier to take. But I'm not saying it won't. Anyway, it felt good that night." When it ended, no one clapped: "That silence was evidence of an angry America." Then the orchestra played "God Save the King"; again there were no cheers. The audience took their seats, O'Hara wrote, "in cold silence."

Aided by police detectives, FBI agents continued to round up Japanese nationals on their watch list, along with some Germans and Italians just in case. All day, the Bureau's switchboards were swamped with tips from helpful citizens who claimed to have witnessed "suspicious" behavior by people who at least looked like enemy aliens. By Monday afternoon, nearly a thousand had been arrested, and the number continued to rise as police and federal agents in some areas decided to seize everyone of Japanese descent and let immigration officials and the Justice Department sort them out. Tennessee authorities skipped a step and simply declared "open season on Japs," informing the state's hunters they need not purchase a special license to shoot any Japanese they saw.

With all Japanese banks and businesses closed by federal order, Little Tokyo in Los Angeles seemed nearly deserted. Extra teams of police patrolled the district, and impromptu "No Parking" signs along the main streets deterred both curiosity seekers and large gatherings of Japanese. Post Office authorities provided an element of absurdity by prohibiting the publication of all Japanese-language local newspapers until the publishers provided "an American translation." (It was not at all clear how postal officials—who apparently could not read Japanese—would have known if the proffered "American" translations were accurate.) A delegation from the Japanese American Citizens League met with the mayor and assured him of their members' loyalty, and Nisei students at Los Angeles City College publicly denounced the attack on Pearl Harbor. "This is the opportunity for all loyal Americans of Japanese descent to prove that they are Americans," one female Nisei declared. "Any Japanese-Americans who are not loyal should be reported and placed in Army custody . . . so as to protect the large majority who are real Americans."

Governor Olson wanted to order all Japanese in California to remain indoors for their own protection, but the State Council of Defense argued that such a move would deprive Californians of the vegetables raised by Japanese farmers. (The state was preparing a petition to federal authorities to permit Japanese vegetable farms and markets—which provided the majority of fresh produce in southern California—to remain in operation.) And so Japanese American children went to school in Los Angeles on Monday morning in the usual numbers, albeit "with a great deal of trepidation"; the older children, according to city schools superintendent Vierling Kersey, "were in a state of hysterical quiet." A few children whose parents spoke no English appeared at school with no knowledge of Sunday's events. In some schools, Nisei met with threats and insults from white students and parents, fueled by rumors alleging fifth-column Japanese activities, gossip which school officials termed "simply vicious." Kersey attempted to calm tensions by reminding everyone that "the children are Americans, and we do owe them a square deal." But before the day ended, the school system received nearly a thousand calls from frantic parents asking what to do "when the bombers arrive."

That evening, all hell broke loose on the West Coast.

It began in San Francisco. The city's nerves had been on edge since the first reports from Pearl Harbor; all Sunday night and the following day, residents stayed close to their radios expecting news of Japanese attacks on California. Less resolute souls fled eastward, creating a heavy stream of traffic across both the Golden Gate and San Francisco–Oakland Bay Bridges. (Sentries stopped cars driven by Japanese and searched for explosives.) By noon on Monday, the area had worked itself to the edge of panic. Rumors of approaching Japanese submarines and bombers convinced city officials to close schools early; many of the city's children spent the rest of the afternoon roaming through the streets calling out "Air raid! Air raid!" while growing increasingly hysterical.

Just after sunset, radar screens at Army posts in the San Francisco area picked up signals which military officials interpreted as Japanese airplanes about one hundred miles west of the city. At approximately the same time, they received an unverified report of a Japanese submarine in the vicinity of the Golden Gate Bridge. Perhaps because they knew how thin the U.S. coastal defenses were—troops equipped with 1903 Springfield rifles, artillery that dated back to the turn of the century, a relative handful of naval vessels to patrol more than a thousand miles of coast—Army commanders decided to take no chances, and ordered all local radio stations off the air so enemy bombers could not follow the radio transmission beams to their targets.

At once all the radios in San Francisco went dead, right at dinnertime. Puzzled residents waited for further instructions; there were none. At 6:20 p.m., police officials ordered a blackout, but San Francisco's three air raid warning sirens could be heard only in the immediate downtown area. Police and fire department vehicles tried to spread the news by speeding through the streets sounding their own sirens, but that merely compounded the confusion. The lights along Market Street, the central and most brilliantly lit thoroughfare, remained on—power company technicians needed to turn them off individually—as did the neon lights throughout the business district, most of which were on time-lock devices. (One insurance company sign brightly spelled out "S-A-F-E.") No one seemed to have the authority to turn off the lights atop the towers of the Golden Gate Bridge. Prison officials at Alcatraz, in the middle of San Francisco Bay, flatly refused to douse their floodlights for fear of a riot.

Even though airplane spotters on rooftops throughout the region never saw or heard a single enemy plane that night, Army officials at the Western Defense Command announced that two squadrons of Japanese planes—thirty planes altogether—had been launched from aircraft carriers five hundred miles off the coast and were approaching San Francisco and San José. Antiaircraft searchlights from the Presidio crisscrossed the sky, lending credence to the reports. San Francisco police called off the initial blackout at 7:30 p.m. and then imposed another blackout minutes later. At that point, the frontier tradition of vigilantism seized control of the city. A University of San Francisco student later recalled driving downtown that evening: "Market Street was bedlam. The United Artists Theatre had a huge marquee with those dancing lights, going on and off. People were throwing everything they could to put those lights out, screaming Blackout! Blackout! . . . No cars could move. The streets were full of people, blocking the tracks, the trolley line. People were throwing rocks, anything they could find. A streetcar came along, one of the old-fashioned, funny San Francisco streetcars. It had a big round light. A man ran up with a baseball bat and smashed the light."

"The Japs are coming!" people shouted. "The Japs are coming!" Someone said the Golden Gate Bridge had been bombed; but there were guards at the bridge, turning away drivers who attempted to cross. At the San Francisco–Oakland Bay Bridge, a California Home Guard sentry fired at an automobile and killed a twenty-seven-year-old female passenger whose husband failed to hear a command to stop. (Sentries also mistakenly fired upon a team of painters working on the bridge, but no one was hurt.) A rumor spread that Japanese troops had captured the Presidio, and ROTC troops were called out to repel the invaders. A taxicab with its headlights out collided with another car without lights in Alameda, killing both drivers; before the night was over, eleven other people were injured in auto accidents in the Bay Area. "Don't think this is sheer dramatics," a young woman in Berkeley wrote to a friend back east; "it's too horribly frightening to be good drama." The next morning, people flocked to newsstands to find out precisely what they had lived through.

Eight hundred miles to the north, Seattle—which also harbored a substantial Japanese population—experienced its own nightmare Monday evening when military authorities mistakenly thought they detected enemy planes headed their way. During the ensuing blackout, a crowd of well over a thousand people rampaged through the city's streets, smashing the windows of more than two dozen stores whose lights remained on, and sometimes helping themselves to the merchandise inside. Leading the mob was the nineteen-year-old wife of a Navy sailor. "We've got to show them they can't leave their lights burning," she announced proudly. "That's my patriotism." A combined force of American soldiers and British sailors stationed nearby finally restored order.

A thorough search by American military planes of the waters off the northern California coast the following day revealed neither Japanese ships nor Japanese planes. Skeptics doubted that Japan would dispatch reconnaissance planes or bombers to attack targets so far away from its primary interests in East Asia, especially when its forces already were spread thinly across the Pacific. War Department officials in Washington quickly concluded that there had been no enemy planes along the coast, but Lieutenant General John DeWitt, the head of the Western Defense Command, refused to concede any error. "Those planes were over our community," DeWitt insisted on Tuesday. "They were enemy planes. . . . Why bombs were not dropped, I do not know." In any event, the general evinced far more concern about the "criminal, shameful apathy" of some

San Franciscans who failed to heed the blackout than the violence of the mobs. Addressing a meeting of the San Francisco civilian defense emergency committee, DeWitt argued that "it might have been better if some bombs had dropped to awaken this city."

Ernie Pyle arrived in "bomb-expectant San Francisco" on Tuesday. "There is suspense here," he wrote, "and wonderment of what the night will bring, and a feeling of drastic urgency." That night, the city endured another pair of air raid alarms and blackouts, but this time there was no panic, save for one would-be soldier who ran about waving a bow and steel-tipped arrows he planned to use against "them Jap parachutists."

Nevertheless, when Alistair Cooke tuned in that evening in Washington to hear the latest news on his radio—"our inseparable daily drug"— he was stunned to hear "a sentence more bizarre than any that dramatist Orson Welles had used to terrorize a continent. It was an announcer smoothly saying, 'We now take you to news of the Far Eastern battle zone. Go ahead, San Francisco.' Even the West Coast had betrayed us, the traditional country for escape was blacking out too. There was suddenly no place to go to get away from it all." It was, Cooke decided, "as low a point as American morale could ever fear to touch."

Los Angeles experienced its first full-scale blackout on the fourth night of the war. A thunderstorm that afternoon put nerves on edge—hundreds of residents called police to see if they were being bombed—especially after the FBI chief in San Diego announced that the agency had received "persistent reports that bands of Japanese, some armed, were roaming in Baja California near the United States border."

About 8 p.m. on Wednesday night, Army observers reported unidentified planes in the vicinity of Los Angeles. Having recently emerged from emergency meetings with the high-strung La Guardia, military officials ordered a blackout from Bakersfield to the Mexican border, and eastward to Nevada. Radio broadcasts ceased. A number of defense plants in the Los Angeles area shut down and sent their workers home, losing hundreds of thousands of man-hours on aircraft production. (Several West Coast defense firms subsequently raised the legal question of whether they needed to pay workers for time lost to air raids or blackouts. Labor Department officials ruled that they did not.)

Traffic signals in downtown Los Angeles went dark. Police stood at intersections with flashlights and told drivers to proceed home with their headlights out. Not surprisingly, over a hundred people were injured; Los Angeles hospitals reported more than five times the usual number of evening calls for ambulances due to traffic accidents. One man was killed when his car collided with a streetcar; both vehicles had been traveling with their lights off. Here, too, a mob roamed through city streets smashing advertising signs and the lights in shop windows, causing thousands of dollars of property damage. Stumbling blindly through the darkness, even in the familiar surroundings of their own homes, residents reported "a sense of terror, bewilderment, and limitation." In the community of San Pedro, near Los Angeles harbor, authorities congratulated themselves on a successful blackout until an observer noticed one electric sign that remained brightly illuminated on the roof of the Chamber of Commerce Building: WELCOME TO SAN PEDRO.

"When you swing from a peace basis to a war basis there's bound to be a certain amount of stumbling, bumping and fumbling of the ball," wrote columnist Bill Henry in the *Los Angeles Times* on December 10. "It seems likely that this particular point in our history—from December 7 to date—is to be known as the Era of the Grand Bungle."

Military authorities continued to make dangerous errors. On the evening of December 12, San Francisco experienced more turmoil during a two-and-a-half-hour blackout inspired by "verified reports of unidentified airplanes flying over the area," some of which purportedly had dropped flares. "People were running around like wild," smashing lighted store windows, a bystander reported. Some frightened drivers abandoned their autos; others tried and failed to make it home on the dark, rain-slicked streets. "There were accidents from all kinds of things—autos and street cars," noted one hospital employee.

On the following evening, antiaircraft batteries outside of Los Angeles suddenly opened fire on phantom enemy planes. One three-inch shell landed, unexploded, in the backyard of a house in nearby Highland Park; police returned it to the Army. Later that night, an overzealous Army sentry on Highway 101 in Hermosa Beach—who had no orders to stop any vehicles—shot and killed a woman passenger in a car that failed to halt on his shouted command. (The husband, who was driving, said he thought the soldier was a hitchhiker seeking a ride.)

The incident persuaded Governor Olson to declare a state of emergency. California officials publicly condemned "marauding gangs of self-appointed air raid wardens" and "hoodlums masquerading as patriots" who attacked citizens and property during blackouts. In southern California, police and civilian defense authorities imposed a blackout speed limit of ten miles per hour in cities, and fifteen miles per hour in the countryside. And merchants began closing their stores early, typically at 4:30 p.m. (even though it was still the Christmas season), so shoppers could return home before dark.

New Yorkers had the good fortune to experience their first air raid alarm in the daytime. Around eleven o'clock on the morning of December 9, U.S. First Army headquarters on Governors Island received a call from the War Department in Washington, checking on a report of unidentified planes heading toward Manhattan. Air Defense Command authorities mistook the question for a warning, and immediately ordered their planes at Mitchel Field on Long Island into the air.

All radio stations within a hundred miles went silent. Civilian planes in the New York area were grounded, and incoming flights were diverted. Most public schools in the city dismissed their classes, sending students home just as parents were heading to school to pick them up. The city's makeshift air raid siren system proved signally ineffective: New York officials attempted to employ a special sequence of fire and police sirens as an alarm, but residents were so accustomed to hearing those sounds amid the usual cacophony of the city streets that many simply ignored them, if they heard them at all.

Unlike their counterparts on the West Coast, however, New Yorkers seemed "more bewildered than alarmed," more confused than panicked. For every pedestrian who took shelter, several more—apparently unclear on the concept of air raids—ran into the streets to see what was happening. Curious office workers simply stuck their heads out of windows and stared up at the sky. Police attempted to evacuate Times Square, but many pedestrians ("the recalcitrant, the blasé, and the plain stupid," grumbled one disgruntled bystander) stuck around to read the news bulletins. A policeman stopped two city buses near City Hall and told everyone to get out and take cover; following a five-minute argument, not a single passenger had budged. "What was I to do?" the cop asked a reporter. "Use my gun on them?"

After hearing a radio warning that enemy planes would bomb Manhattan within the hour, columnist and bon vivant Lucius Beebe hurried to the fashionable restaurant "21," where he was joined by other society notables "desirous of being blown to bits in their best Daché bonnets and smartest clothes," accompanied by a host of news photographers. "It was a very pleasant and exciting lunch," Beebe noted, "pregnant with expectancy and eventual anticlimax, but it gave the room a satisfactory sense of being already in combat." Clearly, Beebe concluded, "the invasion was going to be a social success."

Movie theaters decided to let their films run on, although ushers stood by the emergency exits just in case. Amid the skyscrapers of Wall Street, an elderly lady paused, listened for a moment, put up her umbrella, and proceeded calmly on her way. Virtually the only site of real panic was, predictably, the New York Stock Exchange. The market had weathered a shaky Monday, watched closely by NYSE officials prepared to suspend trading if a post–Pearl Harbor rout developed. But the more severe losses occurred on Tuesday, when the sirens and reports of "unidentified planes" scared some brokers into dumping shares at any price before heading for cover. In very heavy trading, the market suffered its worst decline since the fall of France in May 1940.

When Boston's Mayor Maurice Tobin received a Navy warning that afternoon that enemy planes had been sighted two hundred miles from his city, he mobilized the entire Boston police force and ordered the officers to get all private cars off the streets. Police promptly proceeded to stop air raid wardens, Red Cross nurses, and defense workers from reaching their destinations. Both the Boston Navy Yard and the Bethlehem Steel shipbuilding plant in Quincy were evacuated; inside the plants, furnaces shut down and vats of molten steel cooled, rendering work on nearly $5 billion of defense contracts impossible until the night shift began. On Martha's Vineyard, Charles Lindbergh reported that "people here actually expect to see enemy planes flying overhead, and they believe there is grave danger of the town being bombed." That evening, a journalist noted that Boston's streets were "as stripped of motorists as a desert, . . . as clean as the ice surface between periods of a hockey game."

Nearly everyone was at home, listening to President Roosevelt's latest fireside chat. Earlier that day the president had held his customary Tuesday press conference, looking "calm, rested, cheery [and] buoyant," while affably parrying reporters' questions about military affairs. Roosevelt did confirm that *war* production—the word *defense* was officially out; *war* and *victory* were in—would be expanded and speeded up, with every factory that was producing defense/victory materials placed on a 24/7 schedule, which would require either a lot more overtime, or a lot more workers, or, most likely, both. Meanwhile, White House windows were fitted for blackout curtains, the Secret Service doubled its guard around the mansion, and soldiers in steel helmets manned machine guns on nearby rooftops because there were no antiaircraft guns available.

In his address that evening to a radio audience estimated at 90 million Americans (virtually every adult in the nation), Roosevelt acknowledged that "so far the news has all been bad." He promised that the government would provide more details on U.S. losses at Pearl Harbor—so far the published reports were sketchy—as the Navy completed its investigation, but the president added that he would release no information that would give aid or comfort to the enemy. And while Roosevelt assured his listeners that "we are going to win the war and we are going to win the peace that follows," he urged them to put aside any thoughts of an easy victory: "It will not only be a long war, it will be a hard war. . . . On the road ahead lies hard work—grueling work—day and night, every hour and every minute."

Two days later, Germany and Italy declared war on the United States; Congress immediately reciprocated. "Now, all that I feared would happen has happened," Charles Lindbergh wrote in his diary. "We are at war all over the world, and we are unprepared for it from either a spiritual or a material standpoint."

"Each man was pretty much alone with his thoughts last week, turned inward, considering things privately," mused the *New Yorker*, "adjusting his life to a new set of conditions, not yet completely understood. . . . People met and talked as they always had, but they thought separately. Everybody exchanged military opinions based on what little information there was (it was a lovely season for clichés and false premises), but no one was very attentive, each busy with his own need to grasp the real dimensions of what had happened, to define his own relation to it." In unguarded moments, thoughts of war disappeared amid the comfort of daily routines. But "this happy state was always brief. There was always something to bring back the consciousness of total separation from the past."

Usually radio provided the jolt. For the past week, numerous radio network executives had interrupted their usual slate of comedies and dramas—which they felt might appear "impertinent" under the circumstances—with a steady diet of news bulletins, special reports, and all-night vigils from the Philippines, or perhaps California. Invariably the news was bad: the surrender of American forces on Guam; Japanese bombers pounding Nichols Field, the U.S. Army air base outside Manila; the British battleship *Prince of Wales* sunk off the coast of Malaya; Japanese forces landing on Luzon.

But the confused lines of communication in the early days of the war, and widespread official reticence to acknowledge losses (the War Department did not issue *any* communiqués until December 10) meant that the radio reports were typically sketchy. So newspaper offices were flooded with telephone calls from readers wanting the latest updates; the *Chicago Tribune* alone received over fifty thousand calls in the first three days after Pearl Harbor. Others simply dialed 0 and asked an operator for news from the front, even though telephone operators were even more isolated than nearly anyone else. Washington hostesses in search of a scoop invited all the military officials they knew to their parties. "It has been nothing but war, war, war," observed one exhausted society columnist, "speculations whispered over chicken patties at women's luncheons; umpteen versions of 'what really happened,' according to anonymous high officials, exchanged at afternoon gatherings."

Attendance dwindled at movie theaters and nightclubs; tickets for Broadway shows went begging, even though some theater owners interrupted their shows to read war bulletins to their news-hungry audiences. Hopes for a record-setting Christmas shopping season plummeted, as department stores reported empty aisles. "When I did my shopping," reported Hedda Hopper from Hollywood, "you could have fired off a gun and not hit anybody but the clerks."

"This is not good for us," insisted a social worker in Boston. "It is not even conducive to winning the war. . . . Let us get just enough of war news to be conversant with the main facts." The radio networks' practice of "breaking into routine programs with only vague 'flashes,'" charged one media critic, "was thoroughly upsetting to nerves already stressed." If it continued, "the vital work all America is engaged in could be bogged down easily in a welter of nerves and anxious listening." At the end of the first week of war, Chicago's Mayor Edward Kelly suggested that it was time for Americans to "get away from the radio and get to work."

Gradually the networks resumed their normal programming, and began to release war bulletins in a more orderly fashion in regularly scheduled news spots. Guidelines for wartime news reporting issued by the National Association of Broadcasters advised stations to avoid sensationalism, and to "report war news calmly, slowly, and deliberately, so as to avoid horror, suspense and undue excitement." They were also requested to stop broadcasting unconfirmed reports or enemy communiqués, and to refrain from second-guessing American military officials. Audience participation and ad-lib programs were discouraged, in case someone unwittingly blurted out classified information: "An open microphone accessible to the general public constitutes a very real hazard in times of war."

Several Philadelphia stations agreed to drop their all-night record-request programs, to prevent enemy agents from using songs to send coded messages. Dramas about the military were out, replaced by realistic stories describing the war's effects on the home front, or talks on the contributions women could make to the war effort. Comedian Fred Allen's variety show abandoned its signature introduction of a wailing siren, for obvious reasons. NBC's *The Treasury Hour* replaced its variety and comedy segments with serious music, presumably excluding the vast majority of war songs written in the first week after Pearl Harbor—most of which were simple-minded exercises in Japan-bashing and soon forgotten: "Taps for the Japs"; "I Wouldn't Want to Be a Jap for All the Tea in China"; "You're a Sap, Mr. Jap (to Make a Yankee Cranky)"; and the unfortunate "We're Going to Find a Fellow Who Is Yellow and Beat Him Red, White and Blue." Lyrically speaking, the war was not off to a great start; Irving Berlin recommended waiting until the nation's nerves calmed down. "The thing doesn't come," Berlin acknowledged. "You can't just say,

'Let's go kill the Japs.' The newspapers can do that better. A song's got to be something different."

Anti-Japanese outbursts far outweighed any public expressions of hostility toward German or Italian culture. Along the Tidal Basin in the nation's capital, a gang of youths cut down four Japanese cherry trees—two were part of the emperor's original gift from 1912—during a partial blackout on December 9. "To hell with those Japanese," they scribbled on one tree. To prevent similar acts of vandalism, the city's Freer Gallery of Art removed all Japanese paintings, prints, and sculptures from its displays; the Boston Museum of Fine Arts followed suit. The New York City Department of Parks demolished the Japanese Pavilion in Flushing Meadow Park, one of the last remnants of the 1939 World's Fair. City officials also changed the sign on the pen housing the Japanese deer in Central Park to "Asiatic deer."

In Montpelier, Vermont, complaints from residents led town authorities to take down the Japanese-manufactured silver bells used for holiday street decorations. (More problematic were the whistles used by many air raid wardens in New York City, which bore the legend "Made in Japan.") In New Orleans, the congregation of the Rising Sun Baptist Church unanimously voted to change its name to the Pentecost Baptist Church. Author John P. Marquand announced that he would write no more Mr. Moto detective novels: "He seemed a really nice fellow," Marquand confessed to a reporter. "But now it seems I had him all wrong. A veritable wolf in sheep's clothing, so to speak."

Repertory companies across the country canceled productions of Gilbert and Sullivan's *The Mikado*, despite the fact that the musical satirizes Japanese culture (and, in a deeper sense, Victorian institutions). In Washington, the Gilbert and Sullivan Opera Company proceeded with its performance a week after Pearl Harbor, but changed the words of the opening chorus from "We are gentlemen of Japan" to "We are gangsters of Japan." In case anyone missed the message, the program notes stated that the opera correctly portrayed Japanese as "sly, wily and deceitful, unconscionably corrupt, and treacherous. . . . With a dagger between the teeth, a sputtering bomb held behind the back and the outstretched hand dripping with blood."

Under orders from their companies' headquarters, five-and-dime chain stores removed all Japanese-made merchandise from their shelves. Most of it they simply destroyed. "We even burned up Santa Claus," chuckled the manager of one Woolworth store after consigning a cotton Santa from Tokyo to the flames. In one Michigan town, authorities built a bonfire out of five thousand calendars made in Japan, while Detroit shoppers smashed Japanese-made china plates on department store floors, or used them as clay pigeons. Families who had already purchased Christmas ornaments from Japan threw them into the trash. "If we can't get American-made decorations," proclaimed one New Englander, "the tree will stand as she is." The purge was emotionally satisfying, perhaps, but hardly prudent. "We do not want to follow Hitler in book burning," warned the director of civilian defense in Kansas City. "To destroy articles of Japanese manufacture would not hurt Japan now. It would in fact help our enemies, for such articles would be replaced by our own factories and out of materials we need elsewhere."

Justice Department officials asked Americans to abstain from "direct action" against Japanese aliens or Nisei, and newspaper editors and columnists reminded their readers that most of the Japanese in their midst were loyal Americans, especially since the FBI continued to apprehend enemy aliens it deemed dangerous. Indeed, "Japanese who aren't in [the] wrong," declared a U.S. attorney in southern California, "can be treated as if they are still human."

Yet insults, threats—"Free shaves for Japs," proclaimed the sign in a barber shop in Bayonne, New Jersey, "Not responsible for accidents"—and reports of "vigilante justice" by "misguided mobs" prompted non-Japanese Asian Americans to devise means of identifying themselves. Some wore handwritten signs ("Don't shoot! I'm a Chinaman!"), while others carried hastily printed badges or identification cards. The most popular option was a lapel pin showing crossed American and Chinese flags, and the word "China" printed (in English and Chinese) on a white background, issued by the Chinese consul general in New York City.

Alarmed by the "distressing ignorance" displayed by white Americans on "the delicate question of how to tell a Chinese from a Jap," both *Time* and *Life* magazines published photo spreads with detailed recommendations on how to distinguish between the two national types: Chinese tended to be taller (average height five foot five), while "virtually all

Japanese are short"; Chinese men typically were slender and had "long and delicately boned" faces, compared to Japanese males' "squat, long-torsoed build, a broader, more massively boned head and face . . . and heavier beard"; and Chinese facial expressions were more likely to be kindly and open, while Japanese were "more positive, dogmatic, arrogant." Finally, Chinese men were less hairy, "seldom grow an impressive mustache," generally "avoid horn-rimmed spectacles," and were more relaxed in social situations. Japanese, on the other hand, "are nervous in conversation," and "laugh loudly at the wrong time." A Harvard professor of Eastern languages added that Japanese "shuffle along more," and "are likely to be bow-legged and ding-toed . . . as a result of their ceremonial posture of sitting on their legs."

On Monday, December 15—Bill of Rights Day—Americans celebrated the 150th anniversary of the ratification of the first ten amendments to the Constitution. Although federal officials canceled the celebration planned for Washington (to avoid large crowds in case of air raids), Senator Hiram Johnson of California reminded Americans that "if you forget the Bill of Rights in the days to come, you will have fought this war in vain, and deny the very things for which you are fighting."

# 4: Holiday Wishes

## DECEMBER 15–31, 1941

*I think we need a good shaking up and it*
*looks as though we are going to get it.*

—THEODORE DREISER, DECEMBER 1941

Looking back over the first seven days of war, the *Washington Post* decided that it had been "the most fateful week in United States history." So much had changed in the wake of Pearl Harbor that the final month of peace seemed "as remote from our present as the Minoan civilization." Eleanor Roosevelt agreed. "It seems like a completely changed world," she told a friend upon her return to Washington from the West Coast.

At the White House, the president worked behind locked gates, drawn curtains, and lowered blinds. Heavily armed soldiers ringed the mansion; no private cars or cabs passed through the iron gates manned by Secret Service agents, and delivery vehicles were rerouted to a garage six blocks away. Police blocked both East and West Executive Avenues to traffic. The airspace above the White House became a no-fly zone. Inside, a second-floor room had been transformed into the president's "battle room" (with maps and telephones for up-to-the-minute reports), fire buckets filled with sand stood ready at strategic points on both levels, and the sign "We Ain't Mad With Nobody" had disappeared from the pressroom. At night, passersby remarked upon the "eerie spell" of a White House in utter darkness.

Throughout the still-southern city, everything suddenly was moving at a frenzied pace. (Everything except the traffic, which routinely jammed when Army trucks stalled at the narrow approaches to the Potomac River bridges. "The Nazis couldn't invade this town," muttered one disgruntled cabdriver. "Not in the rush hour.") A growing sense of urgency, of making up for lost time, galvanized officials involved in the war effort. "The expansion of personnel is such that nobody can keep up with it," reported one journalist. "Everyone is up to his ears in the next ten minutes, tomorrow, next Tuesday, a week from today at the latest." Virtually every government office wall bore a reminder that "TIME IS SHORT" in block letters a foot high. "The frenzy of wartime Washington is such that nobody ever has any time for anything but frenzy," observed a reporter for *Life* magazine. "It means that anything beyond right away is too remote to bother with, that nobody, from the President down, has any time to sit and think. . . . 'Don't ask us where we're going,' they say, 'get out of the way and let us get there.'"

There was not even time for practice blackouts, although military officials acknowledged that Washington ("the nation's administrative nerve center") was "not only a possible but a likely object of attack." Unfortunately, the city's only air raid siren—discarded nine years earlier by a volunteer fire department in suburban Maryland—emitted nothing more than "an unappealing, disillusioned and funereal moan," with a range of about three blocks. Meanwhile, local residents stocked up on pistols and rifles, presumably to fend off enemy parachutists, and debated the best choices for ad hoc air raid shelters. (Suggestions included the basement of the Post Office Department—thirty feet below street level, and equipped with a cafeteria—or the subterranean Mayfair cocktail lounge, whose manager promised to "serve hot soup to everybody.")

Much to Franklin Roosevelt's consternation, a presidential bomb shelter—condemned by one Republican congressman as an "unnecessary nondefense expenditure"—was being constructed in an underground vault in the Treasury Building. The shelter's site was hardly a military secret; professional tour guides routinely pointed it out to tourists. For his part, the habitually optimistic Roosevelt told Treasury Secretary Morgenthau that he refused to go down into the shelter "unless you allow me to play poker with all the gold in your vaults."

Despite Mayor La Guardia's insistence that residential areas did not yet require private air raid shelters, apprehensive Americans began making their own preparations. The simplest option (recommended by some

Army officials) was a series of outdoor zigzag trenches with sloping sides, covered with heavy wooden planks or sheets of corrugated iron. The Los Angeles Department of Public Works distributed pamphlets with plans for concrete shelters, to avoid using scarce metals. Or one could build a simple shelter of bricks; "after all, these shelters don't have to be A-No. 1 to serve their purpose," noted the head of Baltimore's Bureau of Buildings. A New York construction company promised to convert (for $200) a residential basement into a bombproof refuge by adding new walls of reinforced concrete, strengthening the roof, and adding armored double doors. Four thousand dollars bought a more commodious shelter equipped with circulating air, a bathroom, and accommodations for fifteen to twenty people. One Los Angeles home construction company quickly transitioned from building "California Cottages" to "American Bomb Shelters"—the standard model cost $585, but the builders cheerfully suggested that if enemy planes failed to appear, the shelter could easily be converted into "a swimming pool or a sound-proof rumpus room."

Critics called it a case of war jitters, arguing that "the materials, labor and energy which might be put into building home shelters wholesale will serve a far better purpose building factories or tanks." The OPM complained that it was overwhelmed with requests for steel for private shelters in the first weeks of the war, but the Office of Civilian Defense had warned 50 million Americans (more than a third of the nation) who lived within three hundred miles of either coast that they resided in "theoretical target areas," and state and local government officials repeatedly reinforced the message with their public statements. "The Germans can easily reach our shores with bombers," proclaimed J. W. Farley, director of Massachusetts's Committee on Public Safety, "and it is highly probable that they may try to slip an airplane carrier close enough to our shores to launch an attack." In ordering practice blackouts for every community of more than five thousand residents, Maryland's Governor Herbert O'Conor declared that "our people are in danger" due to the numerous defense plants around Baltimore: "It is only reasonable to assume that our State now occupies a prominent point in German and Italian war plans." Not to be outdone, Governor Lehman of New York issued his own decree mandating immediate blackouts for every city in his state (except New York City, which was a separate civilian defense jurisdiction).

Even though some Americans dismissed these warnings as "jittering dramatics [and] . . . grandmotherish harangues," few communities deemed themselves unworthy of being bombed. "It can happen here!" insisted civilian defense officials in Tuscaloosa, Alabama, "and it may happen in Tuscaloosa!" (Efforts to mobilize Alabama civilian volunteers were complicated by the decision to establish a separate defense program for African Americans.) Texas towns throughout the Lower Rio Grande valley staged blackout tests, as did numerous communities along the Colorado River. For the first time since a riot by inmates twelve years earlier, authorities at Auburn prison in upstate New York turned off their giant searchlights for a fifteen-minute blackout drill; the convicts remained quiet. In Gary, Indiana, Army officials attempted a daylight "smoke blackout" to hide a massive Carnegie Illinois Steel Corporation factory from enemy planes by burning tar and oil in twenty furnaces, and running twenty locomotive yard engines—burning coal doused with oil—back and forth across the six-square-mile mill yard for fifteen minutes. An umbrella of dense black smoke hid the plant for a few minutes, until a strong breeze blew the soot away—and onto a neighboring town. (After a second attempt went similarly awry, authorities gave up on the idea, concluding that the smoke probably would be more likely to attract bombers to the factory than to camouflage it.)

It soon became clear that most cities were incapable of defending their citizens. "One of the main differences between this war and all others," noted one veteran journalist, "is the fact that in this war civilians must look out for themselves." Eleanor Roosevelt's tour of the Pacific coast states had convinced her that "so much equipment was lacking that they could not do many of the things that were considered essential." The same was true in the East and Midwest. In Massachusetts, the state fire coordinator announced that between 60 and 75 percent of Boston's firefighting equipment was obsolete. "For all practical purposes," admitted the *Baltimore Sun*, "Baltimore today still has no civilian defense program ready for an emergency." A *Detroit Free Press* columnist warned that the area's numerous defense plants—and their workers' tightly packed residences— would be sitting ducks for Nazi planes: "Enemy bombers could fly as low and as straight as they pleased—and with murderous certainty." Effective air raid sirens were nowhere to be found in any part of the country; local authorities were forced to improvise with substitutes such as locomotive whistles, drawbridge bells, motorcycle policemen driving with their sirens blaring, or volunteers in rural areas banging on iron wagon wheel rims and anvils.

More vigilante groups arose to take up the slack. Forty Chippewa women in Pontiac, Michigan, formed a rifle brigade to battle any Axis troops that might parachute into their area. "We have rifles, we have some ammunition, and we know how to shoot," promised Mrs. Charles Matteson (aka Princess Silver Star). "We are disappointed because our fighting women cannot go to the front." In response to rumors that Japanese agents ("and other aliens") might be flown into southern California to destroy strategic bridges, cut military communications, or create traffic bottlenecks on vital highways, a captain in the San Diego County sheriff's office organized the Minute Man Rifle Corps, a "highly mobile" band of eighty volunteers, including many members of the West Coast Rifle and Revolver Club. "Unhampered by red tape," the captain boasted, his force "could break up such attempts before they have a good chance to get under way and could leave mopping up operations to the Army." At his sixty-acre farm outside of Arlington, Vermont, artist Norman Rockwell reported that local patriots were preparing for Hitler and his panzers to try to roll through town on Route 7: "Those stiff-necked Vermonters will finish Hitler. He'll never get past Arlington." Meanwhile, inmates at Sing Sing prison in Ossining, New York, reportedly were "spreading out a welcome mat for any unexpected visitors," particularly Axis paratroopers.

"Logic (and the military experts) told us that there was no appreciable danger," admitted an anxious New Yorker, "but the peril was too far outside our experience—something that might come in from the sea without warning, very high and nearly silent, as impersonal as lightning. The wail of sirens coming up thinly from the street, the controlled voice on the radio telling us of destruction already conceivably on the way, even the drumming of our own planes patrolling the threatened city—none of these was particularly reassuring." So Americans welcomed the pamphlets and posters from the OCD—distributed door-to-door by Boy Scouts—and the daily installments of instructions in newspapers with detailed recommendations on "What To Do In An Air Raid": "The safest place in an air raid is at home. . . . Mother makes the best air raid warden. . . . If bombs start dropping near you, lie down. . . . A cold, damp cellar during a blackout is more dangerous to your health and life than all of the bombers Hitler and the Japs can send over here. . . . You don't stand over a stove during an air raid—you get under it."

Newspapers and magazines presented silhouettes of Japanese planes, to help Americans identify and respond to enemy bombers. "If you see the full underside silhouette," warned *Life* magazine helpfully, "a bomb may hit near you in the next split second." (Unfortunately, many of the silhouettes were of outdated Japanese aircraft built nearly a decade earlier.) Civilian defense experts and science professors offered insights into the "anatomy of bombs"—"People are afraid of bombs because they do not understand them"—by outlining the potential damage from fragmentation, incendiary, armor-piercing, and high-explosive demolition bombs. Firemen demonstrated the proper use of gas masks; businessmen studied camouflage techniques, and attended classes on defensive measures against chemical attacks. Educators recommended that children be kept as busy as possible during bombing attacks, preferably wielding hammers on pint-sized construction projects to drown out sounds of destruction. SPCA and Humane Society officials instructed pet owners to give their dogs and cats aspirin or sodium bromide to quell any anxiety. (Not all pets were as fortunate as the retired Triple Crown racehorse Seabiscuit, whose owner reportedly was building him a bombproof stable on a northern California ranch.)

Journalists who had experienced air raid alerts in Europe provided their own practical suggestions. For pedestrians walking along sidewalks during blackouts, Tom Treanor of the *Los Angeles Times* recommended "a special kind of blackout walk" to avoid injury when they inevitably fell off the curb at unseen intersections—"a sort of shuffle," explained Treanor, "with the knees bent and the body crouched forward. This absorbs the shock to some extent." Treanor also advised walking behind someone smoking a cigarette whenever possible: "You can keep a nice distance behind, just far enough so you can hear him grunt if he steps off an unexpected curb." Night-vision experts instructed Americans to look "around" objects during blackouts, instead of directly at them—"practically the reverse of daylight seeing." They could practice by viewing winter trees on moonless nights, gradually discerning smaller and smaller branches, until their eyes reached "full blackout acuity."

Armed with lists of essential blackout items, shoppers dutifully began buying up all types of black cloth (including black petticoats) to cover their windows, along with flashlights, candles, portable radios, garden hoses, fire buckets, and shovels. Merchants quickly recognized an opportunity. "Bloomingdale's is prepared to help *you prepare* for possible emergencies," read one ad, with window shades and drapery fabric for make-your-own blackout curtains, flashlights with mirrors ($1.75), Bakelite air raid whistles, one-hundred-pound bags of sand, asbestos gloves, and black rubber boots. Kresge's opened special "blackout shops" in a number of stores, offering black sateen for curtains, oil stoves, canned goods, bottled water, white raincoats, and white umbrellas. Claiming that it was America's "Headquarters for Official Blackout Necessities," Hammacher Schlemmer advertised firefighter's axes, first-aid kits, stirrup pumps, sterling identification tags ("necklets and bracelets"), and windproof lanterns. Fashion designers devised air raid alarm suits of waterproof gabardine (all-in-one outfits designed to be donned in thirty seconds), blackout dinner costumes ("the sort of thing one could wear to a shelter if suddenly called out of one's home"), "defense-all" outfits (modified overalls with small bags attached at the waist to keep jewels safe in the dark from "blackout snatch-thiefs," while leaving both hands free to crawl down the cellar stairs), and new lines of women's hats—some padded for protection against falling objects, and others made of asbestos and glass to resist flames. And con men went door to door, selling gullible homeowners "chemically treated" sand to help extinguish fires from incendiary bombs.

Enough Americans took civilian defense warnings to heart that authorities in Washington grew alarmed, particularly those responsible for war production. As flashlights and batteries flew off store shelves, the Office of Price Administration (OPA) found it necessary to freeze the price of both items. Surging sales of black cloth led Office of Production Management spokesmen to beg Americans to stop buying new fabric—which the OPM wished to reserve for military uniforms—and instead construct blackout curtains from material they already owned: "blankets, quilts, bedspread, carpets, rugs, draperies or even overcoats." The present wave of buying, the OPM declared, "will seriously hinder our war effort." When those appeals failed to dissuade shoppers, authorities enlisted the Better Business Bureau to try to convince the public that there was no such thing as "official" materials for blackouts.

All to little effect. On December 21, the *New York Times* reported that sales of blackout equipment remained strong across the country, and supplies scarce. "If a couple bombs fall in Washington and everybody wants to blackout," sighed one harried department store manager in the nation's capital, "I don't know what we'll do."

By the third week of the war, a visitor to the Pacific coast found Americans there still waiting for . . . something: "They didn't know what. They feared almost anything. Maybe the Japanese would bomb San Francisco, Portland or Seattle. Maybe Jap planes would hedgehop up from hidden bases on the peninsula of Lower California, attack the airplane factories of San Diego and Los Angeles. Maybe there would even be an enemy landing somewhere on the 1,300-mile coastline from Puget Sound to Mexico." Arriving in Chicago on December 22 following a two-week stay in Hollywood with her friend Mary Pickford, actress Lillian Gish told a reporter that "the California coast is in a panic. They are expecting air raids hourly." Stores closed before five o'clock every afternoon, added Gish, and almost no one ventured out after six o'clock; reservations on eastbound trains were increasingly difficult to obtain.

From their ranch outside Los Angeles, actress Carole Lombard and her husband, Clark Gable, proclaimed their eagerness to defend their property against Japanese paratroopers. "Let 'em come!" Lombard told reporters. "Pappy and I haven't been banging away at ducks and skeets all these years for nothing." Three hundred miles north, at Tor House atop a rockbound promontory on the shore of Carmel Bay, Una Jeffers (wife of poet Robinson Jeffers) calmly awaited the enemy. "We've had much excitement here & arrangements for blackouts & so on. People mostly behave very well, a few hysterics," she told a friend. "It is really very thrilling to walk around the Point at night and not see a pinpoint of light anywhere even in Pebble Beach. We have our guns loaded, daggers at hand, & required shovel, rake, pick axe, {&} sand prepared, and sit cozy and snug inside our shuttered windows. Oh and I have one weapon forbidden by law," added the fifty-seven-year-old Jeffers, "a brass knuckles."

Army officials on the West Coast discouraged any gathering of more than ten thousand people, fearing that large crowds would attract enemy bombers, clog the highways, and tie up too many police resources. Such a policy clearly threatened the Rose Bowl, the area's premiere holiday event, which traditionally drew crowds of ninety thousand college football fans. The New Year's Day matchup that season featured Oregon State, champions of the Pacific Coast Conference, and an undefeated Duke University squad. Although Duke players professed their willingness to play the game at its traditional site in Pasadena, California—"Heck no; we're not scared to go out there," chirped one Duke running back—the War Department insisted that the game be either canceled or moved. Reluctantly, the Tournament of Roses Committee agreed in mid-December to hold the game at Duke's stadium in Durham, North Carolina, although experts estimated the shift would cost California nearly $1.4 million in tourism revenue. To Tom Treanor, the loss of the Rose Bowl—combined with the Army's recommendation to cancel the Santa Anita horse racing season for similar reasons—"brought war home to Southern California with a vividness that nothing short of a bombing could have achieved."

Plans for other sporting events were either changed or canceled. The national figure-skating championship, scheduled for Berkeley, California, in February 1942, was moved to Chicago. Baseball owners vetoed a proposed deal to move baseball's St. Louis Browns—an aesthetic and financial embarrassment to the rest of the American League, frequently drawing Sunday crowds of fewer than a thousand fans—to Los Angeles; no owner wanted to subject his players to the threat of Japanese bombing raids. Restrictions on private civilian planes persuaded Miami officials to shelve their annual All-American air races. Due to the shortage of rubber and metal for wheels, the Soap Box Derby was canceled for 1942, and Eddie Rickenbacker, owner of the Indianapolis Speedway, suspended the annual Indy 500 auto race for the duration of the war.

Military manpower requirements threatened to dismantle collegiate and professional sports rosters. Already twelve members of Fordham's Sugar Bowl–bound football team had enlisted in the Navy, and fourteen members of the Naval Academy's gridiron squad expected to be on active duty within a month. (According to sportswriter Grantland Rice, General Douglas MacArthur believed that football players made the best military officers.) At the National Football League's annual draft of collegiate players—held on December 22, one day after the Chicago Bears won the NFL championship before a minuscule hometown crowd of fewer than fourteen thousand fans—teams hunted for athletes whose Selective Service status would allow them to play at least one season of professional football. Deferments overshadowed talent; married players, especially those with dependents, proved especially popular, along with linemen whose height and weight made them ineligible for military service. (Sometimes the strategy backfired; Brooklyn selected a hefty tackle from the University of Tennessee who turned out to be a minister who refused to play football on Sundays.) Meanwhile, Heisman Trophy winner Bruce Smith, a senior running back from the University of Minnesota who held a 1A military draft classification, fell all the way to the 119th pick.

"Uncle Sam will have more to do with determining the 1942 champion of professional football than any coach in the league," predicted sportswriter Shirley Povich. "He'll be dictating next year's lineup." If too many talented players disappeared into military service, Chicago Bears owner-coach George Halas suggested cutting roster sizes: "We used to play with 14- and 16-man squads. We can do it again." Major League Baseball faced a similar future, although—as Grantland Rice pointed out—there were more decent baseball than football players over the age of thirty. "This is going to be an old ballplayers' year," wrote a *Boston Globe* columnist. "If the war is as bad as it looks, there won't be any young ones around to play ball very long." By the time the World Series rolled around, the victor would be the club "which rakes up the best collection of antiques."

In the closing months of World War I, the federal government had nearly shut down professional athletics by insisting that all able-bodied adult American males either "work or fight." Sportswriters urged the Roosevelt administration not to issue a similar order; they argued that competitive sports enhanced civilian morale, and contributed to the development of an aggressive wartime mind-set—what Harvard president James Conant termed "the psychology of attack." Syndicated sports columnist Bob Considine urged the nation to go even further and throw out its outdated notions of good sportsmanship. "This is a Galento war," declared Considine, citing a boxer ("Two-Ton" Tony Galento) known for his willingness to employ dirty tricks in the ring. "This is knee-in-the-groin, thumb-in-the-eye, clip-'em-from-behind, beanball, tripping, roughhouse, gutter principle war. The umpire is dead." America's salvation, Considine concluded, lay "in forgetting everything that sports has taught us about fair play, and wading in with a lively imagination for coining new fouls, new ways to break the sacred rule of giving the other guy an even break, a fair shake."

Perhaps the process had already begun. "You may have noticed that the past couple of years have made us callous to death," wrote Tom Treanor from southern California. "I have heard fewer exclamations of sheer horror over the sudden slaughter of our own soldiers than I heard when the first deaths were reported from Europe" in the late summer of 1939. "Now we expect it. . . . We're more hardened in the fire of war than we realize." Perhaps; or it may simply have been youthful bravado that led a New York youngster to accompany his Christmas list to Santa Claus with the following threat: "You better bring all this stuff or I'll beat you to a pulp."

On December 15, Secretary of the Navy Frank Knox at last released his report on the American losses at Pearl Harbor: one battleship, three destroyers, and a mine layer sunk; 2,731 sailors dead and 656 wounded. Although the casualty figures were much higher than preliminary accounts had indicated, Knox's report—issued reluctantly and only after threats of congressional investigations—reassured many Americans who had heard rumblings that the Navy's losses had been even worse. "I saw nothing in it," concluded Wendell Willkie after meeting with Roosevelt at the White House, "to give any reason for the wild rumors afloat." Yet the rumors persisted, especially since Knox's report deliberately understated the damage to Navy ships.

Throughout December, detailed and accurate news bulletins (particularly on military developments) remained scarce and specifics scanty. "Phrases, phrases, phrases," observed a frustrated journalist, "and the citizens of Pocatello, Idaho, and Punxsutawney, Pa. are still in the dark, still wondering what's going on." Paraphrasing Winston Churchill, *Life* magazine complained that "'never before in history have so few kept so much from so many.'"

Instead of establishing a single office for disseminating war news, Roosevelt allowed each executive department to decide for itself what information to release. Confusion ensued; as one critic pointed out, "nobody knows just who is to tell whom what." With the War Department and the Navy controlling (with an iron hand) the release of military information, the press occasionally was led to publish stories that overstated American achievements. "Enemy Routed in Luzon Fighting," read a typical headline. "Philippines Situation Reported Well in Hand."

"The newspapers are winning the war for us," noted Charles Lindbergh wryly. "I wish our military forces could keep up with them. From now on it will be extremely difficult to find out what is really happening in the war." More than one journalist warned that any attempt to mislead the American people about the course of the war would rapidly destroy confidence in the Roosevelt administration. "If the government knows what's good for it," wrote Bill Henry in the *Los Angeles Times*, "it won't try to kid the public."

In explaining the reasons for American losses at Pearl Harbor, Knox had exaggerated the impact of military intelligence provided to Tokyo by Japanese civilians on Hawaii. It was, Knox declared, "the most effective fifth-column work done in the war with the possible exception of Norway," adding that American authorities had been "much too generous" in their treatment of Japanese on the islands.

Knox's charges fueled the existing suspicion of Japanese nationals and Nisei in the United States, particularly on the Pacific coast. Already California had been swept by whispers that local Japanese farmers had poisoned the vegetables they sold to white customers; state officials received so many queries about this purported conspiracy that they conducted hundreds of chemical tests on two thousand samples of suspected produce—and found nothing amiss. A subsequent rumor claimed that Japanese saboteurs in California packing plants had tainted the nation's seafood supply. "The entire country has been flooded by reports of glass being found in canned seafood, especially canned crab," announced a Food and Drug Administration official; the offending substance turned out to be struvite, a harmless crystalline compound. Reports that Japanese bombers planned to attack agricultural labor camps in the San Joaquin Valley provoked a mass exodus of migrant farmworkers back to Texas and Oklahoma, until state authorities announced that "it is preposterous to believe any foreign power would waste military equipment endeavoring to bomb our farm labor camps." Californians peppered FBI switchboards with questions: "Can I still buy my groceries from my Japanese?" "Should I fire my Japanese gardener?"

Eastern and midwestern authorities focused on the danger of subversion by agents of the European Axis powers. "We are loaded to the gills with Germans and Italians," proclaimed J. W. Farley from Massachusetts, "and can expect plenty of sabotage which will be serious." On December 16, Navy officials closed the port of Boston indefinitely to private shipping in the evenings and during dense fog. Three thousand U.S. Army troops were stationed at key points throughout New York City, including federal buildings and the waterfront. Police banned pedestrians from the walkways over all East River bridges at night, and transportation authorities sealed all parcel lockers in the city's subway stations. "Beware of inquisitive women," warned notices posted at Navy offices in the New York metropolitan area. "Women are being employed by the enemy [as spies] . . . on the theory that they are less liable to be suspected than male spies." While reluctant to quash legitimate criticism of the government (particularly in bars), the New Jersey Licensed Beverage Association advised tavern owners "to be on the watch for spies and subversive whisperers." Businessmen who preferred to deal personally with saboteurs could purchase "plant protection rifles" from the R. F. Sedgley company in Philadelphia: "Springfield military-type, caliber 30-06, complete with sling, bayonet and scabbard—Immediate Delivery." ("Tear gas pistols also available.")

In Chicago, where Mayor Kelly daily expected attempts to poison the water supply, a new federal grand jury was sworn in to deal with cases of sabotage and espionage. Chicago police were swamped with requests to guard river and highway bridges, defense factories, railways, power plants, and other strategic locations which one civilian defense official claimed were "in constant danger of sabotage." Sometimes nerves frayed. A sentry at the Naval Reserve Armory on Lake Michigan shot and killed a duck hunter whose motorboat pulled alongside a Coast Guard training ship;

suspicious of strangers before dawn, the sentry said he had fired two warning shots, then fired again when the boat failed to stop.

Photography became a dangerous pastime for Americans. Police arrested civilians for taking photos of sensitive subjects such as a steel plant near Chicago, or the armed guards at the Fourteenth Street Bridge in Washington. In Worcester, Massachusetts, a filmmaker shooting a documentary for the Office of Emergency Management was taken into custody when police mistook his movie camera for a machine gun. New York City authorities banned cameras from all bridges within the city limits; Navy guards later seized the cameras of more than twenty visitors to New York's waterfront. The police chief of New Britain, Connecticut, went a step further and prohibited anyone from taking photos of anything anywhere in the city, except on one's own property.

Detailed weather forecasts vanished for the duration of the war. On December 16, the U.S. Weather Bureau announced that it would release only minimal information in its predictions, to avoid providing any data that might help enemy forces plan an attack. No weather maps would be printed in newspapers, no display maps would be posted in public places. Radio broadcasts would be limited to warnings of serious conditions: heavy snows, floods, hurricanes, or severe cold waves. Gone were observational reports, charts, and weather summaries, including the movement of warm or cold fronts, and specific statistics on wind conditions or barometric pressure. "Cloudy and warmer Monday," read one typical forecast, "moderate to fresh winds."

Christmas was no time for Americans to relax their guard. "The pagan enemy will not respect our most important religious festival," insisted one Pacific coast newspaper. "On the contrary he is likely to choose that day for special surprises and bloody stratagems." Army officials instructed all teams of military and civilian aircraft observers to maintain a 24/7 watch throughout the holidays; "No one," snapped La Guardia, "can fathom the deviltry of the Nazi command." Secretary of War Stimson advised defense contractors and government agencies to "increase their vigilance during the coming holiday season to the end that we shall not be the victims of treachery from within." On December 23, state troops in Virginia began stopping and searching all cars at bridges and other unspecified "vital points" to help deter sabotage. Military and civilian authorities in Buffalo claimed to have received information "from a very reliable source that an effort will be made to sabotage certain industries December 24, 25, and 26," particularly defense plants near the Canadian border. (They also warned that a new, cone-shaped Christmas tree light manufactured somewhere in Asia "is being sold and is in reality a time bomb," even though none had been found in the Buffalo area.)

"We hear from every delivery boy, postman, doorman, store clerk, taxi driver, superintendent, and next door neighbor," sighed one rumor-weary civilian, "that we are going to be bombed, shelled, or gassed Christmas Eve." Americans listened dutifully to the warnings; then they went out to shop.

Two weeks after Pearl Harbor, the holiday shopping season was nearly back in full swing. Once again department stores (which, outside of the West Coast, had resumed their evening hours) were thronged with customers eager to part with their cash. "You can sell 'em anything this year," marveled a salesgirl in Baltimore. "They've got the dough and they're crazy to get rid of it." Although retail sales lagged behind prewar expectations, they remained on track to surpass every Christmas since 1928.

But the war already had created subtle differences. There were more strangers among the holiday crowds—men in military uniforms, and defense workers recently arrived in new towns. Although everyone seemed imbued with goodwill (at least toward other Americans), some observers sensed a lack of the usual holiday camaraderie. "Everybody appeared to be intent on his own business and interested only in those with him," noted one journalist in an East Coast city. Passing through a New York department store, a visitor was struck by "a general look of doom on the faces of floor walkers, and a tendency of the salesgirls to leave you flat and rush to the windows at the sound of every passing fire engine," to check for falling bombs. Somehow the season's customary greetings seemed out of place in what literary critic Brooks Atkinson called "the hideous world of 1941." At a Salvation Army party in Washington, Eleanor Roosevelt wished everyone "a happy and hopeful Christmas." "I don't think," she added, "that it will be possible for any of us to say this could be a 'merry Christmas.'"

Children found fewer department-store Santa Clauses—gone to the

Army or better-paying defense jobs—to take their requests, and street-corner Santas occasionally abandoned their posts to scan newspaper headlines for the latest updates on the war. In Chattanooga, Tennessee, an anxious six-year-old boy wrote to his local newspaper to ask if the rumor about Santa Claus being drafted was true: "If so, what does Uncle Sam think us little boys are going to do for Christmas?"

Practical (and grimmer) presents dominated the last-minute rush: heavy slacks, warm underwear, housewares, cotton stockings, and oversize pocketbooks with room for first-aid kits. Diamonds, rubies, and furs went begging. Ignoring government pleas, shoppers continued to snap up blackout cloth—tucked into gift boxes with a red-white-and-blue ribbon and a sprig of artificial holly—along with flashlights and garden hoses. One concerned Californian decided to go even further and dig an air raid shelter in his backyard as a Christmas present to his wife and daughter.

Defense bonds and stamps became all-purpose presents for casual acquaintances, replacing gag gifts, suddenly rendered inappropriate. Employers used defense bonds as Christmas bonuses (which were plentiful); sports tournaments awarded them as prizes; holiday travelers gave defense stamps as tips. Businesses promoted them in advertisements—"No Christmas tree is complete without Defense Stamps and Bonds," proclaimed Filene's department store in Boston—and even recommended bonds above their own product. "If you want cameras for Christmas . . . Ritz has them," noted an ad for Ritz Camera Centers. "But buy defense bonds first!"

Toy sales were still running far ahead of 1940, even though some manufacturers could not complete all their orders due to the shortage of materials. Military toys continued to dominate the market. In Manhattan, Lucius Beebe reported that the "most prominent feature in the toy shop windows this season is lead soldier outfits with tanks, tank cannon, anti-aircraft rifles and mobile artillery units." Close behind were "Flying Fortress" bombers with twenty-seven-inch wingspans, model antiaircraft guns that fired wooden bullets ("Turn the crank and watch the bullets fly!"), and windup tanks that spat out sparks from machine guns as they clambered over obstacles in their path.

Consumers scoured the dwindling stocks of durable goods: refrigerators, vacuum cleaners, phonographs, radios, and washing machines. ("The time may come," predicted Bloomingdale's, "when the gift of a washing machine may be more precious than a rare jewel!") As federal officials put the finishing touches on plans to convert automobile factories to war production, automakers urged Americans to buy new cars while they could. "Any way you look at it, there's a long, long trail ahead of the next car you buy," warned a Buick ad.

New tires already were gone. On December 17, OPA director Leon Henderson announced that the existing ban on tire sales would be extended to January 4, when it would be replaced with a rationing scheme that Henderson called "the most drastic rationing program Americans have ever known." Civilian consumption of rubber products would be cut by 80 percent, effectively prohibiting the sale of new tires to private automobile owners for the duration of the war. ("Stop unnecessary driving immediately," Henderson advised the public, and "double up.") Exceptions included doctors' cars, ambulances, police and fire vehicles, school and city buses, industrial and construction equipment, and tractors (on farms)—but not taxis, delivery trucks, or hearses.

Some rural counties were entitled to only one new tire per month; the entire territory of Alaska would be limited to about one hundred. Retreads, which used only 40 percent as much rubber as new tires, would still be available, but one industry expert estimated that only half of the tires on America's 32 million cars could take new treads, largely because they had consistently been driven while underinflated. And nearly all the secondhand tires on the market had disappeared by the end of December. (A number of Americans had seen the "tire famine" coming and had stocked up with spares; Firestone Tire and Rubber Company's 1941 net sales were "the largest in the company's history.")

The ripple effects of rubber rationing threatened a wide variety of businesses, starting with those who sold new tires: garages, filling stations, repair shops, and, of course, tire salesmen. As Americans scaled back their driving (a peacetime average of nine thousand to ten thousand miles annually, nearly half for pleasure), tourist camps and resorts would suffer; so would highway maintenance, which was typically dependent upon revenues from state gasoline taxes ($65 million per year in New York State alone). A small number of retail merchants who made home deliveries began buying horses and mules for fifty to two hundred dollars apiece, but as one businessman complained, "we can't fight a war hiring mules and riding around in buckboards."

Perhaps the most critical problem would be simply getting to work. Polls revealed that slightly fewer than half of American workers drove to their jobs or rode in someone else's car, while 34 percent walked and 18 percent used public transportation. Most of those who commuted by auto said they could find alternative ways to get to work, but more than one-fourth could not. For the war effort, the problem was especially acute in rural areas, where the government had deliberately (for security reasons) built defense plants away from population centers. But workers also faced commuting challenges in certain cities such as public transportation–starved Los Angeles—"the original drive-in town"—or Detroit, where many of the largest defense plants were located on the outskirts of the city, far from existing bus or streetcar lines; Ford's massive new Willow Run bomber plant, for instance, lay nearly thirty miles from the downtown area.

Rubber rationing also threatened to end the production of bathing suits, women's foundation garments, galoshes and boots, elastic waistbands, pencil erasers, rubber bands (Americans used 30 billion per year), bathtub toys, and balloons. *Time* magazine envisioned an average American male, "his pants and socks dragging, . . . his wife bulging in the wrong places, his balloonless children teething on wood, his car tireless in the garage, riding off to work on a hard-benched bus or subway, unable to erase mistakes, or snap a band around them." Sports fans braced for another hit. New signs appeared at National Hockey League games: "Notice: Because of the increasing scarcity of rubber we would greatly appreciate our patrons returning any pucks which might be shot into the audience in order that we may be sure of enough to finish the season."

But no sport faced a greater threat than golf. When Henderson suggested that production of golf balls (a "nonessential luxury") would be suspended for the duration, panic-stricken golfers besieged sporting goods stores, country club shops, and department stores to stock up on the precious commodity. On the morning of December 18, Abercrombie & Fitch in Manhattan sold more than twenty-four thousand golf balls before 11 a.m.; by noon all of its stock was gone. In Chicago, A. G. Spalding & Brothers was forced to refuse orders from desperate retailers across the Midwest. Searching for used balls for resale, sporting goods executives sent scouts to Florida to collect rewashed and repainted balls from puzzled greenskeepers. It was, noted the *New York Times*, "one of the greatest buying rushes ever noted in the sporting goods field." Retailers soon restricted customers to a dozen balls apiece, but the spectacle of panic buying struck many Americans as distinctly antisocial. "Anyone buying beyond his immediate needs," complained one disgusted New Yorker, "steals from his fellow-citizens and deserves their contempt." In an editorial titled "Rationing Ahead," the *Times* predicted that the golf ball debacle was a sign of things to come. An informal rationing system had sufficed in this case, the *Times* noted, "but it would not do if the rush of excited buyers and hoarders were after something more essential."

"What Americans wanted, as would any people newly at war, was to feel some certain pride in their Army and Navy," reported Alistair Cooke. But no one could disguise the grim news from the Pacific: American troops, under the command of General Douglas MacArthur, engaged in a desperate defensive action against a far superior Japanese invasion force in the Philippines; Japanese bombers repeatedly pounding outnumbered and outgunned U.S. Marines on Wake Island; British forces retreating before a final Japanese assault on Hong Kong. "From the Allied point of view," observed columnist Barnet Nover, it was a picture of "almost unrelieved gloom."

Closer to home, Japanese submarines launched a campaign against American oil tankers off the coast of California. The first attacks occurred on December 20; two of the three American ships escaped unharmed, but the SS *Emidio*—sailing from Seattle to San Francisco—was struck by shells and a torpedo as it passed Cape Mendocino. Five of its thirty-six crew members perished; the rest were rescued by a Coast Guard cutter. Over the following seven days, Japanese subs attacked six more American ships, damaging two, and killing one additional sailor. Several of the attacks occurred within sight of shore; "so close," wrote Ernie Pyle, "you could almost hit one with a rock." Meanwhile, Navy officials—who were loath to reveal the precise location of the West Coast attacks—acknowledged that German submarines were operating off the Atlantic coast.

"There have been," wrote Assistant Secretary of State Adolf Berle in his diary, "a number of bad days."

Against this backdrop, Prime Minister Churchill and a team of British military advisers arrived in Washington on December 22 for a series of strategy conferences with their American counterparts during the Christmas holiday. Churchill's voyage had been a closely guarded secret; taken completely by surprise, Eleanor Roosevelt rushed out the next day to find Christmas gifts for her British guests, only to discover that "the shops were pretty well sold out."

Late on the bitterly cold afternoon of Christmas Eve, Churchill joined President Roosevelt on the South Portico of the White House for the annual tree-lighting ceremony—which, to the surprise of nearly everyone in the capital, had not been canceled. Police and soldiers checked each person who passed through the White House gates, confiscating cameras and packages. Patrols of FBI agents and troops armed with rifles and submachine guns kept spectators a hundred yards away from the executive mansion, but the crowd (estimated at twenty thousand) could see Roosevelt and Churchill silhouetted against the lights of the White House.

Shortly after five o'clock, the rector of Catholic University delivered an invocation, followed by four carols played by the Marine Band and sung by everyone on the grounds. Roosevelt and the prime minister each spoke briefly; onlookers noticed that the crowd chattered restlessly while the president spoke, but remained respectfully silent during Churchill's remarks. Some in the audience tried to leave early, but police refused to open the gates until the program was over. As the sun disappeared behind the Virginia hills, Roosevelt pressed a button to light the White House tree a thousand feet away, just inside the south gate. The ceremony had taken only half an hour, but Eleanor was relieved it was over: "There was little joy in our hearts. The cold gripped us all so intensely that we were glad of a cup of tea on our return to the house."

Inside, the Roosevelt family gifts rested beneath a small Christmas tree on the second floor. With no Roosevelt grandchildren at the White House, the only stocking over the presidential mantelpiece belonged to Fala. Throughout the District's downtown area, merchants had turned off their neon lights; windows of office buildings and apartment houses were black, the streetlights darkened. Visitors could hear a steady procession of patrol planes overhead. On the radio, newsmen announced that Wake Island almost certainly had fallen to the Japanese. "The gayety which has usually marked Christmas Eve in the capital," wrote a veteran correspondent, "was ominously lacking tonight."

Across the nation, Americans reached out to one another. The volume of holiday mail set new records, and long-distance calls were up nearly 50 percent over Christmas 1940, despite authorities' pleas to keep telephone lines open for emergencies. "I think it's possible that the people are beginning to realize that this may be the last real Christmas they'll have for many years," one observer pointed out. "And maybe they're determined to make it a real Christmas—for their families and for the men in the services, too." While some Americans canceled their holiday parties "owing to war conditions" and the threat of blackouts—from southern California, Tom Treanor reported that "the Christmas whirl has practically come to a standstill"—others argued that holiday festivities improved morale, especially among young adults "whose nerves," as one mother put it, "are dangerously near the breaking point already. No telling what they'll have to face before this thing's over. We're going to give them all the fun we can."

According to War Department projections, at least 2 million men would be called into military service over the next twelve months, more than doubling the size of the existing Army. Several days before Christmas, Congress voted almost unanimously to expand the military draft to men between the ages of twenty and forty-four. The Senate and the Roosevelt administration originally wished to include nineteen-year-olds, and numerous commentators from Walter Lippmann to the *Chicago Tribune* argued for the draft of eighteen-year-olds as well. "There is no better material for the army than the youth of 18 or 19," claimed the *Tribune*. "He has a man's strength and much more than a man's recuperative powers. . . . He is at an age when obedience comes easily and the capacity to learn and to adapt to changed circumstances is greater than it will be a few years hence." But the House refused to budge below the age of twenty-one—the question, explained one congressman, was "at which age boyhood ends and manhood begins"—until a compromise was reached at twenty.

In light of the Army's manpower demands, even the brisk pace of post–Pearl Harbor recruiting paled; between December 7 and Christmas Eve, fewer than fifty thousand volunteers had enlisted in all the services combined. War Department officials briefly considered halting voluntary enlistments to keep skilled defense workers from leaving their jobs, but Congress's refusal to draft teenagers persuaded them to keep their recruiting offices open, so they could at least attract eager eighteen- and nineteen-year-old volunteers into the military.

Looking ahead, Americans knew that soon they would be looking back. "Christmas 1941—you are sure, by now, that it will have special meaning," predicted a Kodak advertisement for its new Kodacolor print film. "Snapshots never meant so much as now. . . . Every scene and episode will be more than ever important."

On Christmas Day, Roosevelt and Churchill attended church services in the morning, worked through the afternoon (the president did not have time to open his presents until late in the day), and dined on oysters, roast turkey with chestnut dressing, sausage, sweet potatoes, and plum pudding. At the Navy Building on Constitution Avenue, employees dined in the cafeteria on hot dogs and beans. "Hitler is to blame for having your Christmas leave cancelled when you expected to be home with your family," a Washington columnist reminded federal workers. "Get good and mad, if you have to get that way, at Hitler and his war-making pals in Rome and Tokyo."

Fewer traditional holiday radio programs from abroad entertained listeners; the only broadcast from Bethlehem came from the gritty industrial town in eastern Pennsylvania, whose landmark giant steel Christmas star remained dark. Instead, Americans heard mayors answering questions about civilian defense, and talk show guests discussing "What Shall We Teach Our Children About the War This Christmas?" Visiting southern California, John Houseman recalled "listening to a portable radio as one calamity followed another in unknown places halfway across the world. . . . Hong Kong fell for Christmas." Wendell Willkie urged a national radio audience to prepare for years of "Spartan simplicity and hard work"—"We must face the most profound dislocation of our lives"—and Attorney General Biddle cautioned Americans not to "overestimate our capacities to do the job that lies ahead, nor underestimate the evil strength of our adversaries."

By December 25, federal agents had arrested 2,944 "dangerous enemy aliens," mostly Japanese. In Los Angeles's Little Tokyo, stores and restaurants remained closed. The neighborhood's twenty thousand residents lived "under suspicion and police surveillance," wrote a *Los Angeles Times* reporter, "their American trade vanished and their own people cut off from normal income. . . . The faces of those who loiter in doorways and along almost-deserted First and San Pedro Street curbs depict the ultimate in depression—often fear."

To Detroit, Christmas brought fewer paychecks. Since late November, employment in the metropolitan area had fallen nearly 7 percent as the government finally forced automakers to curtail production of civilian cars; on December 22 alone, 20,000 jobless Detroit workers had filed for unemployment compensation. The major automakers still had not devised a coordinated plan to convert entirely to defense production—"an imperative necessity," noted Marquis Childs, "that had been there all the time." State officials predicted that the delay would cost another 206,000 auto workers their jobs by the end of December.

"Christmas this year was a sort of enforced interruption, a necessary observance of a significant occasion," noted the *New Yorker*. It seemed appropriate that the holiday fell in the middle of the week; the festivities were soon over, "and people seemed glad to get back to the matter at hand."

"The weather today will be colder than a Christmas turkey, and the information about it from the Weather Bureau is just as skimpy," read the forecast in the *Washington Post* a few days later. "However, they report, minus the trimmings, that it will be clear and cold this morning. The temperature was expected to drop to somewhat above freezing by dawn."

On Capitol Hill, congressional Republicans laid plans to shatter the post–Pearl Harbor façade of national unity, to launch what columnist Drew Pearson called "a knockdown fight against the Democrats next year." Already a trio of Republican senators—Robert Taft, Styles Bridges, and Charles Brooks—had proclaimed their intention to deliver "constructive criticism" on the war effort, particularly to uncover waste and inefficiency in a defense program expected to cost $100 billion over the next two years.

"Everyone expects the honeymoon to end within months, perhaps weeks," explained *Life* magazine's correspondent in Washington. "Everyone expects that when the honeymoon ends, the dead cats and the low punches will fill the air again and under the cover of honest criticism the men who hate Roosevelt will throw everything they've got into a desperate effort to unhorse him. They won't have Willkie, Landon or Hoover with them, but they will have all the elements which see in Roosevelt's war-presidency a consolidation of his power that no electoral victory could ever give him. . . . Conspiracy is quiescent in Washington, but the stiletto market is booming."

As newspaper headlines conceded the imminent Japanese conquest of Manila, administration spokesmen and congressional Democrats sought to dampen any public expectations of American victories in the Pacific anytime soon. Presidential press secretary Stephen Early warned that effective aid to MacArthur's troops on the Bataan Peninsula could not cross the Pacific for quite some time. "The country must be prepared for losses of men and probably many ships," acknowledged Senator Tom Connally of Texas. Senator Walter George of Georgia, too, felt that "the American people must be prepared for a long period of disappointments." The nation faced "dark, grim days," Federal Security Agency administrator Paul McNutt (a former governor-general of the Philippines) told a national radio audience: "The bell will toll, again and again."

And so Americans sought refuge in movie theaters during the final week of December, to try to forget the war for at least a few hours. Attendance was up nearly 25 percent over the holiday season of 1940, setting new records in one theater after another. Even an undistinguished film such as *Sundown*, a melodrama set in Africa starring Gene Tierney as a "woman of mystery" ("so much banal nonsense," sniffed the *New York Times*), smashed the previous mark for weekend receipts at Loew's Criterion theater on Broadway. Easily the most charming film in release was Walt Disney's *Dumbo*, praised as "an exercise in film magic . . . rich in enchantment": "It's a bit of happy forgetfulness in a world which should be more like a Disney cartoon and less like a horror tale of the Middle Ages." But the film's short running time (64 minutes) left plenty of room for the latest newsreels from the Pacific.

On New Year's Eve, the traditional celebrations seemed "something of an anti-climax," observed the *New Republic*. "Everyone understood perfectly that a new year and a new era had begun on December 7, beating the calendar by three weeks, and that it was a page that would never be turned back." Numerous localities banned the use of fireworks, sirens, horns, flares, and firearms (and, in New Jersey, small cannons) to "prevent alarm and hysteria in a war-jittery population." Hearty good wishes struck many as inappropriate. "'Happy New Year' has to be said with just the right intonation this year," wrote Tom Treanor. "The voice should taper off into a serious note." One telegraph office in Detroit strongly discouraged customers from sending "Happy New Year" greetings at all—"because we don't know," explained the girl working the counter, "if it's going to be a happy New Year, and we don't want to mislead people."

West Coast streets were empty, as military officials prohibited "unnecessary noise" or gatherings of crowds outdoors. "We scared 'em all home," explained a policeman in Portland. In San Francisco, Ernie Pyle passed the time staring at the buoys holding up the submarine net beneath the Golden Gate Bridge: "It makes you realize, more than anything else I've seen, that we're actually at war and in danger right here at home."

Hotel bookings in Chicago were down, after a rash of post–Pearl Harbor cancellations. Many of the private parties that still took place were family farewell dinners for young men heading off to military camp. At nearby defense plants, operating on a 24/7 schedule, factory whistles blew at midnight; workers cheered, then went back to work.

Champagne flowed most freely in Boston, where Mayor Tobin urged residents not to allow "bewildering times" to dampen their holiday celebrations. Still, the war seemed inescapable. Bartenders served red, white, and blue cocktails; women wore corsages in a V for "Victory"; and bakers adorned cakes with the stars and stripes. Partygoers sported buttons that read, "Remember Pearl Harbor" or "To Hell With Hitler." One Bostonian swore he had never seen "such an outpouring of money"; it was, he said, "as though everyone was attempting to enjoy to the utmost what they felt might be their last real celebration for some time."

New York City greeted the new year with less abandon than usual, and fewer arrests for drunkenness or assault. "The superficial celebration features were the same," wrote one reporter, "but overshadowing it all was the tacit regret of war." Authorities spared no precautions against air raids or sabotage. Times Square contained the largest collection of law enforcement officers in its history: over two thousand policemen (and nearly as many air raid wardens), and a substantial share of the city's eight-hundred-man detective force stood watch in the thirty-four-block area, along with two fire engines and special guards from the city's water and public works departments. Street corners bore special loudspeakers to provide instructions in case of air raids, and signs that read "In case of an alarm, walk—don't run," with arrows pointing out of the square.

At nearly two thousand observation posts up and down the Atlantic coast, civilian volunteers kept watch throughout the night.

In Washington, the Capitol was dark on New Year's Eve for the first time since 1918. Streets were crowded, but with more spectators and fewer merrymakers than the previous year. Men in military uniform seemed to be everywhere. At the Mayflower Hotel, larger parties outnumbered reservations for couples: "It seemed," said a hotel official, "that those who would be merry wanted company." While thousands of city residents attended worship services at local churches—the National Cathedral held the first watch-night service in its thirty-five years of existence—the most prestigious private party was held at Evalyn Walsh McLean's estate, Friendship, which was slated to be converted into a thousand-room hotel for single girls working in the capital. Guests included Senate majority leader Alben Barkley, Assistant Secretary of State Dean Acheson, and Assistant Attorney General Thurman Arnold. Adolf Berle was there as well. "Knowing that our boys were being killed by hundreds in the Philippines and that probably Manila was even then being sacked by Japanese troops," Berle wrote in his diary, "I had less than no appetite whatever for this. . . ."

There were no signs of any celebrations at the White House.

# 5: Cloudy, Turning Colder

## JANUARY 1942

*It is not written in the stars that
we shall win this war. Nothing will
save us but ourselves.*

—DOROTHY THOMPSON

It snowed in Los Angeles on New Year's Day. Some neighborhoods received two inches, the first measurable snowfall in the city in ten years, and plenty for kids who had been listening to war bulletins on the radio to pelt one another gleefully with snowballs.

Residents of nearby Pasadena had their city to themselves. No grand parades marched down Colorado Boulevard; the usual 1 million spectators for the Tournament of Roses festivities were reduced to a few early risers out for a stroll. Most of the shops were shut up tight. Replacing the official 150-member marching band, an impromptu troupe of sixteen musicians from Pasadena Junior College bravely soldiered down the street in a ragged V formation, playing whatever songs they knew best, and earning scattered cheers from passersby.

In North Carolina, Oregon State's football team salvaged a measure of West Coast pride by upsetting heavily favored, hometown Duke, 20–16, in the transplanted Rose Bowl game. The contest started in a dreary rain and drizzle, but nothing like the downpour that afflicted the Sugar Bowl in New Orleans, which sportswriter Bill Cunningham described as "the backlash of an Alabama hurricane that kept coming in waves like returning flights of aerial bombers." Struggling to remain upright through the wind and rain and mud, the Fordham and Missouri players slid and skidded on the sodden turf—"a slow motion circus of drowned rats," thought one observer—for the entire game. The only score came when Fordham blocked a Missouri punt, the ball slithering out of the end zone for a safety. Although ballcarriers for both teams repeatedly fell down without being touched, and the game dragged on with frequent delays while officials dried the football, neither radio announcers nor reporters could mention the weather, which remained an official military secret until twenty-four hours had passed.

Defense plants across the nation carried on business as usual. "General holidays are a dangerous form of national self-indulgence," explained a *Washington Post* editorial, "with the country involved in a war in which victory favors the side that can outproduce its enemies." War Department employees in Washington also put in a full day's work as they awaited the latest grim reports from the Pacific. Manila fell a day later, a loss which Mark Sullivan deemed "the worst reverse America has suffered in a foreign war since 1812."

"We have lost the first round," wrote columnist Barnet Nover. "There must be no sidestepping the tragic fact that we have recently suffered the greatest succession of military and naval disasters in our entire history." Surveying the string of American losses in the Pacific, Westbrook Pegler agreed that "there is not a single ray of consolation." More defeats loomed on the horizon. "Every competent person in Washington, I think, is prepared for bad news ahead; thinks the news is likely to be bad for at least three months," predicted Sullivan. "That is the minimum estimate. The news may be prevailingly bad for six months."

Roosevelt took a longer view in his State of the Union address to Congress on January 6. Despite the concerns of congressional leaders who urged him—for security reasons—not to deliver the speech in person, the president arrived at the Capitol in his black limousine shortly before 12:30 on a bitterly cold afternoon. Only twenty or so spectators waited outside to greet him; military authorities discouraged public access to the president. As he began his speech, observers noticed that Roosevelt lacked his customary gusto. "Dark circles ringed tired eyes," noted one reporter. "His face was grayish above the white shirt." Warning that the struggle against the Axis would be "a hard war, a long war, a bloody war, a costly war," the president promised that "as our power and resources are fully mobilized we shall carry the attack against the enemy. We shall hit him, and hit him again, wherever and whenever we can reach him." To provide the requisite striking power, Roosevelt asked Congress to authorize $56 billion worth of arms in the coming fiscal year, a staggering array of weapons that would require 15 million workers in war industries—three times the current number—and a substantial increase in "taxes and bonds and bonds and taxes," along with an end to production of numerous consumer goods. "Let no man say it cannot be done," Roosevelt proclaimed, the strain visibly falling away as he spoke. "It must be done—and we have undertaken to do it."

Polite applause interrupted the president's message thirty times in thirty-five minutes, but the most enthusiastic reception greeted his promise to take the offensive against Japan and Germany. "We are not for defense any longer, we are for offense," swore John O'Ren in the *Baltimore Sun*. "They asked for it, and the state of the nation is a disposition to let them have it."

But at every turn, an increasingly impatient public ("Where is the Fleet? What's it doing?") learned that an all-out offensive remained far in the future. "The miserable truth," acknowledged *Time* magazine, was that "U.S. production of war materials was still nowhere near enough. . . . Bottleneck had become the most hated word in the language, 'too little and too late' a phrase too deep for tears."

One after another, commentators from all parts of the political spectrum castigated the lagging and snarled American production of war materials. "The fact is that the rate of production to date is a disgrace to the greatest industrial nation on earth and a menace to life and liberty," claimed Westbrook Pegler. Misleading publicity photos of tanks and bombers purportedly "rolling off the assembly lines" in rapid succession deceived no one, Pegler insisted, except "the Americans who shouldn't be hopped up with such habit-forming encouragement." Disheartened by the wasted money and energy she saw in the nation's capital, Dorothy Thompson condemned the "terrible overlapping, confusion and petty jealousies" that were handcuffing the agencies involved in the war effort. Ernest Lindley pointed out that the effects already were being felt in the Philippines: "The cost of the smugness and near-sightedness in industry and labor—and in the direction of the arms production program—has begun to be measured in the lives of American men."

"Nobody ever will be able to add up the terrible cost that is resulting, not from bad decisions, but from just plain red tape, delay in paper work, lost messages and orders," reported Ray Clapper from Washington. "Demoralization here has reached the point where it is interfering with the wholehearted, aggressive direction of the total war effort that must be had before the short time that has been left runs out." An interim report by the Senate committee investigating defense production, chaired by Democrat Harry Truman of Missouri, blasted OPM leadership as "shortsighted" and "lackadaisical," and confirmed that "carelessness and inefficiency have already cost us a great deal and, if continued, can cost us much more." The Truman committee was especially critical of the troubled program for manufacturing military aircraft. "Apparently," it concluded, "there never has been and is not now any real planned and coordinated program for the procurement of aircraft."

Four weeks after Pearl Harbor—and more than eighteen months after Roosevelt's declaration of a national emergency—the Office of Production Management still lacked a detailed inventory of American industrial resources. At a meeting with automobile company executives on January 5, the OPM's Knudsen admitted that he had no idea which companies could produce what war materials. Reading from the War Department's $5 billion shopping list of armaments, Knudsen told the assembled businessmen that "we want to know if you can make them or want to try to make them. If you can't, do you know anyone who can?" At one point he seemed more like an auctioneer: "We want more machine guns. Who wants to make machine guns?"

It was the final nail in the OPM's coffin. "No doubt can now remain that [Roosevelt's] Administration is badly organized and inadequately manned to carry out the war program," concluded Walter Lippmann. On January 13, Roosevelt responded to public demands to appoint an armaments czar by creating the War Production Board—the nineteenth major defense agency since May 1940—and naming former Supply Priorities and Allocations Board chief Donald Nelson as its chairman, with full authority over the entire defense production program. One of the few business executives acceptable to both industry and New Dealers, the fifty-four-year-old Nelson was known for his no-nonsense attitude and occasional impatient outbursts. ("Business as usual must go to hell!" "Get the stuff moving and get it moving now!")

Most of the nation's press applauded the appointment of Nelson, a move the *New York Times* described as "a belated but nevertheless highly reassuring step toward bringing the full power of American industry into war production." But as congressmen began to receive a rising volume of constituent mail criticizing the administration's conduct of the war, the sense of national unity instilled by the attack upon Pearl Harbor started to unravel. "If the people become dissatisfied with the way the war is being fought," warned the *Chicago Daily News*, "many new figures could be swept into the House and Senate by public revulsion which is never temperate in wartime."

Few Americans shared a favorable view of the Office of Civilian Defense. As one critic put it, the OCD "has never known what it is doing, what it was meant to do, what it had power to do, or who was to do it." La Guardia responded by denouncing his detractors as "liars" and "swivel-chair scribes," and attributed criticism of his activities to "some Jap or a friend of a Jap" employing a "new technique . . . to create confusion, to continue fear and terror in the minds of our people." In early January, the House of Representatives grew so disgusted with La Guardia's stewardship of the agency that it voted to transfer responsibility for civilian defense to the War Department, despite Secretary Stimson's vehement insistence that the Army already had all the challenges it could handle.

The following day, Roosevelt announced that he was appointing James Landis, dean of Harvard Law School and regional director of civilian defense in New England, as the executive director of the OCD, relegating La Guardia to a figurehead role. The House promptly rescinded its vote.

Every major American city was still struggling to complete its own civilian defense preparations. None had enough emergency equipment to deal with air raids; Boston alone had installed permanent sirens that actually worked. A survey of Philadelphia residents discovered that barely one in twelve homes had taken the necessary precautions against air raids, and only "a pitiful minority" knew what to do if an alert sounded. In Miami, authorities were stumped by the daunting problem of blacking out acres of plate glass windows in the city's 328 hotels, many of which were "glass showcases for the first 20 or 30 feet of their height, with hundreds of windows above that." Officials in Detroit did not get around to soliciting applications for air raid wardens (men only) until mid-January; hoping for 20,000 volunteers, the initial campaign stalled at about 4,300. "The only conclusion possible," grumbled the *Detroit Free Press*, "is that [Detroiters] are apathetic toward warnings that the city may be a target for bombers."

New York City officials lowered their expectations, opting to practice partial "dim-outs" of streetlights instead of complete blackouts. There still were no effective sirens, nor was there even agreement on what the air raid signal would be. (*Vogue* magazine wondered why New York, which "has been making a million ghastly, gratuitous noises all its life, just can't seem to make a noise like an air-raid siren.") Since Pearl Harbor, none of the metropolitan area's 210,000 air raid wardens had received any equipment from La Guardia's administration, save for a few armbands.

But on January 26, city authorities launched a training program for civilian defense volunteers via television broadcasts. Since so few private homes had TV receivers, "viewing posts" were set up in radio dealers' shops and police precinct houses for four weekly thirty-minute broadcasts over the local NBC affiliate, WNBT, with live demonstrations of approved procedures for air raid wardens, fire watchers, and rescue squads. (The general public was invited to look in as well.)

An informal national poll of civilian defense authorities named San Francisco "the worst managed civilian defense set-up in the country." The director of the city's Civilian Defense Council had resigned at the end of December, following revelations that the council had purchased no emergency firefighting equipment, and fewer than 10 percent of enrolled volunteers were receiving training in emergency procedures. The lackadaisical response to yet another mistaken air raid alert on January 3—the city's seven new sirens were drowned out by traffic noise—made it clear to one reporter that "there was little sign that the city was any more prepared for war than it was five weeks ago." A week later, exasperated residents launched a movement to jettison Mayor Rossi ("Recall Rossi and Save San Francisco") for his "mishandling of civilian defense preparations and his general incompetence."

San Franciscans' anxiety over a possible Japanese bombing attack seemed "to ebb and flow with the tides of war on the other side of the Pacific," observed Ernie Pyle in early January. "But right now, I believe the San Francisco public mind has settled down to a resigned but firm belief that sooner or later this city will have a taste of it." Across the country, military and political officials (and private citizens) continued to issue warnings that American communities remained vulnerable to Axis assault. Admiral Chester Nimitz, the new commander in chief of the U.S. Pacific Fleet, declared that it was "not beyond the bounds of possibility that Japanese submarines operating off the West Coast of the United States may attempt to lay their shells into cities before they leave." The Pacific Ocean, he said, was "too big to prevent it entirely."

"An effort will, of course, be made by the enemy to take us again unawares," insisted Eleanor Roosevelt, "to raid some city where there is a big defense industry." Military authorities claimed that the possibility of a Nazi zeppelin attack on the East Coast was "definitely in the cards," and the Massachusetts Committee on Public Safety cautioned that German bombers could attack coastal cities "more easily than we think." The American Red Cross War Fund campaign resorted to blatant scare tactics, sponsoring an advertisement with a drawing of a little girl looking up at bombers in the sky and asking, "Are they coming over here to fight, daddy?" No, her father responded, "but they may try. If they try, some may get through, for it is a wide sky, and bombs may crash here as they crashed on far-away Hawaii and in the distant Philippines."

More easily organized than major metropolitan centers, smaller inland communities—many of them miles from any viable military objectives—persevered in their own preparations. Residents of Florence, South Carolina, realized that they might not be a primary bombing target, but they believed that they still stood a reasonable chance of getting hit if enemy planes struck the East Coast. "We're pretty well on the alert here," declared a local spokesman. "We've figured that, if a plane got slightly lost and had to lighten its load, this is a perfect place for the pilot to get rid of his bombs. . . . We're in just about as much danger here as the folks are anywhere else." A journalist traveling through the southeastern states encountered similar convictions in every town he visited: "You might just as well tell them that their town water is polluted or that their grade schools are inadequate, as to even hint that they are safe."

There were, of course, occasional dissenters. "This war is driving me out of my mind," complained a woman in the town of Goshen, Massachusetts. "All the rich people in Goshen have literally taken it to their bosoms. They're having the time of their lives . . . [with] their uniforms and meetings and knittings and first-aid classes and air-raid warden courses and civil defense preparations. . . . It's one air-raid drill after another. . . . Hell, I could scream with the futility of it. . . . And who in the name of heaven wants to bomb Goshen anyway?" The governor of Colorado was equally skeptical about the value of practice blackouts for his state. "People are nervous enough," he decided, "without exciting them further."

Yet even those who believed themselves safe from bombing raids received a jolt when Surgeon General Thomas Parran told the U.S. Council of Mayors on January 12 that the enemy "has planned, and in my opinion will use, bacteriological warfare whenever possible." Local governments, Dr. Parran recommended, should "begin at once to take every possible precaution." Suddenly an object as innocent as a bottle of milk delivered to the front door became a potential danger. "No prospect strikes greater chill," concluded the *Washington Post*, "than that of mass attack by bacteria so deposited as to insure a maximum of casualties."

Since War Production Board officials refused to release steel or other scarce building materials for the construction of public (or private) shelters—and since wartime budgets already were constrained by other demands—state and local officials dispatched teams of architects to determine the safest existing buildings for improvised protection against enemy attacks. Frequently the search ended at the nearest prison, typically a sturdy concrete-and-steel structure. So New York State officials authorized the use of "prison housing, feeding and hospital facilities" for law-abiding citizens during air raids; if necessary, prisoners would be asked to double up to provide room for "outsiders." In Louisiana's notorious Angola prison, inmates were given the opportunity to fill out applications to share their quarters with civilians, "just in case."

One of the most extensive networks of private shelters in the nation belonged to Hollywood, where film executives—fearful that enemy pilots might mistake sprawling soundstages for defense factories—adapted their studios' spacious basements and carpentry shops for the emergency. Warner Bros. alone boasted four shelters, reinforced with sandbags, for its three thousand employees. Each shelter reportedly was equipped with beds, a kitchen, water, air-conditioning, a telephone system, a piano, a jukebox, hospital facilities, dominoes, and playing cards, with plain wooden benches along the walls. (Warner executives enjoyed their own exclusive "closet" bomb shelter.)

War had already brought a host of changes to the movie industry. Shooting schedules began earlier, typically at 8 a.m.—which meant actors often had to awaken around four o'clock to be in makeup on the set by eight—and typically ended by 5 p.m., so employees could return home before dark, in case of blackouts. To avoid disclosing strategically valuable information to saboteurs, Army authorities banned filming near railroad tunnels or bridges; nor could any movie show American harbors, airports, or defense plants. Sirens were out, as were automobile chase scenes (a staple of gangster pictures). Dwindling supplies of lumber and metal meant that studios had to recycle old sets as much as possible; even nails were collected and reused. Shortages of guns and ammunition forced tough-guy actors to use children's cap pistols, and costume dramas disappeared along with studios' stores of silk and satin.

Tire rationing eliminated most location trips. The drone of Army aircraft stationed along the California coast frequently penetrated soundstages and interrupted production, while the studios' own planes were grounded, forcing directors to use miniatures or model planes suspended from roofs. (Director Sam Wood received an exemption for a bombing scene in *For Whom the Bell Tolls*, but only after assuring nearby residents the planes were not Japanese invaders.) Studio horses and firearms were requisitioned for military or civilian defense purposes, and the Army reportedly threatened to draft Roy Rogers's prized fleet of carrier pigeons.

Some films already in production had been overtaken by events and needed to be rewritten. Others, including *Call Out the Marines*, were released ahead of schedule. MGM's musical comedy *I'll Take Manila* understandably was retitled *Ship Ahoy*, and the unfortunate *Midnight Angel* became *Pacific Blackout*, complete with bombers "droning menacingly" above a darkened town, and an Axis agent masquerading as a civilian defense official. ("Exactly the sort of picture which should NOT be shown at this time," charged a *New York Times* critic.) Screenwriters rushed to incorporate Japanese villains into their scripts, only to discover that there was, as one observer put it, "an acute shortage of Japs." "Nobody wants to play a Jap," explained Hollywood columnist John Chapman. "Not even the half dozen Japs registered with the screen actors' guild." To complete production on the espionage film *Secret Agent*, studio executives tried to persuade Peter Lorre ("Mr. Moto") to play a Japanese character, but he refused, as did numerous Chinese and Filipino actors.

Service comedies, so popular in 1941 with their irreverent humor and ridiculing of military authority, ended up on the trash heap. In the immediate aftermath of Pearl Harbor, some studio executives (particularly at Warner Bros.) gave a green light to as many war or patriotic films as they could produce. Others heeded Eleanor Roosevelt's advice—"For Heaven's sake, keep them laughing, and they will work harder, fight harder"—and focused on comedies to relieve wartime stress. January brought yet another trend, as one journalist reported that "the boys out in Hollywood are stumbling over one another's scripts in the mad rush to put into production films about our war efforts," especially the contributions of defense workers: *The Swing Shifters*, *Night Shift*, and a Paramount musical with the prosaic title of *Priorities on Parade*. But whatever the genre, Hollywood columnist Jimmie Fidler reminded filmmakers that "screen heroes must temporarily replace absent fathers, husbands, sons and boy friends in the minds and hearts of young and feminine America."

Against the backdrop of war, Hollywood's social scene lost its luster. Lavish parties seemed inappropriate. The Academy of Motion Picture Arts and Sciences initially canceled its annual awards banquet, then substituted instead a less formal dinner (no white ties for men, or evening gowns for women), and the swank Sunset Strip nightclub Ciro's, so chic in prewar days, closed its doors until conditions improved. "Business in the high class night clubs," sighed the club's manager, "is simply shot to hell."

Stars kept disappearing into the military—Jimmy Stewart, Robert Montgomery, and Douglas Fairbanks, Jr., among others—along with directors such as Garson Kanin and John Ford, and hundreds of cameramen, electricians, and other technical experts. And on the night of January 16, a plane carrying Carole Lombard and seventeen other passengers (including a dozen Army pilots) crashed into a mountain thirty miles southwest of Las Vegas. Lombard was on her way home from a tour selling defense bonds in her native Midwest; the previous day, the popular actress had sold more than $2 million worth of bonds in Indianapolis in the space of an hour. Heartbroken, Clark Gable could not be consoled. He began drinking heavily, and spent his evenings watching Lombard's films. White House officials wanted Gable to keep making movies: "Gable's one of the people's daily habits," a Roosevelt administration official told Walter Winchell. "We don't want to rob them of their daily habits all at once." But the actor began making plans to join the Army Air Corps, even though he was too old to serve as a pilot.

"The more we whip up the tempo of the war effort, the more accidents there are bound to be," predicted the *Washington Post* in mourning the loss of Lombard. Indeed, the National Safety Council reported that Americans had set an all-time record for traffic deaths in 1941—up 16 percent from the previous year, an increase the council attributed largely to "the ever-increasing tempo of national defense." The *Post* envisioned more of the same: "War urgencies so greatly multiply the burden on transportation personnel and equipment that a rising incidence of accidents is inescapable."

On January 14, a Navy spokesman warned the American public that German submarines were operating "all up and down the Atlantic Coast." Within hours, a U-boat torpedoed the Norwegian tanker *Norness* sixty miles southeast of Long Island. The following day, another tanker was sunk by a German sub in the same area.

Reluctant to provide details about the sinkings or the American response, Navy officials acknowledged that the submarine threat had grown "increasingly serious." The U-boat attacks, claimed a *Boston Globe* editorial, "brought the war closer to this country than it has been in the present struggle" (at least for the East Coast). By the end of the week, two more tankers had been torpedoed off the coast of North Carolina, and twenty-nine sailors were dead or missing. "Every sailor I have talked to," said one survivor, "says subs are now thicker along the Atlantic coast than fish."

Initially there were only five U-boats, the opening salvo in Germany's "Operation *Paukenschlag*" ("Drumbeat"), designed to pick off inviting targets such as oil tankers making their way laboriously up the eastern seaboard to storage depots and refineries. Beyond depriving the United States of vital resources (more than 90 percent of the oil and gasoline used on the East Coast came via tankers from ports in the Gulf of Mexico), the U-boats aimed to heighten anxieties among the American public, and tempt Navy authorities to divert protection from the Allied convoys carrying supplies to England.

By January 31, the Navy had confirmed the sinking of ten American or Allied merchant ships off the Atlantic seaboard, with nearly a hundred sailors dead or missing. (In fact, thirty-five ships had been sunk.) In hopes of calming coastal communities—residents of Atlantic City could hear the explosions as a series of torpedoes slammed into one tanker—War Department officials declared that joint Army and Navy forces had established a "closely coordinated defensive and offensive network system" to fight the invaders. But the evening lights from carelessly illuminated cities along the East Coast—sometimes visible for ten miles or more at sea—silhouetted the tankers and created "a neon shooting gallery" for the U-boat commanders. (Unofficially, the campaign was known among German sailors as "the American Turkey Shoot.")

"I wouldn't be a bit surprised if some of the present torpedoing so close to your shores were due to fifth-column work," noted a British merchant marine sailor visiting Manhattan. "New York is full of loose talk. In restaurants and bars I have heard your sailors and dock people unthinkingly give out information of vital importance to the enemy." Pleading with the public to abjure careless talk about troop movements or shipping timetables and routes, the Navy launched a campaign known informally as "Shut Up, America." Seagram's Distillers volunteered to design and distribute cautionary posters to taverns, and Bristol-Myers did the same for drugstores. In Los Angeles, Navy officials enlisted actress Jane Russell ("the Hush-Hush Girl") to pose with her finger to her lips above the slogans "Serve With Silence" and "A Slip of the Lip May Sink a Ship."

To prevent radio stations from inadvertently broadcasting sensitive information, the recently established federal Office of Censorship issued formal regulations on January 16 to supplement the previous recommendations of the National Association of Broadcasters. The new guidelines prohibited interviews at airports or train terminals, and suggested that stations "steer clear of dramatic programs which attempt to portray the horrors of combat," and "avoid sound effects which might be mistaken for air raid sirens." They also banned any "appeals for missing persons and lost dogs," or birthday party announcements that might actually be coded enemy messages, particularly those that instructed a listener to "look under the chair" or "on the mantel" for a surprise.

As the censorship office exercised a firmer hand over the release of war-related news, reporters scrambled to find anyone in an official capacity willing to provide accurate information, especially since (as *Time* magazine noted), "the publication of virtually any news about the United States war effort is now forbidden unless specifically sanctioned by the Government." Cabinet members and civilian and military department spokesmen held fewer news conferences; "no comments" flew thick and fast. Government press officials had learned that "they may get into trouble if they answer questions," claimed the *New York Times*, "but not if they say they cannot." Roosevelt himself—despite his obvious joy in jousting with reporters—canceled two press conferences in early January and ended another after three minutes, refusing to answer any direct questions.

"The Japs know when they attack," wrote one angry Californian from Los Gatos. "Withholding the facts can mean only that those in authority must feel that Americans can't take it, that they are not adult." Walter Lippmann concurred. "Mr. Roosevelt has a long, hard, bitter war to conduct," Lippmann noted, "and he cannot conduct it successfully without explaining it continually to the people. . . . The American people are not children, and they will have to be treated as adults if they are to face the grim future as men and women."

Worse, the news the government chose to release continued to paint the military situation in a far too optimistic light. Every day, complained the *Washington Post*, military authorities released accounts of real but relatively minor American achievements: "a prolonged artillery duel, the regaining of a few temporarily lost outposts, the recapture of a few square miles of jungle, the sinking of a few enemy ships." Precluded by censors from discussing truly important military developments, newspapers presented these triumphs as brilliant victories. "They are misleading," charged the *Post*, "in the sense that they are utterly out of proportion." As a result, "the public . . . has received through the press an impression of war progress which, to say the least, is unjustifiably optimistic."

Radio announcers presented an equally rose-colored view. "For Heaven's sake stop this silly feeding of honeyed buncombe over the air," pleaded columnist Chapin Hall in the *Los Angeles Times*. "The fact remains that the five weeks since the Japs stabbed us in the back at Pearl Harbor have been disastrous and humiliating, and it is no time to feed the public lollypops or lead the unthinking into a belief that the invincible Uncle Sam is ready to 'mop up.'" The president seemed unwilling to right the balance; even Eleanor Roosevelt acknowledged that her husband lacked Churchill's dexterity in presenting uncomfortable truths to the public.

Numerous observers noted the complacency that ensued. "It is shocking," complained the *Chicago Tribune*, "to observe the citizens of this country going about their business and their pleasures apparently unmindful of the soldiers who are dying in the Philippines." "The time has come," declared Governor O'Conor of Maryland, "for our people to change radically their point of view. There is too much indifference, too general a willingness to let the other fellow do the job." From Tennessee, World War I hero Alvin York remarked laconically that "it looks like some people haven't waked up yet."

"In Heaven's name, let's get mad!" demanded a full-page advertisement by a Cleveland defense firm in *Newsweek*. "Don't you want vengeance?" In its list of wishes for 1942, the *Detroit Free Press* hoped for a "greater realization on the part of the general public of what it will take in money, men and effort to win this war." From Los Angeles, Chapin Hall added that "there is too much general apathy loose in the land, especially along this [Pacific] coast," accompanied by "a growing tendency to shrug off the war as something apart that will be attended to in due time by the country's armed forces."

"If we were literally besieged or beleaguered, the dissemination of bad news might properly be regarded as inimical to our morale," wrote former New Deal adviser Raymond Moley. "But at the moment there is no danger that our morale will not bear up under bad news. There is no danger that we will take things too seriously. The danger is that we are not yet taking them seriously enough." In a commentary entitled "A War We

Can Lose," Hanson Baldwin—the *New York Times*' foremost military analyst—agreed that "we are still complacent; we still display . . . 'the valor of ignorance'; we are still 'slothful with fat pride.'" The Roosevelt administration, Baldwin charged, needed to awaken Americans "to the fact—which, to too many of them, seems fantasy—that we can lose this war, that nothing is foregone, except struggle."

Tire rationing was off to a rocky start. "A motor-minded public," reported the *Baltimore Sun*, "seems to find it difficult to adjust itself to the plain facts of the tire situation." While a substantial majority of Americans agreed that the rubber shortage made rationing necessary, drivers in one region after another demanded exemptions from the government's ban on sales of new tires; "everyone," complained William Knudsen, "seems to want to get from one place to another sitting down." The president of the Chicago Motor Club insisted that "since Chicago and vicinity are more dependent upon the passenger automobile for transport than New York City, due to less extensive public transportation facilities, our need for tires is far greater." (Chicago automobile owners had purchased a prewar average of more than 70,000 tires per month; their January 1942 allotment was 2,523.)

One southern California congressman announced that there would be "hell to pay in my district" if defense workers could not get new tires for the cars they needed to get to and from work. An American Federation of Labor spokesman argued that tire rationing was "the most unreasonable program that has yet been devised by any government agency," because it threatened "to upset our entire civilian economy" by denying new tires to delivery vehicles (typically driven by members of the Teamsters union). All across the state of Maryland, motorists telephoned the governor directly "to ask him to intercede for them" in obtaining tires. Massachusetts's state tire-rationing administrator reported similar pressure from local politicians, but "there is no sense exerting pressure, because pressure rolls off us like water off a duck's back."

Motorists who attempted to get their tires retreaded found that auto shops had order backlogs of several months, and were running low on materials. So many were charging exorbitant fees that on January 11 the federal government slapped price ceilings on retreading and recapping services. On the same day, the OPA's Leon Henderson announced that since profiteering in used tires "already has reached serious proportions," he would set maximum prices for them as well. Price-gouging by tire shops, Henderson promised, "cannot and will not be allowed to continue. . . . The public must be protected from exploitation."

"The average citizen has little or no conception of the rubber situation," observed a member of the tire-rationing board of a New Jersey town. "Many think that rationing will be temporary. . . . Others have the attitude 'they can't do this to me,' and believe that if they pay enough they can get new tires some way." And some could. *Time* magazine called tire rationing "the most magnificent opportunity for bootlegging since prohibition days," and OPA officials acknowledged that "complaints alleging violations have been quite numerous." On January 18, the *Los Angeles Times* reported "accumulating evidence that hoarding is going on. . . . Reports persist that rationed tires are being acquired by persons all over the country who already have good rubber to ride on." British journalist Alistair Cooke admitted that several gangsters of his acquaintance had started a competition to see "who could most frequently drive out in the morning with a new set of white-walled tires."

Tire thefts soared. "A bird with a broken wing doesn't look any more helpless than a car with two of its wheels missing," wrote one alarmed motorist in Los Angeles. "And it's a sad sight that's greeting many a motorist these mornings." The president of the American Automobile Association charged that a "wave of tire thievery [was] sweeping the country": some thieves stripped tires from cars; some stole both cars and tires; and some swiped the cars, removed all four tires, and abandoned the cars in remote locations. More brazen gangs stripped tires from cars in the open and replaced them with old, worn replacements, while passersby assumed they were merely changing a flat.

For the first half of January, auto thefts were up nearly 50 percent in ten of the nation's largest cities. Los Angeles authorities reported an average of fifteen incidents of tire theft per day, three times the normal rate. So many tires were pilfered in Philadelphia that police began putting them on the daily list of valuable hot items—along with jewelry and antiques— for special attention by patrolmen. In Chicago, thieves stole the rubber-tired wheels from a baby carriage. A team of criminals in Norfolk, Virginia, reportedly heisted one car's tires but ignored a diamond ring on the front seat: "Roses are red, violets are blue," read the note they left behind, "we like your jewels, but your tires are new."

Judges imposed the maximum penalties permissible: a year in prison for stealing a used tire in Virginia; two and a half years for the theft of two spare tires in Michigan; two years in jail in Delaware, plus ten lashes at one of the state whipping posts. Legislators in New York and Illinois made tire theft a felony, so prison sentences could be extended to five or ten years. Inspired by comments equating tire theft to horse rustling in the Old West—"You will recall they used to string men up sometimes then," noted one magistrate—Firestone tire dealers began using electric irons to brand new tires ("Safti-Brand Service") with their customers' initials. "While the brand of three initials may not be as picturesque as the Circle R or the Bar X brands of the cattle range," announced Firestone, "it serves the same purpose by establishing ownership."

Searching for silver linings, government experts predicted that tire rationing would decrease gasoline consumption by 35 percent in 1942, reduce traffic congestion, increase carpooling and the use of public transportation, and make Americans more fit by encouraging walking or bicycling. Moviegoers were treated to publicity newsreels of Leon Henderson riding a recently designed "Victory" bike—lighter, with less metal, smaller wheels, and thin tires of reclaimed rubber—in front of the Capitol steps, with his female secretary perched awkwardly in a basket on the handlebars. ("He didn't ride very well," a six-year-old girl pointed out. "He wobbled all over.")

Officials of the Council of State Governments advised the nation's governors to lower speed limits on highways—a few had already done so—partly to save rubber, but also to save lives, "because if people do drive fast on old tires their worries about rubber conservation may cease abruptly." Some observers foresaw a return to neighborliness as Americans were forced to rely on one another for transportation. "We've been living too much apart," noted Tom Treanor, "as if we were high blood pressure neurotics and couldn't stand the wear and tear of human relationships." Perhaps Americans already were making new friends; a classified advertisement in one small-town North Carolina newspaper read: "Lady with good car desires to meet gentleman with four good tires. Object—Miami."

Henderson advised motorists not to expect the end of tire rationing anytime soon. "We'll be very lucky indeed," he told reporters in mid-January, "if two years from today we have as much rubber for tires as we have at the moment." In the meantime, Firestone and Goodyear announced plans to produce tires made from reclaimed rubber (dubbed "Victory" and "War" tires, respectively), which were safe only when driven at low speeds—thirty-five miles per hour or less.

Automobile rationing came next. Effective January 2, sales of new cars were prohibited until rationing rules went into effect on January 15. (Used car prices promptly jumped by 10 percent for older models, and 25 percent for newer ones.) Production of civilian cars continued through the month, but as January came to an end, the last civilian vehicles rolled off the assembly lines, leaving nearly 400,000 American autoworkers unemployed, at least two-thirds of them in Michigan.

Rising unemployment in "the former automotive city" led labor and management to resume their pre–Pearl Harbor bickering. In a half-page advertisement published in numerous newspapers and magazines, the Congress of Industrial Organizations blamed the delay in converting to war production on automobile companies' selfishness and incompetence, and demanded equal influence with management in coordinating the long-delayed conversion process. The Automobile Manufacturers Association responded with anti-left rhetoric straight out of the 1930s, hinting darkly that the CIO's criticism of the auto industry's war effort was "designed to create a division so that certain groups may obtain control of the productive machinery of the United States." The suggestion of shared labor-management control of the industry, added General Motors president Charlie Wilson, aimed at nothing less than the "socialization of industry."

At least the autoworkers could readily transfer their skills to defense production once conversion finally occurred. Over a hundred thousand automobile salesmen who had lost their jobs in the nation's forty-four thousand auto dealerships (probably for the duration) faced a more difficult path. "Apparently," concluded Newsweek, "no one in Washington has thought about the need for finding a job in the armament program for such displaced white-collar workers."

Rationing rules reserved the 650,000 new cars still on hand for government use, including Lend-Lease shipments to Europe. Despite persistent rumors to the contrary, Henderson assured the public that the government had no plans at that time to commandeer privately owned automobiles if the stockpile of new cars ran out—although, he added, "that's a gloomy possibility." "Depends on the Japs," Henderson explained. "I don't know how soon we can lick them."

Nearly 60 percent of the nation's 35 million families owned at least one passenger car or truck. Asked how they planned to adapt to wartime exigencies in 1942, slightly more than half of car-owning families told Gallup pollsters they planned to significantly reduce their driving, by an average of 45 percent—which approximately equaled the leisure share of their prewar driving mileage. Many Americans had already canceled their winter vacation plans. Driving from Washington, D.C., to Florida, a journalist noted that traffic on the highways was more sparse than he had ever seen: "Gas station attendants in North Carolina were complaining about the light trade. So were the roadside eating places of all kinds. The same went for tourist camps and hotels."

"The 1942 winter season in Florida is considerably below par," observed one onlooker, who ascribed the decline to tire rationing and "the factor of fear," including "all sorts of silly rumors about barbed wire on the beaches, together with the East Coast submarine scare." As bookings dwindled by an estimated 20 to 30 percent, Miami hotels found themselves with "a bad case of January jitters"; to reverse the tide, the city's hoteliers cut prices and sponsored ads to remind the rest of the nation that "V stands for Vacation as well as for Victory."

A group of western states launched similar campaigns to lure tourists: "See the Old West—Travel Strengthens America," and "Turn your back on winter worries under the soothing desert sun." But Joseph Eastman, the recently appointed federal director of defense transportation, advised Americans that "travel for mere pleasure or sight-seeing . . . must be curbed and brought within much narrower bounds."

Enemy aliens could not leave town at all without the permission of the Justice Department. On January 1, Attorney General Biddle announced that citizens of the Axis nations who wished to travel from one U.S. city to another—by car, bus, or train, because air travel was still forbidden—were required to apply for government approval (explaining the route and purpose of the trip) a week in advance. Officials applied the order indiscriminately; seventy-five-year-old Arturo Toscanini, the guest conductor of the Philadelphia Orchestra and an Italian national, needed permission to travel from Philly to Washington to perform at a sold-out concert at Constitution Hall on January 13. Since each form had to be filled out in quadruplicate, Ezio Pinza (Italy) and Lotte Lehmann (Germany) needed to fill out eighty-eight forms each for a twenty-two-city Metropolitan Opera Company tour.

By the first week of January, the FBI had detained slightly more than 3,000 of the 1.8 million enemy aliens in the United States as suspected saboteurs or spies. Those not in custody faced increasing restrictions beyond travel limits. As rumors continued to swirl about the role of Japanese fifth columnists in the attack on Pearl Harbor, Justice Department officials ordered all enemy aliens to surrender their cameras, radio transmitters, and shortwave receivers. (Anti-Nazi refugees in Hollywood had to turn in their movie cameras; famed photojournalist Robert Capa relinquished his camera as well.) On January 5, Biddle expanded the ban to include bombs, explosives, photographs or maps of military installations or equipment, codes, ciphers, and "papers, documents, or books in which there may be invisible writing." Ten days later, Roosevelt issued a proclamation ordering the registration of all enemy aliens over thirteen years of age; henceforth they would need to carry identification cards with their photograph, signature, and index-finger print.

Having encouraged the public's suspicions about Axis nationals, Biddle requested the U.S. Conference of Mayors to protect loyal aliens against attacks by "amateur detectives, the super-patriot, and the self-appointed sentinel." In a national radio address, another top Justice Department official advised Americans not to follow the lead of "misguided patriots [who] like to display their Americanism by smearing shop windows, or making insulting remarks in public about persons of foreign birth." Such irresponsible acts, he added, "are only slightly less reprehensible than those of the saboteurs and spies you have vowed to suppress."

Reports also reached the White House of employers firing alien workers, a practice which Roosevelt termed "as stupid as it is unjust," especially when the war production program needed every skilled worker available. In California, a labor supply commission spokesman warned that industry's refusal to hire enemy alien workers was slowing the defense effort, and he condemned the dismissal of "local and patriotic American citizens who are regarded as having 'foreign names,' whatever that may mean in a country which has drawn its people from all parts of the world."

"If one loyal group is to be designated as fair game for super-patriots, or persons of uncontrollable emotions," wondered the *Detroit Free Press*, "where will the line finally be drawn?"

Driving along the Pacific coast between San Francisco and Seattle at a leisurely pace in late January, Ernie Pyle reported that "the small towns have not changed much in appearance from peace time. . . . People on the streets act as they used to. . . . Life, even on the 'front line' here, has been disarranged very little by the war so far." But Pyle also noticed the decline in population in the coastal towns ("Despite denials, it is true that many people have left the Coast"), the growing and "ghastly" traffic problem near defense plants, and a dearth of full-fledged enthusiasm for the war: "War is talked at parties and wherever two persons get together, of course, but the man with zeal in his eye is a rare one. War fever is not at the 1918 pitch."

Similar observations came from other parts of the country. "There has been very little whooping and general spread-eagleism in the first days of this affair," noted columnist John O'Ren in the *Baltimore Sun*. "It's a nasty job and everybody knows it: so why waste time by using euphemisms to camouflage hard facts?" Tom Treanor, too, noticed the lack of flag-waving demonstrations in the Los Angeles area. "I haven't heard a band on the street in this war," Treanor wrote. "We're going at it without illusion that it's going to be fun." Returning to his home on Martha's Vineyard from a visit to Washington, Charles Lindbergh did encounter an actual "war parade" in Fall River, Massachusetts, but the spectacle left him unimpressed: "Bands and 'Legionnaire' girl band leaders with short skirts and very red legs. (It is one of the coldest days of the winter.) Behind them marched crowds of citizens carrying small flags. I could not help feeling that the American spirit was there but that it was without direction or leadership. . . . In a few minutes it would be over, and they would return to their homes and shops and offices, back in the routine of their old lives."

What the American people needed, decided Congressman J. Parnell Thomas of New Jersey, was "a good five-cent war song." "The nation is literally crying for a good, peppy, marching song," declared Thomas, "something with plenty of zip, ginger and fire." Songwriters had moved beyond simple-minded bashing of Japan, but the overall quality of new tunes ("I've Changed My Penthouse for a Pup Tent") remained dismal; an RCA Victor spokesman said his company received an average of five patriotic songs a day, and "most of them are terrible." Warmed-over songs from World War I—including "Over There" and "Keep the Home Fires Burning"—staged a brief comeback, while gangs of kids on city streets sang their own anthem, adapting the seven dwarfs' marching song from the Disney film *Snow White*: "Hi-ho, hi-ho / We're off to Tokyo / We'll smash the Japs / Right off the map / Hi-ho, hi-ho!" Disappointed with the musical effort ("dribble") to date, bandleader Paul Whiteman suggested that the nation needed a war song in swing tempo to really grab both soldiers and civilians. "I wish Tin Pan Alley would get busy. Or inspired," Whiteman grumbled. "It's enough to make a band leader lose weight."

Perhaps the patriotic love song "He's 1-A in the Army and He's A-1 in My Heart" (recorded by Harry James and His Orchestra) came closest to capturing the mood of swing music fans, as record numbers of young American men and women continued to flock to marriage license bureaus. The Census Bureau reported an all-time high of 1.5 million marriages in the United States in 1941, and the hectic pace spilled over into January 1942. In some cities, marriages were up by 150 percent since Pearl Harbor. "It may be the draft, it may be the war, or it may be love," sighed a Baltimore civic official.

Soldiers and sailors flooded city marriage bureaus in San Francisco, Seattle, and San Diego, in the heaviest rush for wedding licenses the West Coast had ever witnessed. Magistrates across the nation noted a substantial increase in grooms wearing military uniforms, rushing to get married before being shipped overseas. The *Detroit Free Press* called it "the day of living in an age of swift meetings and swifter farewells"; time was so short that the mayor of Utica, New York, waived the usual twenty-four-hour waiting period between issuing a wedding license and conducting the ceremony, because some servicemen had no time to wait. Seeking to stem the tide, Eleanor Roosevelt implored college women not to drop out of school "in a patriotic fervor" or change their life plans "because your beau is going into the Army." "The hysteria of war," agreed a professor at Mills College in northern California, "is likely to make many couples rush into a marriage that has been ill-considered, based on brief acquaintance. . . . Marry in haste and repent in leisure, an adage proven true in peacetime, is ten times as true in times of war."

On the other hand, a growing number of men were marrying to evade military service. For the first fifteen months of the draft—between October 1940 and December 1941—Selective Service officials routinely granted deferments to married men on the assumption that a wife depended upon her husband's civilian income; some Army officials also believed that "a peacetime soldier would not be much good if he had a wife to worry about." Altogether, about 7.5 million men had received dependency deferments. "We have leaned backwards," admitted Selective Service director Lewis Hershey, "and have not argued about when a marriage took place, or whether a husband actually is supporting a wife, or whether a wife might not be able and ready to return to her normal job and support herself, thereby releasing her husband to the army."

But as draft calls increased, and authorities discovered what one Colorado official termed "an alarming tendency to use marriage as a method of draft evasion," Hershey announced in early January that local Selective Service boards would crack down on new deferments. "Dependency is relative," he explained. "We will not do anything to disrupt the institution of the family. But we will have to determine whether it is a family in fact, or simply has the appearance of one." Draft officials in New York City adopted new procedures that required husbands "to establish to the satisfaction of the members of his local board that his marriage was contracted in good faith and in the natural course of human affairs and not for the purpose of evading service." Authorities in other states decided that any draft registrants married on or after December 8, 1941, were automatically disqualified for dependency deferments. "It makes no difference," shrugged the Illinois state director of Selective Service, "whether or not the marriage is contracted in good faith."

Girls who chose not to marry their boyfriends before they entered military service could join the "Always in My Heart Club" founded by a group of young women in Los Angeles in January. Members wore heart-shaped lockets containing their boyfriend's photo and the motto of the club, signifying their commitment to be true for the duration. "We hope this will keep the boys happy," chirped the club's commanding officer, who hoped to establish branches across the country. "We have heard so much about their being afraid we'd forget them, once they were out of sight. This ought to be good for soldier morale." Club rules actually encouraged dating other members' beaus: "Members in each city will entertain the boy friends of members in other cities, remembering at all times whose property a particular boy friend is."

Any plan that would help slow the rising incidence of venereal disease in the United States was welcomed by the surgeon general, who deemed syphilis "the most urgent public health problem in this country today." In his January 12 speech to the U.S. Conference of Mayors, Dr. Parran declared that commercialized prostitution—"one of our most expanded war industries"—was responsible for as much as 75 percent of all new cases of venereal disease, and he urged local authorities and military officials to crack down on vice, especially in areas around military bases and defense "boom towns."

Parran's office dispatched specially trained medical officers to Army camps, launched new education programs for the troops, and established "prophylactic stations" available to soldiers and sailors, but some base commanders refused to shut down the brothels in their area, claiming they were necessary to maintain troop morale. Even when military authorities cooperated, the problem did not disappear; in a conversation with California attorney general Earl Warren, Parran estimated that "ten to fifteen per cent of all servicemen would find a woman to consort with even if it was necessary to jump off a ten-story building."

Public health experts feared long-term damage to the nation's well-being from the 50,000 draftees already rejected by the Army because they displayed symptoms of venereal disease, men whom Parran referred to as "smoldering incendiaries." To heighten public awareness, a coalition of health, welfare, and civic organizations sponsored "National Social Hygiene Day"; the Public Health Institute sponsored educational advertisements ("Syphilis Is Sneaky!") and offered complete exams and treatment "at very low cost"; and the Metropolitan Life Insurance Company provided free copies of their booklet *The Facts About Syphilis*. "I cannot urge too strongly on the people of this state," declared New York's Governor Lehman, "how vital is this menace."

Progress would be hindered by the growing shortage of doctors for the civilian population. In early 1942, there were about 186,000 licensed physicians in the United States, of whom 13,000 had entered military service. Experts estimated the Army and Navy would need another 19,000 by the end of the year, bringing the total to over 17 percent of the nation's supply. Rural areas would feel the drain most keenly. Even before the war began, nearly a third of the nation's counties lacked any public health services; in eighteen of the most thinly populated states, the ratio of doctors to the general population ranged from one physician for every 901 residents all the way to one doctor for every 1,532 people.

Nurses also were in short supply. So many girls were leaving high school or college for defense jobs that nursing schools found it difficult to recruit students to replace the experienced nurses who were joining the armed forces. A desperate New York State legislature voted unanimously to suspend the State Nurses Practice Act, which had required all nurses practicing in the state to be registered and licensed.

"The medical profession," announced the editor of the *Journal of the American Medical Association* grimly, "[is] closer to scraping the bottom of the bucket . . . than any other occupation, trade or profession."

# 6: An Unquiet Feeling

JANUARY–FEBRUARY 1942

*One by one the comforting notions vanished,*
*leaving behind them the pained, familiar*
*feeling that this was not the way things were*
*supposed to happen at all.*

— *THE NEW YORKER*, FEBRUARY 1942

Authorities across the country implored Americans to get in shape. "The Germans and Japanese have been trained for years in physical fitness, while we have been loafing," observed John B. "Handsome Jack" Kelly, the director of the Office of Civilian Defense's nationwide "Hale America" campaign. Local defense council representatives joined the movement by encouraging their civilian volunteers to adopt exercise routines "to make up for the soft life that most Americans have been living," and to "save car tires by walking off your spare tire." It would be no easy task; a Gallup poll showed that nearly half of Americans did no outdoor walking at all outside of work, and only 42 percent took systematic exercise of any kind.

As former top-ranked tennis player Alice Marble pointed out, Americans simply sat too much. "It's very serious," noted Marble, who was serving as OCD's assistant director of national defense in charge of physical fitness. Americans sat "in offices, on subways, in cars, at home, and at the movies. The machine has made them sluggish." (Double-feature films were a particular bête noire for Marble.) "All we want," she concluded, "is for people to get up off of their easy chairs and do something"—albeit within reason. "Rope-skipping," Marble cautioned, "is only for people in good condition, or it's likely to kill you."

And so a team of OCD representatives toured the nation, spreading the gospel—via radio broadcasts and lectures—that "in a total war no one can sit in the bleachers." To "toughen up everybody in America," specialized exercise routines were developed for various groups: air raid wardens, housewives, senior citizens, draft rejectees, and office workers "who bend over defense plans all day." A separate OCD branch, headed by Olympic star Jesse Owens, promoted fitness among African Americans. Defense contractors were advised to "intensify the emphasis on sports and recreation so that healthy Americans can keep planes flying, ships floating, and the tanks moving."

Hale America sponsored track meets and golf tournaments—although sporting goods dealers warned that the supply of golf balls might disappear altogether by midsummer—and planned a nationwide bowling program so Americans could "keep them rolling" and "hit the head-pin with Uncle Sam." The OCD scheduled major-league baseball players to speak at recreation centers and conduct informal instructional clinics before ball games. ("It's going to be torture for most of them," predicted sports columnist Bob Considine. "Few of them are speakers. Few of them are at ease among fans. . . . It's going to be a tough season for a lot of players who for years have studiously avoided the public that pays their salaries.") Colleges and high schools opened their gymnasiums to the public for calisthenics and basketball games on a twenty-four-hour basis; defense workers who needed to unwind after eight hours on the midnight shift played in "Dawn Patrol" basketball leagues, while their spouses ("midnight wives") enjoyed badminton, volleyball, and tap-dancing classes.

Challenged by the NCAA "to lure the man in the stands out on the field," college administrators adopted intensive physical-training requirements for their students. Columbia University dropped classes in badminton, table tennis, and bowling, and replaced them with boxing, wrestling, and long-distance running as part of a three-times-a-week compulsory program. At the University of Southern California, male students spent Friday afternoons dashing through mazes, vaulting fences, running relays, and practicing carrying their "injured" colleagues. And Yale University officials implemented a mandatory "training and toughening" plan for undergraduates, including manual labor activities such as chopping wood, excavating, and ditch digging, along with bodybuilding exercises, wall climbing, swimming, jujitsu, rugby, and hockey—sports that would "teach men how to take punishment as well as give it," noted one sportswriter, "a valuable lesson in this put-and-take war where the enemy is just as smart and just as brave and has the advantage of a breath-taking head start."

Occasionally the physical-culture proponents went too far. In early February, the fifty-three-year-old Kelly—a former Olympic rowing champion turned Philadelphia politician whom President Roosevelt had chosen in September 1940 to lead the national physical-preparedness campaign—suggested that American society put "too much emphasis on the brain and not enough on the body." In short, said Kelly (who had quit school at the age of sixteen), Americans needed to become "a little dumber and much stronger." ("Could we be dumber than we have been?" wondered Senator Carter Glass of Virginia, speaking for administration critics everywhere.) Dismissing Kelly's comment as "grotesquely naive," the *Baltimore Sun* pointed out that the choice between intellect and muscles was not a zero-sum game: "By all means let us seek national physical fitness, but let us not deceive ourselves that we shall find salvation in a gymnasium alone."

But fitness was more than exercise, and Americans were bombarded in early 1942 with advice on proper nutrition—particularly since poor diets accounted for nearly one-third of Selective Service physical exam failures. "Never before in the history of our country," swore one enthusiast in the *Washington Post*, "has the 'right' food been of such vital importance." Grocers distributed pamphlets on "nutritional intelligence" to customers, and city health departments provided booklets on foods that would "make you fit for defense." Women's clubs, church groups, and civic organizations such as the YWCA sponsored evening classes in nutrition. The Campfire Girls dedicated themselves in 1942 to learning how to "fortify the family" by shopping for vitamin-rich foods, and then cooking dinner once a week so Mom could spend a full afternoon volunteering for war work.

Diet experts provided tips for "wartime vitality": give up fried foods; don't overcook vegetables; and eat carrots at least three times a week (or more if you lived in an area with frequent blackouts). Restaurants joined the chorus—"Dining is Defense when you dine on our health and morale-building 'Victory Victuals'"—as did corporations such as Campbell's Soup Company ("Uncle Sam says 'Eat more tomatoes'") and the Metropolitan Life Insurance Company, which reminded American housewives that "'plenty to eat' does *not* always mean 'well fed.'"

For homemakers, the ultimate goal was "nutritional defense": to serve healthy foods and still leave enough funds in the household budget to purchase defense bonds and stamps as well. And so each week, thousands of letters poured into government offices—there were fifteen different federal agencies claiming to provide nutritional expertise—from women asking advice on what food to buy and how to conserve leftovers. The Office of Defense Health and Welfare Services (which was trying to wrest nutritional oversight from the OCD) responded by mailing more than 200,000 posters promoting a list of essential foods, and by producing a two-reel film entitled *Hidden Hunger* (starring Walter Brennan) "to aid the average citizen in eating sensibly during wartime."

To maintain peak efficiency in war production plants, New York State legislators proposed a special nutritional program to improve the diet of defense workers in communities where boom conditions had raised the price of healthy foods to exorbitant levels. Nutritional advice seemed particularly essential for recently hired defense workers who had suffered from poor eating habits during long years of joblessness. As one government nutritionist explained, "You can't take people off relief rolls, place them in war industries and expect them to be efficient and accurate."

Dwindling stocks of sugar on grocery store shelves bothered nutritionists not at all, especially since Americans had consumed 114 pounds of the sweetener per person in 1941—twice as much as any other country. The post–Pearl Harbor wave of sugar panic buying persisted throughout January and February, with widespread reports of women pushing grocery carts piled high with five-pound bags, sometimes purchasing one hundred pounds at a time. Grocers posted signs that read, "DO NOT HOARD—REMAIN CALM," but news of American military reverses in the Philippines, which provided 15 percent of the nation's annual sugar supply, exacerbated the stampede. Women's clubs sponsored speakers who declared that "she who hoards is Public Enemy Number 1," and authorities compared hoarding sugar to helping Hitler. To no avail. Housewives established gossip grapevines to alert their friends when the neighborhood grocer received a new shipment of sugar, and when merchants restricted purchases (typically two to five pounds of sugar per customer for each visit), some shoppers bought their share and then dispatched every available family member—"cousins, daughters, uncles and aunts"—into the store to buy more; then they moved on to the next store.

By mid-January, many grocers were refusing to sell sugar to anyone except their regular customers, and even then they imposed restrictions. "We don't have any sugar half the time," explained a clerk at the Roosevelt Market in Washington, D.C. "If we let customers have sugar one day, we won't let them buy any more for two or three days, but, nevertheless, some people are really piling it up."

Hotels removed dishes of individually wrapped sugar cubes from their rooms (easy "souvenirs" for guests when they checked out), and replaced them with less portable partially full bowls of granulated sugar. A restaurant in South Carolina posted a sign asking coffee drinkers to "Go easy on the sugar, boys, and stir like hell"; public health authorities estimated that the nation annually wasted twenty-five thousand tons of sugar stuck to the bottoms of coffee mugs and teacups. Cafeterias and diners that formerly provided unlimited sugar with cups of coffee or tea took away the sugar bowl entirely, forcing customers to ask waiters or counter clerks for a spoonful of sugar—few had the nerve to ask for more than two. Many restaurants stopped serving the traditional free second cup of coffee, because there would be no free second helping of sugar. One chain of Boston restaurants experimented by offering sugar in small glass bottles with a shaker on top, on the theory that it took so long to shake out a spoonful of sugar that diners would give up in frustration. The experiment ended when customers simply slipped the shakers into their coat pockets as they left.

Newspapers and magazines published scores of recipes on "How to use Less Sugar and like it": sugarless pies, cookies, cake (including pork cake), crullers, chocolate pudding, and salad dressing. Instead of sugar on breakfast cereal, the OPA recommended raisins, dates, prunes, and apricots as substitutes. Demand for honey neared an all-time high. Food processors increasingly turned to corn syrup to sweeten their products; to persuade the public, highway billboards proclaimed that "Corn Sugar is Better for You." Eleanor Roosevelt vowed to serve more fruit salad at the White House in place of dessert. (She also recommended potatoes as an alternative source of energy, but it was not the same.)

Any chance of curbing the panic buying vanished when Secretary of Agriculture Claude Wickard appeared on Mrs. Roosevelt's weekly radio program on January 18 and—after weeks of denying rumors of a sugar shortage—acknowledged that "there just won't be enough sugar for our usual consumption" in 1942: "We'd better prepare for some belt tightening." Wickard blamed the shortfall on reduced imports, military demands (including the manufacture of explosives), Lend-Lease shipments to Britain and Russia, and hoarding—by individuals as well as by candy and soda producers, some of whom reportedly had stockpiled two years' worth of sugar. (Wickard neglected to mention the stores of sugar amassed by moonshiners. When police raided one small-time bootlegger's apartment in the Bronx, they discovered a still and nearly 4,500 pounds of sugar. For more ambitious operations—such as the recently uncovered illegal liquor ring in New York State which Treasury Department investigators deemed the largest in the nation's history—experts estimated that a thousand-gallon still might require 80,000 pounds of sugar every week.)

Faced with a new surge in purchases (and prices, which had risen more than 50 percent in some areas), Leon Henderson finally announced on January 24 that the government would impose sugar rationing within the next few weeks. Since the nation's supply was estimated to be one-third below the 1941 peak, Henderson proposed that each American, including children, would be allowed to buy only two-thirds of the seventy-four pounds of sugar the average citizen had purchased the previous year. Their actual ration allotment would be slightly lower—perhaps three-fourths of a pound per week—to account for the granulated sugar they would consume in restaurants and cafes. Food producers would have their supplies cut by 20 to 35 percent; on Wall Street, Pepsi and Coca-Cola stocks promptly sank to a twelve-month low.

Admitting that "there has been a considerable amount of hoarding in recent weeks," Henderson—who considered such behavior almost "traitorous"—declared that consumers would need to sign a certified statement confirming the amount of sugar their family possessed when they registered for their booklets of ration stamps. More than two pounds per person would be considered hoarding, and rationing authorities would withhold an appropriate number of stamps. OPA officials indicated that they expected "relatively few cases of falsification in reporting the amount of sugar in the possession of any family"—the penalty for false reports ran as high as ten thousand dollars and/or ten years in prison—but they did not explain how they would verify individual claims. Rumors spread that FBI agents had begun to interview grocery store owners about their customers' buying habits, and that air raid wardens planned to search kitchen cupboards as part of their routine blackout inspections. "A house to house search will not be tolerated," insisted one Chicago homemaker who had purchased more than her family's fair share of sugar. "If our government had had the foresight to prepare for the present emergency as our housewives had done, we would not now be suffering the embarrassment of having both cheeks slapped and a boot in the rear besides by the Japanese."

For the moment, Henderson advised sugar hoarders to "sell some of it to your neighbors who may be without or sell it back to your grocer." Government officials expected the appeal to recoup 265,000 tons of hoarded sugar; several weeks later, however, the "Sell It Back" campaign seemed to be foundering. One chain of East Coast grocery stores reported that "only a negligible amount of sugar" had been returned for resale. Some housewives in small towns reportedly threatened to destroy their sugar stockpiles, to avoid the disgrace of being publicly branded as hoarders; others boiled down their sugar in hopes that syrup would be exempt from rationing restrictions. (It wasn't.) On the other hand, sales of powdered ant poison were increasing, to keep insects out of kitchen larders stocked with sweeteners.

"Winning back the Far East is the hardest job we ever undertook," warned columnist Raymond Clapper. "The battle is going against the United Nations all around. We cannot view with any optimism whatever the position of General MacArthur in the Philippines. Singapore is in grave danger." Throughout January and February, American troops in the Philippines retreated gradually and grudgingly down the Bataan Peninsula, inflicting substantial casualties on the Japanese invaders; but the Japanese army received reinforcements, and the Americans did not. By the end of January, State Department officials in Washington were wondering whether they could get MacArthur and his family out of the Philippines alive.

Enjoying nearly total air supremacy in Southeast Asia, Japanese bombers pounded the key British island-fortress of Singapore and strategic Allied targets in the Dutch East Indies, striking as far as northern Australia. Japanese invasion forces landed in the Solomon Islands, on Sumatra, on Borneo and Celebes and Java—the last Allied defensive stronghold between Burma and Australia—and continued their advance through Thailand and Malaya. "If there has been any lingering belief on the part of the American people that the tide of battle in the Pacific would turn automatically in our favor once Japan's 'first strength' was spent, that belief ought by this time to have been dissipated," declared the *New York Times*. "We are face to face with one of the great crises of our history."

News from other fronts was hardly reassuring. In the second week of February, the German battleships *Scharnhorst* and *Gneisenau* evaded the British fleet that had kept them penned in at Brest, and sailed through the mists of the English Channel to Norway, to prey on Allied convoys bound for the Soviet Union. And German submarines continued to ambush tankers steaming slowly up the Atlantic coast of the United States. "There was a melancholy tune being picked up every night in the Navy Department," noted Alistair Cooke, "from the wireless messages of oil tankers going down off the coasts of New Jersey, Delaware, and the Carolinas." By mid-February, the Navy acknowledged the sinking of fifteen "large vessels" in American waters, totaling over 113,000 tons, with 438 sailors dead or missing. The real toll was closer to fifty ships.

"Lunching by one's self with the newspaper propped up against the sugar bowl," remarked one despondent writer in New York, "is very bad for morale." At his home in Oxford, Mississippi, William Faulkner was less polite in his assessment. "This world is bitched proper this time, isn't it?" wrote the novelist to a friend on January 21. "I'd take all those congressmen who refused to make military appropriations and I'd send them to the Philippines. This day a year and I dont believe there will be one present second lt. [lieutenant] alive."

A licensed pilot who had been trained in the Royal Canadian Air Force in the closing days of World War I, Faulkner already had organized air raid observation posts in the area around Oxford, in the event Axis bombers struck northern Mississippi. But as he completed work on his latest novel, *Go Down, Moses*, the forty-four-year-old Faulkner—who never saw combat in the previous conflict—sought a more active role in the war effort. "I have a chance to teach navigation (air) in the Navy as a civilian," he told publisher Robert Haas. "If I can get my affairs here established, I think I'll take it."

After traveling across the country for much of January, newscaster Edward Murrow concluded that most Americans lacked Faulkner's sense of urgency; rather, they seemed to view the war as a spectacle, and themselves as mere spectators. "We do not fully appreciate the need for speed," said Murrow. "We do not quite understand that if we delay too long in winning the victory we will inherit nothing but a cold, starving embittered world. . . . Already there are signs that we're coming to accept slavery and suppression as part of the pattern of living in this year of disgrace. . . . There is the danger that we may become brutalized."

From nearly every quarter came charges that the American public remained complacent, even in the face of a nearly unbroken string of disasters overseas. "Reports from the country continue to assert that the spirit of urgency and alarm, so needful for a successful war effort, is not rising at the pace of war production," wrote Arthur Krock. "It is still lagging and sluggish, and susceptible of easy relapses." Upon completing his own cross-country journey, Walter Lippmann lamented "the unawareness, the overconfidence, and the complacency" of Americans, who seemed to have adopted "the notion that the war is something which MacArthur is fighting, or that the President is fighting, while the rest of us sit in the bleachers."

"I find all around me a smugness and satisfaction which to my mind are entirely unjustified," declared William Batt, director of the War Production Board's materials division. "Not since the days of the Revolution have we ever had much of a chance to lose a war. And we have a chance to lose this one." The *Washington Post* agreed. "It is no secret, that, by and large, the American people have not yet settled down to the grim task of fighting for their freedom and their lives," noted the *Post* with a palpable sense of frustration. "Pearl Harbor was a jolt," added the *New Republic*, "but there is plenty of evidence that the jolt was not strong enough. We must get down to taking the war seriously; and we must do it in a hurry." Former New Dealer turned conservative commentator General Hugh Johnson was more succinct. "The general public," Johnson grumbled, "simply does not seem to give a tinker's damn."

On Capitol Hill, legislators of both parties chastised Americans and challenged them to cast aside their unwarranted sense of security. Texas congressman Hatton Sumners, who had served in Congress since the early days of World War I, informed his colleagues in the House that "I do not see yet that vital, stirring consciousness of responsibility, consciousness of danger . . . which we have got to have. . . . We have been losing this war from the time we began it, literally losing this war." In the Senate, Massachusetts Democrat David Walsh decried the "general smugness of the American people," and Scott Lucas of Illinois warned a national radio audience against "armchair complacency": "We in America must get down to bed rock. . . . We must go on the theory that [war] can be lost, and not sit back quietly and say, 'Well, it may be a long war, but eventually we will win.'" Americans needed to "face the facts," argued Republican Robert Taft of Ohio, "and forget the artificial creation of morale. Our people are not discouraged. They are too complacent."

After touring defense production plants on the Pacific coast and in his home state of Texas, Congressman Lyndon Johnson concluded that many Americans still were not certain what the war was really about. "The fact that they don't know is in evidence in every plane plant—on every ship ways," Johnson wrote to Sam Rayburn in February. "Their physical appearance shows lack of understanding. Their lack of mental concern is evident on every facial expression. Their complacency, indifference, and bewilderment are an open invitation to [enemy] direction."

By far the most prevalent explanation for the public's "dangerously complacent" attitude was the continuing refusal of military censors ("blind, stupid or arrogant," claimed Arthur Krock) and administration spokesmen to acknowledge the ominous significance of the nation's succession of staggering defeats, particularly in the Pacific. "The war is unreal and remote from the great mass of our people," noted one critic from Massachusetts. "It could hardly be otherwise, muffled in a shroud of witless censorship. Those who do appreciate the gravity of our position do so in a sense of utter helplessness and bafflement."

Pressed by reporters, Roosevelt admitted that some of the criticism of the nation's complacency was justified, but the president suggested that Americans were growing more realistic about the military situation every day. Other observers were less sanguine. "The people's emotions are not yet fully enlisted in this fight," concluded military analyst Hanson Baldwin, "and the people's confidence in their government's word is not so firm and implicit as it should be because the people suspect, with reason, that they are not being frankly dealt with." Military and civilian officials alike, charged James Reston, still had not learned "one of the most fundamental psychological lessons of the war: that the Anglo-Saxon peoples will not make the revolutionary sacrifices that are now necessary until they understand that the position of their countries is not only bad but desperate."

Nor had newspapers and radio stations ceased their practice of exaggerating minor American victories—dismissed by conservative journalist David Lawrence as "sporadic triumphs here and there"—in a misguided attempt to bolster morale. "They persist in this idle sugar coating," complained a *Detroit Free Press* editorial, "in the mistaken belief that the people of this country can't take the 'bad news' and that to tell the truth would materially injure their morale."

Such misleading coverage only fueled Americans' overconfidence, their conviction that "one American can lick ten Japs or five Germans and that is all there is to it." Their sense of national superiority had made Americans "lethargic," argued Admiral William Standley, whom Roosevelt had recently appointed ambassador to the Soviet Union. "We've been too damned successful in previous wars," added Standley. "Now too many of us are sitting with our hands complacently folded while we wait for 'George' to win the war." British visitors to the United States confirmed that "the American people are looking at the war through rose-colored glasses." "Their idea of a long, hard war is one punctuated by a steady succession of smashing victories for the United States and its allies," claimed one Englishman after a stay in the States. "The people themselves prefer to buy newspapers and listen to radio programs which have the rosiest news."

Perhaps Americans were beguiled by "the sumptuous publicity," as Alistair Cooke put it, that accompanied the nation's war production program. Ever since Pearl Harbor, newspapers and magazines had regaled the public with "luscious three-color charts and graphs showing the American production spiral, starting down with everybody else's but zooming by the end of the current year, at latest, into the stratosphere. . . . We here in the United States," Cooke concluded, "studied our own production story and assumed the victory."

"The truth is that we have never fought against an outside enemy for our lives since the Revolution," wrote playwright Maxwell Anderson, author of the 1934 play *Valley Forge.* "Our one weakness as a belligerent is that we still think of war as it was when it last touched us closely. . . . We must wake our imaginations to conceive the hell that has been poured over the Serbs and the Chinese or we cannot properly realize our own danger, cannot find the anger and the resolution needed to keep that hell from our own country."

Donald Nelson urged Americans to make the requisite adjustments as quickly as possible. Upon completing his first month as director of the War Production Board, Nelson warned the public that "complacency has no place in America if we mean to win the war." Designating 1942 as "the critical year in the existence of the United States," Nelson urged Americans to "stop thinking about what we can do to the enemy in 1943 and start thinking about what we're going to do to him in February and March of 1942."

They could begin, suggested Treasury Secretary Henry Morgenthau, by investing more of their earnings in war bonds. Although Americans bought $1 billion worth of defense bonds and stamps in January 1942—a considerably higher amount than in any previous month—Morgenthau judged the response insufficient. Only one in seven American wage earners had purchased any bonds at all, and relatively few bonds had been sold in denominations of $100 or less, which meant that workers in lower-income brackets (whose purchasing power was increasing most rapidly, thanks to expanding war production) seemed to be particularly remiss in their patriotic duty. Worse, a significant percentage of American consumers who *were* buying war bonds were using their savings to make the purchases, thereby defeating one of the two main purposes of the bonds, which were designed not only to help pay for the conflict, but also to soak up discretionary income and keep a lid on inflation.

"We must have every income earner in the country saving regularly on a week-to-week basis," insisted Morgenthau, "if we are to finance this war without bringing the evils of inflation upon us." Hence the ubiquitous advertisements and relentless campaigns to promote bonds throughout the early months of 1942, which struck some observers as palpable evidence of the public's complacency. If the average American were truly alive to the threat posed by the Axis, explained one irritated New Yorker, "it would not be necessary to ding into his ears practically at quarter-hour intervals throughout the day over every network the crying need for him to buy defense stamps and bonds."

Instead of war bonds, Americans were purchasing more stuff. Indeed, American shoppers had embarked on a record-setting buying wave that began in early January, when department store sales typically fell into their post-Christmas doldrums. But OPM officials let slip a prediction that the Army would receive 50 to 75 percent of the nation's wool supply over the next twelve months to outfit 2 million new soldiers. (Each recruit in training purportedly required 160 pounds of wool annually for clothing—including uniforms, overcoats, and socks—and more than 270 pounds per year while on active duty, compared to a mere nine pounds for civilians.)

Cuts in civilian clothing production appeared inevitable. Fearing higher prices and future shortages in menswear, consumers hurried to department stores to stock up, often buying three or four suits at a time, along with two overcoats and perhaps a dozen shirts. Merchants in Los Angeles reported "a rush of retail buying," with sales at their highest level since the week before Pearl Harbor. "We have been having a bigger clothing business recently," boasted one leading Chicago store, "than for any similar period for which we have records."

Quickly the movement spread to other goods which consumers expected (logically or not) to become scarce: nylon stockings, soap, radios, blankets, woolen skirts, rugs, carpets, and even imported medical drugs. "Department store counters were jammed with hoarders," reported *Time* magazine, "laying in supplies of everything from cotton sheets to wool socks." Fearful of rubber rationing, women shoppers targeted brassieres and girdles, which many considered essential to their health and comfort, especially in defense jobs. The scramble for foundation garments, reported one California observer, did not quite rival the previous summer's silk-stocking panic, "but it's respectable and provides a lively scene."

According to the Federal Reserve Board, department store sales nationwide during the first week of January rose 26 percent above the same period of 1941 (when business already had been robust); for the second week of January, purchases were 32 percent higher, a buying spree which Dun & Bradstreet declared an all-time record, as many stores reported the largest weekly sales volume in their history. The only holdout appeared to be Mississippi, where one retailer acknowledged that "we haven't even had a run on silk stockings."

As January came to a close, the buying wave was still going strong. In the nation's capital, department store sales jumped 66 percent above the previous year; in Cleveland, sales were up 45 percent; Boston saw a rise of 40 percent. "It's coming in without the slightest effort on our part," shrugged one executive. Across the country, statistics revealed that retailers sold more merchandise to consumers in the first month of 1942 than in any January in American history. It was clear to contemporaries that much of this purchasing consisted of "stocking up." "The major portion of the increase in retail sales can be attributed to advance buying and plain hoarding," noted the Retail Merchants Association. "Americans are on a buying spree," agreed the *Los Angeles Times*, "and a substantial part of what they are buying is going into the pantry, the clothes closet, the tool chest and a dozen other home hideaways and not into immediate consumption."

This was precisely the sort of behavior Roosevelt administration officials hoped to discourage. Because civilian goods were necessarily becoming more scarce, the buying splurge was bidding up the price of consumer goods as well as exacerbating existing product shortages or creating new ones. "Foolish Spending Is Sabotage!" insisted an advertisement for the Savings Bank of New York State, and other observers chimed in with similar denunciations. "It is no part of patriotism to store up staples like a squirrel does nuts," charged columnist Chapin Hall in Los Angeles. "You cannot buy victory and luxury in the same market at the same time," proclaimed the *New York Times*, and a *Washington Post* editorial noted that "some citizens are pitifully slow to shake themselves out of the habit of grabbing while the grabbing seems to be good." From Chicago, Mayor Edward Kelly pointed out that "some of our people are hoarding soap, sugar, fats, oils, hosiery, and other commodities" against future troubles: "Not a pound of sugar nor a pair of hose should be bought unless the need is immediate. Hoarding is equivalent to treason."

Even some retailers, reported Dun & Bradstreet, "tended to regard the trend as not only abnormal, but unhealthy," and sought to stem the tide. ("They don't want a riot in the girdle section," explained one journalist, "or a mob scene in the overcoat division.") On February 13, a dozen department stores—including Bloomingdale's, Saks Fifth Avenue, Macy's, B. Altman and Company, and Gimbel Brothers—issued a joint appeal to consumers in the form of a newspaper advertisement featuring Adolf Hitler presenting an iron cross to an American couple standing by a jumbled mountain of merchandise with an inscription that read: "For Distinguished Service to the Axis—for Hoarding." "Play your part by buying only for your immediate needs as usual," urged the stores. "Being a good American citizen, you want no advantage over your neighbor. Think it over. You'll probably want to conclude that you want to share wartime inconveniences, when and as they materialize."

Groundhog Day in 1942 lacked its usual cachet. The government's ban on real-time announcements of weather conditions left meteorologists in a bind. The best they could do, wrote one frustrated forecaster, was to suggest that "if a certain furbearing animal comes out of his habitat (description and location undisclosed), and the sun is ——ing, he will cast a —— which will frighten him back into his habitat (location still undisclosed) and we will have —— weeks more of (censored) weather." With long-range atmospheric predictions (even by rodents) forbidden, Punxsutawney Phil's findings remained a military secret.

Wartime exigencies also colored Valentine's Day celebrations. Since commercially produced greeting cards were usually designed eighteen months in advance, lovers found few "servicemen's valentines" to send or receive. Those that were available sold briskly, including one with a young lady in the embrace of a soldier: "It's O.K. to be prepared, but the only arms that interest me are yours." ("I wish I had 5,000 of those," sighed a sales clerk. "That's how fast they are moving.") Retailers also reported

heavier than usual sales of "slams" or "torpedo" greetings—cards that began innocently on the front, and then delivered an insult on the back.
More endearing was the personalized greeting sent from a Harvard
undergraduate to a Radcliffe student. "I'm sending you my sugar ration," it
began, "not just today, but for the 'duration.' / Now my coffee won't taste
so fine, / So please, won't you be my Valentine?"

New Orleans's annual Mardi Gras festivities, scheduled for February 17,
were canceled for only the third time in eighty-five years. (There had been
no celebrations during the Civil War following the Union occupation of
the city, or in the closing months of World War I.) The carnival's govern-
ing committees concluded that holding the usual parades and balls "would
not be consistent with the present status of the nation." Instead, local residents held parties in private homes and clubs, and staged a more sub-
dued procession that ended at booths selling defense bonds; but estimates
of lost revenue approached $1 million.

Ten weeks after Pearl Harbor, New Orleans's civilian defense program
remained significantly short on volunteers, and many of those who had
signed up for duty in the first rush of patriotic fervor never appeared for
training classes. It may not have mattered anyway; city authorities lacked
the necessary equipment, and had to issue an appeal to the public for one
hundred movie projectors to show OCD training films to prospective air
raid wardens. "Unquestionably New Orleans has lagged behind the rest
of the state," acknowledged Governor Sam Houston "Sweet-Smellin' Sam"
Jones. And preparations across the rest of Louisiana left much to be
desired. In early February, Jones charged that "Louisiana is not fully awake
to the fact that this country is deeply involved in a war whose issue is freedom or slavery," a condition the governor found particularly troubling,
since military officials deemed the state's Gulf Coast oil fields "splendid
objectives for saboteurs."

Although a number of jurisdictions in the United Sates had made noticeable progress in their civilian defense preparations—devising evacuation plans, teaching techniques for traffic control during blackouts, and
training dogs to "sniff out spies and saboteurs" in restricted areas—many
state and local programs remained beset by internal divisions, misman-
agement, and public indifference. In early February, James Landis conceded that cities along both coasts still were not prepared for bombing

raids, partly because authorities often refused to cooperate across political lines. "In some portions all have not wakened to do anything about the situation," Landis said. "I don't know whether they will wake up unless something happens to make them do so. Some sections of the country don't think we are at war." The national commander of the Veterans of Foreign Wars charged that many civilian defense organizations were "infested with politics," an accusation borne out by the byzantine infighting in Detroit, which replaced San Francisco as the worst-prepared city in the country. "Civilian defense has failed to crystallize in Detroit, the great central arsenal of the United Nations," complained the *Detroit Free Press*. "Everybody knows it." The city's mayor quarreled with the governor; the State Defense Council fought with the police commissioner; and the Board of Commerce battled the mayor. As a result, residents had received no instructions on how to behave in an air raid. (Leaflets were promised by mid-March—perhaps.) State legislators and Detroit authorities could not even agree on whether to join the rest of the nation in adopting "war time," the year-round daylight saving time recently approved by Congress for the duration of the war. Frustrated by the interminable bickering, local labor leaders sent a formal request to President Roosevelt to intervene and impose some measure of order.

Meanwhile, authorities repeatedly insisted that the nation remained disturbingly vulnerable to enemy assault. "We haven't any protection at all on the West Coast," claimed Senator Hiram Johnson of California in mid-February. "I see in the future another Pearl Harbor within the continental United States unless something is done." In a meeting with high-ranking military and civilian defense officials from eight southeastern states on February 13, a regional director of the OCD warned that "we are totally unprepared" to meet Axis attacks on the Atlantic coast. "It is an open secret," he said, "that if the Atlantic seaboard were attacked, either from within or without, today or tomorrow, we would be wholly unprepared to meet it."

"Don't let anyone tell you that you are too far away from the battle for aerial attack," declared Chicago's Mayor Kelly. "Chicago is a danger zone. . . . If the Japanese can go 4,000 miles to strike by air at Hawaii, it is also possible for them to strike at Chicago, and they may do it." The chief air raid warden for the District of Columbia predicted that the capital would be bombed "mercilessly" within the next six months; "I believe we are going to die by the thousands here on these streets," he told a gathering of civilian defense volunteers. New York State's newly appointed defense council chairman announced that "the United States Army definitely believes that this area will be bombed," and the *New York Times* reminded its readers that if the enemy "tries hard enough, he can destroy some buildings, wound some of us, kill some of us. We can't help it." President Roosevelt agreed. In the course of a press conference on February 17, Roosevelt noted in a matter-of-fact tone that under certain conditions, enemy ships could shell New York City (perhaps tomorrow evening, he added helpfully), or Axis planes might drop bombs on Detroit. Pressed by anxious congressmen, Secretaries Stimson and Knox indicated that the nation's limited military resources would remain focused on battlefields abroad, and not on defending the United States' coasts. "We've got an awful lot of bread, and very little butter," Knox explained, "and it will have to be buttered very thin."

Left largely on their own, Americans gradually adapted the details of their daily lives to the disruptions created by the threat of enemy attacks. Instructors from the University of California Farm Extension Service taught fifteen hundred dairy farmers how to milk cows in a blackout. (One tip was to place empty pails over lanterns to reflect light downward, leaving the essential parts of the cow plainly visible.) Women's organizations sponsored judo and jujitsu classes to train female air raid wardens to fend off unwanted romantic advances during blackouts. Colleges devised rules to govern examinations interrupted by air raid alarms; Harvard administrators decided that tests within a half-hour of completion might count toward a final grade, "provided, of course, the proctors were able to collect the blue-books." On the other hand, the administrator of St. Patrick's Cathedral on Fifth Avenue in Manhattan announced that air raid alarms would not interrupt the Mass; parishioners were free to leave, but the clergy at the altar were not. Recognizing that patrons' appetites might be spoiled by the approach of enemy planes, the New York State Restaurant Association suggested that cafés "prepare smaller quantities of food when advance warning of air raids was given." (Since "honest but panicky guests" often left without paying when an alarm sounded, the association also recommended that "service might be discreetly arranged on a pay-as-you-go basis.")

Retailers offered more sophisticated blackout products, including fluorescent-treated satin tablecloths and ashtrays, luminous cloth for hatbands, and ninety-eight-cent flashlights that fit around a wrist: "It lights the way . . . And leaves both hands free!" But as Americans commenced in late winter to refurnish and redecorate their homes—possibly for the duration—they turned away from black fabrics and iron buckets and fire extinguishers, or anything else that would transform their comfortable nests into fortresses. "Instead," observed the *New Yorker*, "people are acknowledging their awareness of possible bleak days ahead chiefly by purchasing things like unelectrified candle brackets, old-fashioned oil lamps, parlor stoves, and similar homely symbols of a safer day, clearly looking to them less for a feeling of actual protection in emergencies than for the kind of comfort that a night light provides in a nursery. Right or wrong, this is the trend of the moment, and there is at least this much to be said about it: anything which provides a measure of comfort is not entirely without value."

"The typical sight in Washington these days is a line of persons," wrote a visitor to the capital: queues at cafeteria counters, at drugstore registers, at taxi stands and theaters and telephone booths. "There is waiting for a seat at the movie, for a chance to cross the street, for the completion of a new building into which to move." And if one managed to squeeze onto a bus or streetcar, there were lines of standees there, too. "We have the most damnable system of transportation in the country," grumbled a congressman from the Midwest. "Riding the Burma Road is a pleasure compared to riding streetcars in Washington."

With an infrastructure designed to provide for a population of slightly more than a half million, the District of Columbia was rapidly approaching 800,000 residents. Military personnel and new government employees—mostly clerical workers for the War Department—poured into the city at the rate of four to five thousand each month, and the pace was increasing. There were already more than 200,000 federal workers in Washington in January 1942 (nearly half of whom had arrived over the past eighteen months), and U.S. Bureau of the Budget director Harold Smith estimated that another 85,000 would arrive by the end of the year—perhaps a third of them with their families. Along with the requisite number of teachers, public service employees, retail clerks, waiters, and construction workers, authorities expected a total of 250,000 additional arrivals in the next twelve months. "The ugly fact that no one can ignore," contended *Washington Post* columnist Merlo Pusey, "is that new residents are streaming into the city much faster than we can possibly take care of them."

Hotel rooms—often subdivided into cramped "single" cubicles—were booked months in advance, and locals joked that private baths had gone out with Hitler. Some business travelers on overnight, round-trip visits took to sleeping in Union Station, curled up on benches. Apartments were nearly impossible to find; the percentage of rental vacancies was less than 0.5 percent, with lengthy waiting lists. Low-income families could find no housing in the city at all.

"House and room overcrowding," claimed one D.C. official, "have reached menacing proportions." A congressional committee investigating the capital's housing shortage heard reports of thirteen people living in one room, of six adults and four children living in a three-room apartment, of five families in a seven-room house, and eighteen people in a wretched six-room house with a single outside toilet. The deputy general manager of the Home Owners' Loan Corporation declared that Washington's housing woes were "a problem almost unparalleled anywhere in the country"; in one eighty-five-block section near Capitol Hill, the buildings were "all rapidly deteriorating and a considerable part already disreputable . . . a breeding place for disease and crime." And in January, a local housing authority put all of its slum-clearance efforts on hold for the duration.

"Slum conditions in many spots are as bad as any in the United States," confirmed former congressman Maury Maverick, a high-ranking official with the Office of Personnel Management. Maverick also found health care in Washington sorely lacking in comparison with other American cities; beyond an acute shortage of hospital beds (hundreds of obstetrical-care cases were turned away each year), and clinics that operated only part-time for lack of nurses and doctors, the overcrowded conditions and constant influx of newcomers facilitated the spread of contagious diseases.

"Syphilis and tuberculosis run riot here," charged Pusey, backed by statistics that showed the syphilis rate in Washington was more than three times the national average: "It makes little difference whether an American soldier is shot down by the Japanese or falls victim to syphilis while visiting the National Capital."

City commissioners issued a formal proclamation asking every D.C. homeowner to rent "decent living accommodations" to at least one government war worker for the duration of the war. But while a sizable majority of the new federal workers searching for living quarters were women (most under the age of twenty-seven), nearly three-fourths of local householders who offered their spare rooms requested "men only." Landlords complained that women tenants took longer baths, talked to their friends on the phone at all hours, entertained guests in the parlor or living room, stayed home nights and ran up the electricity bill, burned the furniture with their cigarettes, and washed their undergarments in the bathtub or sink and left them hanging to dry in the bathroom. "In contrast to nearly all of the men roomers I have had," huffed one landlady, "they are what would be called uncultured in the home."

"It's downright unpatriotic," responded one defense housing official. "What if girls are more trouble? Everyone else is making sacrifices nowadays. . . . These girls are taking the place of men who are fighting. If we don't get places for them, there can't be any war."

Opportunities for recreation and relaxation were rare, and not only because many government workers spent ten hours a day at the office, six or seven days a week. "There isn't enough to do in Washington for the thousands of boys and girls (mostly girls) who are pouring into the capital to typewrite World War Two into submission," wrote Bob Considine. "There are no beaches, few gyms, no big-league fighting, hockey, basketball, few tennis courts, few golf courses the clerks can afford." Professionals were no better off. Stress levels were so high that one local physician claimed that the occupational diseases of Washington were "peptic ulcers and coronary thrombosis." The superintendent of St. Elizabeth's Hospital, the local mental health facility, advised "high-strung, frail and eccentric people" to stay away from the city, which already owned the highest rate of insanity in the country. "A visitor would stake his life," noted a reporter for *Life* magazine, "on the assertion that there is more liquor, more black coffee, more cigarets and cigars and, on top of it, more sedatives consumed among the middle-income people in Washington today than anywhere at any time in history."

To ameliorate the shortage of office space, temporary government buildings—white, two-block-long structures known as "tempos"—sprouted throughout the downtown area; in February, construction crews were digging up the Mall between the Lincoln Memorial and the Washington Monument. But the scarcity of adequate housing posed a more complex problem. As the coordinator of defense housing informed a congressional committee on January 29, the city could provide a maximum of only 10,000 additional houses and 4,500 "temporary shelters" for government workers without causing a complete collapse of Washington's utilities, schools, hospitals, sewer lines, and police and fire protection. Any further construction, he predicted, would "seriously overtax the facilities of the District."

In a press conference the following day, President Roosevelt (who was celebrating his sixtieth birthday, which he termed "the dark age") proposed one solution: everyone not actively contributing to the war effort should pack up and leave Washington. During wartime, the president explained, there was no place in the capital "for people here merely 'to watch the show,' participate in social events, or live with too much space around them in 20-room homes on Massachusetts Avenue." To Roosevelt, such residents were "parasites," and he suggested that local newspapers run headlines at the top of their front pages asking, "ARE YOU A PARASITE?" Roosevelt hoped that such treatment would embarrass enough native Washingtonians into leaving, but the president reminded reporters that his war powers enabled him to commandeer hotels and office buildings if necessary and, he thought, private homes as well.

Reaction followed swiftly. Longtime residents peremptorily rejected Roosevelt's "get-out-of-here" proposal. "I've lived here all my life," exclaimed one outraged woman, "and I'd like to see anyone put me out!" Newspapers revealed exactly who owned some of those spacious mansions in fashionable northwestern Washington: the list included the president's fifth cousin, Alice Roosevelt Longworth (who lived in a four-story home on Massachusetts Avenue); the king of Belgium; Joseph Davies (former ambassador to Russia and the husband of Marjorie Post Hutton Close

Davies, whose estate included a private golf course); and Democratic senator Peter Gerry of Rhode Island, who had purchased Herbert Hoover's former home. (Gerry took it all good-naturedly; Republicans, he said, had called him far worse names than "parasite.")

"Everybody in Washington thinks everybody else is a Parasite," noted the *Washington Post,* which flippantly asked its readers to "send in names of Parasites you would like to run out of town.... We will show you a purge that is a purge! California, here they come!" In the midst of a slow tourist season, the mayor of Fort Lauderdale encouraged Washington's "non-production residents" to relocate to Florida, and the Miami Chamber of Commerce placed an ad in the District's newspapers inviting Washingtonians to "Move to Miami 'for the duration'": "You'll find it's actually sensible, economic, and patriotic to move to Miami.... You'll be more than welcome. Come on down."

Roosevelt's ploy seemed a clumsy and self-defeating attempt to inspire the public to make sacrifices for the war effort. "If the President had spent hours thinking up ways and means of pouring cold water on the patriotic spirit," wrote Merlo Pusey, "he could scarcely have produced a more effective word" than "parasite." Numerous commentators suggested that instead of running private citizens out of town, Roosevelt might more profitably dismiss or reassign thousands of New Deal bureaucrats who appeared to be rendering no real contribution to the war. Indeed, some critics claimed that efforts by the New Deal's "alphabet" agencies (including the Works Progress Administration, the Civilian Conservation Corps, and the National Youth Administration) to carry on business as usual was diverting precious resources from the nation's war effort. It was time, argued longtime budget hawk Senator Harry Byrd of Virginia, "to strip the government of nonessentials so we can devote all our energies to winning the war."

Congress's first target was the Office of Civilian Defense, particularly after word leaked out in early February that the agency had hired a diminutive former nightclub dancer named Mayris Chaney—a close friend of Eleanor Roosevelt and a frequent guest at the White House—as director of children's activities in its physical fitness section. Appointed to her post in November 1941, Chaney received a salary of $4,600 a year (nearly three times the average annual income in the United States) for her work at the OCD under the first lady's supervision. At the same time, the press disclosed that the administration had hired another of Mrs. Roosevelt's friends, actor Melvyn Douglas (whom conservatives claimed had "amply demonstrated his very left-wing tendencies"), to lead an arts council within the OCD.

Eager to put a human face—other than their own—to the nation's troubles, congressmen wasted no time in denouncing both appointments as examples of "boondoggling" within the national civilian defense program. They questioned Chaney's qualifications and her salary ("Billions for defense, not one cent for poppycock"), and wondered what possible role storytelling and children's exercise routines played in the nation's defense against air raids. Senator Millard Tydings of Maryland dismissed the OCD as "a social reformatory," while one California congressman denounced the agency as a "pink tea party." The controversial chairman of the House Committee on Un-American Activities, Texas Democrat Martin Dies, announced that he possessed evidence that communist sympathizers were "trying to take over the Office of Civilian Defense," and were "making pretty good progress."

News reports revealing that the OCD was funding other "lighter aspects of bolstering morale"—including music, town-hall meetings, games such as marbles and horseshoe pitching, and a special "Know Your Government" division—produced a flood of outraged letters, telephone messages, and telegrams to legislators protesting the presence of "parasites and leeches" on the agency's payroll. The public's indignant and seemingly disproportionate reaction, noted one journalist, "pointed to a demonstration of hostility hitherto unknown in the prosecution of the war effort." (One wire to a Missouri congressman came from the nation's foremost stripper, Sally Rand, who offered to replace Chaney and serve for free: "Will change name of fan dance to 'Nude Deal,'" she promised.)

In the end, Congress settled for passing an ostentatious amendment to the OCD appropriations bill banning the use of its funds for "instruction in physical fitness by dancers, fan dancing, street shows, theatrical performers or other public entertainment." The vote was largely symbolic, since the legislation contained no funds for such activities anyway, and recently appointed director James Landis conceded that "it is urgently necessary that OCD be stripped down immediately for emergency action."

Observers feared that the Chaney-Douglas incident might further dampen popular enthusiasm for the war, especially if Americans concluded that the administration eschewed the sort of sacrifices it demanded of everyone else. "It is the poor example which the Government is thus setting which has the most demoralizing effect upon a people girding themselves for war," concluded Merlo Pusey. Arthur Krock accused the administration of allowing "carelessness, waste and favoritism . . . to clog the war effort," and Raymond Clapper claimed that the Office of Civilian Defense was becoming "a kind of personal parking lot for the pets and proteges of Mrs. Roosevelt."

Stung by the unusually harsh and personal criticism leveled against her and her friends, Mrs. Roosevelt insisted that the attacks were "purely political, and made by the same people who have fought NYA, CCC, WPA, Farm Security, etc." Nevertheless, she announced her resignation from her civilian defense post on February 18, and Chaney followed suit. ("To know me," the first lady sighed, "is a terrible thing.") Mrs. Roosevelt blamed the controversy on "a small but very vocal group of unenlightened men" who were attempting "to renew, under the guise of patriotism and economy, the age-old fight for the privileged few against the good of the many." Novelist Rex Stout, who headed a prowar writers' group, saw it the same way. "It was a symptom," wrote Stout, "of a deep and dangerous disease which the smoke of Pearl Harbor momentarily obscured but did not cure, and did not even affect. . . . Most of the appeasers and isolationists and home-grown Fascists, and certainly the worst of them, are today exactly what they were before Pearl Harbor."

The *New Republic* concurred. Congress, it argued, remained as "basically and bitterly anti-Roosevelt and anti–New Deal" as it had been before the war, awaiting only an acceptable target for its hostility: "For two months now its resentments have been growing, like the accumulating lava in a slumbering volcano." But since the president remained virtually untouchable—his approval rating had soared to a high of 84 percent—his opponents chose "the easy and vulgar path of attacking a few unimportant appointments."

Behind the anti-Eleanor outburst in Washington stood a substantive minority of the wealthy class and business community, who, one conservative commentator noted, "still get the creeps from the Administration."

Sharing a suspicion that Roosevelt had maneuvered the nation into hostilities for his own political ends, they remained "not absolutely sure," as Walter Lippmann put it, "whether they are more concerned about the Japanese and the Nazis or about the New Dealers."

Whatever remained of the post–December 7 political truce vanished in February. Former Republican presidential candidate Alf Landon used his party's annual Lincoln Day celebration to launch the 1942 congressional election campaign with a speech excoriating the Roosevelt administration for its "incompetent and unskillful leadership" of the war. Speaking to a nationwide radio audience on the NBC network, Landon charged New Dealers in Washington with plotting to use "the colossal dislocation this war is going to bring into our lives" to install a permanently collectivized economy—"a totalitarian collectivism"—in the United States. The *Chicago Tribune* concurred. "The war has been taken as an excuse to continue and expand the wasting of our national strength and resources," declared the *Tribune* in an editorial. "Those in Washington who have long striven to establish an economic dictatorship are having a field day. The war is made to order for their purposes."

"This campaign of unfair, poisonous sniping is dividing America in its fight against the Axis," replied House majority leader John McCormack of Massachusetts. "Something must be done to expose the repeated efforts of members of the House and others to undermine confidence in the Commander-in-Chief." Accusing the GOP of attempting to "destroy and disunite our people," Democratic National Committee chairman Ed Flynn proclaimed that "it is now plain that the Republican Party is not so much interested in winning the war as it is interested in controlling the House of Representatives."

# 7: The Golden West

## FEBRUARY–MARCH 1942

*The firefly lights that used to line the long shore*
*Are all struck dumb; shut are the shops, mouse-dark*
 *the houses . . .*

—ROBINSON JEFFERS, "PEARL HARBOR," 1942

"I am not one of the jackasses who think Frisco can't be bombed," wrote playwright Eugene O'Neill from his farm in Contra Costa County, thirty miles east of the Golden Gate Bridge. "I think, sooner or later, it will be. The Japs hate California more than all the rest of the U.S.A. and it would be a big boost for their morale to sneak a carrier within range to do the job—worth the risk of losing the carrier, I should say. All I hope is, it doesn't happen before they get civilian defense well organized in Frisco—or there will be a terrible mess."

O'Neill found it increasingly difficult to concentrate on any new dramatic endeavors in early 1942. He had recently completed a first draft of *A Moon for the Misbegotten*, but O'Neill admitted to his son that so far the play was not nearly as good as its title—"Much work to do before it will be anything." The author had begun to display symptoms of Parkinson's disease, which inevitably hampered his writing; but "even if I were fit," he confided to a friend, "I couldn't concentrate now. Or kid myself that plays matter a damn. The mind is in Pearl Harbor, the Philippines, Singapore, etc. I can't take anything else seriously. As far as I'm concerned, the drama is dead for the duration, and what of it?"

Halfway down the California coast, just south of Carmel, poet Robinson Jeffers spent one night a week—from midnight to 6 a.m.—alone in a tiny sentry box high atop a cliff overlooking the Pacific Ocean, watching for signs of Japanese raiders. Armed with expertise gained from an advanced course in first aid, Una Jeffers had joined a medical team on call for war emergencies one week each month; in March she planned to start a course in motor repair. But the couple seldom strayed far from home. "We were caught short on tires," Una explained to editor Bennett Cerf in New York. "For many years we have never averaged less than 1500 miles a month, usually a lot more, & feel rather crippled by the rationing. We are walking more than ever."

They also enjoyed fewer visitors. Tourism in California dropped by nearly half in early 1942, curtailed by tire rationing and persistent rumors of "danger, attack and terror" on the Pacific coast. One business promoter complained that prospective travelers from the East and Midwest "actually believed that we were undergoing 'blackouts' every night and were in imminent danger of bombings, that our highways were barricaded, gasoline scarce and travel restricted even to the point of women and children [being] barred from the State." Desperate for customers, California hotel executives insisted that gasoline filling station employees stop gossiping about war rumors with motorists passing through the state, and business leaders launched a national newspaper advertising campaign reassuring the rest of the country that folks on the West Coast "are on the alert, but living normally—night and day."

Unless one's ancestry was Japanese. Throughout January, enmity toward both foreign-born Japanese (Issei) and Nisei escalated quickly among whites in California, Washington, and Oregon—fueled partly by headlines and newsreels of Japanese military victories over American forces in Asia, and partly by the publication of a more thorough (albeit not entirely accurate) investigation into the Pearl Harbor debacle, with its undocumented allegations of fifth-column activities by the Japanese population of Hawaii. Anti-Japanese feeling on the West Coast appeared "to cluster in the low income, poorly educated groups," noted Archibald MacLeish, head of the federal Office of Facts and Figures. "They are the ones who are most suspicious of local Japanese in general." But the reaction was becoming more widespread than administration officials realized.

Branding Japanese nationals on the Pacific coast "a menace to this country," an association of western farmers asked the federal government to immediately intern enemy aliens in the region and impound their property (presumably so it could be distributed to white farmers). Rumors of arsenic-poisoned produce revived among the public. Wary San Francisco officials recommended that an embargo be imposed on all fruits and vegetables brought to market by Japanese farmers (nearly 50 percent of the state's output); dozens of vegetable stands in southern California sprouted signs saying, "Chinese Operated. No Japs Here"; and the state board of health—fearing sabotage in the form of an outbreak of botulism—forbade the employment of enemy aliens in cannery food-sterilization operations. Occasionally anxiety descended into paranoia: in the San Joaquin Valley, the district attorney of the city of Visalia accused Japanese truck drivers of planting tomatoes in a pattern that formed an arrow pointing to a nearby air-training field.

In southern California, the Los Angeles County Board of Supervisors dismissed all forty-nine of its Nisei employees, while the city's workers of Japanese descent were "encouraged" to give up their jobs for the duration. "We just felt that for the safety of the city it was best to remove all employees with Japanese connections," explained Mayor Fletcher Bowron. "Many of them had access to important city records, maps, and other valuable documents." Taking no chances, the Los Angeles Chamber of Commerce suggested that everyone of Japanese descent be expelled from the city.

State Attorney General Earl Warren—a member of the influential and xenophobic fraternity known as the Native Sons of the Golden West—charged that the Japanese population in California represented the "Achilles' heel of our whole civilian defense effort. . . . Unless something is done about it, it may possibly bring a repetition of Pearl Harbor." Warren warned especially against Nisei who had spent considerable time visiting Japan, absorbing foreign ideals that made it impossible to distinguish "between dangerous enemy aliens, of whom we are sure there are many here, and Japanese-American citizens genuinely loyal to the United States."

Pressured by anti-Japanese sentiment from his southern California constituents, Republican congressman Leland Ford called for "the movement of all Japanese people to whatever location the military authorities think they ought to be in." When other Americans were risking their lives in military service, Ford argued, "it is not asking too much of the Japanese to make [a sacrifice] in the form of permitting themselves to be placed in concentration camps, although they may be loyal."

Privately, Governor Olson informed General DeWitt that white voters' hostility toward "the Japanese" was nearing dangerous levels. Californians "feel that they are living in the midst of enemies," Olson said. "They don't trust the Japanese, none of them." They objected especially to Japanese living and working near vital defense installations. "It is scarcely believable," wrote columnist Tom Treanor, "that we can go through an entire war permitting thousands of an enemy race to move at will through the most vital military sector in the United States. . . . There is all sorts of current information which must be going out daily, to our great disadvantage."

Backed by a growing public clamor, War Department officials persuaded a reluctant Attorney General Biddle on January 29 to order all Axis nationals to evacuate eighty-eight designated military zones along the California coast by February 24. Prohibited regions included the San Francisco waterfront, Los Angeles harbor, and the land surrounding every nearby airport, dam, power station, and defense plant. This concession slowed the anti-Japanese drive not at all. Critics pointed out that Biddle's order covered only enemy aliens—not the Nisei—and allowed both groups to remain in the coastal area, albeit outside the prohibited zones. And many deemed Biddle's deadline far too lenient. "A great deal of damage could be done by saboteurs between now and February 24, particularly if they are goaded by the thought that their opportunity for destructiveness will be curbed then," argued the *Los Angeles Times*. "Hesitation on the part of the government has continued too long. California has a right to expect, now that a start has been made, that the job will be completed quickly, and that it will be a thorough one."

Yet Biddle continued to resist, armed with confidential FBI reports that essentially dismissed the risk of sabotage from the Japanese American community. (J. Edgar Hoover blamed the pressure for mass evacuation on "public hysteria" and "the comments of the press and radio announc-ers.") In a radio speech on February 1, the attorney general assured the American people that the federal government was "taking every pre-caution to guard against espionage, sabotage, or other fifth column activities" on the West Coast: "We don't take chances." Biddle added, however, that "the persecution of aliens—economic or social—can be a two-edged sword. Such persecution can easily drive people, now loyal to us, into fifth column activities." To intern every enemy alien in the nation, he warned, would be "profoundly unwise" and "profoundly un-American."

Biddle's attempt to adopt an evenhanded approach served only to con-vince Californians that he failed to grasp the urgency of the situation. *Time* magazine reported that "Francis Biddle's measures struck most West Coast citizens, indeed, as wishy-washy." After traveling up and down the Pacific Coast, columnist Henry McLemore claimed that he had yet "to meet a man, woman or child who doesn't think that Mr. Biddle's handling of the bow-legged sons and daughters of the Rising Sun is mighty ridicu-lous," treating the Japanese menace "with all the severity of Lord Fauntle-roy playing squat tag with his maiden aunt." The *Los Angeles Times* accused Biddle of "looking at the Japanese situation in this country through the eyes of a lawyer; through the eyes of an ultra-liberal lawyer"—a failing which fostered a "growing uneasiness" among West Coast resi-dents "on the subject of Washington's failure to comprehend the Japanese problem."

Congressional criticism also was rising. Columnist Drew Pearson re-ported "a mounting undercover feeling on Capitol Hill that the spy and fifth column problem in this country is not being met with the rigorous realism needed," and that some federal officials "seem more concerned about what they term 'civil liberties' than the security of the nation." HUAC chairman Martin Dies denounced the Roosevelt administration's "maudlin attitude toward fifth columnists," and warned that unless the government changed its course, "there will occur on the West Coast a ca-tastrophe which will make Pearl Harbor sink into insignificance." Re-spectable observers who typically dismissed Dies's conspiracy theories decided that this time the Texas congressman might be correct. The no-tion of a rising by "America's Nipponese" was "certainly not as fantastic as talk of an attack upon Hawaii would have seemed two months ago," cautioned the *Washington Post.* "Potential enemies within our gates must be dealt with as such. They cannot be left at liberty until their destructive work has been done. From now on it must be the United States and its security which are given the benefit of the doubt."

In southern California—where about 80 percent of the state's Nisei population resided—local governments stepped up the pressure. After Earl Warren proclaimed California wide open to the threat of sabotage, a Los Angeles County grand jury voted unanimously in the first week of February to ask federal officials to move all Japanese aliens away from the Pacific coast, and give "serious consideration" to removing the Nisei as well. The Los Angeles County Civilian Defense Council requested that the Army declare martial law and ship all enemy aliens to inland concentration camps for "productive agricultural labor"; it suggested that Nisei also "be invited to take residence and occupation in such internment areas." After voting to move "all persons of the Japanese race" at least two hundred miles farther inland, the Ventura County Board of Supervisors warned that "the temper of the people of the Pacific Coast has risen to such a point that it is becoming dangerous for loyal Japanese to reside in close proximity to the Pacific Ocean."

Throughout the nation, enrollment in colleges and universities continued to fall. When spring semester classes convened in February 1942, some schools found that their undergraduate population had declined by as much as 20 percent, depleted by military enlistments, the Selective Service—especially after Congress lowered the draft age to twenty—and the lure of defense jobs. Administrators responded by accelerating their courses of study, telescoping four years of undergraduate classes into three (and sometimes two) to persuade students to stay in school and complete their studies, or at least provide better-educated dropouts for the military. Leisurely summer vacations vanished, replaced by a third academic semester; winter and spring holidays were sliced to a few days apiece; and instructors condensed course material into the bare essentials. Long-standing social rituals of peacetime (such as Dartmouth's Winter Carnival) fell by the wayside, victims of crowded schedules and students' determination to focus on "the more serious aspect of college life."

Professional schools followed suit. The Association of American Medical Colleges announced that seventy-six medical schools—including most of those on the East Coast—agreed to intensify instruction so doctors could complete their studies in three years instead of four. Law schools went from three years of study to two. Easing the path to advanced degrees even further, Harvard opened its graduate schools to students who had not yet obtained a bachelor's degree.

New war-related courses dotted undergraduate schedules: studies in explosives, military psychology, war gases, Soviet history, military French, modern war strategy, military math, the principles of sea power, ballistics, current Latin American trade problems, military communications, and music for drum majors. Before Pearl Harbor, fewer than a dozen American universities offered Japanese language classes—Archibald MacLeish told Congress in early 1942 that he could find only three non–Japanese Americans who could read and write Japanese, which was only a slight exaggeration—but now demand boomed for courses in the spoken language. Federal officials especially applauded colleges' efforts to improve prospective soldiers' knowledge of world geography. "I think apart from some backward nations," complained Dr. John Studebaker, U.S. commissioner of education, "we are more illiterate in geography than any other civilized nation."

To those who felt that the speed-up and curriculum changes represented a misguided effort to make "war colleges of our institutions of higher education," University of Chicago president Robert Hutchins suggested that colleges needed to sacrifice long-run goals for short-term objectives in wartime. "We have stood for liberal education and pure research," declared Hutchins. "What the country must have now is vocational training and applied research." Paul McNutt was more succinct. Academics needed to leave the "ivory tower" of "puerile pacifism," the head of the Federal Security Agency told a conference of educators: "Whether you like it or not, whether you wear a uniform or not, you're in the Army now. That—or a Nazi strait-jacket later."

Wartime pressures led public school administrators to alter their schedules as well. In some rural areas, summer vacations were extended from May to November, so teenagers could help plant and harvest crops on farms facing an acute labor shortage. Other districts tried to rush their students through the system more rapidly; Georgia officials introduced Saturday classes and summer courses on a statewide basis to allow students to graduate months earlier, a policy assailed by child advocacy groups. "Hurrying boys and girls through school does not in itself make adults of them," warned the president of the National Congress of Parents and Teachers. "Not in spite of the war, but because of it, we dare not deprive our children of one iota of the education and training they should have. . . . There would be little purpose in our winning a war to provide security for a sickly and ignorant generation."

Curriculum changes followed quickly. Nearly everyone agreed that the war required greater emphasis on science and mathematics; Navy officials said they had rejected an alarming number of otherwise qualified recruits because they lacked basic arithmetic skills. The Army requested more intensive instruction for future draftees in foreign languages and recent history, especially for long-neglected Asia and Latin America. Courses in aviation mechanics, welding, machine tool operation, and ship carpentry appeared on high school schedules. As mothers spent more time outside the home, Boston schools made sure that every girl in fourth grade and above completed a course in preschool child care. Baltimore students learned to "sing for defense," particularly American folk songs; "in time of air-raid warnings," said a city school official, "there's nothing like singing to steady the nerves." New York City's superintendent requested the reinstatement of military training in high schools to instill a more aggressive attitude in students, and Philadelphia's public schools chief suggested that educators should encourage "the desire to destroy the enemy," if not outright hatred of the Axis. "I don't see anything undemocratic about shooting rats," he declared. "It is high time that American schools find a dynamic, virile part in this war. The trouble with many superintendents is that they are piddling while Rome burns."

No school system topped Los Angeles County in adapting to the war. Vowing to make his students "the most health-adequate youth in America," Superintendent Vierling Kersey ordered a physical examination of all the county's ten thousand high school seniors—with free dental and medical care for children who could not afford it—and threatened to make physical fitness tests a requirement for graduation. Teachers in academic subjects were instructed to return to the basics. "We're not depriving kids of their freedom when we demand that they know how to find 1/2 of 3/8," argued Kersey. "A good part of this war depends on competency in computation." Older elementary school students were asked to write the superintendent a letter explaining what they were doing (or planned to do) to help win the war. And to instill a sense of initiative, Kersey encouraged students to raise livestock in their backyards; by the late winter of 1942 they were caring for more than seventy-five hundred rabbits and chickens, and a thousand pigs.

As course offerings multiplied, teaching staffs shrank. Under the pressure of the draft and multiplying classroom responsibilities—new subjects to teach, student morale-building, citizenship training—the supply of qualified teachers diminished rapidly; experts estimated that rural schools (with their lower salaries) could lose half of their teachers by the end of 1942. "We are faced, therefore, not only with an immediate shortage," proclaimed the executive secretary of the National Education Association, "but also with the possibility of a shortage of such proportions as to curtail many educational programs or to close many schools."

Social workers and boys' club volunteers also departed for war plants and the Army, leaving male teenagers with fewer adult role models outside the family. Looking ahead, a spokesman for Big Brothers foresaw trouble, fueled by "the sudden acquisition of disproportionately large wages [in defense jobs] among boys of 16 to 18 years of age," and "the impetus of war excitement." Indeed, court officials in Los Angeles, Baltimore, and Washington, D.C., reported that juvenile delinquency had already risen significantly since Pearl Harbor.

In communities that attracted an extensive influx of defense workers, local social welfare agencies for youth were simply overwhelmed. "In many of the approximately four hundred war production and defense areas throughout the country," noted Secretary of Labor Frances Perkins, "conditions seriously detrimental to the welfare of children exist, and in many of these areas . . . local services for children are almost entirely lacking." To Paul McNutt, such conditions were "the swamp which breeds the mosquitoes" in the form of rising numbers of teenage prostitutes: "Packing-box shanties, far from schools. Boys and girls that do not have a chance at sound training for jobs. Towns that think they cannot afford recreational facilities but let honky-tonks and roadhouses serve as a substitute." No one could doubt, concluded McNutt, that "the impact of defense conditions and of war has borne heavily on children."

Alarmed by what he called "the blighting of the seed corn," novelist Theodore Dreiser wrote to Eleanor Roosevelt, asking her help in obtaining radio airtime for a series of broadcasts on the dangers facing American children in wartime. "There are one million children below fourteen years who are picking cranberries in Cape Cod, shelling pecans in Texas, and hundreds of other jobs that bring them nothing but bent backs and piecemeal education," Dreiser told the first lady. He proposed to develop scripts for programs about malnutrition in children, the effects of slum housing, the plight of children working in fields and factories, and the neglect of education for the sons and daughters of migratory workers. Government safeguards for children were clearly in the national interest, Dresier reasoned, since "it has always been true that yesterday's child is tomorrow's soldier." But the White House did not respond.

Just outside the Baltimore city limits, several thousand defense workers and their families lived in a jumble of forty or more makeshift trailer camps. Drawn to the region's shipyards and aircraft plants from farms and small towns up and down the East Coast and as far away as Iowa and Nebraska, they had been unable to obtain affordable housing in the city; rents in low-bracket dwellings in Baltimore had surged by an average of 25 percent since Pearl Harbor, sparked by increased demand from both defense migrants and record numbers of newlyweds.

So a growing number of Baltimore war workers in the nearby communities of Middle River, Patapsco Flats, and Curtis Bay resided in boxcar-like vehicles that often lacked toilet or bath facilities, or even running water. (Community outhouses and "utility houses" with showers served their needs.) Some couples saved money by living in trucks or junked autos with wheels but no tires (ground rent eight dollars per month) and of course no electricity; roofs were buttressed with cartons tacked down to keep out the wind. Many of the migrants had forsaken marginal farms at home to earn money on production lines while they could. "When I begin to grumble," confessed one woman in her mid-thirties from North Carolina, "my husband says with a smile, 'Well, we are not up here for our health.'"

Women in the camps complained of loneliness above all. Often the men in neighboring trailers worked (and slept) on different shifts, leaving their wives few opportunities to visit one another. Instead, women passed the time alone, knitting or doing their washing; one said that her main source of amusement was "seeing couples move in and out of trailers." Recreational facilities for children were scarce or nonexistent, and cautious parents hesitated to turn their kids loose amid a host of strangers. One mother admitted that she was afraid to take her two small children anywhere "for fear of running into some kind of disease. They have never had anything but red measles."

Baltimore native H. L. Mencken watched the migrants pour into the city and its factories and regarded them with contempt. Mencken was offended especially by the "filthy poor whites from Appalachia and the Southern Tidewater," whom he described as "thin and evil-looking," "shabby, ill-fed," and "true savages." "Some instinct forces them to destroy every green thing," Mencken grumbled. "The Negroes are much more civilized." By the end of summer, an additional eighteen thousand war workers were expected to arrive in the Baltimore area.

Detroit suffered similar overcrowding. In early 1942, thousands of families already were crammed into shacks and trailers on the outskirts of the city, but the situation promised to deteriorate further as construction proceeded on the Ford Motor Company's massive Willow Run bomber plant about an hour's drive away. Ford officials anticipated a total of nearly 100,000 workers when the plant reached full production levels, although there really was no place to put them. The nearby town of Ypsilanti (population fifteen thousand) was swamped with construction workers and the first wave of aircraft employees, while grandiose federal plans to construct an entire new city—with dormitories and homes for all of Willow Run's workers and their families—remained bogged down in a snarl of red tape and bureaucratic quarrels.

Occasionally the war-production program devoured entire towns. In the first months of 1942, ten thousand demolition and construction workers descended upon Letterkenny Township in southern Pennsylvania, leveling more than 350 buildings and uprooting the entire population of one thousand people—including a substantial community of Mennonites—to make room for an Army ordnance storage depot. Schools, barns, and churches vanished. Officials in the nearby town of Chambersburg feared they, too, would be overrun by the influx of workers. "It also will be very bad," mused the secretary of the local Chamber of Commerce, "if this project attracts any considerable number of Negro workers from other parts of the country, because accommodations are extremely limited for them in this part of the state."

Ernie Pyle saw his hometown of Dana, Indiana, devastated by the construction of a munitions factory just north of town. "A great defense plant anywhere near us means the end of the close-knit, kindly, simple, honest community that I and my father and my grandfather knew," wrote Pyle. "It means that people like my father will have to sell and move off the land they have trod a lifetime. . . . They will become refugees, bewildered and sad." As longtime residents left town on two weeks' notice, Army officers and engineers moved into the more desirable farmhouses; other homes were torn down. It was, Pyle decided, "a tragedy—the planned and necessary execution of an old community." He predicted that Dana would soon become "a boom town, roaring, crowded, strange. . . . Strangers will open juke joints; prices will skyrocket. . . . Farmers for the first time in their lives will have to lock their houses against the 3,000 'foreigners' who will swoop in and devour our community." The war, concluded Pyle, "is beginning to hit close, now, to many of us."

"If Lincoln were alive today, what would he do . . . to defend the nation against the Japanese horde?" asked Los Angeles Mayor Fletcher Bowron in a radio address on Lincoln's birthday. To Bowron—who preferred to communicate with his supporters directly via radio, since he believed the major newspapers failed to report his words accurately—it seemed clear that Lincoln "would make short work of rounding up the Japanese and putting them where they could do no harm." Convinced that Los Angeles represented "the nerve center" of a Japanese spy network, the mayor claimed to have received "hundreds of letters, messages, phone calls, [and] personal appeals" supporting the evacuation of Japanese aliens and Nisei to "a place of safety" several hundred miles inland. "Those little men who prate of civil liberties against the interest of the nation and the safety of the people will be forgotten in the pages of history," the mayor predicted, "while an executive in Washington who will save the nation against invasion and destruction will be entitled to a secure place beside Lincoln."

One day earlier, Bowron had met with General DeWitt, urging him to recommend the evacuation and internment of all Japanese aliens and Nisei living in the Los Angeles area. On February 13, an ad hoc conference of congressmen and senators from California, Washington, and Oregon— many of whom, according to Department of Justice officials, were "just nuts" about the Japanese threat—overwhelmingly approved a resolution asking President Roosevelt to order "the immediate evacuation of all persons of Japanese lineage" from the Pacific coast. Similar measures were passed by representatives of the County Supervisors Association of California ("It is impossible to know Japanese who are loyal from those who are disloyal") and the League of California Cities. One California legislator warned that the public was losing patience with the federal government's dilatory tactics: "We're splitting hairs and providing traitors and enemy aliens opportunity to perfect plans that we know have been going right ahead for months."

A joint statement issued by Attorney General Biddle and Secretary Stimson affirming that "there has been no substantial evidence of sabotage" by Japanese on the West Coast only heightened suspicions. In testimony before a congressional committee, Earl Warren argued that the "very absence of sabotage" was actually "the most ominous sign in the whole situation." "I believe we are just being lulled into a false sense of security, that our day of reckoning is bound to come," concluded Warren. "The sabotage we are to get will be timed just as at Pearl Harbor and in the invasion of France or Denmark."

After visiting the West Coast in early February, Walter Lippmann decided that the alarmists were correct. "The Pacific Coast," he wrote, "is in imminent danger of a combined attack from within and without. . . . It is a fact that communication takes place between the enemy at sea and enemy agents on land." (Numerous military and civilian authorities doubted that such contact occurred.) Like Warren (who was, in fact, one of the columnist's sources), Lippmann believed that the absence of Japanese attempts to disrupt American war production in California "is not, as some have liked to think, a sign that there is nothing to be feared. It is a sign that the blow is well-organized and that it is held back until it can be struck with maximum effect."

A new series of raids by FBI agents and local police on Japanese communities across California reportedly uncovered enough firearms, ammunition, binoculars, maps, "secret documents and uniforms," cameras, and "signaling devices" to confirm Lippmann's judgment. The publication in newspapers of the first official, detailed photos of the bombed USS *Arizona*—afire and listing on its side—and the arrival in northern California of part of the wreckage of American planes destroyed at Pearl Harbor inflamed tensions further. Discarded on a dock in Oakland, the piles of twisted metal from the aircraft seemed to one observer "a sinister reminder to West Coasters of what neglect and apathy can do in wartime."

Then Singapore fell. On February 15, Japanese forces captured the supposedly impregnable island's massive naval base—the keystone of Allied strategy in the Pacific war—and took prisoner eighty thousand British, Australian, and Indian soldiers. "This is one of those moments of awful disaster that make your stomach sink," wrote Raymond Clapper. "Japan controls now the whole other side of the Pacific." The date soon became known as "the second 'Jap Sunday,'" exactly ten weeks after Pearl Harbor.

"This was the worst week of the war," mourned *Time* magazine in the aftermath of Singapore's loss, which capped a string of days that included the sinking of more American tankers by U-boats off the Atlantic coast, and the burning and capsizing of the massive troop ship *Lexington* (a partially converted French passenger liner) at its pier in New York City. "The nation took one trip-hammer blow after another—vast, numbing shocks. It was a worse week for the United States than the fall of France; it was the worst week of the century. Such a week had not come to the United States since the blackest days of the Civil War."

Perhaps *Time*'s editors exaggerated—but not by much. "The considered judgment of responsible officials in Washington is that the fall of Singapore marks the darkest moment of the war for the United Nations," reported the *New York Times'* James Reston. "It is virtually conceded that Sumatra, too, must inevitably fall, cutting the United Nations off from their main supply of oil in the Southwest Pacific and leaving the Japanese free passage into the Indian Ocean, from where they can raid the Allied supply lines to China, Suez, and the Persian Gulf." Allied resistance on Java, too, was expected to collapse. And soon thousands of Japanese troops would be shifted from Singapore to the Philippines to reinforce the offensive against MacArthur on Bataan.

From Washington, OCD Director James Landis warned Americans that Singapore's fall meant that "the battle front will move nearer this country—possibly 3,000 miles—and will mean a longer war." Eleanor Roosevelt assured the readers of her daily newspaper column that the president had anticipated the loss of Singapore, but she understood that many Americans had not. "Perhaps it is good for us to have to face disaster," she suggested, "because we have been so optimistic and almost arrogant in our expectation of constant success."

Two days later, Senator Thomas Stewart of Tennessee introduced legislation "to imprison all Japanese Americans for the duration of the war." The following day, Congress appropriated $300,000 for a federal investigation of Japanese fifth-column activity in California, Oregon, Washington, Hawaii, and Alaska. "If we don't move in advance of sabotage," insisted Representative John Costello, whose district lay just east of San Francisco, "Pearl Harbor will be insignificant to what will happen here." Veteran race-baiting congressman John Rankin of Mississippi—whose constituency included no Japanese at all—urged the Roosevelt administration to drive "all the Japs out from under the American flag for their treachery and perfidy." "Once a Jap, always a Jap," Rankin declared. "You can't any more regenerate a Jap than you can reverse the laws of nature."

No investigation would be required. For the past week, Stimson had been wrestling with the problem of evacuation of the Nisei, trying to balance the threat of Japanese invasion aided by fifth columnists—which he felt was very real—with his conviction that the wholesale removal of American citizens from their homes on racial grounds "will make a tremendous hole in our constitutional system." Stimson tried to pass the buck to the president, who passed it right back to the War Department with a suggestion to "do anything you think necessary. . . . But it has got to be dictated by military necessity."

In the aftermath of Singapore, Roosevelt made his decision. On February 17, the president approved the removal of both Japanese aliens and Nisei, and asked Stimson to draft the requisite paperwork. Roosevelt signed Executive Order 9066 two days later, although it was withheld from publication for twenty-four hours. In the two-page, five-paragraph document, the president provided Stimson (or designated military commanders) with authority "to prescribe military areas . . . from which any or all persons may be excluded," in an effort to take "every possible protection against espionage and against sabotage to national-defense material, national-defense premises, and national-defense utilities."

Administration spokesmen made it clear that the order would apply only to the West Coast, and that only Japanese (not Germans or Italians) would be evacuated. Biddle claimed that "the move has been taken largely for the protection of the Japanese themselves," but no one was fooled. Mayor Bowron deemed it "a step in the right direction," a phrase that was repeated verbatim by a number of legislators from the West Coast who impatiently awaited the next step.

At a mass meeting of Nisei in Los Angeles, Japanese Americans lined up to sign a pledge of loyalty to the United States. "We know we are loyal to the American flag," noted one Nisei journalist, "but race hatreds are being stirred up now in the Fascist pattern." From the top officials of the Japanese American Citizens League in San Francisco came a plea for calm. "We have advised our 20,000 members not to become overly alarmed or panicky," they wrote. "It is difficult for us to conceive that our government, with its vaunted heritage of democratic ideals, would break down the equality that has always existed between its citizens and discriminate against one bloc of them."

"After Singapore," wrote Tom Treanor, "the things I cannot take are certain silly little, cheery little patriotic pepper-up songs concocted by Tin Pan Alley. . . . War isn't a musical comedy and the songs we sing should have, at least, dignity, even if the words and tunes are no good." And most were not. American songwriters still had not caught the nation's wartime mood. "The big dance bands, as if you didn't know, are bombarding us with war-song records," wrote a music critic in the *New Yorker*. "So far, however, the boys have been badly stumped by a lack of good words and/ or music, and none of their martial output has been of a nature to bring a tingle to the old spine." A *Chicago Tribune* editorial dismissed such tepid tunes as "Uncle Sammy, Here I Am" and "Good-by Dear, I'll Be Back in a Year" as "panty-waist numbers": "Add a crooner," the *Tribune* scoffed, "and get out the aspirin."

Aspirin came in handy when radio stations played Irving Berlin's latest song, "I Paid My Income Tax Today," written at the request of Treasury Secretary Morgenthau to encourage Americans—7 million of whom were earning enough to owe federal income taxes for the first time in their lives—to pay up promptly, or even ahead of schedule. "We must pay for this war somehow," Berlin's tune reminded taxpayers. "Uncle Sam was worried but he isn't now / I paid my income tax today." A later verse added, more ominously, a lyrical warning to Washington: "I never cared what Congress spent / But now I'll watch ev'ry cent / Examine ev'ry bill they pay."

To assist the 22 million Americans who would be filing federal returns under the new and higher tax rates, Walt Disney studios produced a cartoon short starring Donald Duck navigating his way through the short-form paperwork. (By February, Disney's staff was dedicating three-fourths of its time and manpower to wartime production, including training films for the Army and cartoons for the State Department's goodwill program toward Latin America.) Initially vexed by the question of Donald's marital status, Treasury experts decided that he could file as "the head of a family," since he supported three adopted nephews "for whose maintenance he has a legal and moral obligation." With a declared income for 1941 of $2,501—low for a Hollywood star, but Walt Disney explained that "we don't want to spoil him"—Donald ended up owing $13 in tax, which he was happy to pay once he heard a radio voice reminding him that the government used everyone's "taxes to beat the Axis!" Shown in twelve thousand movie theaters, the cartoon earned high marks from audiences and critics, but in a fit of post–Mayris Chaney pique, Congress refused to reimburse Disney for its production costs.

Other Hollywood filmmakers offered their talents to elevate the quality of the government's propaganda efforts. Director Frank Capra—newly enlisted and assigned to the Army's Special Services Branch headquarters—was asked to produce a series of documentary films that would explain to millions of American soldiers exactly why they were fighting. As General George C. Marshall pointed out, most of the Army's recruits had never even seen a gun. "They were being uprooted from civilian life and thrown into Army camps," Marshall told Capra. "*And the reason why* was hazy in their minds." Invited to Washington to tackle a similar assignment in pamphlet form—to "explain to a great many young men why they are about to get stuck in the stomach"—essayist E. B. White decided that the sobering task called for "no pretty writing." "It is dangerous to get playing with words on the very highest of planes," White noted, "because they become (unless you are careful) like checkers men and eventually take charge."

In a fireside chat on the evening of February 23, President Roosevelt gave the American public his own account of the stakes involved in the war, and the challenges the nation faced. It was an opportunity for Roosevelt to confront charges that his administration refused to publicly acknowledge the dire military situation facing the United Nations, particularly in the aftermath of Singapore's fall. "The swiftest and simplest way to build the type of morale which we need at this moment," declared a *New York Times* editorial, "is for the President himself to tell the country plainly that the United Nations have met with terrible reverses," and that "the dangers we now face are grave in the extreme." "The people wanted to hear the worst—and they wanted to hear it from their President," agreed *Time* magazine. "Preach hell to us upon every occasion!" implored a frustrated Virginian. "Preach the terrible hell of Axis world domination—the permanent damnation of Axis victory!"

None of the 70 million Americans who heard Roosevelt's speech that evening knew exactly where the president was. (Security precautions precluded the usual radio introduction—"Now we take you to the Oval Room of the White House.") As Roosevelt began, some listeners thought he seemed "unusually grave"; the president rushed through the first part of his speech, coughing frequently, the lingering effect of a recent cold.

"We Americans have been compelled to yield ground," the president acknowledged, "but we will regain it." There was no hell, nor damnation—only a dispassionate exposition of the reasons for the recent Axis victories, the present difficulties facing the United States, and the hardships that lay ahead. It struck one reporter as a "great geography lesson," as the president repeatedly turned to the seven-foot map behind him and asked his audience to follow along on their own maps at home to comprehend the vast distances involved in the war. (Map sales had soared in anticipation of the speech.) There was no mention of Singapore, only a condemnation of former isolationists and America Firsters who still favored a defensive "turtle policy." "We prefer to retain the eagle as it is," insisted the president, "flying high and striking hard." Praising recent gains in wartime production, Roosevelt pledged that "we shall not stop work for a single day," although earlier that day 3,500 workers had walked off their jobs at a shipyard in San Pedro, California, in a dispute over a ten-hour day.

In the end, Roosevelt promised that though many obstacles remained, the democracies would win the war if they remained united. ("It will be sort of like Lent, only longer," surmised one young woman in the radio audience.) The *New York Times* remained unimpressed. "We still find a tendency on the part of the Administration to believe that bad news must be broken gently," the *Times* complained on the following day. "There is still much to be done. . . . And the President alone can lead the way."

During the president's speech, a Japanese submarine surfaced a half mile off the coast of southern California, about seven miles north of Santa Barbara, and lobbed two dozen five-inch shells in the general direction of an oil refinery. Most of the shells exploded harmlessly in fields, ditches, or on a nearby ranch; one fragment reportedly caused minor damage to a piece of pumping equipment. Civilian defense authorities waited until Roosevelt concluded his talk before ordering local radio stations off the air, but by that time the submarine had disappeared.

It was the first enemy attack on the American mainland, but there was no panic. The *Los Angeles Times* dismissed it as "a hurried and nervous nuisance raid" by an enemy who displayed "execrable marksmanship." To some, the incident cast further suspicion on the loyalty of neighboring Japanese Americans. "There is reason to believe," muttered the *Times*, "that this submarine attack was aided if not actually directed by signals from the shore."

"I think there'll be a lot more submarine activity off our shores," predicted Los Angeles columnist Bill Henry, "before this mess is over."

"Any day now I expect a forty-pound shell to come hurtling through my roof and announce the arrival of the Mikado," wrote Groucho Marx from Hollywood. "In a way, it would be a blessing. The indifference, the blasé attitude and the smugness that seems to pervade this whole coast can only be cured by shell shock." Besides, Groucho added, "I have invested a fortune in blackout curtains, candles, lump sugar, rubber tires, kerosene lamps and pemmican and I'd like to get my money's worth out of them."

As Groucho prepared to move back to Manhattan, Hollywood's studio executives resumed their search for the pulse of the wartime public. "On the one hand," noted a film critic, "the picture writers continue their relentless unearthing of saboteurs; on the other, they furnish comedy to take people's minds off their troubles." Few observers offered a kind word for the tired "lone-hero-outsmarts-the-bumbling-Gestapo" formula. "Such films," concluded the *New Yorker*, "seem a bit cocksure for the present precarious moment in history; the privilege of making them should be considered one of the fruits of victory." Perhaps they even encouraged overconfidence among moviegoing Americans. "This contempt for the Nazis leads to a complacency which has proven disastrous," wrote one reader to the *New York Times*. "This attitude could not be more successfully executed if there were a secret Nazi agent in each [studio] front office suggesting plots." Others pointed to the similarly deceptive effects of newsreels such as *Tanks*, which showed American factories churning out row upon row of armored vehicles, accompanied by Orson Welles's "concise and comforting commentary."

And yet there were signs that Americans' nerves were not as steady as they seemed. Often complacency resided side by side with war jitters in what S. J. Perelman described as "a strange blending of tension and apathy." Physicians reported a sharp increase in cases of insomnia, making it "Public Illness Number One," affecting an estimated one-third of the adult population. Americans worried about the draft, and about loved ones in military service whose whereabouts were seldom known. "One of the minor difficulties of being a non-combatant in a time like this," admitted the *New Yorker*, "is that curiosity becomes an aggravating burden hard to carry around, almost impossible to sleep with."

War workers fretted about finishing their jobs on schedule and with sufficient precision, and middle-class Americans lay awake at night wondering "how in thunder they're going to pay those income taxes next year." Sundays no longer offered a respite of peace and quiet, especially along the coasts: "Almost always somewhere in the clouds," reported one journalist, "the roar of a big plane, and often a group of ships, can be heard. . . . There's no way of telling what they are or where they are going." One sleepless woman in Baltimore imagined hordes of Germans invading the city and looting grocery stores, leaving her children to starve. Sales of cigarettes and sleeping potions soared; massage therapists tripled their business; department stores offered hundreds of devices to encourage drowsiness; and patients flocked to psychiatrists, psychoanalysts, and "professional listeners."

As in the days immediately following Pearl Harbor, radio was blamed for exacerbating the nation's anxieties and creating what the *Washington Post* termed "the prevailing mood of gloom and foreboding . . . a sort of utterly irrational and thus quite dangerous state of 'funk.'" Psychiatrists claimed that listening to bleak, repetitive news broadcasts for prolonged periods produced a disordered mental state known as "radio fatigue," which "uses up the energy and wastes the emotional drive that should go into the war effort." (It was no accident that Alka-Seltzer ran two ads in the space of fifteen minutes on the NBC evening news roundup.) Regular news breaks were bad enough, but many stations continued to interrupt scheduled programs for the latest "flash" bulletins. "We're jumpy enough," complained the *New Republic*, "without hot bricks being set in our path."

A steady diet of radio soap operas (which filled 80 percent of the networks' daytime schedules) apparently made the condition worse. One Manhattan psychiatrist found that women patients exhibited particularly acute symptoms of anxiety following exposure to a steady diet of serial melodramas peopled with characters "in perfectly awful trouble," ranging from fear, frustration, and insecurity to sexual jealousy, revulsion, and rage. "I started this war with a morale as good as anybody's," claimed a female listener in Idaho, "but it started slipping after a few days of steady 'washboard weepers,' and by the end of a week I was ready to surrender." "Haven't the American people enough to weep over without our radios blaring out sorrow?" asked an exasperated housewife in Michigan. "For heaven's sake, can't someone stop them? Give us something to laugh about."

To calm their workers' nerves, defense plants began piping in sing-along music; popular choices included "Swanee River," "Sweet and Low," and "I've Been Working on the Railroad." (President Roosevelt's favorite sing-alongs at the White House were "Home on the Range" and "Anchors Aweigh.") For those listening at home, experts suggested "something quiet and nostalgic. . . . Keep on the slow ones till you calm down." Assured by Arthur Murray studios that "dancing is the best tonic for physical and mental health," community recreation agencies sponsored weekly square dances to fight the jitters and build group morale. ("People must mix in a square dance," explained one YMCA official. "They can't be standoff-ish.") Newspapers advertised booklets on *How to Avoid and Overcome Nervous Troubles*, while the National Noise Abatement Council announced a campaign to help ease "the nervous strain resulting from noise during the war emergency." Desperate for tourists, Florida advertised itself as a nerve tonic, where visitors seeking rejuvenation could join six thousand kindred and calm souls playing shuffleboard "all day in the warm sunshine in a five-acre tropical park."

On the West Coast, Army officers and Los Angelenos provided a disturbing demonstration of just how dangerous wartime jitters could be. Shortly before 2:30 on the morning of February 25, military authorities in the Los Angeles area issued an air raid alert prompted by the approach of what they perceived to be one or more hostile aircraft. All-night local radio stations went silent, air raid sirens sounded a constant wail (at least the sirens that worked, which was fewer than one-fourth of those the city had recently purchased), streetlights went dark, and several dozen searchlights stabbed the sky, reminding some observers of the world premiere of the latest Cecil B. DeMille movie.

For nearly two hours, Californians from Long Beach to Santa Monica could hear the pounding of antiaircraft guns, and see the golden streaks from tracer bullets and the orange bursts of exploding shells. (It was, someone said, "the first real show of the second world war, on the U.S. mainland.") Despite repeated instructions on how to behave in an emergency, many people took precisely the wrong actions. Some stood on front porches in their pajamas, watching the sky; others climbed to rooftops to track the searchlights. Instead of leaving phone lines free for emergency services, people flooded police and newspaper switchboards asking what the hell was going on. Clusters of spectators gathered in the streets until whistling shell fragments sent them scurrying for shelter. (One woman dressed in a nightgown stood obdurately in the middle of Catalina Street, "screeching like a bloody owl," despite her husband's repeated pleas to "come backta bed.")

Police and civilians alike swore they saw enemy bombers, but no bombs fell from the sky. One policeman told a reporter he had seen 150 or 200 planes: "They came in great dark clouds." Others said "there were seven planes, maybe nine," or perhaps twenty-seven. ("Roaring out of a brilliant moonlit western sky," claimed the *Los Angeles Times*, "foreign aircraft flying both in large formation and singly flew over Southern California.") Rumors that a Japanese plane had been shot down sent sightseers rushing to view the debris. One cop thought he saw American planes engage the invaders in dogfights, but no American aircraft ever left the ground. Nor did any of the 1,430 rounds of antiaircraft ammunition strike its intended target, although the shells did plenty of damage to nearby neighborhoods. A hail of shrapnel knocked down telephone wires, shattered windows, and littered the ground around Los Angeles Municipal Airport. One shell exploded in the kitchen of a doctor's home, and another in a private garage; no one was injured in either case.

Unexploded shells landed in a downtown intersection, along a roadside near a golf course, and in a Santa Monica driveway, not far from the beach house where William Randolph Hearst and his longtime lover, actress Marion Davies, had sought refuge after evacuating the publisher's ornate and brilliantly lit castle at San Simeon. "I was having a dinner party," Davies later recalled. "All the lights in the house went out, and I jumped under the table." Hearst, meanwhile, stood on the beach house balcony to watch the show. "You never heard so many guns in your life," said Davies. "People were fainting. There was firing up and down the whole coast."

When Los Angeles columnist Bill Henry awakened to the sound of gunfire, he glanced out his window and noticed several large objects in the sky, drifting placidly down the coastline in a straight line. He understood at once they were not Japanese bombers. "Airplanes, particularly enemy airplanes, don't move that slowly or steadily when under fire," Henry pointed out. "It looked to me like a batch of balloons just floating along on the strong night wind." Indeed, the purportedly hostile planes were nothing more than a string of weather balloons, equipped with lights, which recently had been launched by military authorities.

Amid the confusion, three people lost their lives in automobile accidents, all of them driving without headlights. Two more suffered fatal heart attacks—an air raid warden, and a truck driver who was transporting a load of ammunition. More than a dozen Japanese Americans were arrested by FBI agents and police after paranoid residents reported suspicious-looking Asians purportedly waving flares on hilltops or flashing apartment lights to signal the way to military targets. Since police refused to allow civilian vehicles through the city streets until the all clear was sounded (belatedly, at 7:30 a.m.), a massive traffic jam ensued at rush hour, preventing thousands of defense workers from reaching their jobs.

Within twenty-four hours, Secretary of the Navy Frank Knox admitted that it had all been "just a false alarm": "Our understanding is that no planes were over Los Angeles, and none have ever been found in that area." But the War Department stubbornly insisted that the threat had been real, and Army officials fabricated details to try to make their version more credible. Several days after the incident, Secretary Stimson told reporters that as many as fifteen planes "operated by enemy agents" may have flown above the city at speeds as high as two hundred miles per hour in an attempt to identify the location of antiaircraft batteries and to frighten West Coast civilians.

More dangerous to the nation's morale was the military's inability to tell the public the truth. "Conflicting statements from the heads of our armed forces," noted Wendell Willkie, "tend to discount what they may say in the future." California congressman Leland Ford angrily accused the War Department of issuing "fake reports"; according to Ford, the civilians on the coast were not jittery, but "they are beginning to believe that the Army and Navy are." Others were more distressed by the Army's failure to get even a single American plane in the air to identify or pursue the mystery aircraft. "This incident is a cause for grave misgivings," concluded the *New York Times*. If Japanese aircraft had actually flown over Los Angeles, American defenses had been "completely ineffective"; and if no enemy planes were present, the entire fiasco was "a sign of expensive incompetence and jitters."

"The Negro people are not sold on this war," proclaimed the Reverend Adam Clayton Powell, Jr., to a Boston audience in early February. "They are not sold on it because they remember the last war, to make the world safe for democracy," a spurious crusade that brought African American veterans home to face "the same old pseudo-democracy at home" and "the worst race riots the country has known." Recently elected to the New York

City Council—the first African American to gain that office—Powell challenged the United States to "make America safe for democracy before you go out to make the world safe for it. . . . This war for democracy must be recaptured by the people."

Evidence of disaffection among the black community was not difficult to find. A conference of eighteen national African American organizations (including the NAACP and the National Urban League) reported in January that their membership was not "whole-heartedly, unselfishly, all-out" in favor of the war. British journalist William Hickey came to the same conclusion following a four-month tour of the United States; a "radical, nationwide change of heart," Hickey realized, "is needed to ensure total Negro co-operation in the war effort and to immunize America's 13,000,000 colored folk against effective and subtle enemy propaganda." Although African Americans widely despised Hitler and Nazi Germany (knowing murderous racism when they saw it), the conflict in the Pacific seemed less clear-cut. A poll of Harlem residents in early 1942 found that approximately half of respondents believed that they would be treated better by the Japanese than by white Americans; the same survey also disclosed that many African American children preferred to play the roles of Japanese soldiers in war games, so they could exact revenge upon whites.

Discriminatory hiring practices by defense contractors fueled blacks' anger. Hearings by the president's Fair Employment Practices Committee (FEPC) in January and February elicited evidence of racial bias by such prominent war-production firms as Fairchild Aviation, Stewart-Warner, Buick Aviation, Sperry Gyroscope, and Allis-Chalmers. Witnesses testified that a number of defense plants openly advertised for and employed only white workers for skilled positions; qualified black applicants were routinely ignored, or relegated to jobs as janitors or porters. Sometimes companies also restricted their trainee programs to whites, or directed nearby vocational schools to accept only white students.

One East Coast aircraft factory employed seventeen thousand workers, only ten of whom were African American. A midwestern defense plant employed eight thousand whites but not a single black. "We have no written nor stated policy against hiring colored," the personnel manager explained. "It is just one of those things that just hasn't happened." (By contrast, Ford led all war contractors with eleven thousand African American workers.) The Nordberg Manufacturing Company, based in Wisconsin, reportedly prohibited blacks from even entering its plant to apply for jobs.

New Jersey's war factories were operating at only 50 percent of capacity, and War Production Board chairman Donald Nelson admitted that one reason was "that our records show a considerable degree of racial discrimination" by the state's manufacturers. "We have loads of discrimination," acknowledged New York State's attorney general, blaming defense firms' hiring practices for a "very dark" landscape of stalled assembly lines and idle machines in munitions factories. "To deprive America's production efforts of needed skilled hands because those hands are black," charged educator Mary McLeod Bethune, a close friend of Eleanor Roosevelt, "is to thrust a knife of disloyalty into the back of Uncle Sam."

Sometimes labor organizations left employers little choice, since dozens of local unions—particularly those affiliated with the American Federation of Labor—excluded blacks from membership. A few unions explicitly established race as a criterion for membership in their constitutions; others shunted African Americans into auxiliary organizations, with equal dues but less generous benefits. Occasionally white workers threatened job actions if their company employed blacks. In February, six hundred white female workers at a chemical plant in New Jersey informed management that "they would walk out in a body if any colored girls were hired." ("I'll guarantee that if they don't admit colored, I'll lift their charter," replied a top AFL official.) By the end of the month, the FEPC had cited two West Coast locals of the International Association of Machinists for effectively barring "qualified and needed workers from employment in defense industries solely because of their race," but the committee chairman conceded that it would take "a good many years" to eliminate discrimination in the labor movement altogether.

Black workers who did obtain skilled defense jobs faced an even greater challenge in finding decent housing. In Detroit, most found themselves crowded into the densely populated ghettoes of Black Bottom and Paradise Valley on the east side of the city. Federal authorities had attempted to ease the pressure in late 1941 by approving two separate housing projects for local defense employees—a large group of homes for white workers (many of whom were recent arrivals from the rural South), and a smaller one for blacks. The Detroit Housing Commission strongly recommended that the African American workers' development (known as the Sojourner Truth Housing Project) be located in Black Bottom, but officials in the Office of Emergency Management's Division of Defense Housing decided to put it on an eighteen-acre tract in an all-white area, just across the racial boundary.

Although more than a hundred units were completed shortly after Pearl Harbor, the Sojourner Truth project remained unoccupied until late February, while Detroit officials—fearing a backlash from white neighborhoods—implored Washington to turn the development into white-only housing. Federal authorities briefly relented, then reversed course again and insisted that it remain reserved for African American workers. White protestors picketed City Hall, swearing they would never allow blacks to enter the project. In hallways outside the city's council chambers, several dozen white women screamed insults at Mayor Edward Jeffries, who supported the African American residents (as did the United Automobile Workers local at Ford). "This is no longer a question of housing," explained Jeffries. "This is a question of whether Government can publicly discriminate against the Negro."

On the evening of February 27, the night before the first African American tenants were scheduled to move in, about 150 whites with picket signs ("We want White Neighbors") gathered at the site. Some of the protestors erected a twenty-foot cross, soaked it with gasoline, and set it afire. By dawn several hundred more whites—including women and children—had joined the lines marching in front of the project. The first moving van arrived at 9:30, followed by three more trucks with black families and their possessions. Despite the presence of more than a hundred police, white protestors blocked the road; both sides traded insults until whites began smashing headlights and throwing bricks and chunks of concrete blocks at the blacks' trucks.

Mayor Jeffries issued orders to call off the moving vans, but the confrontation quickly deteriorated into a general melee. Vehicles were overturned; furniture smashed. Reinforcements for both sides arrived, armed with rifles, shotguns, clubs, steel bars, and pipe. By noon more than a thousand rioters were trading blows. At least two shots were fired;

several people suffered knife wounds. When mounted officers broke up the crowd, the battle resumed in the side streets. Police finally dispersed the mob with three rounds of tear gas.

Authorities arrested 108 people; charges ranged from inciting a riot or carrying concealed weapons to felonious assault. Fifteen rioters and three policemen were hospitalized. Fearing disorder might spread to other cities with similar housing situations, federal officials postponed indefinitely any attempt to move black tenants into the project. Roy Wilkins, assistant secretary of the NAACP, dispatched telegrams of protest to President Roosevelt, Mayor Jeffries, and Attorney General Biddle, but Sojourner Truth remained vacant as white pickets resumed their vigil. "There is no use moving these people in if you need an army to protect them," shrugged Detroit's police commissioner.

"The Army is about to take me to fight for democracy," declared one young African American caught up in the struggle. "But I would as leave fight for democracy here."

# 8: Dark Tidings, Straight, No Sugar

## MARCH–MAY 1942

*The nation still stirs uneasily, like a man*
*half-awake on a morning of disaster, still*
*half-hoping that the evil thing is in the dream*
*and not a reality.*

— *THE NEW YORK TIMES,*
MARCH 8, 1942

At the end of February, Alistair Cooke set out to find wartime America. After spending the initial months of the war in Washington, the British-born journalist decided that he wanted "to see what the war had done to people, to the towns I might go through, to some jobs and crops, to stretches of landscape I loved and had seen at peace; and to let the significance fall where it might."

Driving on four retreaded secondhand tires, Cooke headed south and west, nearly alone on the highway in the tire-rationed Virginia country-side. "I drove almost a dozen miles without seeing more than one truck and one private car coming or going," he wrote. "It was a curious new feeling, like driving in Europe—in England—on Monday morning." Stopping for lunch in the small mill town of Luray, Cooke noticed that "the town was deserted. On the way out, you learn that yesterday they lost sixty boys to the draft."

In Rainelle, West Virginia—once home to the largest hardwood sawmill in the world—Cooke saw lumber companies struggling to keep up with the escalating wartime demand for wood as a replacement for steel and metal. The hectic pace of life left Cooke with the impression of "a town doing business a little brisker than it can comfortably manage," especially as the town's best carpenters departed for better-paying jobs in aircraft factories, and its mechanics for East Coast shipyards. Certainly there was little time to follow the latest news on the Pacific war: "You smell around the town for the always elusive odor of 'morale.' It is a meaningless scent. In the close embrace of the mountains, in which most of these men and women were born and will die, there is little call to know much about the war or any geography but your own." The war had, however, made native-born townspeople wary of recent immigrants. "A distrust has been building of homegrown fifth columnists," noted Cooke, "and the Italians who live in coal-mining camps are the special victims of local suspicion."

Nightfall of the second day brought Cooke to the town of Huntington, where billboards called upon residents to protect their families by enlisting as civilian defense workers, and nearly three thousand already had, even though the community lay three hundred miles from the East Coast. Scarcity was beginning to pinch: nurses at the local hospital complained of a shortage of doctors, and restaurants rationed sugar and asked customers to order only one cup of coffee "in the interests of national defense." When Cooke requested a drink at a soda fountain, the boy behind the counter pointed to a sign on the wall: REGRET. OUT OF COCA-COLA. "To an Eskimo," sighed Cooke, "this may seem a trivial anecdote. But I walked sadly back to the hotel, convinced that the war was beginning to—if not at least push us around with a velvet glove—administer a gentle nudge to the American way of life."

People and goods were disappearing across the nation. "The thing that startles is the vanishing of a face long familiar," noted one New Yorker. "Inevitably the old civilian routine must come to depend more and more on new faces"—a new bank teller, grocery clerk, or elevator operator: "We are so constituted that a small break in the daily routine will bring things home more sharply than a world-shaking event some distance away."

Sometimes no replacements could be found. As Americans abandoned their peacetime jobs, shortages appeared in occupations from Colorado cowboys to beauticians in Detroit (two hundred of the city's beauty shops already had closed for lack of staff), and household help just about every-where. Social Security officials estimated that the United States had 2.5 million domestic workers in 1940, but war work depleted their ranks and raised the demands of those who remained. Homeowners in 1942 would need to pay their maids and cooks considerably more than the pre-war average of ten to fifteen dollars for a six-day week. "The docile maid-of-all-work, the pivot of middle-class households from time immemorial, is vanishing from the American scene," proclaimed the *Los Angeles Times*. In Hollywood, Groucho Marx lost so many servants to the lure of aircraft plants and shipyards that "I now have what is known as the servant-of-the-week," he told a friend. "If it keeps up, I'll either join the Army or subsist entirely on canned foods for the duration."

Eugene O'Neill could not afford to be so flippant. Too ill to manage his own household chores, O'Neill feared that if his handyman was drafted, he could never replace him. "It is practically impossible to hire anyone now to do anything," the playwright wrote. "They are all in the ship yards or in the service. It's a tough time to own a farm. . . . All the farmers in this valley are rapidly going nuts wondering how they can work and harvest their crops."

By the early spring of 1942, nearly 5 percent of hired agricultural work-ers had left American farms. Although agricultural wages had risen nearly 30 percent in the past year, they remained substantially below the boom paychecks of defense factories; in some parts of the country, work-ers in war plants earned as much in one week as farm laborers did in a month. California farmers faced an especially daunting labor challenge, since all the Japanese and Nisei who formerly worked for white landown-ers were scheduled for internment.

But hired labor performed only about one-fourth of the work on the nation's 6 million farms. The rest was done by farmers' family members, and enlistments and escalating draft calls were draining more and more farm boys from the land, especially since Selective Service officials in many areas refused to grant agricultural workers the same "essential labor" deferments as defense employees. Congressmen from rural districts implored General Hershey to help stem the losses; meanwhile, newspa-pers in the South and Midwest carried page after page of classified ads offering family farms for sale.

Department of Agriculture officials predicted that summer would bring the nation its worst farm labor shortage in history: a rural workforce 10 percent smaller than in 1941. At the same time, the Roosevelt administration expected farmers to boost production by 15 percent in 1942—to feed American soldiers, provide supplies to Britain and the Soviet Union, and satisfy industrial workers whose rising incomes enabled them to enjoy a richer diet than ever before. "Your duty is to produce everything you can regardless of the circumstances," the assistant secretary of agriculture told a conference of farmers. "You're going to have to carry on against such odds as never before."

To meet the federal government's goals, Kentucky authorities paroled petty criminals to help with spring planting; Maryland officials suggested using war prisoners, once they got some. In Minnesota, businessmen volunteered to pitch in on a part-time basis. The New York State legislature approved a measure allowing students who were fourteen years or older an additional thirty days' leave from school to work in the fields in the fall. (Denver officials went a step further and proposed a children's "victory army" to aid farmers, but parents vetoed the plan because it too closely resembled Nazi youth indoctrination programs.) So many women took up lighter farm chores that females formed nearly 15 percent of the rural labor force—substantially more in some southern states—compared to 1.5 percent in spring 1941. Those who wished to take on more strenuous jobs could enroll in the International Harvester Company's free training courses for farm women ("tractorettes") at its 6,500 dealerships, complete with manuals detailing how to drive tractors, operate power plows, and repair a variety of mechanized equipment. But purchases of new farm machinery to replace human labor seemed out of the question, since the War Production Board's priorities reserved nearly all the nation's steel and iron for defense production.

Orders issued by the WPB in March and April also ended the manufacture of a wide variety of metal and plastic consumer goods for the duration. Once supplies were gone from store shelves and warehouses, American shoppers would see no more new refrigerators, radios, electric mixers, radiators, lawn mowers, electric toasters, roasters, fishing tackle (except for hooks), dishwashers, tin soldiers, percolators, phonographs, pinball machines, dinner bells, Christmas tree bulbs, electric razors, television receivers, metal zippers, sewing machines, bronze caskets, jukeboxes, flashlights, irons, vacuum cleaners, electric trains, and plastic or metal ashtrays and coat hangers and playground equipment. ("In effect," observed *Time* magazine, "the United States citizen could go stand in a corner for the duration. And even if he sat quiet, he must watch the lights to save electricity.") In a thinly veiled "or else" threat to American industry, Donald Nelson announced that the WPB expected "the complete conversion of the men, materials, and machine tools formerly devoted to these pursuits to war production."

To preserve dwindling supplies of tin ("Tin for Tokio"), WPB officials required the return of one empty collapsible tube of toothpaste or shaving cream for each new tube purchased. There would be few tin cans (which were nearly 99 percent sheet steel anyway) for food or beverages; beer migrated into quart glass bottles, to save metal on bottle caps. Razor blade production was reduced to one blade per adult American male per week, which gave unshaven faces a vaguely patriotic cachet. Nylon hosiery followed silk into oblivion, once the WPB announced that "most, if not all, of the nylon supply will soon be needed for military requirements." With the supply of shellac—nearly all of which came from India—reserved for military and essential civilian purposes, WPB officials ordered phonograph record companies to reduce their output by 70 percent. ("This means a cut in rug-cutting," complained one music lover, "and no good news for highbrows either.") And American distilleries that could turn grain into 190-proof ethyl alcohol—needed for smokeless powder—were ordered to make nothing else, effectively shutting down wartime production of bourbon, rye, and gin. Experts estimated the nation's stockpiles of whiskey would last another four years; "despite all the wars and rumors of wars," crowed H. L. Mencken, "the supply of sound liquor in this great republic remains almost infinite."

"Never announce to the American public an impending shortage," recommended the *New Yorker*, but government officials did precisely that, and consumers resumed their panic buying of goods slated to disappear. As "crowds of typical Christmas size" invaded shopping districts, department store sales throughout March ran about 25 percent above 1941 levels; in Philadelphia and Cincinnati, merchants ran advertisements asking customers to stop buying so much. Shoppers were determined to purchase what they could while they could, noted *Time* magazine: "They knew that next year's income tax would make this year's look like a dime lost in a subway grating. Now they meant to have some fun." Easter set off another shopping spree, with stores throughout the nation setting all-time sales records for the season.

Sales of men's clothing remained robust, as customers purchased two or three suits at a time, along with multiple pairs of shoes, or a half dozen shirts—particularly after a March 3 WPB order that mandated changes in the design of men's suits to conserve wool and cotton. Effective March 30, American clothing manufacturers would have to eliminate pleats, trouser cuffs, shoulder padding, and patch pockets; narrow the width of trousers by four inches from knee to ankle; shorten the length of suit coats; narrow the width of collars and lapels; and abolish the usual second pair of pants. What remained was dubbed a "Victory suit."

"It's not flashy," admitted Illinois congressman Cecil Bishop, a former tailor. "It's conservative." A skeptical Henry McLemore warned his readers that "the only way for a man to look good in a 'Victory Suit' is to get himself in shape." The new suits, McLemore pointed out, neither flattered nor concealed. "If you are too skinny, they make you look like a scarecrow on a day off from the fields. If you are too fat, they emphasize each extra ounce. . . . The Victory Suit does everything but point an index finger at the excess baggage." WPB authorities subsequently issued a clarification barring anyone from buying pants with unfinished hems and adding cuffs at home. Shoppers promptly stormed department stores to purchase another round of cuffed trousers before they ran out; the *Wall Street Journal* reported that the nation's clothing sales for March equaled eight months' worth of purchases in peacetime.

To encourage women to spend as little as possible on clothes, WPB officials simply issued an edict in early March to "freeze the existing silhouette"—waistlines and hemlines would stay pretty much where there were—and prevent any "radical changes in fashion that might render obsolete and therefore useless any existing clothes in women's wardrobes." Minor variations in the basic outline were permitted, but not extraneous frills such as balloon sleeves, French cuffs, flared skirts, or all-around pleating ("Taste without waste"). Simple and functional outfits seemed to fit the nation's mood anyway. "The overdressed woman will be as unpatriotically conspicuous," sniffed celebrity journalist Adela Rogers St. Johns, "as though she wore a Japanese kimono."

"We're going to be more svelte, more colorful, more alluring in cotton than we ever were in silk," predicted Edith Head, one of Hollywood's leading costume designers. Recommending brightly colored clothes in "clear, pretty pastels," Head reasoned that "cheerful colors make cheerful people, and that's what we all must be in this great national emergency." Choices narrowed after WPB officials reserved ten basic dyes (especially browns) for military wear, leaving shoppers to choose from alternate hues such as Gunpowder Gray, British Rose, Pan-American Red, Russian Green, or American Wine. Navy blue was in—"Suddenly, nothing suits you except a navy suit!"—but black was reserved for widows.

Before the war, few adult women outside the South or college campuses wore slacks in public; in the spring of 1942, females of all ages and sizes took to wearing them, particularly civilian defense volunteers. One Washington retailer claimed slacks represented "a new kind of living . . . a studied casualness—an effort toward functionalism that comes to the surface in wartime." Fashion critics were appalled. Disdaining the trend as "an affectation which is supposed to denote earnest concentration on the war effort," one New York fashion writer insisted that "this emphatically must stop. . . . There isn't one woman in two hundred who looks as well in slacks as in skirts." ("Rule 1—Don't wear slacks if you are the large majestic type," advised the *Boston Globe*'s fashion columnist. "Slacks will look even worse if you're large and not majestic.") Emily Post deemed them acceptable for country life during the day—a symbol of "the simplification of modern living"—but Eleanor Roosevelt demurely refrained from joining the trend. "I don't think slacks would be very becoming on me," the first lady cheerfully admitted. "You have to be young and thin to wear slacks—and if you are I think you look very nice."

"At night, when we get back to our prefabricated home," wrote S. J. Perelman from southern California, "we just about have strength to pick up the evening paper, get the latest disaster straight between the eyes, and totter off to bed." Surveys revealed that the average American was spending an additional thirty minutes every day reading the newspaper, and the news from the Pacific was—as German émigré Lotte Lenya put it—"so terrible discouraging."

In late February and early March, United States naval forces suffered yet another defeat, this time as part of an ill-fated American-British-Australian-Dutch effort to slow the Japanese invasion of Java. Over three days, the United Nations fleet was decimated. Details emerged slowly through the cloak of Navy censorship, but by mid-March it was clear that the setback in the Java Sea represented "the most serious naval defeat . . . since Pearl Harbor." Three months after the attack on Hawaii, Japan controlled the entire southwest Pacific except Australia. "And Australia," warned *Time*, "is in peril."

"We have been pounded by a barrage of bad news as new and shocking in our experience as if it were a range of bombs," concluded the *New York Times*. In his diary, Charles Lindbergh noted simply that "at present we are losing the war about as rapidly as we can." One journalist suggested bitterly that "the ban on new radios will be no hardship to the listening public. The old sets are plenty good enough for the third-rate news we are getting these days."

Government censors' persistent attempts to manipulate public opinion by selectively releasing war news left Americans wondering what even worse disasters remained hidden. "We are discouraged and dissatisfied with the kind of news which has been handed us since Pearl Harbor," snapped the *New Yorker*, accusing authorities of vacillating between "the mysterious silence of the censor and the lyrical scream of the propagandist. It has been baffling, contradictory, and tentative."

Few responsible reporters questioned the government's right to withhold details of military encounters to avoid disclosing sensitive information to the enemy. But "unnecessary suspense, unwarranted delay and confusion over what the Navy Department actually does release," claimed the *New York Times*, "is not calculated to stiffen American morale in a long, hard war. Democracy cannot function efficiently in the dark." Playwright Maxwell Anderson discerned in Washington "an unfortunate implication that our fellow citizens and allies are to be told what is good for them, and that somebody should be delegated to decide what is good for them." A democracy "will defend itself best when it knows what's going on," Anderson insisted. "A free people is capable of free discussion of uncensored news, and that's its strength."

Heavy-handed propaganda did not play well with the American public either. "Ballyhoo doesn't win wars," argued columnist David Lawrence. "Yet the tendency in Washington now is to turn on the ballyhoo. . . . It is nothing short of tragic that the Administration has failed to understand either how to get unity or to preserve it." Artless patriotic appeals and slogans ("Let's go to Tokio," "We're in it, let's win it") struck many Americans as unseemly. "The feeling that it is being fully informed probably would do more for the public morale than all the pamphlets and radio shows the government can contrive," maintained Ernest Lindley. Americans were weary "of doubletalk . . . of those phony Whitmanesque radio programs which ring in Valley Forge, Gettysburg, San Juan Hill, with boastful asides to Adolf, Benito, *et al.*," agreed an angry New Englander. "Instead of facts we get dreamstuff."

By springtime a significant segment of Americans remained disconnected from the war effort. "Here on the East Coast the war seems enormously far away," wrote H. L. Mencken to Theodore Dreiser in early April. "People talk of it vaguely, as they might talk of the Judgment Day." Business executive Philip Pillsbury encountered a similar sentiment while touring the Midwest; civilians in the heartland, Pillsbury claimed, believed "that we're in for a short war which we can listen to on the radio." In Louisiana, Governor Jones grew so alarmed at his constituents' lethargy that he mounted a three-week, statewide tour in a sound truck with the words "Awake America" on the side. "Things are not good in this nation; we are not awake," Jones confessed. "It is going to be necessary to turn our whole thinking, feeling and talking about this war upside down and face it with a new solemn dedication."

From southern California, Ernie Pyle reported that "despite submarine shelling and 'air raids,' I can't sense that the war has changed the people." Perhaps, Pyle suggested, it was simply the wrong time of the year for wartime fervor: "It is good to be alive in the spring, when warmth comes again to the earth. Maybe that's what's the matter with America. Maybe we're all too pleased at just being alive."

Perhaps. But the Roosevelt administration's management of the war risked alienating public opinion even further. "For too long this war seems to have been considered by Washington as its own private affair," complained one critic in the *New York Times*. "There is a good chance of its being lost unless it is made the business of all the people." All the wintertime accusations of complacency only deepened the divide between Washington and the rest of the country. From coast to coast, newspapers, magazines, and congressmen received letters from ordinary citizens defending their patriotism. Some reversed the charges—"I wonder why we are constantly bombarded with admonitions to wake up when it's the Government in Washington that needs to wake up"—while others blamed a "lack of leadership and information" that consigned the public to "bewildered, distrustful despair."

"People are not 'excited' and are 'silent' about the war because they are sad, embarrassed, and confused," suggested a writer from Galveston, Texas. The average citizen "hasn't the whole picture, he doesn't know what his part is," acknowledged one midwesterner. "Meanwhile, without fidgeting or hysteria, he is trying to mind his own business and keep his shirt on. Don't scold him for it."

Declining war bond sales provided hard evidence of the public's disaffection. In January, Americans purchased $1.075 billion worth of bonds; February sales totaled only $711 million; March fell to $565 million. (Some people reportedly hesitated to buy bonds because they believed that Roosevelt was putting the cash into his personal savings account.) Nor were Americans rushing to invest on Wall Street. Stock prices had been falling since Pearl Harbor, and in mid-April they hit their lowest average price level since April 1933—the depths of the Great Depression. Under the pressure of dismal war news and the virtually inevitable prospect of increased taxation (and therefore lower dividends), blue-ribbon stocks such as United States Steel, Boeing, Westinghouse, Bethlehem Steel, Southern Pacific, and Kennecott Copper all registered new lows.

Currency had been flowing out of U.S. bank savings accounts since the war in Europe began, and at a faster rate over the past three months. Although most of this money helped finance industrial expansion, higher wages, and increased consumer spending, Federal Reserve officials concluded that a substantial quantity of cash withdrawn from banks was simply being hoarded. Uneasy about the future, and fearful that the Roosevelt administration would confiscate their bank accounts, a growing number of Americans appear to have buried their cash behind the walls of a safe (rentals of safe-deposit boxes surged) or stuffed it in a sock, instead of lending it to the federal government or putting it to productive use. "Hoarded dollars are idle dollars, slacker dollars," one New York bank reminded its customers: "Dollars withdrawn from circulation hinder and delay the building of planes, ships, tanks and vital armaments. . . . Hoarding money in times of war amounts to sabotage against the Government." Still the drain continued; by mid-April, Americans were hoarding an estimated $500 million to $1 billion. "Some bankers," reported *Time*, "think even small bills are going into mattresses now."

Upon leaving West Virginia, Alistair Cooke entered the Ohio Valley and northern Kentucky, rolling through hilly country "with more unpainted barns and abandoned shacks than I had ever seen in the Dust Bowl." The region's typical tobacco farmer—subsisting on marginal land—appeared only slightly concerned with "what the radio commentators tell him about the war for democracy"; instead, farmers feared that Washington's wartime preoccupation with crops of military value (such as soybeans) would reduce their tobacco acreage and render their struggle for subsistence even more difficult. "The young ones," Cooke added, "know that there is nothing much ahead for them but the draft."

Louisville on a Saturday night was brimming with soldiers on leave from nearby Fort Knox. "It is the first town we have seen that looks as if it might be a city in a battle zone. The streets are rolling with dumpy broad-faced girls, sometimes pretty in a poorly rouged way, spanning the sidewalk six or seven of them arm in arm, breathing a kind of giggling defiance of the loitering soldiers." Many of the girls, Cooke noted, "are enjoying the new thrill of being able to pass up not one male but droves of them."

There were also crowds of newcomers who slept in Louisville but worked across the river. "Early every morning you will see their cars, like a reincarnated junk pile, file in thousands across the toll bridge over the Ohio River, meet another convoy of cars in Jeffersonville, and go on north up Route 62." They were headed for Charlestown, Indiana, and the world's largest smokeless powder plant, twelve miles across the Kentucky line. In 1940, Charlestown had a population of 939—"the sort of town that is too small to get on anything bigger than a state map," thought Cooke, "and when it does they spell it wrong." Then the government chose it as the site for a powder plant, and by early 1942 there were fifteen thousand people in Charlestown. Workers came from Vermont and Colorado, from Oregon and Kansas, many arriving in trailers "till every muddy patch of brown ground was black with them." Those who could not afford even to rent space in a mobile home ("fifteen dollars a week for one end of a trailer with an old sheet dividing it half-way") ended up sleeping in barns, in store cellars, or in Sears and Roebuck tents down by the river.

Then Cooke swung down through southern Kentucky, where state officials sought vainly to persuade hardscrabble farmers to grow at least one acre of sorghum for syrup to replace the sugar in their own diets. "This prospect," Cooke observed, "does not greatly excite the farmers. They don't honestly believe that America will have to go short of sugar. . . . 'But hell,' they say, 'they's plenty of good syrup in the drugstores, and if they's one thing America at war don't need to start it's rationing.'" But rationing was well on its way.

OPA officials had delayed the start of sugar rationing for several months, while they decided precisely how much sugar to allow individuals, restaurants, and industrial users. Authorities also needed time to complete "the greatest single job ever tackled by the Government Printing Office": over 700 million booklets, forms, and cards, including 190 million copies of the basic fifty-six-week ration book (including extras for lost or stolen books)—enough to form a tower of paper fifteen miles high. The OPA finally settled on an allowance of one-half pound of sugar per person (including kids) per week, which translated into forty-eight teaspoonsful, or forty-two "ordinary lumps." Families who typically purchased baked goods would notice little change; those who baked their own desserts would feel the pinch. Restaurants received 50 percent of their 1941 supply, and commercial firms—bakers, candy makers, and soda bottlers—got 70 percent of their previous year's allotment.

Americans registered for sugar ration books in the first week of May at their local public elementary schools, with more than a million teachers volunteering to collect forms and distribute books. It was, the *Wall Street Journal* observed, the sort of exercise that Americans "instinctively resent—going to a specified place, at a specified time, standing in line and answering questions, which, while harmless enough, the interrogated regards as nobody's business but his own." Applicants were required to state how much sugar they had stockpiled (including the last-minute rush of panic buying in late April); those with six pounds or more per person did not receive a ration book until their "household hoard" dropped below five pounds. With no systematic way to investigate anyone's statement, authorities relied on the public's patriotism and Leon Henderson's warning that "the country is in no mood to let chiselers get away with it. Our policy will be to hit chiselers, hit them hard and fast."

It all came off with only minor glitches and mild grumbling, although some teachers found it "remarkable how many of the registrants had no sugar." Nationwide, fewer than 5 percent of Americans admitted hoarding more than the six-pound limit; the largest stash belonged to a forty-one-year-old New Jersey electrician who had accumulated 15,500 pounds of sugar because he was "thinking of going into the food business."

Restaurants adjusted their menus by cutting out sauces that required sugar, and introducing fig pudding and date pie for dessert. The Horn & Hardart Automat in Manhattan eliminated baked apples with syrup (six teaspoons of sugar per apple) for the duration, but provided a table staffed by pretty "sugar girls" who doled out a teaspoonful at a time for grapefruit or coffee. One Chicago restaurant asked patrons to "kindly report persons who thoughtlessly put sugar bowls into their pockets." The silver sugar bowls in the House of Representatives dining room abruptly vanished; congressmen had to ask waiters for a lump. Film studios sought substitutes for clear sugar panes in breakaway windows, while Hollywood cafés and soda fountains suffered a Coca-Cola drought. ("Our volume has been reduced," acknowledged a Coke advertisement, but "the character of Coca-Cola will be unimpaired.") In Philadelphia, inmates of the Eastern State Penitentiary launched a hunger strike to protest their reduced sugar rations; when the warden rejected their demands, nine prisoners in an isolation block set their mattresses afire in defiance. One inmate suffocated in the smoke, and seven others were hospitalized.

Americans' supply of tea and coffee was dwindling along with sugar. Japanese victories in Asia had cut off nearly a third of the United States' tea imports, and several waves of panic buying—sales were up more than 40 percent for the first quarter of 1942—reduced the nation's tea reserves to a three-months' supply. To ensure that stocks lasted through the end of the year, the War Production Board decided in late March to slash deliveries to retailers. Starting in April, grocery stores and tea shops would receive only half of the tea they had purchased in the same month of 1941; storekeepers were expected to limit sales to customers accordingly.

Coffee posed a different sort of challenge. Americans drank nearly ten times more coffee (an average of twenty cups per week) than tea; half of the nation's supply came from Brazil, another 25 percent from Colombia, and the rest from other Latin American countries. By April, civilian consumption was being crowded out by the Army's increasing demand for coffee—five large mugs a day for each soldier—and, more ominously, by the U-boat menace off the East Coast. Nazi sinkings of Brazilian freighters led the government in Rio de Janeiro to pull its ships back to home ports; American vessels could not pick up the slack because Washington needed every available cargo ship to carry vital war materials. Fearing a worse shipping crunch to come, WPB officials ordered a 25 percent reduction in wholesale deliveries of coffee, beginning in May, to conserve existing supplies. Grocery stores limited customers to one pound per visit, and restaurants encouraged restraint by reminding patrons of the risks sailors took to bring coffee through U-boat-infested waters.

Operation Drumbeat's primary target was not coffee, of course, but oil. In two months, German submarines sank enough tankers off the Atlantic seaboard to reduce petroleum shipments to the eastern states by 45 percent. Railroads and pipelines—which in peacetime carried only about 5 percent of the East's supply—dramatically increased their shipments from Gulf refineries, but they could meet only a quarter of the daily demand. The East's reserves continued to decline; by early March the region had only one month's supply on hand.

"Oil is ammunition: Use it Wisely," suggested an oil company advertisement in eastern newspapers. "Maybe you <u>can't</u> carry a gun," added an Esso ad, "but you <u>can</u> save oil." According to the National Safety Council, Americans actually were driving *more* frequently in early 1942, due to increased activity by war production workers and civilian defense volunteers, as well as "tourists bent on having a few last rides," and curiosity-seekers gawking at lines of bombers as they drove past aircraft plants. ("If you're careless today," warned Texaco, "you may be car-less tomorrow.") But motorists seemed to be traveling shorter distances, as evidenced by a slight reduction in gasoline sales in most states, and at least some of them were driving more slowly. By early March five states—all in the East—had reduced their speed limits to forty miles per hour or less, and on March 14 Roosevelt asked the governors of the other forty-three states to follow their example. (Fifteen states still had no fixed maximum speed at all, relying instead upon drivers to engage in "reasonable, prudent driving.") Besides saving gas and rubber, slower driving speeds might also curtail the public's "frantic and purposeless scurrying to and fro," suggested the president of the American Automobile Association: "You will find that slowing down in driving will help you to maintain a degree of calm and composure so necessary in these times of wild rumors and war jitters."

It would also preserve automobile tires; experts claimed that tires wore out almost twice as quickly at sixty miles per hour as at forty. "Conservation of tires is still the No. 1 war problem for all America," claimed the *Detroit Free Press*. "It is more talked about than any other, and there appears to have been less done about it," partly because administration officials could not agree on the severity of the rubber crisis. Optimistic forecasts from Vice President Wallace and Secretary of Commerce Jesse Jones claimed that synthetic rubber could be manufactured "quickly, cheaply, and without impairing the national war effort." It could not; production was far behind schedule and mired in controversy and overlapping bureaucratic jurisdictions. Yet after meeting with Wallace, Senator Truman confidently assured reporters that "if the people become aroused and demand rubber tires, they can get them because we have everything it takes to make them."

But Donald Nelson insisted that there would be no new rubber tires for civilians for at least the rest of 1942, and probably for the duration. "Everyone of us who is used to riding on rubber without giving the supply a thought," noted Nelson, "should look at his tires and say: 'That's all there is. There isn't any more.'" And perhaps less. In early March, Leon Henderson informed a Senate committee that the rubber shortage was growing so acute that the federal government might soon need to requisition tires from the cars of nonessential civilians (i.e., most Americans) to keep "essential vehicles" on the road.

As a first step to conserve both petroleum and rubber, Secretary of the Interior Harold Ickes announced on March 14 that deliveries of gasoline to service stations in seventeen eastern states, the District of Columbia, and Oregon and Washington would be reduced by 20 percent, beginning March 19. (Many of the tankers upon which the Pacific Northwest normally relied for oil had been diverted to military assignments.) It was clear "beyond all argument," explained Ickes, who also served as petroleum coordinator, "that some curtailment in the use of gasoline for ordinary civilian purposes is now necessary." Filling stations were limited to seventy-two hours of gasoline sales per week, and operators were instructed to give priority to the needs of essential vehicles such as ambulances, school buses, and cars driven by doctors and government officials.

To avoid overtaxing alternative means of transportation, motorists were urged to not overreact and abandon their automobiles altogether. "Real conservation requires that you keep your car in service for the duration of the war as part of America's essential transportation system," suggested the United States Rubber Company. "Don't think of it as a 'pleasure car.' It's a war car now." Yet Americans reportedly were retiring their cars at the rate of several hundred thousand every month, and transportation experts estimated that 87 percent of cars used by war workers would be out of service within a year due to worn tires. Public transportation in many cities already was stressed: in San Diego, bus and trolley traffic was up 76 percent in the first three months of 1942; in Seattle, it rose 51 percent; in Washington, D.C., 44 percent. Local authorities dragged thirty-year-old trolley cars out of retirement, but the crowds continued to grow faster than the available vehicles, especially since a number of cities had torn up their streetcar tracks for scrap metal. Desperate to add new emergency bus service lines in the Boston area, the chairman of the Massachusetts Planning Board announced that the state might need to employ "anything from a beach wagon to a covered truck with seats in it." And beyond the nation's major cities were 70 million Americans who lacked access to *any* public transportation other than cross-country trains and intercity bus lines.

Railroad passenger travel had increased between 40 and 60 percent since December 7; with no steel available for new locomotives or railcars, overcrowding became inescapable. On a six-week tour of the West Coast, Duke Ellington's band discovered that their usual private Pullman cars had been requisitioned by the Army. "We had to travel just like everybody else, sometimes in a railroad car, sometimes by bus," lamented saxophonist Harry Carney. "The trains were so packed some times we had to sit in the aisles. We really missed those Pullman cars." Air travel proved even more difficult for civilians. In the first quarter of 1942, the nation's sixteen commercial airlines carried 42 percent more passengers than during the same months in 1941, providing priority seating to military personnel and White House officials. After requisitioning a few dozen planes from the airlines in January and February, the War Department announced on April 10 that it was taking over one-fourth of the country's 340 domestic commercial airliners to transport soldiers and material. Army personnel proceeded to tear out the seats of the commandeered planes, install oversize doors and hatches, and paint everything olive drab.

That left only bicycles, and in mid-February Americans began buying adult bikes at more than twice the normal pace. Many were purchased by middle-aged commuters who pedaled inexpertly—dressed in business clothes, with briefcases dangling from the handlebars—to and from suburban train stations, creating traffic headaches along the way. By the second week of March, sporting goods stores from coast to coast had run out of bikes altogether. "The bicycle situation is bad," reported Ernie Pyle from California. "If you're lucky, you might just happen onto one at some small store. But as a general rule you can't buy a new bike in Los Angeles today." Or in the East. "It's no use rushing around trying to buy bicycles now," admitted one bike-shop owner in Baltimore. "You just can't get them. Neither can we."

Alarmed by the sudden stampede, WPB authorities issued an order on April 2 "freezing" bikes—prohibiting the sale, shipment, or delivery of new adult bicycles, effective immediately. "The order was issued," explained one official, "because of the terrific rate at which bicycles have been going to people who don't need them, with too few going to people, like defense workers, who have to have them now or soon will need them." Future production would be limited to the lightweight "Victory" model, with output reserved for war workers and essential civilian personnel.

"The worst possible [censorship] policy," warned the *New York Times* in early April, "is to make public only the favorable facts about our preparedness and to suppress the unfavorable. Such a policy would breed a false public confidence regarding our position and then, when bad news shattered this, would undermine the public's confidence in their Government's statements."

On April 9, American resistance on Bataan collapsed. After withstanding a Japanese siege for ninety-eight days, the American-Filipino lines finally broke. Nine thousand American soldiers and twenty-seven thousand Filipinos surrendered, as much to disease and malnutrition as to enemy guns; between three and four thousand Americans managed to escape to temporary refuge in the island fortress of Corregidor in Manila Bay. The agony had played out for weeks in newspaper headlines as if in slow motion, with front-page accounts of American heroism and short-lived victories ("Yanks Smash Bataan Attacks") alternating with terse reminders of vastly superior Japanese forces and, occasionally, the inevitability of defeat.

"Americans did not yet believe what Pearl Harbor and Wake and Guam told them," noted one correspondent. "They did not believe it because these first reverses of the war had a newsreel quality of unreality." But Bataan seemed different; the surrender carried far greater emotional impact than any previous American defeat, as communities across the nation counted their losses—76 young men from a single small town in Kentucky; 140 from Salinas, California; several thousand from New Mexico. "Perhaps we are now fully awake to the immensity and the perils of the struggle in which we are engaged," declared the Washington Post. "Certainly there should be no illusion left as to the hell through which Americans must pass to save our civilization. . . . Yet we have scarcely begun to approach our war tasks in the spirit of Bataan."

By April, nearly 10 percent of American males between the ages of twenty-one and thirty-five were in military service. With the Army inducting 300,000 men each month, experts predicted that number would rise to one in six by the end of the year. "We should honestly face the fact," noted Selective Service director Lewis Hershey, "that every young able-bodied man eventually will enter the war."

Nine million men aged twenty to twenty-one and thirty-six to forty-four registered for the draft in February, including Supreme Court justice William O. Douglas, Charles Lindbergh, and Thomas E. Dewey.

(When S. J. Perelman filled out his forms, the Selective Service clerk stared at his last name suspiciously. "Perelman, Perel-Man," he muttered. "Kind of a Japanese name, isn't it?") Most men in their late thirties or early forties—"men who had been just old enough to get into one war and just too young to stay out of another"—would not be slated for combat duty, but author E. B. White promised they would be prepared if needed: "We are the tough old campaigners—a little puffy round the girth strap, faltering a little at the top step of the long stairway, subsisting on bicarbonate of soda and ephedrine sulfate, our pocketbooks lined with silver and our back teeth with gold, but ready to go forth again to distant peninsulas against old enemies."

White's enthusiasm notwithstanding, the Army preferred younger soldiers—ages eighteen to twenty-three if possible. To widen the pool of selectees from that bracket, it eased the physical standards for induction, notably for vision, blood pressure, and mastication. With more than 20 percent of physical-disability rejections due to dental problems, military authorities decided they would no longer require draftees to possess any minimum number of teeth, so long as they could subsist on Army rations. "The attitude now seems to be that men without teeth can live just as well in the Army as they have up to now out of the service," explained Hershey.

While the War Department cherished youth, Selective Service officials continued to base their deferment rulings largely upon registrants' family status, particularly the number and type of dependents. Both the draft boards and the Army assigned a lower priority to occupations, which meant that thousands of highly skilled workers in essential civilian jobs were joining the military either by choice or by compulsion. War production suffered as a result; a federal survey of seven hundred defense contractors in the spring of 1942 discovered that a shortage of skilled labor had forced 384 companies to curtail operations.

"Labor dislocations are daily becoming more serious," charged the *Washington Post*, and the deputy director of Selective Service acknowledged that "the man-power situation will be acute by fall." Experts estimated that the nation's war industries would need to hire 10 million to 13 million war workers over the next twelve months, at the same time that the Army would be drafting 2 million to 3 million more men; but there were no clear guidelines to let young workers or middle-aged men know whether they were more valuable in the military or staying on their job. "As a rule, there is no one to tell them what to do," wrote David Lawrence. "Uncertainty, bewilderment and confusion therefore arise at a time when the production machine should be functioning smoothly."

To instill order into the labor mobilization process, Roosevelt created yet another agency—the War Manpower Commission—on April 18. Headed by Federal Security administrator Paul McNutt, the commission was tasked with determining the labor needs of industry and agriculture for the duration, and directing other government agencies to ensure those needs were met. (It did not, however, possess authority over Selective Service's classification and deferment decisions.) To provide a comprehensive inventory of skills among older Americans (and a pool of prospective workers for defense plants or civilian defense jobs), 13 million men between the ages of forty-five and sixty-four registered with Selective Service on April 27. McNutt considered but ultimately deferred a similar registration for women, although he conceded that "women have shown that they can do, or learn to do almost any kind of work."

At the same time, Selective Service officials agreed to separate the ranks of men with dependency deferments, placing those who worked at essential war jobs in a new category (3-B) and leaving the rest in the more vulnerable class 3-A. Professional athletes fell into the latter category. By the time major-league baseball opened its regular season on April 14, sixty-four players already were serving in the Army or Navy. The woeful Washington Senators took the worst hit, losing twelve men—including their best player, shortstop Cecil Travis. Detroit and Cleveland also saw their stars depart (Hank Greenberg and Bob Feller, respectively), but the world champion New York Yankees lost only a part-time first baseman, and the Chicago Cubs lost no one at all.

More ballplayers would go, of course, as the season wore on. Clubs took to posting a player's draft status in their press guides, alongside the usual vital statistics (height, weight, batting average), but no one could tell who would be wearing khaki by August. Inevitably teams would need to reach deep into their minor-league systems, which were even more depleted by draft calls and the lure of war-plant wages; ten minor leagues already had disbanded. "The bars are down for guys who normally couldn't bribe their way onto a big league club," observed sports columnist Shirley Povich. "In fact, the only thing big-leaguish about dozens of players in the big league uniforms this year will be the uniforms they'll wear." Even Babe Ruth—old and ill at forty-seven years—joked about making a comeback "if I can get someone to run for me."

President Roosevelt gave baseball a green light to operate for the duration ("I honestly feel that it would be best for the country to keep baseball going"), and two-thirds of Americans supported his decision, but owners claimed to be apprehensive about attendance amid so many distractions. They also recognized an opportunity to turn the wartime spirit of sacrifice to their advantage by slashing player payrolls. "There are owners who are not above sandbagging a player into line under the cloak of national emergency, and pocketing the money saved," confirmed Bob Considine. The Detroit Tigers reportedly cut *all* of their players' salaries, even though owner Walter Briggs's manufacturing firm was earning millions of dollars making tanks for the Army.

Nevertheless, numerous players held out for better deals in spring training, none more famously than Joe DiMaggio. The best baseball player in the world (although not the best-paid), DiMaggio had earned $37,500 in 1941. The Yankees offered $40,000 for the new season, but Joe turned it down and spent much of training camp relaxing in a Lido Beach penthouse on Florida's Gulf coast. The public sided overwhelmingly with the Yankees, especially considering DiMaggio's Italian American heritage. (Joe's fisherman father, Giuseppe, arrived in the United States from Sicily in 1898 but had never applied for American citizenship. An enemy alien in San Francisco, the elder DiMaggio was subject to travel restrictions and a nightly curfew, and was barred from the family's restaurant on Fisherman's Wharf, just a few hundred yards from his home inside the West Coast war zone.) Yankee executives made certain the public knew about a telegram sent for Joe by several soldiers stationed at Camp Blanding, Florida: "We cordially invite you to a tryout with the 143rd Infantry 36th Division—the fightingest regiment in this man's army. The pay is only $21 a month but that is better than nothing. Please advise." In the end, DiMaggio settled for $42,500—as critics pointed out, about $34,000 more than General MacArthur's pay—and made himself a target for outraged fans for the rest of the season.

Opening Day brought a host of changes to the national pastime. "The Star-Spangled Banner," previously played only on special occasions, was heard more frequently, occasionally accompanied by Irving Berlin's "Any Bonds Today?" More night games were scheduled—seventy-seven in the American League alone—to increase attendance and permit day-shift workers to watch their favorite teams, although some club executives remained skeptical of the experiment. ("This is a daytime game," insisted Yankees' president Ed Barrow. "The Yankees will never have lights as long as I'm associated with the team.") Due to the rubber shortage, teams asked fans to return any balls hit into the stands, so they could be donated to recreation programs at Army training camps. In an effort to speed up the game, National League president Ford Frick banned managers from stepping onto the field to protest umpires' decisions. "Play will be enlivened," explained Frick hopefully, "and time, an important factor in these war days, will be saved for the fans." ("It is probably the hysteria of the times," grumbled Povich, who felt the ban on arguments would simply make games duller.) And if a game was called due to rain, restrictions on weather reports permitted radio announcers to tell listeners only that "because of circumstances beyond our control at the scene of the game, and because of the censorship regulations, we are concluding our broadcast of today's ball game at this time."

Some ballparks hired their own air raid wardens and set out sand bins, buckets, red-painted barrels of water, and fire extinguishers in case of enemy attacks. Fans were advised not to leave the stadium if an air raid siren sounded; stickers on the back of their seats provided emergency instructions, and red and green arrows directed them to shelter beneath the steel-and-concrete stands. According to a high-ranking OCD official in New York, air raid alarms would not be allowed to disrupt afternoon games. "The ball players will be the soldiers in that situation," he told reporters. "They must stay right there and take it, if it comes, up to a certain point. The show must go on. Otherwise it would be like actors rushing off a stage. If they show panic, you can see what might happen."

It took the Army more than three months to move nearly 110,000 Japanese Americans from the West Coast. When Roosevelt signed Executive Order 9066 on February 19, the War Department was unprepared to supervise, much less enforce, a wholesale evacuation of Japanese and Nisei. Instead, General DeWitt encouraged them to voluntarily emigrate from the region designated as Military Area Number One: the western half of California, most of Oregon and Washington, plus the southern third of Arizona.

Few western communities wanted to take them in. "The attitude of the interior states was hostile," the War Department reported with marked understatement. "The evacuees were not welcome." Fearful of violence and foreseeing a future with no home, driven perhaps from town to town through the West like the Okie migrants of Steinbeck's *Grapes of Wrath*, most Japanese Americans refused to set out on their own—only eight thousand left the coast during the first three weeks of March. Nor did pressure from Congress or the Army persuade local political officials to accept the evacuees. "We don't want them buying or leasing land and becoming permanently located in our state," declared the governor of Idaho ("The Japs live like rats, breed like rats and act like rats," he added, suggesting that the federal government "send them all back to Japan, then sink the island.") Arizona's governor announced that he would not turn the rest of his state into "a dumping ground" for enemy aliens; privately, the governor of Wyoming informed an official in Washington that "if you bring Japanese into my state, I promise you they will be hanging from every tree."

Unwilling to press the issue—and not particularly interested in the matter anyway—Roosevelt created a new civilian agency, the War Relocation Authority, and entrusted it with the headache of supervising and controlling the displaced Japanese Americans after troops removed them from the coast. The mandatory evacuation process began in late March and proceeded in stages, starting with the areas that military officials considered most sensitive: Bainbridge Island (in Puget Sound, Washington); Los Angeles County; San Diego; and the San Francisco waterfront. Authorities typically gave evacuees only one to two days' notice before they had to leave their homes, and permitted them to take only the possessions they could carry. (Any farmers who plowed under their crops before they left would be charged with sabotage, warned DeWitt.) In Los Angeles's Little Tokyo and Japantown in San Francisco, "For Rent" signs seemed to appear everywhere, along with storefront notices that read, "Evacuation

Sale—God Bless America, The Land We Love," and underneath, "Twenty Percent Off."

Each day, an average of 3,750 Japanese Americans were taken from their homes and escorted under guard to Army-supervised "assembly centers," mostly local racetracks and fairgrounds, where they waited while WRA officials selected sites for their long-term incarceration. "Now they have to give up their farms and move out," noted Ernie Pyle grimly, "which is all right with practically everybody, including me." Eleanor Roosevelt simply shrugged. "Unfortunately, in a war," she wrote in her "My Day" column, "many innocent people must suffer hardships to safeguard the nation."

After trying and failing once more to persuade western governors to relent and resettle the refugees within their predominantly white agricultural communities, the WRA built its first three "relocation centers": in Manzanar (a sparsely settled section of the desolate Owens Valley in eastern California); Parker, Arizona (on the Colorado River Indian Reservation); and along the Gila River, forty miles southeast of Phoenix. The agency later added seven more centers, all in remote areas east of the Sierra Nevada and west of the Mississippi River, and all ringed by fences and patrolled by armed troops.

"Most of us understand the necessity for evacuation," acknowledged a twenty-three-year-old Nisei at Manzanar. "But the immediate reaction is, we have got *some* rights as Americans. . . . The whole thing's a mess and we'll just have to take it." A Nisei gardener with two brothers in the U.S. Army was less charitable. "Why should we support anything in this country with a whole heart?" he asked a reporter. "I don't mean any of us give a damn about Japan. We hope they get licked. But . . . nobody ever let us become a real part of this country. . . . If they want to take away all we've got and dump us out in the desert, we've got no choice. But we don't like it."

Army authorities completed the evacuation in early June, and then turned to Military Area Number Two, which included the rest of California. By that time it was clear to the head of the WRA, Dr. Milton Eisenhower, that most Japanese Americans would remain in his agency's relocation centers for the foreseeable future. Already Eisenhower was "sick of the job"; after the war, he predicted, "we as Americans are going to regret the avoidable injustices that may have been done."

# 9: Games of Chance

APRIL–AUGUST 1942

*Never before had the average U. S. citizen
been forced into such personal intimacy
with his Government.*

— *TIME*, JUNE 1942

By all accounts, the 1941–42 Broadway season was a flop. Critics agreed that it was the worst in memory, a "disastrous" and "sadly disappointing" theatrical display. For the first time since 1919, the Pulitzer Prize Board bestowed no award for the best new original American drama; nor did the New York Drama Critics' Circle. Out of the season's sixty-six new plays—including works by John Steinbeck, Clifford Odets, George S. Kaufman, and Ben Hecht—only six were deemed hits by *Variety*, and none of those had debuted since December 7.

American playwrights seemed unable to craft a compelling wartime drama. "The war is a tremendous theme," acknowledged *New York Times* critic Brooks Atkinson. "It distorts dramatic proportions. It throws everything out of balance. . . . It is very difficult to say anything about the war without repeating familiar clichés or without sounding breathless." Since Pearl Harbor, American authors had produced nine plays about the war, none of any stature; one reviewer claimed that they seemed "more like idle discussions by a parlor strategist than orthodox theatrical fare." *Time* magazine's theater critic concluded that the war exerted "a slightly paralyzing effect on playwrights": "Serious writers have found the world's present plight too big to cope with." And it would remain so, suggested veteran reviewer John Mason Brown, until writers managed "to put some personal ceiling under this vast impersonal sky of grief."

But vaudeville was back and in full swing. Over the first six months of 1942, the two most popular stage productions in the United States were *Keep 'Em Laughing*—a hectic musical comedy revue featuring comedian Zero Mostel, a troupe of xylophonists, plenty of pretty girls, plus "unquestionably the best trained-dog act in the history of the theatre"—and *Priorities of 1942*, a similar song-and-very-old-joke variety show. "Vaudeville never died; it was in a dim-out," declared veteran comic Ed Wynn. "Whenever hysteria or fear are close, laughter comes easily."

Across the nation, nightclubs were jammed to capacity nearly every evening. The fun was sometimes a bit more frantic than usual, perhaps due to audiences filled with soldiers and sailors on leave. "There still seems to be plenty of money in circulation," observed Lucius Beebe, "and the soldiery, knowing that it may not be of any use to them tomorrow, is anxious to dispose of what they have at hand." Fights broke out more frequently, even in the better nightspots, although Beebe thought that civilian patrons appeared less boisterous than before the war. "The gloomy implications of disaster have begun to cast their shadows over the last citadels of mirth," he wrote. "Not military disaster, but the disaster of the times." To escape the constant drone of news reports in hotel bars or taverns, more Americans took to drinking at home—"where, for a little bit," noted Beebe, "they don't have to listen to the radio and sense the implications of futility that are almost tangible in public places."

Increasingly the war invaded even the entertainment portions of radio schedules with dramas that one critic described as "well-meant, sometimes brilliant, but often talky, overdone, and unrealistic." War Department–sponsored soap operas such as *A Man and His Army* and *Chaplain Jim—U.S.A.* provided listeners with a hint of life in military training camps, at least according to Army censors. On Saturday nights, all four major networks and numerous independent stations carried *This Is War!*, a dramatic anthology produced by the Office of Facts and Figures which debuted with a warning that "what we say tonight has to do with blood and with bone and with anger." Classic literature was in; one of the more surprising hits of the spring was a weekday show in which Pulitzer Prize–winning poet Mark Van Doren read aloud Nathaniel Hawthorne's

*The Scarlet Letter*, fifteen minutes at a time. ("Hawthorne would hardly know what to make of it," mused Van Doren.) Radio comedians made feeble jokes about the Japanese, but seldom mentioned Nazis. And sponsors annoyed just about everyone by returning to their practice of intermingling the exploitation of their products with sobering news reports from the war.

Americans *still* lacked a "decent, catchy song" written for the war, notwithstanding such well-intentioned if eccentric efforts as "Buckle Down Buck Private" and "Little Bo Peep Has Lost Her Jeep." (One of the most popular songs associated with the war, "Don't Sit Under the Apple Tree (with Anyone Else but Me)"—a major hit in the summer of 1942—was actually a slightly revised version of a song written for a musical several years earlier.) "For some reason this war, far from inspiring the composers, seems to have struck them almost dumb," observed the *Baltimore Sun* in May. "One of the difficulties," explained songwriter Louis Alter, "is that in this war we have no particular front. It is a 'total' war and this demands a 'total' song. How are you going to write a 'total' song? You can't do it just by calling it 'Everywhere.'" Even Cole Porter, increasingly prone to depression, found himself unable to make any meaningful contribution to the war effort, spending his time instead composing uninspired melodies for mediocre Hollywood and Broadway productions.

In New York, left-wing folksinger Woody Guthrie was busy dashing off his own brand of war songs, typically with anti-fascist, pro-labor, and anti-imperialist themes that emphasized "the natural fellowship between the singing constituencies of Roosevelt and Stalin." One of his less radical tunes reminded Americans of the dangers of U-boats off the East Coast: "If a blackout comes to the old home town, / Sally, won't you pull your curtains down. / If a shade goes up, then a ship goes down."

Too often Americans kept their shades up, and merchant ships went down off the eastern seaboard at a devastating pace. Springtime brought more frequent submarine attacks in American waters. Residents of coastal towns from Florida to Maine awakened in the night to the sound of explosions and the sight of ships afire at sea. Sometimes news of an attack brought crowds of sightseers to the beach; sometimes bystanders volunteered to take rowboats into the ocean to look for survivors. The precise number and identity of American and Allied ships torpedoed (nearly two hundred by the end of April) and sailors and passengers killed (more than four thousand) were still hidden behind Navy censorship; Archibald MacLeish's confidential estimate was that naval officials remained "about fifty ships behind in announcing sinkings of freighters." Discussions with naval experts left Walter Lippmann shocked at "the ghastly and humiliating things" which were taking place. "There is no use building ships in sixty days for the Germans to sink in twelve minutes," wrote Lippmann. "There's no use building ships without providing the means to protect them."

Traveling across Florida, Alistair Cooke met the owner of a small fleet of tankers that carried oil from the Gulf Coast to New Jersey. "He confesses that since the war began he has been a chronic insomniac," noted Cooke, "waking with a start and wondering 'how many boats I lost last night.'" After starting 1942 with twenty ships, the oilman's fleet was down to twelve by spring. "By the time I git to New Orleans," he told Cooke, "I reckon I'll have eight or nine maybe." Recruiting and retaining crews grew increasingly difficult; even though sailors often were not told where the ships were going, the 100 percent bonuses promised at the hiring halls made it uncomfortably clear. "Might just as well advertise for suicides," the oilman confessed. "Fifty percent of a crew you pick up in Galveston or New Orleans either quit when they reach New Jersey, and take a train home, or they finish the round trip and go look for a job in a shipyard. Can you blame 'em? Ev'y night I wait for a phone call f'om New Jersey. They don't stand a chance."

Despite the horrific toll, authorities were slow to enforce dimout regulations along the Atlantic coast, and civilians proved even more reluctant to obey them. In the early spring, state and local officials from Florida to New York ordered "all potentially dangerous lighting" extinguished or darkened. Compliance was spotty at best. A sailor on a merchant ship passing a New Jersey beach resort town noted that "the lights were like Coney Island. It was lit up like daylight all along the beach." Looking from the ocean toward the Manhattan skyline during a dimout test, a Navy observer declared that "the glare from the city lights was terrific"; another eyewitness claimed that Times Square glowed "like a gigantic furnace."

On April 30, Secretary Stimson announced that since civilian-supervised dimouts had failed, the Army would assume responsibility for darkening the seaboard. New and tougher regulations covered the coast all the way up to Canada. Less than three weeks later, frustrated military authorities issued even stricter regulations—New York City remained a "murderous mound of light"—and formally proclaimed the entire East Coast a military zone to make it easier to enforce the rules. By that time the Navy had implemented an ad hoc convoy system to escort merchant ships up the coast, albeit with limited success at first. U-boat commanders barely slackened their pace, and struck targets even farther afield in the St. Lawrence River and the Gulf of Mexico (where fifteen ships were sunk in May alone), venturing within two miles of the mouth of the Mississippi River. "We are suffering a major defeat. . . . The Navy has failed and those who have even a partial inside picture know it," wrote Ray Clapper in late May. "The time may be close at hand when the Administration will be called to sharp accounting for the poor showing in meeting the submarine menace on our Eastern Coasts."

Americans were well aware of the carnage at sea. "German submarines have been sinking our merchant ships at an appalling rate," charged the *New York Times* on June 6. "We have lost 250 to 300 of them since mid-January, which is faster than we can build them." And yet dimout inspections consistently revealed widespread and "flagrant violations" of Army regulations. "Boston still hasn't completely grasped the meaning of 'dimout,'" charged a high-ranking civilian defense official in late June, adding that store owners were often the most egregious offenders: "These fellows are great ones to salute the boys in the service. They'd do a much better job of saluting if they'd obey the regulations and dim these lights." One military observer deemed the sky glow along the New England shore "at least four or five times greater than it should be for safety." Novelist Booth Tarkington identified stretches of U.S. Route 1 just outside his home in Kennebunkport, Maine, as "good for Hitler" because careless automobile drivers refused to dim their headlights. Throughout the New York metropolitan area, Army observers reported that "whole communities, as if unaware even now of the dim-out regulations, were found ablaze with light." One reporter discovered "a good many violations, some of them deliberate" along Broadway; in Brooklyn, the only truly dark spots were graveyards.

As the loss of tankers drained petroleum stocks in the East, the Roosevelt administration further curtailed deliveries of gasoline to service stations in portions of seventeen eastern states—from Maine to Florida, plus West Virginia and the District of Columbia. Beginning April 16, filling stations in that area received only two-thirds of their usual supply; a few weeks later, deliveries were cut to half. Defending the reductions, an administration spokesman declared that "it is unthinkable that [sailors] be asked to take the risk of going down on a burning ship in order that somebody may have gasoline to go to a bridge party or the ball game."

To obtain the maximum war benefit from the depleted supplies, OPA officials devised an emergency gasoline-rationing system which went into effect on May 15. Automobile owners were classified according to their value to the war program: motorists who did not require their car for business or commuting received "A" cards, which provided minimal gasoline supplies; war workers who drove to work could apply for more generous "B" cards, but only if public transportation and car pools were unavailable (there were three levels of B cards, depending on commuting distance); and doctors, police, ministers, and others essential to the public welfare received "X" cards and unlimited gasoline. Trucks, buses, commercial vehicles, and taxis were exempt.

Since the average American motorist in 1941 had used nearly thirteen gallons of gas a week (and often spent twenty-five gallons per day on long trips), it came as a shock when Leon Henderson announced on May 8 that an A cardholder would be permitted to purchase only three gallons each week—enough to travel thirty-six miles in city driving conditions, or forty-five miles in the country. Henderson's gratuitous comment that the American "pleasure driver" was "getting a damn sight more than he's entitled to in view of the situation" did nothing to ease the blow; "the American public cannot be damned into cooperation," snapped the head of one motorists' rights organization. To *Time* magazine, it looked as if Americans were at last learning "the truth about total war: no matter how bad the experts say things are going to be, they turn out worse."

As with sugar rationing, registration for gasoline-rationing cards depended upon the honor system: to obtain more than an A card, automobile owners swore that they used their cars for war work, and clerks accepted their word. ("This is a test," mused the *New York Times*, "of self-denial and patriotism.") Unlike sugar, however, the gas-rationing system made distinctions among applicants, and OPA officials discovered that an unexpectedly large number of Americans were willing to exaggerate or blatantly lie to obtain more fuel. "The public immorality that went with bootlegging came back to the United States, in one swift week," observed *Time*. "The demand for X cards or the B classification was so tremendous that 'chiseling' was very apparent," agreed the *Wall Street Journal*. Although federal authorities had predicted that 33 to 40 percent of motorists would voluntarily apply for less generous A cards, *Newsweek* pointed out that "only about 25 per cent did, and in some sections only about 10 per cent."

"If we are unwilling to make a little sacrifice like this," asked one Philadelphia driver plaintively, "how can we expect to win the war?" Numerous rationing boards ran out of B and X cards long before registration was complete. Doctors asked for X cards for their wives, and dentists claimed they needed extra gas for house calls. Sometimes motorists listed their station wagons as ambulances or trucks. "By far the majority think they aren't getting enough and try to convince us that they have some special mission which we should consider," reported one official in Baltimore, where police were summoned to several registration sites "because of the disorderly manner in which a great many applicants acted." New Jersey authorities admitted they were "scandalized at the number of applications for B and X cards." In suburban Westchester County, the "unwarranted demand" for X cards struck one local official as "the most disgraceful thing I have heard of in this war or any other war. . . . St. Peter closed the gates on many Westchester motorists today." Albany's defense council directed police to investigate everyone who received an X card, and the United States attorney in Boston promised to prosecute "100 per cent" every gas chiseler he found. Rationing boards in five southeastern states ran out of B cards altogether, while a local official in Springfield, Massachusetts, declared flatly that "rationing is producing a nation of liars."

"Apparently there wasn't as good an education campaign done in this as there was done on sugar rationing," concluded New Jersey's deputy rationing administrator, although the *New York Times* looked deeper and discerned "increasing indications of public resentment against the rationing system and alleged 'discrimination' against the coastal area." Congressmen proceeded to exacerbate the situation by applying en masse for

X cards. OPA authorities claimed that legislators deserved only as much gas as they required to get to Capitol Hill and back—Leon Henderson requested only an A card for the 1935 Lincoln he drove three miles to work each day, and Donald Nelson and Eleanor Roosevelt also applied for A cards—but rationing boards caved in and provided more than 250 senators and representatives (and sometimes their secretaries) with unlimited supplies of gasoline.

"Congress has bungled another opportunity to lead the way toward essential wartime adjustments," declared the *Washington Post*, while the *New York World-Telegram* charged that "very wrong, very foolish, very selfish" congressmen "have earned the contempt of the people by grabbing special privileges—by refusing to accept for themselves the full burden of the sacrifices and hardships which they vote upon the citizens whose faithful representatives and servants they are supposed to be." The *Detroit Free Press* accused congressmen of displaying "a stupidity that is appalling" and urged voters to "change that 'X' to 'Ex.'" Ray Clapper concurred. Dismayed by Congress's "selfish and destructive conduct," Clapper predicted that legislators "are being so stupid in this that a number of them are apt to pay for it dearly at the hands of indignant voters."

A few members of the House bowed to the public outcry and traded down to B cards. "This war can't be won while anyone rolls merrily down our highways on balloon tires, with full gas tanks and an American flag on the radiator cap," proclaimed a repentant Republican lawmaker from Indiana. But Senate majority leader Alben Barkley obdurately insisted that "I am going to take whatever I am entitled to without apology," and California's Representative Leland Ford snapped that it was time Congress demonstrated that "we're not going to take orders from the bureaucrats downtown."

It was the second time since Pearl Harbor that congressmen had invited widespread popular scorn; over the winter, the House and Senate had interrupted their wartime deliberations to vote themselves generous pensions, a masterstroke of poor timing as thousands of young men were volunteering for military service. A Gallup poll found that 84 percent of Americans opposed the pension measure. "As an example of pure boneheadedness," announced one disgusted Michigan voter, "this pension for congressmen should occupy a niche in the hall of fame." From every section of the country, Americans had dispatched facetious "Bundles for Congress" to their "war-stricken" legislators on Capitol Hill—packages of old clothes, moth-eaten nightcaps, false teeth, used razor blades, artificial limbs, and soothing syrup—ostensibly to ease their representatives' anxieties of an impoverished retirement. "Don't worry about the war and taxes," read an accompanying card. "Get that pension—forget the Axis."

After enduring "the bitterest criticism of Congress in years," both House and Senate hastily reversed their pension votes. But when the public assailed their X cards with equal vehemence, numerous legislators concluded that democracy itself (as personified by themselves) was under siege. Speaker Sam Rayburn of Texas claimed that the criticism was part of "a studied effort to destroy [the] faith and confidence of the American people in their elected representatives," and Representative F. Edward Hébert of Louisiana warned that "our whole system of government is going to collapse" unless authorities prevented newspapers from "taking cracks such as this at Congress." Senator John Bankhead of Alabama wondered aloud if the Justice Department might wish to investigate the "seditious conduct" of "newspaper columnists and other writers" who criticized the legislative branch.

Ray Clapper was quite certain that Congress needed no outside help to sabotage itself. "As a force in our Government," noted Clapper, "Congress is sliding downhill. It is endangered not by the executive branch but by its own shallow incompetency. . . . Congress has remained a collection of two-cent politicians who could serve well enough in simpler days. But the ignorance and provincialism of Congress render it incapable of meeting the needs of modern government. . . . What you hear in Congress," Clapper concluded, "is 99 per cent tripe, ignorance and demagogery and not to be relied upon." Of all the Congresses in American history, concluded *Time*, "none had ever been held in lower esteem than the 77th."

Although the OPA initially intended to keep local rationing boards' rulings confidential, popular resentment toward alleged "chiseling" by neighbors (and congressmen) convinced Roosevelt and Henderson to open all rationing records to public inspection. Besides exposing the names of X and B card holders, OPA authorities warned that they would investigate gas-ration application forms for false statements—penalties included confiscation of ration cards, along with fines up to ten thousand dollars and imprisonment for ten years. Prompted by Henderson's assurance that anyone who got unwarranted privileges "through a mistake or misunderstanding of the regulations" could exchange his or her card with no questions asked, thousands of automobile owners rushed to their rationing boards (including 2,500 in New York City in one twenty-four-hour period) to obtain less generous classifications.

In the Philadelphia area, recalcitrant motorists received additional encouragement to trade in their X or B cards when state police and OPA inspectors set up roadblocks on May 17 on two Delaware River bridges and began asking drivers (except for A card holders) for their name, address, place of business, commuting distance, and the purpose and destination of their journey, to make sure they were not using their extra gas quota for a weekend at the seashore. Despite criticism of "Gestapo" law-enforcement tactics, the ploy persuaded more than six thousand local motorists to exchange their cards within forty-eight hours.

It made little difference at the start. In the week before rationing began, so many drivers had filled their gas tanks to the brim—along with five-gallon cans, ten-gallon drums, cider jugs, and an occasional empty milk bottle—that service stations from Maine to Florida were already drained when restrictions went into effect. Others limited sales to regular customers (which was illegal) but even then dispensed only three or four gallons at a time. Cars that ran dry were abandoned on city streets and highway shoulders.

Anyone who could subtract knew that shortages in the East would continue for the foreseeable future. Essential daily demand still easily outpaced incoming supplies from railroad tank cars, pipelines, and the occasional tanker, and the OPA's ration allotments had been based on assumptions that motorists and station owners would not cheat; any chiseling, bootlegging, or favoritism increased the drain from a finite supply of gasoline. "The privileged ones may have cards entitling them to fill up the tank, but they are going to have trouble getting gas anyway because the filling stations are going to be short," warned Ray Clapper. "The average family might as well plan on the most restricted use of its car until after the Axis is licked."

———

President Roosevelt wanted a new name for the war. He told reporters at a press conference in April that he was dissatisfied with both "World War II" and "the Second World War" because they lacked zip, and neither adequately conveyed his view of the conflict's primary theme: the preservation of democracy and the independence of smaller nations. So Roosevelt asked journalists to invite readers to submit their ideas in a sort of popular contest—"as though," grumbled the *Washington Post*, "the war were some kind of soap or breakfast food."

Suggestions poured into newspaper offices and the White House. Most were sincere but lacked flair and were dismissed as "sentimental slush": "The People's War," "The War For Peace," "The Righteous War," and "The Free-Man War." Others struck a slightly edgier tone, such as "The Devil's War," "The Bastards' War," "The Stooge War," and "War-To-End-Wars, Jr." Unmoved by the public's offerings, the president himself subsequently proposed "The Survival War" because "it comes pretty close to being the survival of our civilization, the survival of democracy, the survival of a hemisphere." The public shrugged; Roosevelt's suggestion, reported the *New York Times*, "met a frosty silence." As one New Jersey reader of the *Wall Street Journal* pointed out, "'survival' is a negative term, denoting a defensive attitude. It is not in tune with the American spirit."

"Slogans are not enough, the Four Freedoms are not enough, production is not enough, a war of attrition is not enough, fleets of bombers are not enough," insisted literary critic Clifton Fadiman. "Only offense will win this war for the United Nations, as defense so far has lost it for them." Fadiman's conclusion echoed the arguments of one of the best-selling books in the United States in the early summer of 1942—*Defense Will Not Win the War*, by Lieutenant Colonel William F. Kernan—as well as the thoughts of General George Marshall ("The time has now come when we must proceed with the business of carrying the war to the enemy") and Wendell Willkie. "We should begin to think in terms of attack, not of retreat," proclaimed Willkie. "We should begin to act in terms of striking, not blocking."

On April 18, sixteen American B-25 bombers led by Colonel James Doolittle took off from an aircraft carrier about 750 miles east of Japan and struck targets in Tokyo, Yokohama, Osaka, Nagoya, and Kobe. All of the planes survived the mission, though each subsequently crash-landed—fifteen in China, and one in the Soviet Union near Vladivostok. Out of eighty crew members, seventy-two survived and eventually made their way back to the United States. Americans first learned of the raid from Japanese news sources whose reports were carried by U.S. newspapers; for nearly a month, American military authorities refused to confirm or deny the mission to avoid disclosing information they deemed secret, although both Japanese and domestic news accounts accurately guessed within forty-eight hours that the planes had been launched by carrier and landed somewhere in China.

Even unofficial accounts of the raid—which disingenuously gave the impression that all of the crews had returned home safely—raised American morale. "Morally and psychologically," wrote military analyst Hanson Baldwin, "it has uplifted our hearts"; on Wall Street, stock prices rose for the first time in nearly two weeks. Civilian defense officials warned, however, that the Tokyo raid would increase the likelihood of Axis retaliatory bombings of American cities. "If we can do it," announced New York City's police commissioner, "they can do it, too." (They did not; instead, the Japanese army punished Chinese civilians for sheltering the American fliers.) And numerous commentators reminded Americans that the Doolittle mission, however emotionally gratifying, was only a small step toward reversing the tide in the Pacific. "Air attacks of greater power and persistence," noted the *Boston Globe*, "will be needed before there is any real diminution of Japan's strength."

Confirmation arrived on May 6, with the surrender of the American-Filipino garrison on Corregidor, whose position had been untenable since the fall of Bataan, and really since December 7. Americans applauded the heroic stand of the fifteen thousand men and women on the island (fewer than four thousand of whom were trained combat troops), but the result of the struggle reminded many of Churchill's observation following Dunkirk—that "wars are not won by evacuations." The loss of the fortress and surrounding islands left Japan in possession of Manila Bay's harbor and airfields and nearly the entire Philippine archipelago. "The war in the Pacific," wrote *Baltimore Sun* correspondent Mark Watson, "stretches further and further into the future."

At the same time, American and Japanese naval and air forces were locked in a five-day battle in the Coral Sea, touched off by Japan's attempt to obtain a launching pad for a potential invasion of Australia. The two fleets never came within sight of each other; the combat consisted entirely of carrier-based aircraft fighting one another and bombing enemy vessels. By the time the Japanese invasion force retreated on May 9, the United States had suffered heavier losses in ships, but Japan had lost more men and aircraft. Most important, the Japanese navy had endured its first setback of the war.

Initially the American military communiqués wildly overstated Japanese losses in the Coral Sea, leaving some unsuspecting civilians convinced that the war in the Pacific was essentially over. "With the Americans the confident winners of the first round in the Coral Sea," crowed *Newsweek* at the end of May, "there was hope for victory, perhaps in 1942." *Time* declared that "the Jap had taken a shattering defeat," sparking a surge of optimism across the United States: "Throughout the land, the belief was strong now that the war was not only being won but would end soon."

Others knew better. "As America approaches the seventh month of war, a net judgment would say there is no basis for hope of anything other than a long war and a hard one," wrote Mark Sullivan. "In the name of their lives and freedom, don't keep on telling our people how good we are with unjustified emphasis in stories and misleading headlines," implored war correspondent Nat Floyd, who had spent several months with American troops on Bataan. "The effect of such publicity," charged Walter Lippmann, "is to give the people a false sense of security, and to promote complacency and inertia in the face of a danger which is becoming so acute that it may mean, if not defeat then an unduly long and bloody and costly struggle."

Traveling through western Illinois in June, historian Allan Nevins reported a lingering mood of "apathy that hangs like a blanket of fog over many communities." One local draft board chairman confessed to Nevins that "it is hard to get most people really waked up. People will admit that war was forced on us by a treacherous attack. They admit that it has to be fought through to victory. But they don't realize that the danger is real and immediate; they want somebody else to do the fighting."

"I am afraid that too many Americans are still deceiving themselves about the job ahead," observed U.S. Supreme Court justice William O. Douglas, who felt that the public was preparing "for a 200-yard dash when a grueling mile race lies ahead." Their expectations stemmed largely from the conviction—held by nearly all Americans—that the nation's vast industrial potential ultimately would prove decisive, virtually by default.

For nearly seven months after Pearl Harbor, the Roosevelt administration hid arms-production statistics from the public, explaining that the disclosure of specific figures would provide valuable information to the Axis. Throughout the winter and spring, however, government spokesmen provided reassuring statements about the progress of the nation's conversion to war production—often by comparing output favorably to the slower pre–Pearl Harbor pace of 1941, or overusing adjectives such as "vast," "huge," "enormous," "tremendous," "magnificent," or "immense"— while escorting journalists on carefully managed public relations tours of war plants. ("Everywhere the story was monotonously but encouragingly the same: production ahead of schedule and mounting rapidly," responded one magazine obligingly.)

In April, Donald Nelson announced that the United States was "over the hump on war production," and Vice President Wallace assured Americans that by late summer, the United States would be producing "more war materiel than any nation in the history of the world." The following month, Roosevelt claimed that American shipyards were performing a "near-miracle" by increasing the nation's shipbuilding capacity "more than 500 per cent." At the University of Missouri in early June, Nelson told his audience that "we have found that our total production of war goods is higher than we had any reason to suppose it could be." Later that month, Roosevelt finally provided the program's first set of detailed numbers when he reported May's production figures: nearly 4,000 planes, more than 1,500 tanks, slightly fewer than 2,000 artillery and anti-tank guns, and over 50,000 machine guns.

By August, the United States was outproducing Britain. The automobile industry had converted more rapidly than expected, and a host of innovations on war plant assembly lines cut production time and boosted output. But behind the administration's reports replete with "chocolate-covered facts" (as labor leader Walter Reuther described them) lay conflicts, confusion, and a damaging lack of coordination. If blunders along the way were, perhaps, inevitable, World War I production czar Bernard Baruch insisted that "these trials and errors were many—too many." From his vantage point as the president's top industrial troubleshooter, Baruch subsequently concluded that "our failure to mobilize properly, and in time, cost us billions of dollars. But infinitely more important, it added months to the conflict and names to the casualty lists."

Shortages of raw materials plagued the mobilization program from the start, partly because so many resources had been consumed by the civilian production boom in 1941, but also because competing war plants scrambled to stockpile scarce materials in the aftermath of Pearl Harbor, to ensure that they would have enough supplies to fulfill future arms contracts. Army and Navy procurement officers abetted this practice by issuing "blanket priorities" that enabled manufacturers to jump to the front of the waiting line for critical resources; the result was "unbalanced and useless stockpiles" lodged in factories for months. Had WPB officials possessed timely information on each firm's inventories, they might have transferred hoarded materials to the plants that most urgently required them—but they seldom did. Steel plate for merchant ships was in especially short supply, keeping the delivery of new ships behind schedule throughout the spring and into the summer. Copper, too, was disturbingly scarce, although Nelson suggested communities could help alleviate the shortfall by melting down statues, bronze bank doors, brass nameplates, and ashtrays.

Shipyards reported rising rates of absenteeism, as much as 10 to 15 percent at some yards; by August, Assistant Secretary of the Navy Ralph Bard admitted that that problem was reaching "dangerous proportions." There were charges of deliberate slowdowns as well. "There's too damned much loafing going on in the shipyards right now," charged Admiral Emory Land, chairman of the U.S. Maritime Commission, which oversaw merchant ship construction. After meeting with shipyard workers in San Francisco, Ernie Pyle reported that "ships could be built a lot faster than they are. They say you can't put your finger on it, but things just don't seem to move as fast as they ought to." One worker in a Pacific coast shipyard told a reporter that delays seemed to be built into the prevailing system of cost-plus contracts, whereby the government compensated firms' production costs and guaranteed a percentage profit. "Money seems to be the least of anyone's worries—just like water coming out of a hydrant," he said. "The more errors, the more delays, the more overtime, the more profit, the more wages—the more for everybody except the Navy."

Since the leadership of both the AFL and the CIO had pledged not to call strikes for the duration, actual work stoppages in war plants were infrequent and limited to wildcat strikes—walkouts staged by local unions without authorization from above. Still, the number of man-days lost to strikes in war industries jumped from 46,000 in January 1942 to 255,000 in June. Most were minor disputes over wages, union membership, or payment of union dues, and quickly resolved. Yet the trend troubled public opinion, which remained solidly opposed to strikes in war industries; one Gallup poll found that 86 percent of Americans felt the government should ban strikes in defense plants for the duration.

"One thing that continually amazes me about this regimented wartime life is the matter of strikes," confessed E. B. White to a friend. "We take for granted that no man's life is his own, any more—that is, the army can give him the nod and he has to leave home and family and put on a uniform. . . . But another guy, in an airplane factory, can lay down his tools for a day or a week and thumb his nose at the whole war in the name of organized labor. . . . Our whole life has, in a sense, been drafted, yet we still go on babying the unions." A *Fortune* survey revealed that more than two-thirds of Americans (including the policy-making body of the American Bar Association) favored drafting war workers who walked off their jobs. Five hundred residents of Marion, South Carolina, sent a telegram to Roosevelt condemning strikers as "traitors [who] should be dealt with as such," and one California Republican congressman suggested that if war industry workers struck, they should be placed in concentration camps or in front of a firing squad.

Some strikes stemmed from racial hatred. On June 2, Chrysler transferred twenty African American workers into its Dodge truck plant in Detroit. About seven hundred white employees first threatened to throw them out, then staged a protest that shut down the factory for the rest of the day. "The local will have to accept the Negroes," insisted a union official. "The U.A.W. and C.I.O. policy calls for equal treatment of Negroes, and so does the American Constitution." Two weeks later, the appearance of eight black machinists at the nearby Hudson Naval Ordnance Arsenal led several thousand white workers to lay down their tools. The walkout ended only after the UAW threatened to pull the local's charter, and Secretary of the Navy Frank Knox promised to ban the strikers—whom he called "disloyal"—from employment in other war plants for the rest of the war.

By summer, most war workers were spending between forty-five and fifty hours a week on the job, prompting an ongoing debate over whether they should continue to earn overtime pay during a war emergency for every hour over forty, as required by federal law. (The standard forty-hour workweek was a relatively recent innovation, a product of the Fair Labor Standards Act of 1938.) Reluctant to alienate his labor base, Roosevelt insisted that workers deserved their extra pay—typically time and a half—and Donald Nelson concurred. Reopening the question of overtime pay, Nelson warned, would likely provoke union demands for higher wages for regular time, and lead to strikes or slowdowns that would wreak havoc on production schedules. Abolishing the forty-hour week, Nelson assured Congress, "wouldn't gain one additional hour of work in our war plants."

Republicans and conservative Democrats disagreed, as did most voters: a Gallup poll showed that a majority of Americans favored a forty-eight-hour-week, although some mistakenly thought the "forty-hour week" meant that employees were prohibited from working longer hours. As one observer explained, overtime pay in war plants was "a good thing that looks bad compared to the sacrifices made by the men in the armed forces." Midwestern farmers charged the Roosevelt administration with "pampering" labor and warned that they had no intention of putting their wives to work driving tractors "to produce cheap food for men working 40 hours a week, with time-and-a-half for overtime." A grand jury in Fulton County, Georgia, went so far as to return "special presentments" against the forty-hour week in war industries, terming it "a betrayal of our men on the firing line."

But management in the nation's largest war-industry plants seldom objected to overtime pay. In fact, companies often used promises of extensive overtime—along with wage increases, bonuses, and liquor parties—to recruit skilled workers from other firms. The practice was known as labor piracy, and by summer it was so rampant that a War Manpower

Commission spokesman compared it to the "shanghaiing of ships' crews on the Barbary Coast in the last century." WMC officials complained that incessant job-jumping disrupted production schedules, destabilized wage scales, and created housing crises around the highest-paying war plants. Numerous firms exacerbated the problem by hoarding skilled workers (like raw materials) for future contracts; by mid-1942, 384 out of 700 war contractors acknowledged that they had been forced to curtail production due to skilled-labor shortages.

Nevertheless, government officials constantly bombarded war workers with pleas to step up the pace of production. Holidays vanished; Memorial Day tributes consisted of regular shifts on the assembly line to turn out more weapons. Lunch breaks disappeared as factories adopted "work-while-you-eat" plans. In one bomb-production plant in Pennsylvania, workers brought hot dogs and roasted them over still-warm bombs fresh off the assembly line. ("It makes a good meal instead of the cold sandwiches," swore one bomb spinner, "and it don't take no time at all to roast a dog over one of them bombs.")

Motivational posters ("The Man Who Relaxes Is Helping The Axis") adorned factory walls, along with lurid images of a cartoon character known as "the Tokio Kid": a Japanese face with an exaggerated grin, an apelike brow, pointed ears, and claws and huge teeth that grew sharper and longer as the war went on. (There were no corresponding stereotypical German or Italian characters.) Since British factories had discovered that music played through loudspeakers proved therapeutic, relieving stress and raising output by about 10 percent, American war plants hired live bands to serenade their workers, or piped in recorded songs, usually current tunes by Glenn Miller, Bing Crosby, Kay Kyser, or Artie Shaw. (Classical music generally met with jeers.)

But haste invited accidents. "Workers in munitions factories will be more reckless than in peacetime," predicted the Metropolitan Life Insurance Company's chief statistician, "and there will be a rise in industrial accidents, [and] nervous and mental diseases will increase." In the first six months of 1942, more than 4,300 workers in twenty-three states were killed in industrial accidents, an increase of 13 percent over the same period in 1941, and far above 1940's total. Nationwide, the Department of Labor estimated that more than 110 million man-days of work had been lost to fatal or disabling accidents (most of them avoidable) on the job since Pearl Harbor—enough to build ten thousand medium bombers or fifteen battleships. "No nation, fighting with its back to the wall, can afford to allow this appalling waste of life and productivity to continue," warned a Labor Department spokesman. "There is no excuse for such a record," agreed the *New York Times*. "In time of war, when every man-hour saved, when every scrap of material salvaged, when every moment of production gained weighs in the scales, it is little short of criminal."

Illness, too, took its toll, costing war plants up to 24 million man-hours of work each month. Fatigue increasingly played a role, as did poor nutrition, despite the ubiquitous healthy-meal advice to housewives. More spectacular was the rise of what one observer termed "the pernicious red-light districts that have grown up in mushrooming industrial communities." Surgeon General Parran testified to Congress that highly organized vice rings were operating around war boomtowns from Seattle and Tacoma to Houston and New Orleans, and military authorities complained of "a huge increase in prostitution" in New York City, especially around the Brooklyn Navy Yard. In Fayetteville, North Carolina, the population of prostitutes reportedly had increased from two hundred to more than four thousand.

Precise statistics were difficult to come by; as Alistair Cooke discovered when he arrived in Jacksonville, Florida, communities were reluctant to acknowledge the existence of prostitutes when they occupied apartments and hotels in respectable areas "whose morals had never been formerly called into question." Yet the rate of infection clearly was rising so rapidly—especially in the South—that some state health departments established special venereal disease task forces, aided by grants from the U.S. Public Health Service. (There was also evidence that some men deliberately contracted gonorrhea to avoid the draft, a dodge that ended when the Army began inducting them anyway and then treating the illness.)

After President Roosevelt called for a crackdown to safeguard the "total physical and moral fitness" of war workers, local jails grew so overcrowded with prostitutes with venereal disease that officials put out urgent appeals to federal authorities to take them off their hands. In August, the Office of Defense Health and Welfare Services agreed to open more than twenty-five abandoned Civilian Conservation Corps camps, to serve as detention centers and quarantine hospitals until the women—between one hundred and three hundred per camp—could be cured.

Reports of widespread prostitution seemed to fit the popular image of life in a war boomtown, with factory workers flush with cash and ready to spend it on a good time. Millions of working-class Americans were, in fact, earning more than a subsistence income for the first time in their lives. Newspaper and magazine articles told of factory jobs paying three hundred dollars a month; of women workers from Detroit on buying sprees at exclusive fashion shows at Saks Fifth Avenue; of champagne sales soaring among shipyard employees in Portland, Oregon; of long lines at Chicago bars and strip joints, and jewelry sales up 25 percent over 1941. In downtown Seattle—where an influx of nearly sixty thousand war workers had swelled the population by 20 percent—theaters and restaurants were jammed, slot machines did a land-office business, and arrests for drunkenness in the first six months of 1942 were already twice the total for the previous year. *Time*'s correspondent in Louisville reported that local residents "have more of everything and they are getting more every day," armed with the attitude that "'I'm going to get mine while the getting is good.'" And the migration of a hundred thousand aircraft factory workers to the San Diego area had turned a quiet resort refuge into "a real boom town" which boasted that "every night is Saturday night"—except Saturday night itself, which became "the night before Christmas."

"Never so much money in town," said an attorney in one Connecticut community that boasted a thriving aircraft plant. "Never such buying, never such packed movies. We even got a night club built onto one of our diners! And the town's ruined. The boom's ruining it. The tax rate's going up and the municipal services are going down. Too many transient kids to educate, too many transient fires to put out, too much transient garbage to collect." As in other war boomtowns, housing was growing increasingly scarce. Workers were wedged into "guest homes"—old houses purchased by speculators and divided into as many flats as possible. One guest home included a pair of girls sleeping on cots in the parlor; a husband, wife, and child in the library; five bedrooms with a dozen cots on the second floor; a single bathroom; and a long third-floor room with six cots for twelve or fifteen men—"hot beds," where men took turns sleeping in eight-hour shifts (no meals provided).

Despite Roosevelt's conviction that "more than ever in our history, we need houses to help win the war," the commissioner of the Federal Housing Administration admitted in May that "we are woefully behind schedule in providing for the great army of migrating workers," primarily due to a lack of construction materials. A consultant for the War Manpower Commission testified in June that "it is not only discouraging, but costly, when men and women are recruited and trained for vital war work and sent to plants where they are needed, only to find there is insufficient housing to meet their needs." In the Baltimore area, defense housing construction was running "far behind schedule and far behind needs." The New York State commissioner of housing declared that "acute" housing shortages plagued over forty war industry centers in the state: "Every room in every house that can shelter a war worker has become vitally necessary." Seattle stuffed newcomers into "boats, trailers, garages, chicken coops, attics, and basements," while workers at the Brooklyn Navy Yard rented space in a group of thirteen-story "tenement barracks" that blighted the land, according to one critic, "as badly as any tenement project of the past."

After visiting Alabama, a witness told a congressional committee that "it's a crime the way those employed in shipyards near Mobile have to live." In the Norfolk-Portsmouth (Virginia) area, one hundred trailer camps provided shelter for seven thousand families. Those were the lucky ones; other workers slept in their cars, or paid boardinghouses on a nightly basis for the privilege of sleeping in armchairs. Numerous black workers' families in Norfolk lived in unsafe and unsanitary one-room dwellings, most lacking indoor baths, and hot beds in the black sections of town often accommodated four workers per day. A reporter visiting the city concluded that "housing is not a problem, it's an impossibility." And so each month at the Navy yard in nearby Hampton Roads, six hundred workers quit "because they can find no place to live."

No city, however, surpassed Detroit, where CIO officials formally protested to the Detroit Housing Commission against the "vicious and unsanitary" housing conditions for workers. "Every day more and more workers are compelled to move into trailer camps or 'shack towns,'" reported the *New York Times*, "and public health experts have warned that disease, vice and slack morale will become rampant if relief is not provided quickly." In one month, Ford hired 2,900 new workers, only to lose 3,100—many of whom quit in frustration over housing conditions. "There is hardly a day," admitted a Ford vice president, "that we don't lose more than we hire." No one had yet determined how to transport workers efficiently to Ford's gigantic new bomber plant at Willow Run—twenty-five miles from Detroit, in an area almost wholly bereft of housing. Government officials ordered Ford to haul them in converted tractor-trailers formerly used to carry automobile assemblies, but company management flatly refused. "They're talking about taking piles of junk, hanging some sheet steel on them, and then claiming they have a bus," complained one high-ranking Ford executive. "Actually they would be regular cattle cars, not fit for human beings. They have no head room, they weave around on the highways, and quickly become filled with gas."

At the end of April, a thousand state troops aided by 300 state police and 450 city cops provided protection as fourteen African American defense workers' families finally moved into the Sojourner Truth Housing Project in downtown Detroit. Over the following weeks more black war workers moved in, and by June most of the guard had been withdrawn. But tensions remained high, and African American commitment to the war effort remained shaky. "It is exceedingly urgent that steps be taken with regard to this matter promptly," warned federal field personnel in Detroit. "Indications are that the morale situation among the Negroes is becoming increasingly worse. And if race riots were to break out in Detroit, the feeling of the Negro that 'if I must die for democracy, why not here?' would tend to spread farther over the country." Unless the president or a high-ranking administration official intervened soon, warned a team of federal investigators, "hell is going to be let loose in every Northern city where large numbers of immigrants and Negroes are in competition."

Americans were betting more money on sports than ever before. "People seem to be in a mood to gamble, which is understandable," wrote Detroit sports columnist Dale Stafford. "You'd be surprised to know how much is being bet on fights in Cleveland, New York, Chicago, and Boston," said one boxing promoter. "Everyone, it seems, has money and is willing to bet it on the outcome of a fight." Revenue from dog racing rose dramatically in Florida; and the opening-night crowd at the Wonderland Park dog track in Revere, Massachusetts, in early June easily broke the track's previous total for wagers.

Horse racing raked in the most cash. The *Wall Street Journal* called the spring and summer of 1942 "the golden era" of wagering on horses; as the New York Racing Commission explained, "Nothing takes a man's mind off Manila like betting two dollars on the wrong horse." Wagers at the spring meetings of Maryland's three major tracks—Bowie, Pimlico, and Havre de Grace—ran 25 percent above the previous year. "Taking a quick whirl through the stands at most racing plants any afternoon," observed a reporter for the *Baltimore Sun*, "you'll find any number of fellows fresh from their jobs at factories and plants out for an afternoon's punting." Although the crowd at the Kentucky Derby in early May featured fewer celebrities than usual, Churchill Downs' grandstand was packed with war-production workers who were attending the derby for the first time ("wide-eyed as at a county fair," thought one observer). Bettors wagered nearly $2 million on the race, while booths selling defense bonds at Churchill Downs reportedly took in less than $200 for the day.

One after another, horse-racing tracks across the country broke their own records for betting: Sportsman's Park and Arlington Park in Chicago, Delaware Park, Suffolk Downs, and Rhode Island's Narragansett Park, which took in the largest daily handle ever in New England. The spring meeting at Jamaica Race Course in New York City was "the most successful in the track's history," but it paled in comparison to the action at Belmont Park. On Saturday, May 30—"the gaudiest betting day in American racing history"—a record crowd of 51,903 at Belmont bet a single-day total of $2,176,071 on eight races, an all-time high for any track in the world. "New York," decided Bob Considine, "has gone horse crazy." By the time the Long Island track concluded its twenty-four-day meeting in early June, racing fans had wagered $27,773,297—surpassing the world's record for the largest average daily betting total.

Since most of the East Coast's popular tracks were located in or near major cities, racing enthusiasts took gasoline rationing in stride. Belmont Park set its single-day records several weeks after rationing began, and the betting craze continued during the summer at Aqueduct and Empire City. Decisions by the Office of Defense Transportation and the

Association of American Railroads in late May and early June to cancel most of the special buses and trains to "amusement places"—including racetracks—also failed to diminish either attendance or the public's appetite for wagering. On Opening Day at Garden State Park on July 18, over 31,600 fans showed up despite the absence of public transportation or taxis (cabdrivers were instructed to regard racetracks as "nonessential" trips).

Resorts and beaches in less accessible locations had a rougher time. Once rationing took effect, pleasure driving on eastern highways dropped between 40 and 50 percent. A *New Yorker* writer traveling through western Georgia, South Carolina, and North Carolina found that "motor traffic had virtually disappeared." Scores of filling stations in Georgia had already shut down. "It's you done this to us," snapped an attendant at a still-working gas pump. "You're going to close a lot of us, including probably me. You brought it on. You wouldn't save your tires. You made the government do it for you by this rationing." Other locals treated the journalist's car as a curiosity, waving and shouting as he passed. "The road stretched, sometimes for twenty-five miles, through what could have been a deserted world. It was an automobilist's paradise, a condition previously only dreamed about. Yet the emptiness of the highway was frightening and awesome as well as exciting. It was lonely. After a while we wanted more people, more traffic."

In New England, roads to Cape Cod were "practically abandoned," and out-of-state visitors grew scarce. ("Swim at uncrowded beaches," suggested an optimistic advertisement by the New England Council.) Reservation clerks at hotels in northern New Hampshire and the Adirondacks reported a wave of cancellations, especially from their customary guests from the Midwest. "A survey of the summer resort area in New England reveals a gloomy picture, due almost entirely to gasoline rationing," noted the *Wall Street Journal* in July. Maine—which relied on summer tourism to bring in enough money to tide the state through its long, brutal winters—was especially vulnerable; gasoline rationing, charged Maine's Republican Senator Wallace White, was ruining "a $100,000,000 tourist business."

Atlantic coastal resorts also were "fighting for their existence this year." Beyond gasoline and tire worries, the public was alarmed by rumors that the beaches were strung with barbed wire to fend off invaders, or littered with oil and corpses washed ashore from U-boat attacks; some were convinced that coastal towns had been placed under martial law. Local authorities dismissed the stories as "absolutely unfounded." "We are bathing as usual on our beaches," insisted the mayor of Ocean City, New Jersey, and an advertisement by the recently formed New Jersey Council promised that "there can be no BLACKOUTS of the beneficial rays of the seashore sun." ("And you won't want to miss the fascinating 'dim-out' along the shore, as night begins to drape itself softly around you.")

But bodies had floated ashore as far north as Long Island, and swimmers sometimes had to dodge sodden life belts and drifting bits of wreckage. In small coastal towns such as Manasquan, New Jersey (about sixty-five miles south of New York City), tourism was down by 60 percent. Rentals went begging until heavily discounted summer homes and amusement concessions were boarded up for the duration, and the streets were deserted by 10:30 at night. Atlantic City hoteliers stayed afloat by the grace of the United States Army, which commandeered virtually all of the large beachfront hotels (and numerous smaller ones) to house thousands of Air Force trainees for four weeks at a time. The conversion cost hundreds of hotel employees their jobs (the Army seldom required chambermaids), forced the eviction of the hotels' permanent residents, and led high-end shops along the boardwalk to shutter their windows, as owners complained that "we can't sell our stuff to soldiers who get $50 a month." On the other hand, hot dog vendors, ice cream stands, and movie theaters thrived.

A similar shift transformed Miami Beach (which banned tourists from its barbed-wire-strewn beaches after sunset) from a three-month winter resort into a year-round Army post town, after military authorities chose the city as the site of a new Air Force Officer Candidate School. Although local officials conceded that "the customary tourist business is finished until after the war," hotels that remained in civilian hands could still turn a profit by renting rooms to young women from northern cities who flocked southward after learning that the ratio of males to females in wartime Miami was nearly twenty to one.

# 10: Borrowed Time

## MAY–SEPTEMBER 1942

*It will continue to be an extremely nervous
and anxious summer.*

—UNDER SECRETARY OF STATE ADOLF BERLE,
JULY 1942

In the first week of June, the United States Navy defeated a Japanese invasion force several miles northwest of the island of Midway, in the most critical battle of the Pacific war since Pearl Harbor. The American victory was due in no small part to a team of cryptographers in Hawaii, who partially decoded Japanese radio transmissions and alerted naval authorities to Japan's plans. Armed with advance knowledge of the Japanese fleet's movements, Admiral Chester Nimitz dispatched reinforcements to the northern Pacific in time to catch the overconfident enemy by surprise.

As in their previous engagement in the Coral Sea, the American and Japanese surface fleets did not come within sighting or shooting distance of each other. The crucial damage was done in the space of about five minutes on the morning of June 4, when American dive-bombers sank three Japanese aircraft carriers and heavily damaged another, which sank shortly thereafter. By the time the fighting ended on June 7, Japan also had lost a heavy cruiser and 3,057 men. American losses included one carrier, a destroyer, and 307 sailors and pilots. The battle left the Imperial Navy with only two fleet-class carriers—Japan's overtaxed industrial base could not quickly replace the lost ships—compared to the U.S. Navy's three fleet carriers, with more than a dozen on the way.

Based upon naval communiqués that proclaimed "a momentous victory" marked by enemy losses ten times greater than those of the United States, American newspaper and radio commentators rushed to greet Midway as a turning point in the war, which it certainly was. But Midway's effect on public opinion was blunted by Navy censors—once again, Americans hungry for details had to wait for weeks as information emerged slowly, remaining fragmentary and inaccurate even after the Navy issued its official report in late July—as well as six months' experience of Navy spokesmen issuing "vivid accounts of the annihilation of the Japanese" which subsequently proved misleading. ("I've been buoyed up so many times and fallen so low afterward," confessed one elderly southern gentleman, "that I'm cautious about getting too cheered up by bits of good news.") Meanwhile, military analysts cautioned the public that even a clear-cut victory at Midway did not portend a swift end to the conflict with Japan. "Plainly, the war in the Pacific is very far from won," noted Hanson Baldwin in the *New York Times*. "It will be months before our strength is sufficiently mustered to take the strategic initiative away from the enemy."

Midway's impact on American morale was dampened further by the Japanese navy's attack upon Alaska and the Aleutian Islands in early June. The assault commenced with brief air raids against the United States base at Dutch Harbor on June 3 and 4, followed by successful landings several days later on the weakly defended volcanic islands of Kiska and Attu, at the western tip of the Aleutian archipelago. Timed to coincide with the invasion of Midway, the campaign was intended to hinder any American preparations to use the Aleutians to launch bombing assaults against Japan's home islands, to divert American naval resources from Midway, and to provide bases for Japanese air strikes against the Pacific coast.

Far less strategically significant than Midway, the presence of Japanese troops on Alaskan territory took on considerably greater importance in the American public mind than it deserved. It sparked immediate alarm along the West Coast, particularly in Oregon and Washington, even though Dutch Harbor was two thousand miles from Seattle. Blackouts grew more frequent, and radio stations up and down the coast went silent at 9 p.m. every night. General DeWitt warned civilians to beware of "Japanese marauders masquerading in American uniforms." Fearing a fire-bomb attack against the densely wooded Pacific Northwest, the U.S. Forest Service ordered park rangers to man their lookout posts in the Cascade and Sierra mountain ranges, and arranged fire-protection classes for workers and businessmen. "All it takes is a couple Japs with a load of incendiaries," an anxious lumberjack informed Alistair Cooke. "They could set the whole goddam coast on fire." (And there *were* a dozen forest fires in the region in June—three times as many as usual—but all were caused by cigarettes dropped by careless workers from nearby war plants.)

Self-appointed citizen armies prepared to swing into action, aided by the recent publication of a well-advertised pamphlet titled *Guerrilla Warfare*, written by a Canadian mercenary and available by mail for twenty-five cents. Described as "a civilian's manual of mayhem and informal murder," it taught readers in graphic detail how to derail trains, dynamite bridges, kill an adversary with a cheese cutter, and ambush enemy vehicles ("a wire cable strung across a road at an angle"). The largest vigilante group in the Pacific Northwest was Oregon's Tillamook Guerrillas, an extralegal band of more than a thousand farmers, loggers, and businessmen armed with rifles and shotguns, and assisted by a female auxiliary, the Guerrilla Women. "If the Japanese try to land in the bays or inlets," threatened their leader, a blind World War I veteran, "they will find guerrillas on cliffs, sandpits, and in the bogs." California's foremost paramilitary organization was the Santa Barbara Home Guards, two hundred volunteers who fashioned homemade dynamite bombs, practiced marksmanship on targets floating in the sea, and simulated hand grenade attacks by lobbing Molotov cocktails at discarded machinery in the city dump. (Unfortunately, the Home Guards were under a cloud in the summer of 1942, because two of their founders had recently fought each other in a duel which left one man dead and the other hospitalized.)

California's official State Guard was in woeful condition, understaffed and underpaid as the result of a political quarrel between Governor Olson and the state legislature. San Francisco remained poorly prepared for an enemy attack, lacking a wide range of civilian defense equipment; in the event of an enemy gas attack, air raid wardens were instructed to sound the alert by beating on pans and tubs. "We in San Francisco are feeling the same feeling that a chicken might feel as it looks up from the block—and waits for the ax," claimed one local citizen. Critics charged that the city's fire department was incapable of fighting incendiary bombs ("Why worry?" replied Mayor Rossi. "No bombs have fallen!"), and a federal judge accused General DeWitt of deliberately refusing to authorize evacuation drills for the city's 650,000 residents; in fact, the public had not even been provided with an evacuation plan. "The trouble," concluded *Time*, "seemed to lie in the Army's tell-the-people-nothing attitude."

Throughout the summer, the Navy proved equally adept at not providing information on events in the Aleutians. (Military authorities had barred civilian reporters and photographers from Alaska since December 7, leaving the press no recourse but to await naval communiqués.) Navy spokesmen initially denied that any Japanese landings had taken place; then they belittled the threat by characterizing it as nothing more than a face-saving response to the Doolittle raid on Tokyo. "It's a lot more than that," snapped Washington's Senator Monrad Wallgren. "We've got a war out there and this is the opening foray."

For days the Navy released no authoritative statement on the military situation in Alaska—and when it did release official communiqués, it ordered newspapers not to print them, leaving Americans to exchange rumors and misinformation. "If the public is confused about the situation in western Alaska, then so is the enemy," reasoned one Navy official, "and that is all to the good." Walter Lippmann disagreed, calling the Navy's response "positively alarming in its frivolity." Frustrated by the Navy's silence, residents of the Pacific Northwest grew even more vexed when a Japanese submarine surfaced off the northern coast of Oregon on the night of June 21 and lofted a series of shells in the general direction of Fort Stevens, at the mouth of the Columbia River. None of the missiles damaged any military target, although the backstop at the local baseball field was pretty much ruined.

"The Japs are headed in our direction," warned Congressman John Coffee of Washington, who shared his constituents' "growing concern . . . over the increasing menace of the Japanese war machine." A reporter visiting the Northwest discovered that "gloom and dejection have replaced the optimism that prevailed here a short time ago," following Midway. In late July, the Navy finally released a more thorough report on the initial enemy attacks in Alaska seven weeks earlier—the *New York Times* decried "the remarkable delay in publishing news of the whole affair"—and acknowledged that ten thousand Japanese troops remained ensconced on Kiska and Attu. ("That's 10,000 too many," grumbled Senator Edwin Johnson of Colorado.) A Navy spokesman added brightly that "if we needed Kiska we could take it," but a month later, the Japanese garrison remained firmly in control of the two islands. "I am scared pink for fear we're going to dawdle until the Japs take over the whole Aleutian chain," declared Alaska's delegate in the House of Representatives. Meanwhile the Navy resumed its policy of silence, broken only to celebrate occasional American bombing raids against the entrenched enemy. "The public continued to be fed on rumors and alleged facts," complained the *Washington Post* in an August 26 editorial. "If the Army and Navy are really interested in promoting public confidence in the conduct of the war, they should review their information policy about Alaska and the Aleutians. . . . It stands for all time as a prime example of how not to promote confidence on the home front."

Advertisements with pretty girls and humorous cartoon characters were out in the summer of 1942, replaced by images of bombers, tanks, drill presses, and soldiers in uniform. To E. B. White, it seemed as if the United States was fighting two distinct wars: the real conflict, "bloody and terrible and cruel, a war of ups and downs," and a fantasy war concocted by advertising men to demonstrate how their companies' products supported American troops on the battlefield. "This second war is a lovely thing," White explained. "We are always winning it, and the paint job stays bright on the bombers that gleam in the strong clean light of a copywriter's superlative adventure. . . . We leap rivers with Goodyear and the Engineers, span oceans with Kelvinator and the Air Force, peel off from a fighter formation with the manufacturer of a snap fastener, blow the daylights out of a Jap cruiser with a lens company located in the Squibb Building. . . . When the bomb bay door opens and the hand presses the lever you are never quite certain what is coming out—a bomb or a bottle of cleaning fluid."

Businesses that still had consumer goods to sell highlighted their products' practical benefits for wartime America. Food advertisements touted nutritional advantages for war workers ("These are no times to be a 'breakfast dodger.' Why don't you switch to Wheaties and give yourself something to work on every morning"), while soft drinks claimed to provide a midday pick-me-up on the assembly line. ("Guns, guns, guns! Steady production means 'all out energy'—all we've got! That's why millions enjoy Pepsi Cola daily.") Smooth-gliding pencils made the defense production process more efficient ("No careless toleration now of time-wasting non-descript pencils"), and electric alarm clocks made sure no one snoozed when there were bombers to be built: "Reveille for America is TAPS to the Axis! Every worker on the job on time speeds the defeat of the dictators."

Characters in magazine advertisements were constantly pressed for time, rushing through the day on hectic schedules: "In the tempo we live today every moment counts." No one had time to relax and enjoy leisurely, sophisticated pleasures; the notion seemed patently unpatriotic. In July, the *Washington Post* dropped its high-society column ("For the duration—and probably longer—we are finished with society-as-such"), opting instead to publicize local residents' contributions to the war effort. Evening-wear sales continued to plummet, forcing prominent design houses out of business. Retailers noticed "an evident tendency to retrench" on the part of their wealthier customers, as "made-to-order" consumers switched to "ready-to-wear." "This year," sighed one clothing manufacturer, "we will probably stop making for the public anything which even resembles a luxury."

It was more than a psychological change. "In the wartime United States," noted *Time*, "the poor were growing richer, the rich poorer," and not by accident. Through its tax and anti-inflation policies, the Roosevelt administration left no doubt that it intended to use the war emergency to raise the standard of living of lower-income Americans ("the economic group," said the *Washington Post*, "which has always been the object of President Roosevelt's solicitude") at the expense of the middle and upper classes.

Throughout the spring and summer of 1942, the specter of runaway inflation haunted the president and his economic advisers. "Nothing in the economic field can interfere with the war effort as much as an uncontrolled rise in prices," declared Treasury Secretary Morgenthau. (When someone suggested privately to Roosevelt that "a little inflation would not hurt," the president replied that he was reminded of "a fellow who took a

little cocaine and kept coming back for more until he was a drug addict.")
Since September 1939, the cost of living had risen by 15 percent, led by
increases in the price of food, furnishings, and clothing. As administration spokesmen repeatedly pointed out, the primary culprit was the wid-
ening inflationary gap ($17 billion and growing) between the expanding
purchasing power of American consumers and the rapidly shrinking supply of civilian goods. But not all classes' incomes were rising at an equal
pace, or at all. According to OPA estimates, about 90 percent of the increase in spendable income was going into the pockets of the nation's wage
earners—both war workers (including overtime pay), and other laborers
whose employers raised their wages to dissuade them from joining the
nearest shipyard or arms factory. "There had been war booms before,"
marveled John Dos Passos, "but this was a war boom that reached right
down to the ditchdigger."

Many middle-class and wealthy Americans, on the other hand, expected their disposable incomes to decline as wartime tax rates continued their inexorable climb. They had already paid record amounts in
federal taxes on their 1941 income, but in the spring of 1942 Morgenthau
asked Congress to squeeze an additional $7.6 billion in revenue from in-
dividual and corporate income taxes—partly to help pay for the war, but
also to curb inflation by withdrawing "the greatest possible volume of purchasing power" and preventing consumers "from engaging in the futile
effort to buy more goods than can be produced."

Although Congress would never accept Morgenthau's proposals intact,
it was clear that middle-class Americans' tax bills would be significantly
higher by the end of 1942, no matter what specific legislation eventually
emerged. "The adjustment will be particularly harsh among the middle
income groups," warned the *New York Times*. "Few families in this class
can relinquish a quarter to a third of income without some drastic re-
trenchment." Nor could Ernest Hemingway. "At present my principal
war problem is financial," Hemingway confessed to a friend in late July,
between sailing trips to hunt U-boats in the Caribbean. "Had to borrow
12,000 bucks to pay my 103,000 income tax last year. I have to pay that
back and get enough ahead so I will not be wiped out and broke when [I]
come back from war."

Roosevelt then doubled down on the administration's tax strategy by asking Congress to impose a 100 percent levy on all individual incomes over $25,000 and on married couples' incomes above $50,000—an idea floated a year earlier by the first lady and various CIO officials. "No American citizen," the president decided, "ought to have a net income after he had paid his taxes of more than $25,000 a year," at least not in wartime. Since such a "supertax" would have affected only about eleven thousand people (including Roosevelt, with his private sources of wealth), while bringing in a relatively insignificant $200 million in additional revenue, its effect on inflation and the budget deficit would have been negligible. Columnist Ernest Lindley, who had ties to the White House, claimed that the measure was designed to curb profiteering and "prevent anybody from making much money during the war." Roosevelt himself described the income limit as a "morale-building" measure; the American public would bear wartime sacrifices "more cheerfully," he argued, if they knew "that rich and poor alike are giving up the comforts of peacetime in order that we may more effectively prosecute the war."

Business leaders roundly condemned the confiscatory measure. The head of the New York Board of Trade called it "destructive of American philosophies of government," and the president of the National Association of Manufacturers claimed that it was "unblushingly borrowed from the public platform of the Communist Party in 1928." Press reaction was only slightly more generous. Frank Kent dismissed the measure as "an almost irrelevant tax limitation which has no bearing on inflation," while the *New York Times* denounced its "novel and capricious departure from established tax procedure and established social principles." The *Detroit Free Press* claimed that it threatened to make wartime ally Joseph Stalin "a permanent sleeping partner," while taking "something very fundamental out of American life": "Winning the war comes first but, in the process of winning, our people do not intend to lose their republic."

Beyond its proposals for higher taxes, the centerpiece of the administration's anti-inflation program was the General Maximum Price Regulation (popularly known as "General Max"), which sought to freeze prices on nearly two hundred key "cost-of-living" consumer goods, including clothing, shoes, fuel, and tobacco. Despite the pleas of many of his economic advisers, Roosevelt chose not to impose similar restrictions on wage increases. Political considerations aside, the president was convinced that some pay raises were justified at a time when nearly half of American workers continued to subsist on less than $1,700 a year—the Labor Department's minimum standard for "health and decency."

As numerous observers pointed out, however, Roosevelt's refusal to freeze wages—especially among lower-income consumers likely to spend much or all of their additional pay—doomed General Max from the start. "Either we must drain off into the Treasury a large part of the increased incomes, including the very low incomes," warned the *New York Times*, "or those incomes and all our savings too will be burned up in a ruinous inflation." Walter Lippmann concurred. "Until there is a tax bill which reaches the lower incomes, which have recently been in the aggregate greatly increased," wrote Lippmann, who supported a national sales tax, "the Administration ought not to pretend that it is dealing with inflation."

Congress did its part to sabotage General Max by failing to effectively control food prices. Between September 1939 and the summer of 1942, agricultural prices in the United States rose more than 50 percent, fueled by government purchases of food for the military and Lend-Lease, and by working-class Americans' desire for improved (or at least more expensive) diets. Since food costs represented slightly more than 20 percent of the average American family's budget, newspapers and local governments stepped up their suggestions for cheap and nutritious meals: "175 Ways to Prepare Soups," or "Victory Meals—Spam 'n' Spaghetti." But grumbling housewives were no match for the influence of the farm bloc in Congress, which defended farmers' interests as fervently as the White House protected wage earners'. "The American farmer [was] in clover for the first time since the last war," explained the *Wall Street Journal*—cash income was up 47 percent over early 1941, and seemed likely to reach $14 billion by the end of the year—and rural legislators intended to keep him there for as long as possible.

The administration's tax proposals encountered equally stubborn resistance on Capitol Hill. Congressmen essentially ignored Roosevelt's request for a twenty-five-thousand-dollar income limit, and dragged their feet in drafting a tax-hike bill; it was, after all, an election year. As the tax debate slogged through the summer, special-interest groups battled to protect their vested interests. "Everyone admits that full conversion of the country to war makes sacrifices imperative," observed Budget Director Harold Smith, "but each group tries to shift the sacrifices to others."

"After seven months of war, the Capital does not give the impression of either stability or unity," wrote James Reston. Week after week, congressmen relinquished any pretense of wartime leadership as they allowed controversial issues to drift, preferring instead to settle old scores by abolishing New Deal agencies such as the Civilian Conservation Corps. A frustrated *Washington Post* accused the legislature of "clearly fumbling its responsibility in an hour of national peril," and from his readers' reactions Mark Sullivan discerned "a mood of angry irritation against Congress; the fact not possible to doubt."

"This is the summer when time is the most precious thing there is— more precious than rubber or metal or men," noted the *New Yorker*. "Yet some of our political leaders are throwing time around as though it were confetti. . . . This doesn't happen to be a summer when we feel like being insulted. We happen to be a little edgy this summer—we won't take much more of that sort of insult."

There were no parades through Washington's streets on the Fourth of July, no concerts by military bands, nor any fireworks displays on the National Mall. Few tourists visited the Lincoln Memorial or the Tomb of the Unknown Soldier; a visiting journalist noticed "an almost ominous silence" along the Potomac. President Roosevelt spent the day at his desk in his map-cluttered office, meeting with Donald Nelson and his military chiefs of staff. Roosevelt seldom found time that summer to escape for exercise in the swimming pool in the White House basement, or to relax on fishing trips; he was experiencing more frequent head colds, and they lingered longer. The president's holiday message to the American people urged them to redouble their war efforts, "not to waste one hour, not to stop one shot, not to hold back one blow," and to substitute "the death-dealing reality of tanks and planes and guns and ships" for "the fireworks of make-believe."

Up and down the East Coast, authorities banned firecrackers, rockets, and other traditional noisemakers that could be misconstrued as enemy missiles; as a result, injuries among small children declined dramatically.

Automobile traffic on highways was far lighter than usual, and deaths from traffic accidents were down by a third, although forty-five people were arrested over the holiday weekend for disregarding Army dimout regulations along coastal roads. Bus stations everywhere were jammed—everyone seemed to be in a hurry to be somewhere else—and Pennsylvania Railroad officials reported that July 4 was the heaviest day of passenger traffic in the company's history.

Baltimore held no public celebrations; the city's aircraft factories and shipyards operated on a normal schedule on the holiday, as did war plants across the country. Ceremonies in Philadelphia were limited to a gathering of two hundred young Americans in Independence Hall, in front of the Liberty Bell, for their induction into the armed forces. Guards cautioned sightseers not to photograph the bell, even though its image was readily available in books and magazines and on nickel postcards. (A journalist who defiantly snapped a picture was taken into custody and charged with a "breach of the peace.")

New York City's holiday tranquillity ("as quiet as a cornfield") was broken only by the previously announced test at noon of a massive new three-ton, 115-horsepower air raid "super-siren," designed by Bell Telephone Labs and perched atop the seventy-story RCA Building on Fiftieth Street. Even though people in Edgewater, New Jersey, could hear the 170-decibel blast (purportedly "the loudest sustained sound ever produced by man"), disappointed police experts said the sound still failed to penetrate all the canyons of Manhattan. Along Broadway, observers noted more men in uniforms and women in slacks than usual; downtown hotels were filled with servicemen on leave and their relatives. Traffic through the Holland Tunnel and across the George Washington Bridge was 30 percent below normal, but Coney Island enjoyed its largest crowd of the season, estimated at a million people. (Dimouts were providing teenagers at the seashore with abundant opportunities for casual sex; "Coney Island," confessed one local cop, "is just one big tunnel of love.") That evening, a new military-themed musical revue, *This Is the Army*—featuring songs by Irving Berlin—made its debut at the Broadway Theatre with a three-hundred-member all-soldier cast (mostly privates and corporals), most of whom had been entertainers in civilian life. The *New York Times* immediately dubbed it "the best show of a generation."

Boston authorities staged their customary holiday parade, starting at City Hall and proceeding to the Old State House to read the Declaration of Independence, before finishing at Faneuil Hall. Instead of fireworks, city officials distributed free ice cream to kids at playgrounds and school-yards; the most popular frozen treat was a "MacArthur Sundae": vanilla ice cream with blueberries, strawberry sauce, toasted coconut, whipped cream, and a miniature American flag. Along the banks of the Charles River, Harvard students enjoyed their only scheduled holiday in the new war-shortened summer term. At nearby New Haven, Connecticut, a high-ranking War Department official reminded the men in Yale's incoming freshmen class—the largest in the university's history—that they were attending classes "on borrowed time," with no guarantee they would be allowed to complete their studies.

Midwestern communities enjoyed their usual fireworks displays at public ceremonies, although Cleveland suffered a surprise blackout when a stray cat short-circuited a wire near the municipal power plant, plunging much of the city into total darkness. At Detroit's Ford Airport, 100,000 spectators watched a company of paratroopers of the 503rd Regiment jump from low-flying planes to seize the main terminal building in a nine-and-a-half-minute simulated attack; one observer compared the billowing parachutes to "popcorn being poured from a bag."

One thousand recruits were inducted into the Navy at a public ceremony at Chicago's Soldier Field as part of a rousing nationwide radio program, but Clark Gable spent much of the day alone in the Windy City, strolling disconsolately along the north shore of Lake Michigan. En route by train to his Hollywood ranch after visiting Washington to obtain a commission in the Army Air Forces, Gable still mourned the death of his wife. "I'm awfully tired," he told reporters. "I have nothing to say about my trip to Washington." His publicity assistant acknowledged that Gable was as "down in the dumps as any one I've ever known": "He's an entirely different guy since Carole's death. . . . He just doesn't want to do anything any more."

St. Louis hosted the final appearance of a twenty-two-city, cross-country War Bond "victory tour" of sixteen highly decorated Allied combat veterans. Over the previous four weeks, the soldiers had been treated to a ticker-tape parade through Manhattan, a reception on Capitol Hill, luncheons and dinners with debutantes and models, numerous rallies at baseball stadiums and racetracks, and an evening with Hollywood movie stars such as Betty Grable and Claudette Colbert. The Treasury Department hoped that the soldiers could tell the public about their exploits and "give the war some glamor" to boost bond sales, which continued to falter—in June, Americans purchased only $642 million worth of bonds, considerably below the $800 million quota. Yet the tour took a toll on the heroes; one British soldier admitted that "it's been bad physically and mentally on all of us." In Cleveland, a veteran of Doolittle's Tokyo raid confessed to an audience that he was "disappointed by what I have found since I got back to my country. I'm disappointed at the failure of the people to realize that we are in a war—a war that we can lose. I'm ashamed of myself to be here . . . instead of overseas with my gang where I want to be."

Los Angeles hosted the nation's most extravagant holiday entertainment: an eight-mile-long procession of tanks, howitzers, antiaircraft guns, and armored cars, accompanied by thirty-three thousand soldiers, civilian defense officials, and war workers. It took two and a half hours for the parade to pass by a crowd of 300,000 onlookers. The *Los Angeles Times* called it "the greatest military spectacle in city history," but others feared that a large portion of the southern California population had developed "a state of mind closely bordering on hysteria in the matter of war consciousness."

Options for civilians to visit the West Coast were disappearing. By the first week in July, the Army had commandeered more than half of the planes in the nation's commercial air transportation system. "All routes and services not regarded as essential to the war program will be terminated," announced the War Department. American Airlines, the largest domestic passenger carrier, reduced its timetable of scheduled flights from eleven pages to two. Railroads squeezed in more passengers (and raised their fares by 10 percent), prompting the director of the Office of Defense Transportation to ask travelers to limit themselves to one suitcase apiece to free up space for troops. Since the start of the year, Pullman sleeping cars had carried 2.5 million soldiers; "it seems to be part of the policy of the government," mused Lucius Beebe, "to remove any one in the Army or Navy from his own home community with all possible expedition and, as far as possible, to conduct the war by going places on trains."

"Every train is really a troop train now, and the faces of the soldiers are completely grave and thoughtful," wrote novelist Katherine Anne Porter, after arriving in Boulder, Colorado, for a writers' conference. "Of course, you see them huddled together sometimes carrying on a giggling conversation full of 'And I says to her and she says—' and all too obviously they grab their fun where they can get it, but the real tone is pretty grim, and these boys have grown up several years before their time."

"People, this year, feel that they need vacations more than ever," declared a spokesman for the New England Hotel Association. But sightseers would not travel far. "People who were formerly addicted to tours and cruises are now spending stationary vacations nearer home," noted the *New Yorker*. Department stores began selling "Stay Home And Like It" patio furniture, complete with barbecue grills. Interior Department officials reported that the number of visitors to national parks in the West was down 50 percent, and 75 percent in the gas-rationed East. "Pictures of our great national parks take on this year a charm they have not had before. It is the charm of inaccessibility," remarked the *New York Times*. "People today look at the Grand Canyon or Glacier Park, and they have something of the feeling with which they would look at a picture of the Alps or the Caucasus. . . . This Summer, by the million, people will stay in the old backyard or on the old front porch and look at pictures of the Grand Canyon and Zion National Park a bit wistfully."

Even Eleanor Roosevelt, who typically traveled more than six thousand miles a month, curtailed her schedule of official appearances. "I'm not at all sure any speech I make is a contribution," she admitted, "or that it would make a penny's worth of difference to the war if I canceled all of them." For the first time since moving into the White House, the first lady began spending more time in Washington than on the road.

As travel grew more challenging, Americans increasingly turned to the telephone to stay in touch with family members separated by military service or war jobs. Federal officials were not pleased. Nationwide, Americans were making 50 percent more toll calls than in peacetime (and 80 percent more in large cities), tying up phone lines so thoroughly that it sometimes took six hours to complete a long-distance call. To avoid lengthy delays in transmitting war-related messages, the Board of War Communications urged civilians to reduce their "purely personal" calls—

"War Calls Come First"—or face stringent restrictions. In the meantime, local telephone companies suggested strategies to keep calls short, including an abbreviated greeting: "Don't say 'Hello.' It's quicker to answer with your name, company, department, or telephone number instead."

As the temporary gasoline-rationing program in the eastern states entered its final weeks in early July, OPA officials announced that they had obtained "widespread evidence" of fraud committed by motorists and service station operators. "With a little trouble you can get all the gasoline you want in New York City and [its] suburbs," reported the *Wall Street Journal*. "Filling station attendants 'make mistakes' on the generous side. There's outright bootlegging too." An OPA "sting" operation found hundreds of filling stations in the mid-Atlantic area willing to sell gas to motorists with no ration cards. Reporters for the *New York Times* discovered "a dozen hoaxes to sell more gasoline to favored customers than ration cards allow." Some dealers failed to punch the ration cards of regular customers; others took bribes for additional gas. Taxi drivers, too, bootlegged their extra gas rations.

As gasoline supplies drained away at a higher than expected rate, filling stations up and down the East Coast again ran out of fuel. Signs that read SORRY—NO GAS (or NO GAS HERE. WRITE YOUR CONGRESSMAN ABOUT IT) greeted motorists along highways and city streets. At times nearly all of the stations in the gas-rationed area were dry; almost none opened on the Fourth of July. Drivers began to stalk gasoline delivery trucks and follow them to their destinations. ("Like rats after the Pied Piper," someone suggested.) Often motorists rode for miles and made dozens of stops before they found an open station; other drivers parked their cars at stations and asked for their tanks to be filled when supplies arrived. Lines of fifty cars or more at gas pumps snarled traffic on nearby streets. Sometimes motorists quarreled with station attendants who refused to sell gas to cars with out-of-state license plates, or tried to limit them to three gallons at a time, even with a B or an X card. Sometimes fistfights broke out.

"Hell had seen no furies," declared *Time* magazine, "like the motorists who did not have enough gas left to drive around to a service station for gas that was not there." When employees at war plants began taking days off to search for gas, the Army commandeered a number of gas stations near factories and reserved them exclusively for war workers, which exacerbated the shortage for everyone else. "I can live with any ration," suggested one frustrated Virginia driver, "but I feel that I should not be forced to use rationed material to hunt for the little bit I can get."

The OPA's permanent rationing program, which went into effect on July 22, sought to plug the worst holes in the interim plan. Instead of ration cards, each motorist received a coupon book; the basic "A" book contained eight coupons—good for four gallons of gas apiece—which could be used anytime during a specified sixty-day period, but not before or after those dates. (The OPA's calculations assumed that cars averaged 15 miles per gallon, and that a typical automobile owner drove 240 miles each month—150 miles commuting to and from work, and 90 additional miles of "pleasure" driving, including shopping and school and church activities.) To obtain supplementary coupons for additional gas, motorists needed to fill out a detailed four-page form that asked them to list (among other things) their occupation, the mileage they had driven in the past thirty days for work-related travel, the shortest distance from their home to the nearest public transportation, the distance by public transportation to their job, and the shortest distance from their home to their job. Extra fuel was granted only to drivers who needed to travel more than 150 miles a month for their work, and who had formed a "car-sharing club" of at least four people (all of whose signatures had to appear on the application), or could explain satisfactorily their failure to do so. Any workers who lived near a subway stop or an elevated or suburban railway station were ineligible for extra fuel, whether they created a car pool or not.

This time, two-thirds of eastern automobile owners received A rations (pleasure drivers); 18 percent obtained "B" rations (war workers with lengthy commutes); and 14 percent were granted "C" status (doctors, ministers, farmers, and government officials—including congressmen and other "bona fide" candidates for public office who needed extra gas for election campaigning). Each car received a color-coded sticker reflecting its owner's ration status, and OPA officials hoped that "constant public scrutiny"—finding B or C cars or taxicabs parked at the beach or near racetracks, for instance—would deter flagrant cheating.

Filling station operators were required to collect coupons for every sale of gasoline, and then redeem those coupons to replenish their supplies of gas. There remained no guarantee, however, that there would be enough gas to meet every rationing coupon distributed to motorists, or that allotments for each classification would not be reduced in the future. "Our reserve petroleum stocks in the East are so desperately low that we must use less and less gasoline," announced Leon Henderson just before the plan went into effect. Anticipating trouble, a spokesman for a gasoline dealers' association called the new rationing system a "farce," charging that "there were more tickets sold for the ball game than there were seats."

By midsummer, eastern motorists had reduced their driving by 50 to 60 percent, but mileage was down only 15 to 20 percent in the rest of the country, where gasoline remained plentiful. As a result, the nation's rubber supply was wearing away from passenger automobile tires at a pace that alarmed authorities. "When the rubber is gone," warned officials at the Office of Emergency Management, "there will be no more for a long time." A study by the Brookings Institution predicted that "if normal driving habits continued, the visible supply of tires will not maintain adequate transportation much beyond the first quarter of 1943." More ominously, the military's rubber reserve was shrinking so rapidly that the Army began substituting steel treads for rubber on its new tanks, which slowed their speed by 10 percent. War Department authorities warned that they might need to requisition civilian tires to avoid future cuts in arms production.

To encourage tire conservation, Goodyear assured its customers in a two-page magazine advertisement that "The Rubber Shortage Is More Critical Than You Think," but many Americans remained skeptical. Months of conflicting and misleading statements on the rubber situation had undermined the White House's credibility on the issue. "The Administration has done a miserable job of telling the public what the trouble is," charged the *Detroit Free Press*, and White House press secretary Stephen Early conceded in a memo to the president that "the rubber-gas rationing question has gotten into a badly muddled condition." The resulting confusion, as Ray Clapper pointed out, left the public vulnerable to politicians and commentators who told them "that this is all the bunk about rationing, pay no attention to what the Government says, go on and race your car around all you want to, use up that gasoline and to hell with this bird Henderson or Nelson or whoever it is that is trying to keep you from joy-riding in your car." Anti-Roosevelt newspapers such as the New York

*Daily News* and the *Washington Times-Herald* encouraged the opposition by publishing stories ("Rubber Shortage A Myth") dismissing the crisis as a White House hoax.

When the administration floated the idea of nationwide gas rationing as a means of conserving rubber, a storm of protest followed from every state outside the East Coast. "The resident of the midlands is offended because he knows there is a surplus of gasoline and because he has been assured that the rubber shortage is going to end before his tires are worn to a frazzle," declared the *Daily Oklahoman*. "The Washington dreamers have stated that this war is going to be tough on everybody, and we all know that it is," acknowledged the *San Antonio Light*. "But there is no sense in their getting impatient and setting out to figure ways to make it tougher and sooner." From the Pacific coast, the Auto Club of Southern California denounced gas rationing as "an unwarranted invasion of liberties thinly disguised as a war compulsion," and a spokesman for the Citizens' Committee to Oppose Gasoline Rationing in Southern California argued that "it is a violation of the spirit of our form of government to say that as individuals Americans have not the wisdom to conserve their own rubber." The nation, concluded the *Kansas City Star*, "is getting sick and tired of the present rationing jitters."

On Capitol Hill, a coalition of a hundred congressmen—including a number of longtime New Deal Democrats—approved a statement opposing nationwide gasoline rationing unless the administration could prove that it was necessary to conserve fuel (but not rubber). Claiming that executives from the major rubber companies were controlling national policy, they argued that restricting gasoline sales "would actually cripple the war effort rather than aid it" by increasing unemployment in oil-producing states, many of whose revenues depended substantially on the sale of petroleum products. "I can see no reason for it for the people in those parts of the country where they are wading knee-deep in [oil]," declared Speaker Sam Rayburn, whose home state of Texas provided more than 20 percent of the world's oil. Senator Allen Ellender of Louisiana proclaimed nationwide gas rationing "uncalled for and unwise," and likely to provoke "much unrest and disunity"; Kansas senator Arthur Capper warned that it would be "disastrous" to his part of the country. While they were at it, a number of legislators took potshots at OPA director and rationing czar Leon Henderson, branding him "a dictator," "a bureaucratic monster," "the would-be head of a Gestapo," and "a smart aleck."

"Maybe I was wrong," wrote Ray Clapper sarcastically. "Maybe what you hear in Congress isn't 99 per cent tripe, ignorance and demagoguery. Maybe it's not more than 95 per cent." But the emergence of the first meaningful sign of popular rebellion during the war emergency persuaded Roosevelt to back off for the time being. Disregarding his advisers' urgent recommendations, the president suggested to reporters that drastic measures might yet be avoided if Americans could reclaim enough scrap rubber to meet the country's military needs until the synthetic-rubber program was up and running. Encouraged by Interior Secretary Harold Ickes's entirely unfounded estimate that 10 million tons of scrap rubber might be lurking in American homes, offices, and factories, the president called for "a short, quick and snappy campaign" to hunt for old or disused rubber products. Gas stations and shoe repair shops became collection centers, paying the public a penny a pound for scrap, which was then sold to the government, melted down, and mixed with crude rubber for military equipment.

For two weeks, Americans searched their basements, attics, closets, and garages for old toys, galoshes, bath mats, garden hoses, suspenders, garters, hot-water bottles, and worn-out tires. Fala contributed several of his rubber bones; War Department clerks tossed in hundreds of rubber stamps. Movie theaters accepted used rubber goods as the price of admission. Junk dealers scoured automobile graveyards, women's clubs launched telephone appeals, public-address announcers at baseball games implored fans to pitch in, and Boy Scouts urged motorists at filling stations to donate the floor mats in their cars.

At the end of the campaign, the grand total nationwide was less than 250,000 tons of scrap—far below the 1.5-million-ton minimum set by the president to avoid rationing. Roosevelt promptly extended the drive for another ten days. Radio announcers challenged the public to "get in the scrap to beat the Jap," and promised that "scrap rubber will make the Axis blubber." Collections still lagged. "We suspect that people are hoarding rubber," charged Ickes, "and maybe even people in official life are hoarding." So Ickes personally hauled away a large rubber floor mat from the White House office building, and congressional aides pulled up several hundred black rubber mats from under the seldom-used cuspidors in House and Senate offices and chambers. (It was time, Ickes suggested, that federal employees learned how to spit straight.)

When the overtime drive finally concluded with fewer than 400,000 tons, even Ickes had to admit the results were "disappointing." Americans in non-gas-rationed states—whose motoring future was at stake— had turned in the most rubber per capita: Nevada led the way with 25.65 pounds per person, followed by Oregon, Idaho, Washington, and Montana. Easterners—who had nothing to gain except a sense of unity with their fellow countrymen—trailed significantly behind, with New York, Pennsylvania, and the District of Columbia finishing near the bottom. New Jersey came in dead last, contributing less than two pounds per person.

Still Roosevelt hesitated to act. "President Roosevelt knows our automobiles all over the country are going off the road in large numbers," wrote Ray Clapper. "Taxicabs are dropping out because they can't get tires. Yet he is afraid to do what all his advisers working on the problem think must be done—clamp down on wasteful use of cars all over the country." Instead, the president persuaded Bernard Baruch in early August to head a blue-ribbon committee to conduct a definitive study of the nation's rubber situation. Dr. James Conant (president of Harvard University) and Dr. Karl Compton (president of MIT), along with twenty-five engineers and technical advisers, agreed to join Baruch to provide scientific expertise.

Baruch's committee issued its report on September 10. After reprimanding the Roosevelt administration for the numerous "procrastinations, indecisions, conflict of authority, clashes of personalities, lack of understanding, [and] delays" that had plagued the rubber program in the early months of the war, Baruch and his colleagues concluded that Americans faced a stark choice between "discomfort and defeat." "We find the existing situation to be so dangerous," they wrote, "that unless corrective measures are taken immediately this country will face both military and civilian collapse." Without substantive changes, the committee foresaw "no rubber in the fourth quarter of 1943 with which to equip a modern mechanized army"; by 1944, "there would be an all but complete collapse of the 27,000,000 passenger cars in America." Baruch insisted that a national gasoline-rationing program was "the only way to save rubber," and recommended restricting passenger automobiles to an average of five thousand miles per year; defense workers would be permitted to drive slightly more, and nonessential drivers considerably less. Baruch's report also proposed a thirty-five-mile-per-hour national speed limit, compulsory tire inspections, and an expanded program to produce 300,000 tons of synthetic rubber using petroleum-based butadiene. OPA officials promptly announced that it would require weeks to print up ration booklets and make all the necessary arrangements, which meant that nationwide rationing probably would not go into effect until after the midterm elections in November.

Harold Ross could find no one to write about the war for the *New Yorker*. "I think it buffaloes everybody," Ross told his friend E. B. White. "Either they have no convictions or they haven't confidence enough to put them out there if they have." Certainly White had no desire to take up the challenge. "The war tends to make me (and everybody) lose my perspective, or grip," he confessed to Ross. "Writing any sort of editorial stuff about this universal jam that everyone is in, is for me a grueling and rather frightening job." When he did try to write about the war, White added, "all that comes forth I drop without regret into the wastebasket; nothing seems to make sense, no matter how you spell it or arrange the words. You write something that sounds informative, throwing the words around in the usual manner, then . . . the thing explodes in your hands, and you look down at your hands. As though you had crushed a light bulb and were bleeding slightly."

In his unflattering review of *The Moon Is Down* (John Steinbeck's novel about one European community's resistance to the Nazi occupation), critic Clifton Fadiman suggested that wartime fiction still had not come to terms with the spiritual struggle at the heart of the conflict. "I suppose it is because this war is bigger and more terrible than their authors seem to admit," Fadiman wrote. "If we cease to love freedom, we are lost, but the love of freedom alone cannot win for us. That appears to be the gray truth of the matter, and it is, let us confess, not the kind of truth that inspires exciting plays and novels." Eugene O'Neill agreed that Americans would need far more than love to defeat the Axis. "The one issue we must all keep in mind," O'Neill wrote to his son in the summer of 1942, "is as simple and primitively clear as the issue in a Prohibition gang war—kill or be killed, crush or be crushed. There is no longer any possible choice. We have got to win the war and win it by a complete extermination of the Japanese and Prussian military caste.... We must not stop until their beloved total war is totally crammed down their throats and their racial inferiority (speaking in their terms) whines for mercy. It will be time enough then to remember Humanitarian principles."

Hatred and violence appeared increasingly in American artists' works. "A personal hate so strong that it makes you want to kill in order to keep the people you love from being slaves . . . is in all of my songs these days," wrote Woody Guthrie to his girlfriend. "I pour the hate and murder and killing into them by the truck loads.... Art is a weapon and as deadly as steel cannons and exploding bombs. Art should not be pacifistic nor mystic, but should send fighting people to the field of battle filled with the clear knowledge of what the real enemy is." In a series of seven post–Pearl Harbor paintings entitled *The Year of Peril*, copies of which were displayed at galleries across the country, artist Thomas Hart Benton conjured up horrifying visual images of violence, including a lurid depiction of two American soldiers with bayonets ripping open the abdomen of a monstrous Japanese figure. "Evil and predatory forces are always with us," Benton explained. "Humanity must . . . rise up and tear their evil out of them and kill them. For this task, sensual hate, ferocity and brute will are necessary."

"Anger is what the people want," agreed popular radio dramatist Arch Oboler, "and they want hate, the hate of a determined people who are going to kill.... The public says: make us angry. We like it." Others were less certain. "Our greatest danger is that, in defeating the gangsters in control of Germany and Japan, we descend to their level of bestiality," argued a Presbyterian cleric in San Francisco, and Father Edward Flanagan, the founder of Boys Town, reminded Americans that "we must not permit ourselves to be smeared with the same moral filth we are criticizing in our enemies." Encouraging hatred might help win the war, acknowledged a professor at Chicago Theological Seminary, but "some day . . . it will spread through our own midst and blaze out in race riots [and] in conflicts between Capital and Labor."

Disturbed by a report that the Roosevelt administration had approved the production of Hollywood propaganda films designed to provoke hatred of the Axis enemy, the *Wall Street Journal* warned that such a policy was "both unnecessary and unwise": "Hate and determination are not the same. The difficulty about this hate business is that once the emotion is let loose, it is at that time out of control. Hate can be engendered. It cannot be channeled."

Hollywood executives already had their hands full turning out "Victory Reels," short documentaries narrated by stars such as Fredric March and Spencer Tracy, celebrating the achievements of the nation's war-production effort. The studios also were rushing feature films to completion at a record pace, fearful of impending material shortages—the War Production Board had recently imposed a limit of five thousand dollars on construction costs for any movie set—and the accelerating exodus of their male stars, cameramen, and technicians to the military. (MGM was scrambling to obtain an occupational deferment for its top box-office attraction, twenty-one-year-old Mickey Rooney, on the grounds that his Andy Hardy movies sustained morale and served as a model for war-stressed American families.) By summer the studios had built up the largest inventory of finished but unreleased films in Hollywood history.

To compensate audiences for the absence of so many popular actors, producers were shooting more films in color, perhaps as many as thirty by the end of 1942—an increase of nearly 50 percent over 1941. For most war pictures it made little difference. Bosley Crowther, the *New York Times'* film critic, dismissed Hollywood's war movies in the first six months of 1942 as "wretched little films . . . which show a shockingly fictitious concept of the war." The movies displayed "a disquieting flabbiness," charged Crowther, "indeed, in some cases, such obtuseness as, in wartime, is downright dangerous," because they fostered misconceptions about the intelligence and tenacity of the enemy, and peddled an outdated version of combat that refused to show the horrors of modern war. Filmmakers, Crowther concluded, "have been blind to the immensity of this war and . . . have utterly failed to realize the responsibility of the medium they control."

Other critics concurred. *Time* claimed that the Errol Flynn–Ronald Reagan vehicle, *Desperate Journey*—which recounted the adventures of a downed RAF crew making its way to safety across Nazi-occupied Europe—"well might have been titled the Rover boys in Naziland," complete with "the obligingly obtuse Gestapo." Writing in the *New Yorker*, John Mosher dismissed Republic Pictures' *Remember Pearl Harbor* as a "conventional claptrap adventure," and advised prospective filmgoers that "flimflam with big titles, titles suggestive of great moments and affairs, is something to be on guard against in the movie houses these days." Such films, wrote the *Los Angeles Times*' Norbert Lusk, might please moviegoers "who insist on having narcotic entertainments regardless of the world around them."

But increasingly each month, American audiences everywhere seemed completely absorbed in newsreels that showed American soldiers arriving on foreign shores, watching intently to see if they recognized any of the faces on the screen.

# 11: Last Call

AUGUST–DECEMBER 1942

*We are still losing this war, period. And we*
*should damn well understand it, period.*

—ASSISTANT SECRETARY OF THE NAVY
RALPH A. BARD, SEPTEMBER 1942

Traveling across Alabama and Mississippi in August, passing through rural areas nearly bereft of radios or newspapers, the *New York Times'* Brooks Atkinson reported that "people in the by-ways know that the war is going badly. That worries them, although they blame no one in particular." Most local residents sought to do their part—sending their sons off to war, helping children fill their war savings books with stamps, and dutifully planting more soybeans and peanuts because that was what their government asked them to do. But Atkinson came to realize how hard it was to connect far-flung military operations halfway around the globe with a forty-acre farm in Alabama. "In case a farmer has time to sit on his porch at this time of the year," Atkinson wrote, "it is difficult for him to imagine battles of tanks, planes, ships, guns and rifles in distant parts of a dimly understood war."

As distant as a contingent of eleven thousand U.S. Marines landing on the thickly jungled island of Guadalcanal, in the South Pacific, on the morning of August 7. The invasion represented the United States' first land-based offensive of the war; one observer compared the arrival of the untested marines on Guadalcanal to "a green football team playing its first major game."

One of the largest of the Solomon Islands, Guadalcanal possessed little intrinsic value. It was an insalubrious piece of real estate, consisting of 2,500 square miles of nearly impenetrable vegetation, forests, steep gorges, and a sharp-edged variety of grass that grew taller than most men. Before the war, the island's inhabitants included fourteen thousand natives, six thousand cattle, almost two hundred goats, a dozen mules, and innumerable tree rats. There were few roads. The mean temperature ranged between seventy-five and eighty-five degrees, and it rained a great deal of the time—an average of two hundred inches per year. Tropical diseases, such as malaria and dysentery, were a constant threat.

Guadalcanal first attracted the interest of American military planners in June 1942, when Japanese troops on the island began building an airfield from which they could threaten American communications with Australia. After wading ashore virtually unopposed in early August, the marines captured the airfield with little difficulty, until the Japanese counterattacked. Over the next several months the scope and ferocity of the battle for Guadalcanal steadily and unexpectedly escalated, as both sides poured in increasing numbers of men, supplies, ships, and planes. Repeated and sometimes fanatical Japanese assaults failed to break the American lines, and amid considerable carnage the marines slowly extended their control over the rest of the island.

Americans learned of the battle largely from Australian and New Zealand sources, and occasionally from U.S. newspaper correspondents on the scene. The Navy maintained its usual reticence; a typical communiqué said only that "operations are continuing in the Solomon Islands area." At the end of August, authorities in Washington assured the public that the battle was "a minor affair and does not approach anything decisive."

"Day by day, the task of arms and the price of victory grow greater," declared *Time*. "The early summer's optimism seems childish now."

Shortly before 2:30 on the morning of September 6, an unidentified plane approaching New York City touched off air raid sirens across the metropolitan area. Startled residents promptly forgot any blackout instructions they had received, flipped on their lights, and raised their windows to look into the streets and the sky. Within ten minutes, telephone lines were clogged with frantic calls to police stations, newspaper offices, and radio stations. No one turned off the streetlamps on several major thoroughfares. Bright lights shone from unoccupied office buildings. An air raid warden suffered a fatal heart attack, and one disoriented New Yorker slipped and fell to his death. Some nearby New Jersey communities gave the all-clear signal prematurely; others never sounded an alarm at all. "Alerts were blown so sporadically and confusingly," wrote one observer, "that at some points at least, it was difficult to tell what was an alert and what an all clear." In short, concluded the *New York Times*, "the blackout organization fell to pieces."

Nine months after the Japanese raid on Pearl Harbor, American cities remained unprepared for surprise air attacks. Practice blackouts staged with advance notice generally produced satisfactory results, although they, too, were occasionally plagued by snags, including willful violators who defiantly refused to obey air raid wardens' orders. Sometimes the scofflaws were local authorities; during one blackout in Los Angeles, lights in the twenty-two-story City Hall remained brilliantly ablaze all through the night. ("Our city fathers were all down there," complained Theodore Dreiser, "making or creating *defense plans!*") By autumn the routine of rehearsal alerts grew a bit too familiar, and the public sometimes subjected wardens to good-natured ridicule. "Apparently we look upon air raid protection as a kind of game," charged Slocum Kingsbury, a leading civilian defense expert, "something to relieve us from the strain of thinking too much about the more serious problems which the war has brought to us."

Unannounced blackouts revealed more-dangerous shortcomings. Communications centers remained a particular problem, and many communities still lacked an adequate warning system. Most major cities were short on civilian defense volunteers, partly because a substantial percentage of enthusiastic patriots who had signed up for civic duties after Pearl Harbor never completed their training sessions. (To make matters worse, a distressing number of surprise alerts resulted in one or more fatalities among air raid wardens, either from heart attacks or traffic accidents in the darkness.) Equipment also was in short supply, since the OCD failed to deliver any material until late May—and then it was mostly helmets and armbands for wardens. In Washington, a series of unscheduled blackouts in August produced such discouraging results that local officials suspended further drills for the time being.

Communities and private organizations nevertheless continued to make piecemeal improvements. San Francisco completed an underground bomb shelter (four stories deep) that had originally been designed as a parking garage; Boy Scout leaders taught their troops how to run through debris-littered streets and carry messages in the dark; department stores in downtown Washington modified their delivery trucks for rapid conversion to ambulances in case of emergency; and 3 million Americans completed Red Cross courses in first aid. In Cleveland, seminarians in a Franciscan monastery learned how to douse incendiaries with sand—an especially useful skill, since the Office of Civilian Defense had recently done an about-face on the best way to extinguish firebombs. After seven months of telling Americans to shower incendiaries with a fine spray of water to avoid explosions, OCD officials finally conducted a few tests and announced in August that a strong, forceful jet from a hose actually extinguished the bombs more rapidly and with less water. (All OCD training films on incendiaries were promptly recalled.)

Coastal defenses also were strengthened, especially after the FBI—with considerable help and good fortune—thwarted a German sabotage plot to blow up a number of vital wartime targets. On the evening of June 12, a U-boat surfaced off the coast of Long Island and dropped off four German agents, who rowed ashore in a raft and landed on a beach outside the town of Amagansett. A Coast Guard recruit saw them arrive, but the men escaped before he could summon reinforcements. Five days later, four more German saboteurs came ashore in Florida, a few miles south of Jacksonville. All eight men had lived in the United States and spoke fluent English. They had spent the past several years in Germany, training for a mission to blow up a number of key transportation points in the East and Midwest, including the heavily traveled Hell Gate Bridge in New York City, Newark's Penn Station, and a series of locks and canals along the Mississippi and Ohio Rivers between Cincinnati and St. Louis. They also planned to destroy three Alcoa aluminum factories, and sow panic by contaminating New York City's water supply.

Although the Coast Guard alerted the FBI shortly after the Long Island landing, federal investigators lost track of the German conspirators for nearly two weeks until one of the saboteurs, George Dasch, lost his nerve and turned himself in. Dasch provided enough information about his comrades and their contacts that all of the remaining saboteurs were in federal custody by the beginning of July. A special military commission tried them in secret—Attorney General Biddle had no intention of revealing just how vulnerable the United States' coastlines were. (J. Edgar Hoover reassured the public that FBI agents had tracked the German agents nearly from the start, but they had not.) Six of the German agents were condemned to death and executed in early August; Dasch was sentenced to thirty years in prison, and a comrade who also had surrendered voluntarily received a life sentence.

Suddenly Americans—starved for details about the German plot—saw saboteurs everywhere. Two girls reported that a U-boat had landed near Hyannis on Cape Cod; the submarine turned out to be a reef uncovered at high tide. Rumors of a seaplane dropping paratroopers into the Adirondacks sent investigators scurrying to upstate New York. Then a caretaker on a farm just north of Roosevelt's home in Hyde Park claimed to have seen "five or six" enemy airborne soldiers floating down through the sky. Hoboes with backpacks were mistaken for parachutists, and drifting weather balloons caused no end of confusion. Panic peaked when Army public relations officials released a series of aerial photographs that purported to show "arrows"—empty grain sacks arranged by fifth columnists into a suspicious design, and farmland plowed into a pointed pattern—guiding enemy bombers toward war plants and air bases. Newspapers swallowed the story, until an alert reporter discovered that one of the "arrows" was nothing more than an assortment of fertilizer bags randomly tossed from a farm truck in Virginia; the other was a landscaped feeding ground for birds at a nature preserve in New Jersey.

The incident became known as "the great air marker hoax," but authorities in Washington shrugged off the blunder. In a series of raids, the FBI picked up over two hundred German aliens suspected of Nazi sympathies and sent them to Ellis Island for the duration. On both Florida coasts, Coast Guardsmen armed with rifles ordered bathers to stay off the beaches from dusk until dawn. And the Massachusetts State Guards began their own guerrilla warfare training to repel invaders, learning how to stalk and dispatch an enemy by garroting, gouging, or stabbing with a hairpin.

"We are deep in what may be the decisive year of the war," announced Elmer Davis, the highly respected journalist who led the Office of War Information, an agency Roosevelt established in the summer of 1942 to coordinate and improve the dissemination of news to the public. "We could lose this war. . . . To win a total war we must fight it totally, and we are not yet fighting it that hard. Many individual Americans have made great sacrifices, but as a nation we are not yet more than ankle deep in the war. We are not winning it yet."

Surveying the war-production effort in early August, Davis acknowledged that "we have done pretty well, but pretty well is not enough." Tanks, fighter planes, and various types of artillery all had fallen behind schedule in June. Although the pace of shipbuilding had improved ("Never have ships been built as fast as in America today," crowed one columnist), the devastating losses from U-boat attacks in the Atlantic meant that the United States would not regain its pre–Pearl Harbor total of merchant shipping until mid-1943 at the earliest. "We have never lost a war; but it has been remarked that this means only that our ancestors never lost a war," Davis reminded Americans, "and our ancestors were never up against a war like this."

"America thinks it has got a production machine in high gear. Actually it is just crawling along," charged union leader Walter Reuther. "Unless things going on in the conduct of the war are corrected very quickly, we are going to lose the war." In a controversial article entitled "Detroit Is Dynamite," *Life* magazine reported that "the news from Detroit is bad this summer. Few people across the country realize how bad it is." Alistair Cooke noted that Ford's defense production declined steadily throughout the summer; by autumn, it was producing 10 percent fewer war goods than in June. Ray Clapper, too, concluded that "so many things are wrong with war production." "The first place that you can get admission of these failures is the War Production Board itself," Clapper wrote. "Everyone at WPB knows factories are closing down for lack of materials. They know more shutdowns will occur." Donald Nelson was beginning to feel the strain. "It just takes too damned long to get things done around here," Nelson grumbled at the end of the summer. "There'll be no more alibis. I'm sick of them." Then production in August fell 14 percent below forecasts, with bombers most significantly behind schedule. "The performance," Nelson conceded, "is not one that we can brag about."

The main problem remained a lack of discipline on the part of military authorities and their industrial partners. Not until the autumn of 1942 did War Department and naval planners decide which types of weapons (and how many) American forces needed most urgently. Until then, Army and Navy procurement officers (who were not yet under Nelson's control) kept on ordering as much of everything as they could—"everything," said one critic, "from battleships to pistol cartridges, that might prove useful in any kind of a war anywhere on the face of the earth." And defense contractors continued to hoard raw materials and skilled labor for future projects. The result, noted *Time*, was "the inevitable mess."

Steel presented the most pressing challenge. According to congressional investigators, the WPB had lost track of 20 million tons of the metal, most of it presumably hidden away in war plants across the nation, and steel mills could not produce enough new steel to meet military demands because of a shortage of scrap—old iron and steel which typically was melted down and blended with pig iron on a fifty-fifty basis. A number of steel furnaces, Nelson said, were "operating from day to day and hand to mouth" with dwindling stocks of scrap; as steel output faltered, war plants were forced to reduce operations, and a few shipbuilders resorted to purchasing steel on the black market.

In a series of appeals ("Junk Needed For War"), Nelson implored American homeowners and businessmen to search their premises "with a fine tooth comb" for scrap—obsolete metal equipment, tools, and machinery. The campaign's goal was 17 million tons by the end of the year, but even one old shovel, the WPB promised, would help to make four hand grenades. "If we, as a nation, allow a single furnace to go down for lack of scrap," Nelson declared, "we should, every one of us, have a guilty conscience." And so, throughout the fall, Americans canvassed their homes and ferreted out any worn-out items made of metal (except tin)—discarded radios, broken lawn mowers, old toys, bedsteads, brass chandeliers, curtain rods, meat grinders, gas lanterns, and kitchen sinks.

Since confusion marred many official collection efforts—"ineptitude all down the line," complained the *Washington Post*—local civic organizations took matters into their own hands, sponsoring scrap rallies and house-to-house drives, and establishing drop-off centers in churches and theater lobbies. In New York City, schoolchildren spent their days gathering scrap instead of attending classes (many used the money they earned to go to ball games), and Mayor La Guardia proposed removing all the metal displays from the city's parks and replacing them with relics of World War II. Art lovers across the country suggested melting down "fourth and fifth rate statues" and turning them into torpedoes and tanks as "a double service—to the war and to art." Prisoners in the county jail at Great Falls, Montana, offered to donate the bars in their cells; prison officials countered by turning in a collection of confiscated hacksaws. The *National Geographic* turned in fifteen tons of scrap metal, including a 1914 taxicab, and the Smithsonian Institution contributed one hundred tons of historic weapons, including a German Krupp gun captured during China's Boxer Rebellion. Naval officials began tearing down and scrapping the *Olympia*, Admiral Dewey's flagship from the Spanish-American War. It was barely enough; by October, WPB officials were asking Americans to donate their old door keys.

Labor problems proved harder to fix. In mid-September, War Manpower Commission director Paul McNutt warned that severe shortages of skilled manpower existed in war plants in Philadelphia (which needed an additional 100,000 workers), Detroit (96,000), Seattle (78,000), Baltimore (59,000), and Tacoma-Portland (55,000). The WMC and its subsidiary organization, the United States Employment Service, were supposed to act as a giant hiring agency, guiding workers to areas of need, but Congress—in a spiteful mood toward bureaucrats in general—refused to adequately fund the WMC, and the commission's staff was overwhelmed by the challenge. "It isn't supplying us with either skilled or unskilled labor at present," claimed the general manager of Bethlehem-Fairfield Shipyards in Baltimore. "Our shortages are becoming seriously acute. At this very minute we need 1,500 men, skilled or unskilled. We've learned to take what we can get."

Deteriorating housing conditions in the booming war centers continued to discourage prospective workers—the *Washington Post* called the consequent loss of manpower "staggering"—and rendered any orderly hiring strategy nearly impossible. (Instead of providing "war housing," beleaguered federal officials lowered the bar and endeavored to supply only "war shelter.") Experts predicted that Detroit war plants would require an additional 170,000 employees by mid-1943, but there was literally no good place to put them. "There just isn't such a thing as a place to rent in Detroit," said the director of the city's Housing Commission. "Money and price simply have no meaning." By autumn, newly arrived families were squatting in Detroit's parks, or in vacant store buildings. The superintendent of Detroit's Welfare Department confessed that "we have reached the stage where, whenever possible, we are furnishing these people with railroad fare and sending them back where they came from."

But enlistments and the draft remained the greatest stumbling blocks to the war-production program, especially as Selective Service boards—having scraped the bottom of their 1-A barrels—moved on to other classifications. In the autumn the Army began accepting men who were blind in one eye (if the other was good enough), or completely deaf in one ear, or who lacked a thumb or a few fingers. San Antonio boards reportedly drafted illiterates and expectant fathers; in Atlanta, married men without children were inducted; and a number of draft boards contemplated taking felons who had been convicted only once.

At the end of October, War Department officials publicly predicted that the Army would require a force of 7.5 million men by the end of 1943, which meant that they would need to pull an estimated 3.5 million current or potential industrial workers from their jobs, leaving war workers who had no dependents squarely in the sights of local draft boards. General Hershey made the situation worse when he suggested that "by this time next year, every able-bodied man of draft age, regardless of dependents, will be in either the Army or Navy, or should be prepared to go in soon." Even war workers with dependent wives, Hershey added, should "begin making arrangements now."

Hershey's announcement set off a stampede of war workers to recruiting offices, frantically seeking to enlist as technicians or specialists before they were drafted. Aircraft factories in southern California (which tended to hire young men in their early twenties) were especially hard-hit over the following week, as Navy enlistments in Los Angeles set new daily records, easily surpassing the surge after Pearl Harbor—the *Los Angeles Daily News* termed it a "mass exodus" from the war plants—while the city's Marine Corps recruiters reported their largest single-day totals since December 8. Over the next several months, Douglas Aircraft alone lost eleven thousand workers to the military.

"We must stop inducting men with irreplaceable skills," insisted Senator Claude Pepper of Florida, and McNutt conceded that "turnover in West Coast war plants has reached fantastic heights," as the enlistments prompted a new wave of labor pirating to replace departing workers. Acknowledging that the War Department was "gravely concerned" about the loss of skilled workers to the military, Under Secretary of War Robert Patterson promised that the Army would stop offering commissions to men who "can make greater contributions to the war effort by remaining in their present vital war work." On November 2, a special WMC management-labor committee recommended that Roosevelt protect war industries by abolishing voluntary enlistments immediately. Bernard Baruch gave the president the same advice, as did Senator Harry Truman's defense investigation committee. All the while, public support strengthened for a federal law to conscript civilian labor; in early November, a Gallup poll revealed that a majority of Americans believed the government should have the power to decide how individuals could best serve the war effort, and force them to do so.

Polls also showed that Americans still opposed overtime pay for fewer than 48 hours a week, but war workers continued to pile up additional hours (and pay) throughout the fall. In October, the average workweek in a war plant increased to 45.7 hours, up more than an hour from September. Much to the dismay of administration officials, however, absenteeism in war plants also was rising, reaching nearly 9 percent nationwide in November and as much as 18 percent in some shipyards. The two trends were not unrelated. Fatigue and stress-related illness accounted for a considerable part of the missed time, especially since the shortage of physicians left many war plants without full-time medical care. But workers also frequently took time off to search for better jobs, to nurse hangovers, to have their cars repaired (since no new ones were available), or to search for gas. The start of hunting season brought a surge in absentees, as did most Mondays ("Monday morning sickness") and the day after payday ("Pay-day richness"), when workers typically embarked on shopping sprees.

Sometimes they found nearby stores almost empty. Visiting the ship-building city of Portland, Maine, author John Dos Passos discovered that "the business section, which used to maintain a certain grim decorum, looks as if a tornado had struck it. Everywhere litter and trash, small gimcrack stores, unswept lunchrooms with jukeboxes, decrepit soda-fountains have taken the place of the establishments of the solid merchants. Cigarette ads and crudely lettered signs reading, 'Beer to Take Out,' are in the shopwindow instead of stocks of goods." Store owners made only halfhearted attempts to obtain their usual merchandise, which grew increasingly scarce as the production of civilian goods waned. "People buy whatever they've got anyway," explained one local resident. "Most likely some of 'em feel they've made as much profit as they kin with the new taxes, so why should they make the effort?"

In November, the Truman committee reported that excessive worker absences were reducing production by as much as 10 percent in many war plants—which translated to thirty-five thousand lost man-hours per week in a shipyard of eight thousand workers. One Ford plant in Michigan suffered average daily losses of twenty-three thousand working hours; the absentee rate at the company's huge Willow Run bomber plant approached 25 percent in late autumn. "This is something like going AWOL in the Army," charged one federal labor relations official. "The extent to which absenteeism impedes our war effort is beyond belief," insisted the War Manpower Commission's regional director in Baltimore, "and something must be done about it soon." Federal officials attempted to combat "work skipping" with posters and slogans designed to make absentees feel like slackers, but to little effect. Some employers fired chronic absentees and sent their names to the local draft boards, an approach which Paul Mc-Nutt endorsed. "Any man who practices absenteeism to my mind is not essential in an essential industry," declared McNutt. "I am perfectly willing to ask the director of the selective service system that such a worker's draft classification be changed and that the man be made available for the draft."

More occupations were open to American women in the autumn of 1942 than ever before. As men disappeared into military service, women worked on railroad track gangs, drove steamrollers and garbage trucks, served as traffic cops and auto mechanics, brewed bootleg liquor, telegraphed play-by-play descriptions from major-league-baseball press boxes, and sold Fuller brushes door to door (so long as they wore loose clothing, to avoid distracting customers). In lumberyards they worked as whistle punks; in brokers' offices on Wall Street they replaced "quote boys," posting the latest stock prices. They drove cabs in cities such as Detroit and San Jose and San Diego—although the San Diego City Council refused to let them pick up passengers after dark, and the Seattle taxicab drivers' union stubbornly refused to admit women.

To handle the increasing volume of telegrams across the nation, Western Union expanded its female messenger force (raising the possibility of mixed quartets for singing telegrams); in New York City, however, women messengers could work only during daytime hours and in business districts, to limit the risk of sexual harassment. Oil companies began training young women to replace male filling station attendants, provided the girls wore sensible clothing such as coveralls and heavy waterproof shoes. "We tried flimsy uniforms and bare legs once last year in California," confessed one gas company executive, "and it did not work. Motorists stop at filling stations for service, not to be entertained." Even women who did not work tried to dress as if they did. "This year fashion decrees that you must look useful," explained the editor in chief of *Harper's Bazaar*. "Glamour girls are out—girls who look useless are dated."

Nearly 13 million American women worked outside the home or farm in late 1942—about one-quarter of the women of working age, and slightly over 25 percent of the total number of employed adults. The number had risen steadily but not spectacularly since Pearl Harbor. Most American working women were single. An overwhelming majority left the workplace soon after marriage to raise a family; in 1940, only 15 percent of married women in the United States worked for wages. A Columbia University study, however, indicated that the realities of war already were starting to change the way women viewed their jobs. "They no longer regard them as stop-gaps between school and marriage," reported the study's author. "They know that because of the war they may have to work long after their marriages."

Increasingly they worked at war-related jobs. At the start of 1942, about 500,000 American women were employed in some type of defense work—about 10 percent of the war production labor force. Over the next six months, war contractors hired women in greater numbers, but nearly always for unskilled or semiskilled jobs, since most defense plants initially refused to even consider women for their skilled-worker vacancies.

Aircraft manufacturers often led the way, partly because their manufacturing tasks required less rigorous physical labor, and partly because their male workforce suffered unusually rapid turnover due to labor pirating and the draft. Once they began employing women, aircraft executives acknowledged that their female employees required less supervision, suffered fewer accidents, inflicted less damage on tools, increased their plants' productivity, and were less likely to quit than men. (Companies also noted that their male employees started to wear ties and shave more often.) By summer, Baltimore's Glenn L. Martin airplane plant employed five thousand female factory workers ("Martinettes") and planned to hire thousands more, and the *Wall Street Journal* reported that women formed a majority of workers in numerous aircraft parts manufacturers in the Philadelphia area. From southern California, Tom Treanor reported that "it looks as though women are almost going to take the factories over." The Labor Department encouraged the transition by lowering the minimum age for girls working in armaments plants from eighteen years to sixteen, and numerous state legislatures suspended their laws restricting working hours (especially at night) for women.

Automakers resisted for as long as they could, continuing to give preference to qualified male workers until War Department pressure and the rising impact of draft calls left them few options. Local labor union officials—fearful that women workers would drag down wage scales—typically supported the companies' hiring prejudices. In February, only four or five thousand women were employed in Detroit defense plants, mostly at smaller companies. Ford—which had never hired female workers for its assembly lines—employed fewer than one hundred, and nervously forbade the small coterie of women employees at its new Willow Run bomber plant from leaving their posts and wandering about the facility; they also were instructed to walk to the restroom in pairs. Cadillac hired twenty-five women, but reportedly sequestered them behind a pad-locked door. ("You know how men are," explained a Cadillac spokesman.) The pace picked up after War Department officials ordered Ford to hire at least twelve thousand women for Willow Run, although company officials struggled to define acceptable attire for its female employees. "We are try-ing to bring in a uniform with no sex appeal," announced a plant super-intendent. "We want to keep that out of the picture entirely." Ford finally settled on a combination of slacks, low-heeled shoes, and a short-sleeved blouse or jacket—no pullover sweaters, jewelry, or nail polish—and made the uniform mandatory for all of its female employees. Oldsmobile, mean-while, still had not hired a single female worker by the end of July.

Shipyards were even less welcoming. At the start of summer, fewer than 1 percent of the workers in commercial shipyards were women. Local chapters of shipbuilding unions such as the International Brotherhood of Boilermakers, which exerted a dominant influence in many ports (par-ticularly on the West Coast), refused to accept female members. Publicly, union leaders claimed that shipyards were too dangerous for women. Their real concern was the threat of cheap replacement labor, especially as shipbuilders—led by Henry Kaiser's mammoth yard in Richmond, California—accelerated production with assembly-line methods, which required less skill and experience.

As the manpower crisis worsened in August and September, resistance to hiring women weakened, although employers remained reluctant to hire women over the age of twenty-five. (Perhaps, suggested the dean of Barnard College, businessmen were afraid that middle-aged women "will try to run the whole office or shop.") By late September, 2.5 million women were employed in war-related jobs—about 20 percent of the nation's total war-production labor force—and Paul McNutt announced that at least 3.5 million more women would be needed by the end of 1943. "There are no surplus materials and no reservoir of unemployed," acknowledged McNutt. "We are losing the war. . . . We must scrape bottom." In a fireside chat on the evening of October 12, Roosevelt made it clear that businesses had no choice. "In some communities, employers dislike to employ women," the president told his radio audience. "In others, they are reluc-tant to hire Negroes. In still others, older men are not wanted. We can no longer afford to indulge such prejudices or practices." Even steel mills (whose male employees placed female workers "on the level with black cats in popularity") began hiring women as crane operators. And forecasts of the nation's labor needs kept rising; in early November, the War Manpower Commission predicted that war industries would need to hire nearly 5 million new female workers over the next twelve months.

Few of the war jobs available to women required more than a brief period of training; one observer noted that employers were "rushing them almost literally from the kitchen to war industry occupations." There was a widely held assumption among businesses, unions, and a substantial segment of the public that most female war workers would be employed in factories only for the duration, and so companies felt little need to provide extensive training programs to develop higher-level skills. Nor were the vast majority of women's defense jobs particularly challenging: employers frequently praised their female workers' willingness to tolerate boredom at repetitive tasks, their docility, and their willingness to speed up the pace of production.

But the charm wore off quickly. By November, companies were complaining about the high volume of turnover among recently hired women. Like their male counterparts, some women war workers began taking time off to shop for better jobs, trying out one firm and then moving on to another. Others found the physical strain of production-line labor too demanding. "The women which the [United States Employment Service] has supplied us are not lazy," noted one businessman. "But after the third or fourth day they find the work is new to them, that it is hard for them to stand on their feet, and they soon go back home. The number of women supplied by the service who have stayed on the job is not large." Supervisors grumbled about inappropriate clothing—"peekaboo" sweaters with bare midriffs, and transparent blouses—and accidents caused by women wearing high-heeled shoes. In Santa Monica, Douglas Aircraft (whose workforce was over 25 percent female by late 1942) was forced to close the bomb shelter in its plant because employees were using it for lovemaking during their lunch breaks.

Often expectations got in the way. Few American girls grew up with a dream of working in a war plant, and while patriotic sentiment and wartime exigencies removed much of the class or gender stigma from factory work (at least for the duration), polls showed that only half of American housewives would even consider taking a war-production job. Vigorous recruiting campaigns by the War Manpower Commission and the lure of generous paychecks helped break down their resistance, although women's pay in defense plants seldom equaled male workers' wages. (In November, the War Labor Board ruled in favor of equal pay for equivalent work, then spent months trying to enforce its order.) But by late autumn, the combined effects of boredom on the job, harassment from male colleagues, and fatigue from six-day, forty-eight-hour weeks led increasing numbers of women to start skipping work.

According to Labor Secretary Frances Perkins, rising rates of absenteeism among women workers was by far the most common complaint from war plant executives. Such criticism doubtless rang hollow to women who needed to keep house and cook, care for sick family members, and do most of the shopping while also working overtime on war-production assembly lines. Childless women struggled to meet all their responsibilities; many mothers found it impossible. "Absenteeism is prevalent among women workers largely because employers have not been careful in selecting the right kind of women for available jobs," declared the director of the War Manpower Commission's Chicago office. And the wrong kind of women—as numerous administration spokesmen made clear—were mothers of young children. "Mothers who have a job to do at home should not be made to feel it is their patriotic duty to go out and work," announced the head of the Labor Department's Children's Bureau, and Secretary Perkins herself urged mothers of preschool-age children to remain at home unless the manpower shortage grew desperate.

Although nearly 90 percent of young mothers took Perkins's advice, newspapers and magazines were filled with stories about the "war moms" who tried to balance family and a job, and the deleterious effects on their children. Public or private day care facilities were scarce at the start of the war, and while informal networks of family and neighbors sometimes filled the gap, women who migrated to war boomtowns typically forsook such support.

By the autumn of 1942, the Children's Bureau of the Department of Labor was receiving reports of babies locked in parked cars all day outside of war plants, and toddlers left unsupervised in defense factory yards because their working mothers had no other place to put them. The *Washington Post* reported that "thousands of children are being locked in their homes," and a Children's Bureau official added that "sometimes the mother locks the children out, believing that they will be safer running around the neighborhood." In Massachusetts, referrals to the Society for the Prevention of Cruelty to Children tripled in the first year of the war; often parents had made no provision at all for their children's care. "In the cases of war working mothers where there is neglect," said an SPCC official, "the conditions as far as children are concerned have become worse than ever."

Wartime boomtowns, where the need for child care was greatest, nearly always lacked the resources to provide for the families of thousands of recently arrived workers. Some defense contractors established their own day nurseries, but often they were expensive and open for only a few hours a day. Private charities barely made a dent in the problem. Mounting public pressure finally persuaded Roosevelt to sign an emergency measure authorizing construction of a series of federally operated day nurseries, but the program suffered from a lack of funding, as well as opposition from churches and business organizations who viewed government-sponsored child care centers as "just one more move toward socialism, such as exist in Germany, Italy, and certain other countries, where the children are practically raised by the state."

Instead of expanding their child welfare services, numerous communities slashed their budgets for education and recreation. New York City led the way, cutting funding for nearly "every child welfare and delinquency prevention service," and abolishing its Juvenile Aid Bureau entirely for the duration. Playgrounds deteriorated as wartime materials shortages deprived them of supplies for games or restrooms or even fences to separate children from the street. La Guardia made matters worse by cutting the city's education budget by nearly $4 million, forcing reductions in an already hard-pressed teaching staff.

In numerous ways, education was taking a backseat to other wartime concerns. Instead of welcoming students back for the fall term, towns and cities across the nation closed schools temporarily—so students could help pick cotton or harvest sugar beets—or permanently, due to teacher shortages. Experts estimated that 300,000 children in war boomtowns were off local school boards' books and not attending school at all. The situation did not disturb Harry Hopkins in the least. "High school courses should be shortened so students will have more time to work, especially on farms," wrote the president's closest adviser in the November issue of the *American Magazine*. "Some students should quit high school altogether. A diploma can only be framed and hung on a wall. A shell that a boy or girl helps to make can kill a lot of Japs." General Hershey concurred. "I don't want to hurt education, but the education of our children may have to be confined," the Selective Service director told a war labor conference. "We must realize that we may have to see the time when our youngsters will have to do farmwork or do something else useful four or five hours a day."

Presumably Hopkins and Hershey were pleased that teenage American boys were quitting school in rapidly increasing numbers to join the workforce, often securing unskilled jobs at "unprecedentedly high wages for inexperienced persons" as employers began hiring sixteen-year-olds—or even boys as young as fourteen—instead of men in their early twenties who might soon be lost to the draft. The New York State Labor Department termed the increase in child labor "unprecedented" (and noted an accompanying rising tide of child labor law violations); in Portland, Oregon, an estimated twenty thousand boys between the ages of fourteen and eighteen were working in shipyards or canneries or lumber mills.

There were social costs beyond the loss of education. A Harvard Law School criminologist noted that adolescent boys "are now earning tremendous salaries and are sometimes running amok as a result. In many cases they are earning more than their fathers ever did in one week. They have become, in effect, the head of the family because they control the purse strings," leaving them "less inclined to parental discipline [and] more receptive to many temptations and avid for fun and excitement." The associate chief of the Department of Labor's Children's Bureau discerned a similar trend. "High wages for young people who have had little or no spending money through the depression years, a sudden change in the tempo of their lives with adulthood coming on them prematurely, inadequate recreational facilities, . . . [and] the absence of the father from home and increasingly the absence of the mother," she claimed, "are already creating the conditions in this country that lead to juvenile delinquency."

No comprehensive national report of juvenile arrests existed, but by any measure, delinquency rates were rising—especially in major cities and war boomtowns—and the average age of offenders was falling. In October, *Time* reported that juvenile delinquency was up by 15 percent in Boston over the previous year, although a number of state authorities claimed the actual figure was much higher. A study by the Michigan State Corrections Department revealed that delinquent behavior by minors in Wayne County (which included Detroit) had increased by 45 percent between 1940 and the end of 1942. In the largest defense industry centers in up-state New York, juvenile crime rose between 25 and 30 percent in the first year of the war; two of the state's three reform schools already were filled to capacity. The number of cases prosecuted in New York City's children's court rose by 11 percent in the first eleven months of 1942; one judge acknowledged, however, that "we do not get all the children who are delinquent. We certainly do not know of all the children who have become engaged in delinquent conduct since the beginning of the war." (The only subgroup of New York City teenagers that witnessed a decline in criminal behavior in 1942 was African American males.) In Staten Island—the borough with the highest rate of mothers working in war industry—the juvenile delinquency rate doubled, including gangs of rowdies who mugged their victims under cover of evening dimouts.

Authorities in six Florida cities—including Jacksonville, Fort Lauderdale, and Fort Myers—imposed a 10 p.m. curfew on teenagers to combat "an alarming rise in juvenile delinquency since the outbreak of war." Los Angeles County witnessed a 22 percent increase in juvenile robberies, burglaries, and thefts from January through September; police responded with a crackdown that targeted (often unfairly) gangs of Hispanic teenagers. "Crimes of violence among boys of junior and high school age since Pearl Harbor have shocked us," said one superior court judge. "War does curious things to the minds and emotions of youngsters. Inhibitions . . . are in some peculiar way weakened or released." In Baltimore, arrests of children under the age of 16 jumped by 50 percent in the last six months of 1942. A spokesman for the Washington Metropolitan Police Department announced in early December that juvenile crime in the capital had risen 35 percent over the previous eighteen months, particularly cases of housebreaking and shoplifting; in many parts of the city, children from eleven to sixteen years old reportedly had replaced professional pickpockets. "Since this war is greater than any other, and its social dislocations more severe," predicted the *Washington Post*, "we may expect more and not less reflection of those dislocations in the lives of children."

Using nationwide fingerprint records (which tended to understate juvenile crime rates), FBI officials claimed that arrests of boys under the age of twenty-one increased by 17 percent during 1942, even as the civilian population of young males declined. Arrests of girls increased even more spectacularly, rising by more than 55 percent over the previous year; the most common offenses were disorderly conduct (up 70 percent), drunkenness (40 percent), prostitution and "commercialized vice" (65 percent), and other sex offenses (105 percent). Self-styled "Victory Girls"—typically between fourteen and sixteen years old—dressed themselves "to look eighteen or twenty" and frequented hotel lobbies, or wandered through dimmed-out downtown streets in search of men in uniform. "They think that the boys are here today but may be dead tomorrow," explained one magistrate, "and they reason: 'We'll give them all they want.'" Sometimes the girls were even younger. "There are thousands of 12- to 15-year old girls who flirt with men in uniform," observed a Vassar child-study expert, and in Boston so many of them loitered on the Common and Scully Square that authorities imposed a 9 p.m. curfew on girls under sixteen— which merely moved the parties across the river to Cambridge. (Boston girls generally preferred sailors to soldiers, claiming that Navy men "have more money to spend and spend it easier," and knew more dance steps besides.)

Child welfare authorities reported that in some communities, enthusiastic amateur "pick-up girls" were starting to crowd out older, professional prostitutes. "To their families they are often known as high-spirited daughters full of the joy of life," wrote Alistair Cooke. "To the soldiers they are known as broilers, dishes, bed-bunnies, popovers, free-wheelers, touchable, Susies, teasers, [and] free-lances." An official of the American Social Hygiene Association concluded that "most of them are just healthy, energetic youngsters from farms and small communities. They have a lot of vitality and a normal thirst for social life and nothing is done to satisfy it," because peacetime adolescent pursuits had lost their allure. "Games seem dull and routine," explained a Washington police spokesman. "They played games before Pearl Harbor." Venereal disease rates among fifteen-to nineteen-year-olds of both sexes rose accordingly, as did the number of illegitimate births—the initial wave of "war babies."

"If we win the war and lose our children en route," observed one social welfare official in early December, "it's going to be an empty victory."

"I hardly need to underline the fact that there is little relation between the academic days which lie before you and those of a peaceful college year," President James Conant told the freshman class at Harvard University in early October. "Only a trace of the broadening background of a liberal arts college curriculum can survive in these grim days." Many of the young men in his audience, Conant predicted, would be called to active military service "long before the completion of your college course": "You must consider, therefore, each of you, how you will use most effectively the short academic period which lies ahead."

At his new teaching post at the University of Minnesota, Robert Penn Warren watched students disappear day by day from his English classes. "The war was taking all the bright boys," Warren wrote to a friend. "I have felt all summer and fall that I was in a kind of backwater, and the dwindling classes, and the little boys who, one day, are struggling under my supervision with English Grammar and the next announce to me that they are commissioned in the Air Force or the Navy, don't make me feel any more secure in the hope that the academic life is real and earnest."

Enrollment in American colleges and universities declined by 14 percent in the fall of 1942, as Americans wondered whether (and when) the government would start to draft eighteen- and nineteen-year-olds. War Department officials had been longing to draft teenagers ever since Pearl Harbor: "Their response to leadership, their recovery from fatigue, their enthusiasm or 'flair for soldiering' are exceptional as compared with older age groups," claimed Secretary Stimson. "The simple fact is, they are better soldiers." But a Gallup poll released in June 1942 revealed that a majority of Americans opposed drafting eighteen- and nineteen-year-olds by a margin of 52–42 percent. Throughout the summer, Congress repeatedly brushed aside any proposals to lower the draft age, and President Roosevelt—with one eye on the midterm elections—refused to publicly acknowledge what *Time* called "the realistic but ugly fact" that the Army almost certainly could not defeat Nazi Germany without using eighteen- and nineteen-year-old soldiers.

As the pool of draft-eligible single men dwindled in the autumn, however, the nation faced the stark choice of inducting either teenagers or married men with children. Confronted with those two options, Americans overwhelmingly—by 77 percent to 13 percent—decided that the draft age should be lowered. (Gallup also polled seventeen- to nineteen-year-olds on the question, and discovered that 81 percent of them favored a lower draft age, including many who wished to enlist but were frustrated by their parents' opposition.)

"The time has come," concluded the *Detroit Free Press* in early September, "to quit kidding the kids." On September 7, Republican representative James Wadsworth of New York—who had sponsored the original Selective Service Act in 1940—introduced a measure to lower the draft age to eighteen; South Dakota Republican Chandler Gurney submitted a similar bill to the Senate. "For several months past, the reduction of the age range has been inevitable," Wadsworth told the House. "The sooner it is done the better." The president evinced less urgency; at a press conference on September 11, Roosevelt informed reporters that he thought the Army probably would not need to call the younger boys until early 1943. As thousands of telegrams and letters from mothers opposing the lower draft age began pouring into congressional offices, legislators decided that they, too, saw no need to hurry, and delayed hearings on the proposal until the administration worked up enough nerve to openly request it.

Roosevelt finally acknowledged reality in his Columbus Day radio address. "I believe that it will be necessary to lower the present minimum age limit for Selective Service from twenty years down to eighteen," the president told his audience. "We have learned how inevitable that is—and how important to the speeding up of victory." A small coterie of legislators remained unconvinced. "Has Congress decided to let Boy Scouts fight this war?" asked one Democratic congressman from North Carolina. "It takes a lot of gall to take 18-year-old boys and make cannon fodder out of them, because you know that's what will be done."

"I ask the House to be brave. Let's get this job over with," replied the chairman of the Military Affairs Committee. Bolstered by the reassuring report of a blue-ribbon panel of psychiatrists who concluded that eighteen-year-olds were no more likely than older men to suffer breakdowns under enemy fire, House leaders pushed the measure through in six days, winning final approval by a vote of 345–16. The bill promptly bogged down in the Senate, which displayed no desire to approve anything before the midterm elections. Prohibitionists used the opportunity to introduce an antiliquor proviso to the draft bill, requiring the War Department to establish alcohol-free buffer zones around Army training camps, presumably to protect the virtue of teenage soldiers. Once that suggestion was shuttled off to committee for further review, a more diverse coalition of senators proposed to prohibit the use of eighteen- and nineteen-year-old draftees in combat overseas until they had completed at least a year of training in the United States. "Remember, these are our children," pleaded Senator Hiram Johnson of California, one of the leading pre–Pearl Harbor isolationists. "What will you do when you've sent this generation to war and they exist no more? Give youth some other opportunity than to die."

Despite General George Marshall's warning that such a restriction would impose an "almost impossible administrative burden" on the War Department, the Senate approved the amendment on October 24 largely as a delaying tactic. The vote forced the establishment of a conference committee to resolve the differences between the House and Senate versions of the draft bill, essentially guaranteeing that no final decision would be made until after the elections. A week after the midterms, the conference report struck out the yearlong-training provision. The House passed the measure again by a nearly unanimous voice vote on November 10; a day later, the Senate followed suit, with only a few negative votes. High school students would be allowed to complete their academic year, but there would be no new educational deferments.

"There is a good solid kind of self possession and sensible facing of the situation," wrote novelist Katherine Anne Porter from the University of Colorado. "And every day another boy gets his [draft] questionnaire, and the boys and girls go around singing merrily 'Last Call For Love.'"

# 12: End of the Beginning

## AUGUST–DECEMBER 1942

*This is my country and my night, this is the*
*blacked-out ending to the day, the way they*
*end a skit in a revue.*

—E. B. WHITE, *ONE MAN'S MEAT*, 1942

"As a nation we are undoubtedly short of our normal supply of coffee," observed the *New Yorker* in late August, "but how far short nobody outside Washington knows, as only the War Production Board has any idea how much coffee actually is in the country or on its way here, and the War Production Board is not saying." A shortage of shipping space and the U-boat campaign against Brazilian merchant vessels steadily diminished American stocks of coffee through the summer, while the rapid expansion of the five-cup-per-day U.S. military took much of what remained. On August 21, the WPB reduced the civilian supply of coffee once more, down to 65 percent of prewar consumption—about eight cups per week. "If everybody will be sensible and go without that extra cup now and then," announced a coffee industry spokesman, "the decrease in supplies should hardly be noticeable."

Anxious Americans consumers promptly besieged grocery and department stores to obtain as much coffee as they could hoard, despite the deleterious effects of long-term storage on roasted and ground coffee beans. In a virtual replay of the sugar fiasco, stores attempted to stop the panic by limiting customers to one pound of coffee per sale; then half a pound; then to weekend sales only. Nothing worked. Stores in every part of the country reported "acute shortages" of coffee; many were cleaned out every morning shortly after opening. "Sorry, no coffee," read the signs. "Today's quota sold."

"Please don't be silly about this and start chiseling and buying more coffee than you need," chided Mayor La Guardia on his weekly radio show. "A great many people have done that and that just isn't nice. It isn't patriotic and it shouldn't be done." The public ignored him. A delivery truck that pulled up to a supermarket in the Bronx found a line of seventy-five housewives waiting for it to unload; the entire 160-pound shipment was gone in half an hour. At a store in Dedham, Massachusetts, twenty women tussled and tore one another's clothes in a desperate scramble for coffee. One grocery in Washington, D.C., reportedly sold more than a thousand pounds in less than two hours. Black marketeers in North Carolina offered coffee at two or three times the legal price; desperate for caffeine, some New England coffee addicts turned to a bootlegged brew that federal authorities warned was "unfit for human consumption."

On October 26, OPA officials announced that coffee would be rationed beginning November 28. Every American over the age of fifteen could buy one pound of coffee every five weeks—enough to make one cup a day, said an OPA spokesman, plus "an after-dinner demi tasse" once a week. Newspapers offered numerous suggestions for stretching the ration into additional cups: mixing coffee with chicory (bitter), parched corn (sweet), or perhaps a tablespoon of brandy, which purportedly provided both "considerable stimulation and a suggestion of exhilaration."

La Guardia recommended mixing fresh coffee with used grounds, and even though President Roosevelt (who made his own breakfast coffee on a small stove) followed a similar routine (allowing the grounds to dry out before reusing them at dinner with a pinch of fresh coffee), the National Coffee Association replied that the mayor "might as well have advised shivering New Yorkers to mix a sprinkling of coal with dead, cold ashes and expect a roaring fire." Adding hot water to unwashed coffee pots would make the brew taste different, but hardly better. "Coffee is coffee," insisted a home economics expert at George Washington University. "One is either drinking coffee or something else under its name. It just will not stretch."

Meat rationing came next. Americans' consumption of red meat (beef, pork, veal, lamb, and mutton) had jumped 10 percent in 1941, to an average of nearly three pounds per week per person, fueled largely by increased demand from the "new rich" wage earners in defense plants, many of whom had subsisted on half that weekly amount (or less) during the Depression. Demand continued to rise in the first six months of 1942. "With nearly everybody working and with record high wages being paid, and with many items of normal commerce off the market, people are spending a larger than usual portion of their increased income for meat," noted a satisfied president of Armour & Company.

Even though American ranchers and farmers produced a record-setting amount of beef and pork in 1942, the increased domestic demand—added to the growing requirements of U.S. and Allied troops—created spot shortages of meat in East Coast cities during the summer. Secretary of Agriculture Claude Wickard urged Americans to substitute cheese, eggs, and poultry for red meat, and restaurants promoted "meatless Tuesdays," but the drain continued. At the end of August, administration officials announced that the government would begin rationing meat in early 1943; in the meantime, they asked the nation's 114 million "carnivorous adults" to voluntarily limit themselves to two and a half pounds of red meat per week. Chicken and fish were not restricted, but there was not enough poultry to make up the difference, and the government had already purchased nearly all the nation's salmon, tuna, and sardine catch—which was substantially below prewar volume anyway, since a significant percentage of the nation's fishing vessels were serving as patrol boats or minesweepers for the Navy.

"This is not privation," the *New York Times* reminded its readers, although it also recognized that "to many Americans it must come as almost the biggest surprise of our wartime economy to discover that there is an actual food shortage." OPA authorities launched a "Share the Meat" campaign ("Help win the War! Keep within your Share!"), but less than a month later Wickard opted for coercion, slashing meat deliveries to retailers by 20 percent. (Supplies for each city were based on the amount of meat consumed in the fall of 1941, with no consideration for subsequent increases in population, which meant that residents of war boom communities such as Detroit, Baltimore, and San Diego received quotas far below the national average.)

Consumers found themselves compelled to substitute liver, kidney, brain, tongue, tripe, and sweetbread for their usual fare; a grocery store in Portland, Oregon, obtained a pair of bison from Yellowstone National Park and advertised buffalo meat at fifty cents a pound. "My cook tells me that it is already necessary to take what is in the market, not what one wants," wrote H. L. Mencken in mid-October. ("Popular ballad: Spam 'n' Salad," read one ad.) Restaurant operators were asked to cut their normal servings of meat in half—essentially to serve child's portions to all customers, at lower prices—and to reduce the number of meat dishes on their menus, offering more spaghetti and oysters instead. Nevertheless, meat deliveries to restaurants and butcher shops grew sporadic, and the *Wall Street Journal* reported in late November that supplies of red meat were "awfully short for the armed forces already." On December 2, OPA officials announced that formal meat rationing for civilians would commence in early January; a skeptical trade association of meat dealers warned Roosevelt that the administration's plan would end in "chaos, chiseling and black markets."

One Boston wholesale market offered horse meat for sale (government-inspected, about 25 percent cheaper than beef) in early December and quickly sold its entire inventory, but horses and mules were far more valuable in the East as replacements for motor vehicles. Dairies, laundries, bakeries, and grocery stores increasingly used horse-drawn wagons for deliveries, as did numerous urban newspapers, including the *Chicago Tribune*, which reclaimed fifty wagons from the city dumps and cleaned them up. (No one was making new wagons in the autumn of 1942, due to shortages of metal and wood.) The Pennsylvania Railroad employed horses and mules for some local deliveries, and Roosevelt Raceway on Long Island transported customers to and from the local rail station in horse-drawn carriages. Sales of buckboards, buggies, and surreys at estate sales soared; the price of hay doubled in the first year of the war. Boston civic officials reluctantly granted the Hotel Lenox the first hitching-post permit in the city's history ("Changing times, changing conditions," sighed a member of the Board of Street Commissioners), and drafted plans to install watering troughs at centrally located gas stations, while St. Louis authorities found it necessary to discourage homeowners from converting garages into stables, at least within one hundred feet of someone's house.

Gas rationing knocked the bottom out of the used-car market, although used bicycles continued to command inflated prices. Demand for country homes and "gentlemen's farms" plummeted as wealthy Americans returned to the cities, along with most of the nation's traveling Gypsy population. "This winter New York's going to crawl with gypsies," predicted one of Manhattan's reputed Gypsy kings. "Gypsies are going to head for the nearest slum and hole up." Bus and rail travel kept rising; Greyhound Corporation reported a 30 percent increase in net income in the first nine months of 1942 over the previous year, and the Association of American Railroads announced that its members' profits had risen by more than 50 percent in the first eight months of the year.

Mass-transit ridership in urban areas was up by nearly 50 percent as well. So many commuters were crowding onto buses in the nation's capital that transportation officials reduced the space between seats by ten to fourteen inches, forcing passengers to squeeze together in a sort of "stand-sit" position. Some southern cities found it difficult to enforce Jim Crow restrictions on overcrowded buses where whites and blacks were thrown into unexpectedly close proximity. "There was not yet any organized, or Klannish, objection to the apparent gain in the Negro's social status," observed Alistair Cooke from Houston. "But I overheard plenty of grumbling comments on the emerging fact that 'these damn Nigras are gettin' underfoot. They don't know their place anymore.'"

Automobile accidents declined, but auto insurance payouts actually rose due to an increase in serious accidents resulting from dimouts, fatigued drivers, and worn tires. Convictions for drunk driving and hit-and-run violations also increased. In early November, the National Safety Council termed the nation's manpower losses to accidents in the first nine months of 1942 "a figure which can only be regarded as a disgrace in view of the reduced driving in large sections of the country and reduced speed of operation. . . . It is evident that the individual citizen still has failed to realize the extent to which the Axis is being aided by American carelessness."

As they awaited the advent of nationwide gas rationing (scheduled for

December 1), drivers outside the East Coast continued to ignore government pleas to conserve fuel and tires. Leon Henderson claimed that non-rationed states had reduced driving mileage by less than 20 percent, far short of the administration's goal. When the Washington correspondent of the *Kansas City Star* returned to the Midwest in the autumn, he found that his most vivid impression was of "the profligate use of rubber and gasoline." "The highly-paid war workers," he concluded, "are doing much of it." He was especially surprised by the amount of speeding: "There are many people who refuse to recognize the fact that rubber is probably the most critical item in the whole war production program." In Los Angeles, enterprising motorists began leasing abandoned service stations and filling their five-thousand-gallon underground tanks with gasoline for future use. Songwriter Johnny Mercer—whose "Blues in the Night" was one of the most popular records of 1942—wondered how he would be able to compose any new songs. "Most of my titles and lyrics I make up in my head as I drive," Mercer explained. "When this gas rationing cuts my driving down I don't know what the hell I'll do for inspiration."

OPA officials expected that the thirty-five-mile-per-hour national speed limit, which went into effect on October 1, would curb reckless driving, especially after the federal government gave local rationing boards authority to revoke speeders' gasoline ration books. To further protect rubber inventories, the administration required all passenger car drivers to have their tires inspected every four months for signs of excessive wear. Their condition would be recorded on a tire inspection certificate—no one could legally operate a passenger car without one—which also bore the serial number of each tire. And beginning in November, automobile owners were limited to only one spare tire per car. Designed to recover hoarded rubber, the administration's "Idle Tire" program required drivers to swear that they possessed no more than five tires per car; any additional tires had to be sold or donated to the government by December 1.

Opposition to nationwide gasoline rationing grew more vehement as the December deadline approached. On November 25, a group of congressmen petitioned the administration to delay the program for six months, claiming that rationing was "being crammed down the throats of the American people." Veteran Democratic congressman Hatton Sumners from Texas charged that "this idea of having somebody from Washington telling an individual how to go about his business looks too much like the same bug that bit Hitler is biting some folks in this Government. . . . We're not going to conserve democracy by turning an individual responsibility over to a bureaucrat." Representative F. Edward Hébert of Louisiana accused Leon Henderson of "sowing seeds of disunity and discord" in the nation; Henderson replied in a radio broadcast that opponents of rationing were either "ignorant" or "intentionally traitorous." From Louisiana, Governor Sam Jones reported "almost universal" opposition to rationing, adding that the OPA's plans reflected "the selfish, dog-in-the-manger attitude of a few Easterners who have been running the United States too long."

Recently appointed national rubber czar William Jeffers, president of the Union Pacific Railroad, told reporters that he had received between five thousand and ten thousand printed cards protesting nationwide gas rationing; many came from individuals purporting to be war workers, some of whom threatened to walk off their jobs unless the government canceled its plans. Jeffers blamed the campaign on "an organized opposition using funds furnished by people who should know better." Lashing out at the administration's critics, Under Secretary of War Robert Patterson promised Americans that "we can not and will not deny our soldiers the finest equipment in order to cater to the whims of those who don't seem to realize that their country is at war."

Gasoline rationing would keep Americans at home over the winter; fuel oil rationing would challenge them to keep their houses warm. Since the summer, Roosevelt and Ickes (promoted to petroleum coordinator for war) had been warning easterners that the "increasingly grave petroleum transportation shortage in the East" meant that fuel and heating oil would be in short supply. "Every user of fuel and heating oil should face realistically the fact that there can be no guarantee that he will get enough oil to meet even his minimum needs," the president announced on August 1. Ickes repeatedly urged homeowners who relied on oil-burning furnaces to convert to coal, which was in far more plentiful supply, but by the end of the summer fewer than 1 percent had done so—even though half of their furnaces had originally burned coal. (A significantly higher percentage of commercial and industrial buildings did switch to coal.) Despite an extensive publicity campaign by the Office of War Information's new advertising department, some East Coast residents dismissed the fuel oil shortage as a myth fabricated by Washington bureaucrats. ("Such reports are worse than mischievous," snapped Ickes.) Others simply decided to wait for their neighbors to convert, so they could avoid the inconvenience.

On September 15, Donald Nelson declared that fuel and heating oil rationing would begin on October 1 for thirty states, including most of the East Coast (where two-thirds of the nation's oil-heated homes were located) and in much of the Midwest—from Kentucky to Missouri and Nebraska, and north to the Dakotas. OPA officials initially hoped to provide homeowners with 75 percent of the previous winter's fuel, enough to keep homes at a slightly chilly sixty-five degrees under "average weather conditions." A week before rationing began, however, an unexpected decline in railcar shipments of petroleum to the East Coast led authorities to lower their goal to 67 percent of the previous winter's consumption—and a lower indoor temperature.

Fuel oil allocations were based on a complicated formula that left homeowners frustrated and confused. OPA application forms required them to measure each room in their house (including halls and closets but not attics or basements, unless they were used as bedrooms), add up the square footage, provide detailed information about their furnace and heating system, and explain how much fuel oil they had used the previous year. ("Another bout with the blanks," grumbled the *Boston Globe*.) Households with young children, elderly occupants, or invalids (physician's note required) would receive additional oil; homes with insufficient insulation or inefficient furnaces would not. "The great majority of the consumers are bewildered by the rationing regulations," charged an oil company executive, "and have only the vaguest idea of what they are expected to do." (Fuel distributors faced the same problem; "We've never been able to figure out the OPA's formula for rationing," confessed one Baltimore dealer.) There would be no fuel rations at all for apartment houses, commercial establishments, and industrial buildings whose owners could have converted their heating systems to coal but failed to do so.

By late September, wood-burning stoves had vanished from stores, and firewood dealers in New England reported their lots were nearly empty; there was not enough manpower available to cut more wood on local farms, nor transportation to carry it to consumers. Churches with diminished heating supplies canceled some of their worship services, and scheduled congregational meetings for private homes. Anxious homeowners besieged OPA offices with frantic phone calls asking for explanations of the rationing procedure, especially since the coupon books for heating oil had not yet been delivered—and would not arrive until late November, nearly two months after rationing began. No one seemed to know what to do about the thousands of New England homes heated entirely by oil-burning stoves.

When rail shipments of petroleum to the East dropped further below official expectations in each week of October, the War Production Board decided to reduce fuel oil rations again. ("*Every* girl's a sweater girl now," chirped an ad for Lord & Taylor department store.) Elementary schools in Massachusetts made plans to consolidate students and shut down the remaining buildings; officials at the Boston Rationing Board's headquarters had to call police to quell an angry mob seeking additional oil coupons. An OPA district rationing official in New York cautioned the public that the heating oil situation was "far more serious than the overworked word 'critical' implies": "Before this winter is over people will have to resort to all sorts of extremes to keep warm."

"There is no use trying to conceal the fact that you are going to suffer inconveniences this winter," admitted Leon Henderson. The nation's civilian population, he added grimly, "has barely begun to feel the impact of the war." In Washington, Representative Edith Nourse Rogers of Massachusetts replied that "no one should have to endure unnecessary suffering and illness due to cold," and a bipartisan coalition of New England congressmen denounced "these bureaucrats in their big cars and warm apartments, who may not understand the problem."

"The effects of the war are beginning to show themselves," wrote H. L. Mencken in the early winter. "The American people realize at last that they are in for what may be a long, bloody and immensely costly struggle."

Democrats' prospects for the midterm elections grew darker as November approached. An early Gallup poll of voters in May had predicted that the party would gain thirty-eight seats in the House; two months later, the projected increase was down to eight seats; by September, Gallup projected a twenty-one-seat gain by Republicans. The president's approval numbers steadily declined as well. After peaking at 84 percent early in 1942, they fell to 70 percent in late August. Roosevelt rarely appeared outside the White House anymore. "What he was doing, where he went, what he was thinking, the public as usual was not told," observed *Time* in late August. Even when the president spent the last two weeks of September on a secret tour of war plants across the country, the press obediently kept his whereabouts from the public; most Americans (except for those in the cities he visited) had no idea that Roosevelt had even left Washington until he returned to the capital and gave reporters permission to break the story.

Uncharacteristically ill-tempered at press conferences, the president appeared frustrated by troublesome domestic issues. Watching him spar with journalists, John Dos Passos noted that questions about rationing and economic policy especially agitated Roosevelt: "His manner becomes abrupt. A querulous note of vexation comes into his voice. He won't talk about these things. Congress will have to decide them, he says. His face takes on an air of fatigue, there's a sagging look under the eyes of having been up late at his desk, of sleepless nights."

Roosevelt was especially vexed by a series of brutally honest public appraisals of the discouraging military situation delivered by top-level administration officials in late September. "The tide of war is still running against us. . . . We are beginning to understand that we can still lose," confessed Paul McNutt. "How about, for a change, just saying that we are still losing the war, period? And realizing that we damn well mean it, period?" wondered Assistant Secretary of the Navy Ralph Bard. "The Allies have taken a terrific shellacking all around the globe," admitted Lieutenant General Brehon Somervell, chief of the Army's Service Forces. "We've lost all our rubber, most of our tin, our hemp, our silk. We've lost ships by the hundreds, men by the thousands. We've lost the freedom of the seas. We've lost everything except a smug sense of complacency."

"There has never been so much questioning about Mr. Roosevelt's leadership as you hear around Washington now," claimed Ray Clapper. "Friends of the Administration are asking questions now. They can't understand some of the things Mr. Roosevelt says and does or doesn't do, his seeming confusion and his contradictions." Observers agreed that enthusiasm among Democratic voters was waning. "The Republican drift is unmistakable," claimed Raymond Moley. "Vast numbers of people are dissatisfied with the conduct of the war and at home." In an informal poll, Washington correspondents predicted that public discontent with the war effort would be the most important single factor in the midterm elections; the *New York Times* pointed especially to rationing, inflation, and Americans' "lack of confidence in the accuracy of reports from the fighting fronts put out by agencies of the government."

Between September 15 and October 15, the cost of living rose at an annual rate of 12 percent, leaving the OPA's price ceilings in tatters. Consumers complained increasingly about manufacturers who evaded price regulations by substituting inferior goods made with mediocre materials or shoddy workmanship. Food prices leaped 2.4 percent in September, despite record agricultural production. To harvest the crops, labor-starved rural communities mobilized an ad hoc army of temporary field workers: townspeople, clerks, businessmen, women's auxiliary forces, state government employees, convicts from California's Folsom Prison, the governor of Idaho ("The job isn't exactly what you would call a breeze"), the entire University of North Dakota student body (classes were canceled for two weeks), and thousands of school-age children. "Gentlemen, it is open season on children for you," an embittered general secretary of the National Child Labor Committee told Congress on October 21. "All restrictions are off. Do what you will with them for the duration and we'll look the other way and call it patriotism."

Sometimes amateur farmhands were not enough. Governor Culbert Olson of California pleaded with Washington for the immediate admission of Mexican agricultural workers to help with the harvest. "Without a substantial number of Mexicans," Olson argued, "the situation is certain to be disastrous to the entire victory program." Specifically, what California growers desired was a generous supply of "stoop labor"—"virtual serfs," explained Alistair Cooke, "who traditionally harvest bumper crops for a few dollars a day, and who are not white"—to replace the pickers (mostly Filipinos) who had deserted West Coast farms for war factories. By fall the administration had negotiated an agreement with the government of Mexico to permit the importation of "guest workers" (popularly termed "braceros") to labor in American fields before being shipped back across the border at the end of the season. California and Arizona farmers employed between four thousand and five thousand braceros in 1942, often at lower wages than American workers, despite official promises to the contrary. Ten times as many would arrive the following year.

Growers welcomed the braceros because the average wage for hired farm labor had risen more than 25 percent since 1941. Industrial wage rates rose throughout the summer as well, especially after the War Labor Board granted a pay increase to steelworkers employed by the four "Little Steel" companies (Bethlehem Steel, Republic Steel, Youngstown Sheet and Tube, and Inland Steel), on the grounds that their wages needed to keep pace with the 15 percent increase in living costs since January 1941. The board's decision—which was extended generally to other industrial workers—did nothing to convince critics that the administration had abandoned its prolabor bias. "Labor leaders must learn that their high, wide and fancy decade is about over," warned one dissenting member of the WLB, "and the World War we are now engaged in is actually going on."

In yet another attempt to control the cost of living, the president announced on October 3 an ambitious anti-inflationary program that included the creation of yet another new agency—the Office of Economic Stabilization—headed by Supreme Court justice (and former senator) James "Jimmy" Byrnes, a longtime Roosevelt friend and ally. ("The eternal right-hand man," thought *Time*.) Armed with nearly dictatorial powers over the domestic economy, Byrnes began by slapping a freeze on the price of nearly all food items (except seasonal fresh fruits and vegetables), extending rent controls to virtually every apartment and dwelling unit in the country, and freezing Americans' salaries and wages at their September 15 levels.

Several weeks later, Congress passed "the steepest tax bill in history"; Roosevelt signed the measure on October 20. At 249 pages and 135,000 words, the Revenue Act of 1942 also was the longest piece of legislation ever approved by Congress, as well as the heaviest, weighing nearly nine and a half pounds. ("It's all right," shrugged the chairman of the House Ways and Means Committee. "It was as good as we could do.") Designed to raise an additional $9.7 billion in revenue, the act increased business taxes by imposing a rate of 40 percent on corporate earnings, as well as a 90 percent excess profits tax—a portion of which would be returned to companies after the war.

For individual taxpayers, the news was worse: the Revenue Act lowered exemptions, increased the normal individual income tax rate from 4 percent to 6 percent, raised the graduated surtax (which escalated sharply on incomes above $2,000) to a maximum of 82 percent, and introduced a flat "Victory" withholding tax of 5 percent on all gross earnings over $12 a week. Under the new system, the effective tax rate on the first dollar of an individual's taxable income was 19 percent; a single taxpayer with no dependents who made $4,000 a year saw his tax obligations rise from $296 to $768. Experts estimated that more than 30 million Americans would need to pay federal income taxes for the first time in their lives in 1943. "Nearly every adult American will not only be contributing to the cost of government and war," predicted one journalist, "but will begin to acquire an investment in sound government and sound money." By executive order, Roosevelt also imposed his long-sought $25,000 limit on individuals' after-tax income.

Excise taxes also rose (to discourage consumption) on a wide assortment of items, including cigarettes, telephone calls, telegrams, train and bus and air travel, beer, wine, and liquor. Before the new excise taxes took effect on November 1, Americans swarmed into liquor shops and department stores in cities and towns across the country, and bought cases of whatever alcoholic beverages they could find. Sales in many areas were more than triple their normal volume. "There is no 'shopping' by customers," noted a Bloomingdale's employee. "They are buying anything and everything." Some stores reported customers standing five or six deep at counters; in others, impatient patrons grew so unruly that shop managers called in police or private guards to restore order. A liquor store owner in Chicago swore that sales in the last week of October surpassed those in the week before Prohibition began in 1919. "Liquor buyers must be hoarding it like sugar and coffee," he said. "Many persons appear to be investing their savings in liquor."

In the weeks leading up to the midterm elections, observers noticed "an intense lack of excitement" among the nation's voters. Some commentators concluded that Americans were too busy at their war jobs to give much attention to political campaigns—often workers who had migrated to jobs out of state never bothered to change their voting registration—or perhaps they were preoccupied with military events abroad. Many were simply disillusioned with politics as usual.

Voter turnout on November 3 was unusually light, especially in large cities. Only 26 million Americans bothered to go to the polls—43 percent of eligible voters, the lowest percentage for any election since 1930. And "the great majority of stay-at-homes," concluded the Gallup organization, "were Democrats."

In a stunning rebuke of the Roosevelt administration that easily surpassed GOP hopes and Democratic fears, Republicans gained 44 seats in the House—reducing the Democrats' majority to 222–209, the narrowest margin in ten years—and picked up 9 seats in the Senate. "All the boys who went down were Roosevelt men," claimed Lyndon Johnson, "who have voted with him come Hell or high water." Republican Earl Warren easily won the gubernatorial race in California. Thomas Dewey became the first Republican governor of New York in twenty years, and was immediately deemed the early favorite for the party's presidential nomination in 1944. "There was surely no precedent for Tuesday's balloting," noted the *Washington Post*. "In its snowball proportions, it was far more than a normal 'off-year' swing. . . . There was a very patent dissatisfaction with the conduct of the war."

"Voters felt the war was not being conducted with greater efficiency," agreed Mark Sullivan. The *New York Times* deemed the vote "an important reverse for the Administration," and Arthur Krock attributed the results to public disaffection with "the clearly demonstrated delays in preparation, failures, errors and compromises in performance, group favoritisms, partisan political approaches to problems and tolerated incompetence which have attended the marshaling of [national] resources." Democratic leaders in Congress advised administration officials to begin cutting bureaucratic red tape, eliminating war production bottlenecks, and "speeding war information more promptly to the public." Some commentators also believed that voters were signaling the administration to shelve further social reforms, at least for the duration. "It was a bad election for visionaries," concluded Raymond Moley. "From Massachusetts to California, men of a conservative bent were elected." To one defeated liberal Democrat, it seemed that "reaction is now in the saddle, riding hell-bent for election—in 1944."

There was no formal post-election response from the White House, but Vice President Wallace tried to put a happy face on the outcome. "Under the circumstances of this election," Wallace insisted, "it is a miracle that there was not a Republican House."

"People are affected by this war in a strange way," concluded Ray Clapper. "It is an offshore war and so much is secret that its magnitude is difficult to grasp. So it reaches out like an unseen hand to clutch people by the throat, with rationing, with goods disappearing completely, with sons and husbands disappearing into the unknown where they may be either alive or dead. The psychological strains of such a war are heavy and lead to bitterness against those regarded as the authors of these circumstances."

Several hours before dawn on November 8, a force of nearly one hundred thousand American soldiers launched an invasion of French North Africa. (Although British troops also participated in a supporting role, the invaders sought to give the appearance of a wholly American force to avoid offending French sensibilities.) Plans for Operation Torch called for a coordinated series of landings on thinly defended beaches just outside the key ports of Algiers, Oran, and Casablanca, but almost nothing proceeded as scheduled: boats ran aground on the wrong beachheads in the darkness; infantrymen were dropped into the water too far from shore; and some landing craft sank before discharging their troops.

As American forces stumbled ashore amid the confusion, they encountered little resistance on the beaches. Announcements blasted through loudspeakers and distributed on leaflets (in bad French) assured the local residents that the invasion was designed not to conquer, but to protect them against a German or Italian attack. (Each American soldier carried detailed instructions on how to deal with Algerian and Moroccan civilians. "You must not talk to Moslem women," they were told. "Never, under no circumstances.") Decades of cordial Franco-American relations caused many American soldiers to hesitate before firing upon their erstwhile allies. The scattered French soldiers they encountered displayed no such compunction about firing upon the visitors, however, and the shore batteries at Oran and Casablanca inflicted substantial damage on the Anglo-American task forces that attempted direct assaults on the harbors.

Americans learned of the North African operation at 9 a.m. eastern war time, when the White House released a statement by President Roosevelt (who was disappointed that the invasion did not occur before the election), informing them that "a powerful American force equipped with adequate weapons of modern warfare" had landed in Algeria and Morocco. "This must be the second front," concluded Senator Harry Truman. "I hope we take them for a loop." Military communiqués painted the invasion as a smoothly synchronized series of landings, rather than the mixture of "anarchy and success" it was.

Algiers capitulated in less than twenty-four hours. It took several more days to subdue the coastal defenses at Oran and Casablanca, but by October 11 the French commander, Admiral François Darlan, had agreed to a cease-fire. Allied casualties totaled about two thousand men, including 526 American dead.

"The radio is full of blasts about the invasion of North Africa," wrote novelist Henry Miller to his lover, Anaïs Nin. "Sounds wonderful. The first brilliant stroke on the part of the Allies." It was, claimed one Army spokesman, "the start of the real American war in the European theater of operations. . . . It marks a turning point from the training period to actual fighting." Military analyst Fletcher Pratt was less exuberant. "It is itself only a first step," warned Pratt, "and the easiest one."

As they awaited reinforcements, the American forces prepared to turn eastward and challenge German troops (who were retreating westward from their defeat at El Alamein) for control of Tunisia. "Hazardous as these operations may be, and however long and hard the road that lies ahead," declared the *New York Times*, "we know now that we are no longer merely hitting back on the defensive."

# Epilogue: December 7, 1942

*A year ago we were still hardly*
*aware of the kind of world we live in.*

—ANNE O'HARE McCORMICK,

DECEMBER 1942

There were few parades or speeches to commemorate the first anniversary of Pearl Harbor. President Roosevelt observed the occasion with official silence, "in remembrance of a day of great infamy"; Secretary of State Cordell Hull thought the memory of the attack spoke for itself. Some communities held church services "for victory and peace," while others sponsored special War Bond campaigns, or staged lunchtime rallies of war workers and civilian defense volunteers. New Mexico authorities declared a holiday to honor the families of three thousand soldiers from the state who had fought at Bataan and Corregidor. Naval censors marked the date by releasing more photographs of the attack on Hawaii a year earlier, along with their most candid—yet still incomplete—acknowledgment of just how devastating American losses had been. "It ought to be a day in our history," declared Eleanor Roosevelt, "from which we learn enough to make resolutions that such things will not happen again."

Most Americans spent the day working. It was clear by the first week of December that the nation's war plants would not meet most of the ambitious production goals established by the president at the start of the year; the Office of War Information estimated that the military would receive perhaps 85 percent of the armaments the administration had hoped to deliver. Instead of sixty thousand warplanes, American factories would turn out only forty-nine thousand (although more of them were heavy bombers than originally planned). Tanks and antiaircraft guns also fell short of the administration's targets, and Washington officials acknowledged that the expansion in arms production appeared to be slowing as men and materials grew more scarce. "In 1942 we were still living off our peacetime fat," noted an OWI report. "We are now close to the bare muscle, and we can only proceed by toughening and increasing that muscle."

American casualties in the first year of war totaled 8,192 dead and 6,335 wounded; another 43,562 men were missing, mostly troops from Bataan and Corregidor who were presumed to be prisoners of war. About 1 million United States soldiers were serving overseas in December 1942, almost none of whom had been abroad a year earlier. On Guadalcanal, fifty thousand marines were extinguishing the last remnants of Japanese resistance. The past four months of the battle in the Solomons had been, in Adolf Berle's words, "the damnedest fight there ever was," but the Japanese high command was nearing a decision to abandon the island, providing the United States with its first clear-cut victory on land in the Pacific theater.

The Anglo-American advance in North Africa, however, encountered stiffer resistance than expected, and the offensive was bogged down in western Tunisia. Pummeled by German panzer units and strafed by Luftwaffe dive-bombers, the Allied troops were beset by supply shortages, inadequate ground transportation, negligible air support, insufficient infantry reserves, poor coordination between American and British commands, and the thick, sticky mud that accompanied the start of the rainy season in North Africa. "To land an expedition is one thing," noted columnist Anne O'Hare McCormick; "to keep it supplied and augmented over long stretches of ocean is another." Military censorship with the invasion force was even tighter than usual, and the Army's overly optimistic communiqués once again encouraged American newspapers to mislead the public about Allied gains. Eisenhower believed that Roosevelt and Churchill, too, failed to appreciate the challenges that lay ahead. "The authorities in London and Washington," the general wrote to a colleague, "continue to suffer a bit from delusion as to the extent of our military control over this country."

Instead of uniting Americans behind the political and military leadership of the nation, twelve months of war had opened a rift between the federal government and a substantial portion of the public. No widespread organized opposition to the war existed; there was, rather, a simmering distrust of Congress and especially the administration, sparked by a feeling that officials in Washington did not trust the people, or the people's judgment, especially when dealing with war news and the elusive issue of morale. Efforts to promote patriotic fervor by manipulating reports from the battlefront made Americans "uneasy and suspicious," insisted the *New York Times*; what the public wanted was "to be told something about the war, and not to be preached to."

Doubts about the accuracy of wartime news would not soon disappear. By early December, a steadily growing proportion of articles in American newspapers were little more than heavily censored military communiqués or thinly disguised government propaganda—a trend which enabled administration officials (including President Roosevelt) to dismiss criticism of their policies by charging that outsiders were "not in a position to know the facts," primarily because administration officials limited the public's access to those facts. "In all governmental affairs, the press is free only to report what is officially released," noted Carl Ackerman, dean of the Columbia University School of Journalism. "The plain truth is . . . that the Government is in control of virtually all important sources of news, since in a total war every conceivable form of human activity can be construed as of military significance."

Stung by sharply escalating taxes, rising prices, and the salary freeze, middle-class Americans ended the year with the unsettling feeling that the Roosevelt administration had chosen them to bear the brunt of wartime sacrifices. At his ranch in California, Eugene O'Neill feared that the nation's white-collar workers, professionals, small businessmen (who won few defense contracts), and small farmers (who won even fewer bids to supply the troops) were being squeezed between organized labor and big business. "The people who are the finest types of America are pushed to the wall," O'Neill wrote in December, "while the lousiest type uses Defense work to get rich quick as lazily as possible, hoping the war will go on indefinitely. . . . I am convinced," he added, "there is also a deliberate plan by a Washington clique to use the war to smash this class."

Anti-Washington sentiments pervaded so much of the country that even a loyal Democratic legislator such as Congressman Lyndon Johnson, who had served Roosevelt faithfully in support of New Deal objectives, found it politically prudent to vilify the federal bureaucracy. In a December 7 message to his Texas constituents, Johnson denounced the "overstaffed, over-stuffed government" in Washington, and wondered rhetorically "what to do about rationing that has gone irrational, about administrators who spent too much time laying down the law to us and not enough time in reading up on the law?" At least one bureaucrat agreed. After serving for five months as "acting chief of interpretations in the Rubber Branch" of the Office of Price Administration, Richard M. Nixon resigned to join the Navy; Nixon later wrote that his brief time in Washington had convinced him that his former colleagues at the OPA "were obsessed with their own power . . . and seemed to delight in kicking other people around."

Certainly opponents of nationwide gasoline rationing—which went into effect on December 1—remained unreconciled to the administration's program. Motorists in southern California spent Pearl Harbor weekend slipping across the Mexican border to Tijuana, where they could fill their gas tanks without restrictions. Authorities in Albuquerque, New Mexico, reported a near riot at ration board headquarters by drivers attempting to obtain B or C cards. In Texas, local rationing boards thumbed their noses at Washington by granting a liberal supply of supplemental gasoline to their neighbors—ranchers and large landowners—while vindictively denying the applications of residents who worked for federal civilian agencies such as the Internal Revenue Service, on the grounds that they were "non-essential government employees."

Rationing "will not work," argued Michigan Republican senator Arthur Vandenberg. "It had better be promptly reviewed, before it breaks down, and the country breaks down with it." The *Chicago Tribune* blamed "New Deal tormentors" (and the *Tribune*'s favorite whipping boy, Mayor La

Guardia) for agitating to impose nationwide rationing as part of a "spread the suffering campaign." Other critics thought they discerned ulterior motives behind the administration's policy. "The public thinks that rationing is part of a grand regimentative scheme," insisted the general manager of the Automobile Club of Southern California, "to bring the people to a state of abject submission to the government's dictates."

Along the East Coast, petroleum supplies declined even further as increasing quantities of gasoline and oil were diverted to Allied troops in North Africa. "Our ability to meet the extraordinary military demands of these areas is largely dependent upon cutting down our own consumption here," explained Petroleum Coordinator Ickes. Consequently, A ration card holders found their gasoline allotments reduced from four gallons to three, while bus service in eastern cities was curtailed to further conserve gas.

Rising military requirements for petroleum also threatened further cuts in fuel oil rations. "Unless tankship deliveries can be increased substantially, a prospect that is distinctly improbable, further fuel shortages of petroleum product for the East Coast must be forecast," warned the chairman of the Petroleum Industry War Council. In New York City, the Department of Health received twice as many complaints in November 1942 of insufficient heat in apartment buildings as it had a year earlier, but Leon Henderson left no doubt of the OPA's priorities. "If it ever came to a choice between risking pneumonia and of getting oil to troops going into Tunisia," Henderson told reporters, "I don't think any medical director would fail to choose the latter."

In reviewing the midterm election results, James Farley—Roosevelt's former campaign manager—decided that "it is quite evident that the American people got a little bit tired of being pushed around." They were about to be pushed around even more. To centralize control over the nation's manpower reserves, President Roosevelt issued an executive order on December 5 granting War Manpower Commission chairman Paul McNutt "virtually dictatorial powers" over the Selective Service system and all civilian employment in the United States. Roosevelt's order gave McNutt authority to decide whether each individual citizen would join the military or work at a civilian job; no one between the ages of eighteen and thirty-eight would be permitted to enlist voluntarily in any branch of the military service. For those who remained in the civilian sector, McNutt ostensibly could dictate what job they performed (moving them into or out of war industries) and where they would work. Such a sweeping grant of authority, concluded the *New York Times*, gave McNutt "more power over more men and women than any one has ever before exercised in this country." (Some observers questioned whether it was prudent to bestow such authority upon a man who was widely perceived as harboring presidential ambitions of his own, especially one who decorated his office with a larger-than-life-sized portrait of himself and an accompanying bronze bust by the door.) In Detroit, the president of the United Automobile Workers' Local 600—one of the largest local labor unions in the world—denounced McNutt's appointment as "a slap in the face" to labor. "Before American labor will submit to any dictatorship," he predicted, "labor will strike all across the nation."

One day later, Roosevelt named Secretary of Agriculture Claude Wickard as food administrator, with authority over the production and allocation of the nation's food supply, including rationing and Lend-Lease shipments. Numerous observers pointed out the areas of obvious overlap between McNutt's and Wickard's new powers—whether farmworkers should be drafted, for instance—but Roosevelt waved away such concerns, promising to settle any territorial disputes himself. In his first press conference as America's "food czar," Wickard promised that the United States would remain the world's best-fed country in 1943, even as shortages of canned goods increasingly plagued small towns across the country. Other communities had already expended their entire meat quota for December, forcing residents to adopt meatless menus for the rest of the year; one columnist suggested that "nineteen forty-three, it would seem, will be a banner year for vegetarians."

A year after Pearl Harbor, the most popular war song on American jukeboxes was "Der Fuehrer's Face," a satirical anti-Nazi novelty number originally written for a Walt Disney film (*Donald Duck in Nutzi-Land*), and recorded by hitherto obscure drummer Lindley Armstrong "Spike" Jones and his City Slickers. Full of brass band oompahs and razzing noises from a kazoolike instrument, the song was an irreverent send-up of the Nazi

Party anthem; *Time* called it "a medley of bronx cheers and polka-dottiness that has to be heard to be appreciated." Following close behind in popularity polls were Hoagy Carmichael's "The Cranky Old Yank (in a Clanky Old Tank)," and "Praise the Lord and Pass the Ammunition," with lyrics by Frank Loesser based on a quote attributed to a Navy chaplain at Pearl Harbor.

Asked why American composers still had not produced any wartime song as memorable as "Over There," songwriter-author-politician Donald Richberg suggested that "thus far the thing has been too grim to sing about. When we begin to win, we'll begin to sing."

On December 7, New York City Parks Department employees hoisted a sixty-five-foot Christmas tree into place in front of City Hall, though all its illuminated decorations went dark at dusk, in obedience to a recent Army order prohibiting outdoor holiday lights during dimout hours. Rockefeller Center featured three smaller-than-usual Norway spruces (living trees, for the first time) adorned with red, white, and blue plastic globes but no brightly colored bulbs. Nor would there be any lights on the national Christmas tree on the south grounds of the White House. Across much of the nation, Christmas trees were in short supply (due to shortages of workers on Maine farms and dwindling transportation options) but demand was rising, forcing prices up by nearly 50 percent in some urban areas.

Department store holiday window displays seemed simpler than in previous years, with paper models replacing metal or wooden figures in the dimmed-out storefronts. Nearly every window in Manhattan's famous department stores featured war-related decorations, including Bloomingdale's display of war-stamp corsages impaled upon Army bayonets. Inside the stores, customers encountered long lines and few salespeople; delays of half an hour for counter service were not uncommon. Merchants advised shoppers to buy gifts early, wrap their purchases themselves (Filene's in Boston provided a forty-foot-long self-serve gift-wrapping counter), and forgo delivery: "Rule for a Wartime Yule: Don't Delay! Buy It Today! Carry It Away!"

"Practical gifts are doubly important now," proclaimed Woodward & Lothrop, and so Americans stocked up on flannel pajamas, sweaters ("A good sweater is worth a ton of coal," suggested Brooks Brothers), and electric blankets that "automatically grow warmer as the room grows colder." Alarm clocks were nearly impossible to find. Military toys remained in great demand—shoppers sometimes found life-size figures of Santa Claus and General MacArthur side by side in the children's aisles—but by the first week of December, most of the scarce metal toys (all leftovers from Christmas 1941) were already gone, and production priorities dictated that there would be no more. Instead, shelves were stocked with wooden guns, jigsaw puzzles of General Doolittle and his plane, models of bomber cockpits with instrument panels (so children "can learn the basic facts about operating an airplane"), games that taught kids to identify various types of aircraft, and lots of drums.

Younger children could use toys and games to work off emotional stress from the war, but teenagers could not, and the incidence of juvenile delinquency continued to rise. Movie theaters across the country reported a mounting wave of vandalism by gangs of boys—typically from thirteen to twenty-one years old—who forced their way past theater ushers and proceeded to slash seats with knives or slice chunks out of carpets, and wreck or steal washroom fixtures. Insubordination and violent behavior by teenage students in public schools grew so menacing that New York City teachers appealed directly to the city's police force for protection. "Before the sun sets," reported the *Boston Globe*, "any teacher in a New York public school may end up with a black eye, sixteen stitches in his head, or even as a corpse," as did one junior high school teacher who was fatally shot by a student in a boys' washroom. "There can be no doubt," warned the chief of staff of Children's Hospital in Washington, "that the facilities of our clinics for mental hygiene will be taxed by an increased number of bewildered little minds whose balance has been disturbed by the horrors of war."

"It has been a year in which the American people have come to realize that no nation is unbeatable," wrote Hanson Baldwin on December 7, "that liberty is purchased only at the price of pain, that even the resources of the United States are limited." Most burdensome was the anxiety and sense of dread that accompanied the departure of nearly 3 million more men into the armed forces during the past twelve months, their whereabouts and well-being typically hidden from their wives, parents, and children. Americans knew that the casualty lists from Guadalcanal and the North African campaign portended far greater losses in the coming days.

Since the nation's resources were, in fact, limited, the federal government had become an increasingly intrusive presence in civilians' lives since Pearl Harbor, and Americans were far from happy about the development. "Americans temperamentally don't like much government," Alistair Cooke explained to his British friends. "They think of it as a healthy man thinks of a surgeon's knife." So the first twelve months of total war had been a bumpy road of adjustments. In December 1942, many Americans still refused to give their wholehearted commitment to the war effort; calls for sacrifice often had been ignored, and restrictions evaded. "There's one thing America hasn't yet got around to," claimed the Carrier Corporation in an early December appeal to the public. "We're still waiting for that old-fashioned American 'drive' that hits the line head-on and sweeps everything before it."

Seemingly determined to prove that American democracy is necessarily a messy and quarrelsome business, Congress had spent much of the first year of war promoting narrow parochial concerns instead of the national interest, playing partisan politics and attempting to incite popular resistance to the administration's rationing programs. The November elections provided Republicans with a substantial increase in legislative influence, although the results represented a rejection of the Roosevelt administration far more than an endorsement of Republican policy alternatives—which seemed, at best, difficult to detect. Like many elections, however, the midterms of 1942 bore unintended consequences; by punishing Democratic congressmen for the administration's bumbling direction of the war effort, voters empowered conservatives who wished to use the wartime emergency to turn back the clock and repeal popular New Deal reforms.

Highly organized pressure groups continued to battle one another in pursuit of their own agendas, despite the damage they wrought upon the war effort. Farm lobbyists worked overtime to thwart price ceilings on agricultural goods. Friction between labor and business had steadily increased in the twelve months following Pearl Harbor, with disputes centering on the government's wage freeze and the closed shop. In 1943, coal miners and railroad employees would stage nationwide walkouts, endangering the entire war production program until Roosevelt seized both the mines and the railroads.

Wartime pressures also had brought racial animosities to the surface, supplying cover for nativists who had long wished to rid the West Coast of Japanese Americans. In cities across the country, white anxieties intensified in 1942 as African Americans moved into communities and jobs previously reserved for whites. The following year, racial tensions would erupt in full-scale riots, as Americans fought and sometimes killed Americans in the streets of Detroit, New York City, Los Angeles, Mobile, and Beaumont, Texas.

On December 7, 1942, American military forces faced a far more promising future than they had a year earlier. But on the home front, national unity remained elusive, even in the midst of a total war.

# Acknowledgments

Special thanks go to the staffs of the Morris Library at the University of Delaware, and the Albin O. Kuhn Library at the University of Maryland, Baltimore County, for their kindness and assistance while I was researching this volume. The Public Inquiries Team of the Historical Resources and Information Division of the U.S. Army Center of Military History also provided valuable and prompt information. I owe a special debt of gratitude to my editor, Daniela Rapp, for her support, enthusiasm, and insights, which sharpened my focus and streamlined the narrative. My agent, Daniel Bial, has been my friend and adviser for more than thirty years, and I cannot imagine attempting to write anything without his guidance and encouragement.

Most of all, I want to thank my family, for being there.

# Notes

The first citation of a published source always includes an abbreviated title; subsequent citations employ only the author or editor's last name, unless I have used more than one book by that author or editor.

The following abbreviations are used throughout:

| | |
|---|---|
| BG | *Boston Globe* |
| DFP | *Detroit Free Press* |
| LAT | *Los Angeles Times* |
| NOTP | *New Orleans Times-Picayune* |
| NYT | *New York Times* |
| SUN | *Baltimore Sun* |
| TRIB | *Chicago Tribune* |
| WP | *Washington Post* |
| WSJ | *Wall Street Journal* |

## Prologue

1 "the biggest Christmas rush in U.S. History": *Time*, Dec. 1, 1941, p. 71.
1 "A good long-term investment, no matter . . .": *NYT*, Dec. 7, 1941.
2 "the vanishing last few yards of silk . . .": *TRIB*, Dec. 7, 1941.
2 "stag party": *NYT*, Dec. 5, 1941.
2 "Though one might think . . .": *Newsweek*, Dec. 22, 1941, p. 66.
2 "the modern magic of television": *NYT*, Dec. 6, 1941.
3 "Furious local counter attacks . . .": *TRIB*, Dec. 1, 1941.
3 "Enhanced income and the prospects . . .": Ibid., Dec. 5, 1941.
3 "farm people are able to join . . .": *SUN*, Dec. 7, 1941.
3 "there are more people . . .": Ibid.
4 "in spite of the present low grade . . .": *Time*, Dec. 22, 1941, pp. 56–57.
4 "the country lived better in 1941 than it . . .": Ibid., Jan. 5, 1942, p. 56.
4 "The consistent increase of marriages is due . . .": *NYT*, Dec. 6, 1941.
4 "Prosperity has an unhappy effect . . .": Ibid., Dec. 13, 1941.

4 "the psychological effects of the war": Ibid., Dec. 5, 1941.

5 "Insofar as trade is concerned . . .": *SUN*, Dec. 7, 1941.

5 "This will be a Christmas full of . . .": *WP*, Dec. 7, 1941.

5 "Now we see the distant fire . . .": Clapper, *Watching*, pp. 275–76.

5 "a caroling Christmas" and "that feeling of camaraderie . . .": *WP*, Dec. 4, 1941.

5 "I am astonished at the frequency . . .": *SUN*, Dec. 3, 1941.

6 "A strong automobile industry is the . . .": *Time*, Dec. 8, 1941, p. 1.

6 "Buick Builds for Defense": Ibid., Dec. 1, 1941, p. 8.

6 "when you decide to buy a new Dodge . . .": *SUN*, Dec. 7, 1941.

6 "All the billboards have gone . . .": A. Lindbergh, *War Within*, p. 232.

6 "nauseating with the richness . . .": Ibid., pp. 239–240.

7 "A Patriotic Gift," "A Tip From" and "Hope You 'Fall In'": *SUN*, Dec. 7, 1941.

7 "We pay a tax on holly . . .": Ibid.

7 "Touch it, and it . . .": *New Yorker*, Nov. 29, 1941, p. 83.

7 "Boys' Complete Military Playsuits": *SUN*, Dec. 5, 1941.

## 1: Before Pearl

9 "Throughout most of my childhood . . .": R. Baker, *Growing Up*, p. 248.

10 "arms, ammunition, or implements . . .": Kennedy, *American People*, p. 7.

10 "There are few save propagandists . . .": *SUN*, Sept. 2, 1939.

10 "no blackout of peace": *WP*, Sept. 4, 1939.

10 "I frankly question . . .": *Time*, Sept. 18, 1939, p. 10.

11 "the box we live in": *New Yorker*, Sept. 2, 1939, p. 11.

11 "two bars of music . . .": Ibid.

11 "a big, gray plane . . .": Ibid., Sept. 23, 1939, p. 11.

11 "We try to reconcile . . .": Ibid., Sept. 9, 1939, p. 9.

11 "The machines of war . . .": Ibid., Oct. 14, 1939, p. 13.

12 "Unquestionably, war is going to . . .": *SUN*, Sept. 4, 1939.

12 "The fatalistic feeling that . . .": *WP*, April 21, 1940.

12 "The terrible geography lesson . . .": *New Yorker*, April 20, 1940, p. 13.

12 "the brisk, cultivated voices . . .": Ibid., May 18, 1940, p. 11.

12 "the only good radio . . .": Ibid., June 1, 1940, p. 48.

12 "It was like a newsreel . . .": Childs, *I Write*, pp. 166–67.

12 "Only a miracle . . . can now prevent . . .": *WP*, May 11, 1940.

13 "Congress and the country . . .": *Time*, June 10, 1940, p. 19.

13 "an unlimited expansion of Army warplane . . .": *WP*, May 25, 1940.

13 "whatever is necessary to build up . . .": *Time*, July 1, 1940, p. 18.

13 "largely in the blueprint stage": Ibid., p. 61.

13 "to levels which will make . . .": *WP*, June 12, 1940.

13 "what America must have . . .": Ibid., May 28, 1940.

13 "we need not fear a foreign invasion . . .": Ibid., May 20, 1940.

14 "I am absolutely convinced . . .": Olson, *Angry Days*, p. 103.

14 "the slow-grinding will power . . .": *New Yorker*, May 18, 1940, p. 32.

14 "we are all headed back to . . .": Ibid., May 11, 1940, p. 28.

14 "bleak despair": *NYT*, May 26, 1940.

14 "gloom and terror": *New Yorker*, June 8, 1940, p. 9.

14 "a nation not sure of its way": Ibid., June 15, 1940, p. 13.

14 "We looked at the faces . . .": Ibid., June 22, 1940, p. 11.

14 "all the horrors of this 'total war' . . .": *WP,* June 3, 1940.

14 "SEE the 'Panzer' . . .": *New Yorker*, June 8, 1940, p. 9.

14 "blitzkrieged by the war": *NYT*, June 18, 1940.

14 "a general state of 'jittery' nerves": Ibid.

15 "headaches of unexplained origin . . .": Ibid.

15 "repeated shock to the nervous system . . .": Ibid.

15 "civilian army of modern minute men": *Time*, June 3, 1940, p. 12.

15 "Death Before Surrender": *New Yorker*, June 29, 1940, p. 9.

15 "Enemy parachutists in America . . .": *WP*, June 2, 1940.

15 "acts, threats, or evidences of sabotage . . .": *Time*, June 3, 1940, p. 13.

16 "America isn't going to be any too comfortable . . .": Olson, p. 106.

16 "a muleback army . . .": Childs, p. 249.

16 "among the armies . . .": Wainwright, *Great American Magazine*, p. 103.

16 "The coordination between air and ground . . .": Bradley, *Life*, pp. 88–89.

16 "The German planes have opened the eyes . . .": *WP*, May 2, 1940.

17 "the un-American principle . . .": Ibid., Aug. 1, 1940.

17 "as weird a hash . . .": *Time*, Aug. 12, 1940, p. 12.

17 "the only emergency . . .": *WP,* Aug. 6, 1940.

17 "the use of totalitarian methods . . .": Ibid., Aug. 3, 1940.

17 "the opening wedge to . . .": Ibid.

17 "how to fight and . . .": Ibid., Aug. 13, 1940.

17 "You will have a country . . .": *NYT*, Sept. 15, 1940.

17 "Hushed whispers will . . .": Olson, p. 215.

19 "privileged princes of new . . .": Clapper, p. 87.

19 "To many of his own class . . .": Childs, p. 125.

19 "in a large and powerful class . . .": Clapper, p. 99.

19 "above everything else . . .": Quoted in Polenberg, *War and Society*, p. 7.

19 "manufactured emergencies": *WP*, Oct 15, 1940.

19 "This administration is rapidly pushing . . .": Dunn, *1940*, p. 203.

19 "totalitairrn": *New Yorker*, Sept. 28, 1940, p. 13.

20 "the bells throughout the country . . .": *NYT*, Nov. 1, 1940.

20 "a man who plays with the lives . . .": *WP*, Oct. 26, 1940.

20 "an American brand of fascism": Olson, p. 254.

20 "blitzkrieg tactics": *NYT*, Oct. 26, 1940.

20 "practically a German": *LAT*, Sept. 18, 1940.

20 "Nazi agents in this country . . .": *NYT*, Oct. 26, 1940.

20 "would cause Hitler . . .": Olson, p. 255.

20 "American opinion is today . . .": *NYT*, Oct. 27, 1940.

20 "not to send your husbands and sons . . .": Ibid., Nov. 5, 1940.

20 "your boys are not going to be . . .": Ibid., Oct. 31, 1940.

20 "a return to power voted . . .": Clapper, p. 104.

20 "There was a sense of relief . . .": *Time*, Nov. 18, 1940, p. 15.

20 "Men have been wondering . . .": *NYT*, Nov. 7, 1940.

21 "We have all had our say . . .": *WP*, Nov. 7, 1940.

21 "They keep hearing . . .": *New Yorker*, Nov. 30, 1940, p. 12.

21 "Older folk are rather fed up . . .": *BG*, Oct. 15, 1940.

21 "a determination to cling to sanity": Ibid.

22 "It is next to impossible": Ibid.

22 "Had some forecaster of say . . .": Ibid., Oct. 16, 1940.

22 "Pall Mall is over . . .": *New Yorker*, Nov. 30, 1940, p. 63.

23 "will be something fierce": Ibid., Nov. 16, 1940, p. 11.

23 "If this isn't the heartiest . . .": Ibid. Dec. 14, 1940, p. 107.

23 "to brighten London's Christmas": *NYT*, Nov. 6, 1940.

24 "a blank check book": Cole, *America First*, p. 43.

24 "would bring an end . . .": *NYT*, Jan. 11, 1941.

24 "MOVE OVER . . ." and "BENEDICT ARNOLD": *Time*, Feb. 24, 1941.

24 "if another fellow and I . . .": *WP*, Dec. 31, 1940.

24 "Until we make permanent choice . . .": Ibid., Jan. 2, 1941.

25 "was still producing more bottlenecks . . .": *Time*, Dec. 30, 1940.

25 "From what I saw and heard . . .": Capra, *Name*, p. 311.

25 "was arming to fight . . .": *Time*, Feb. 24, 1941, p. 24.

25 "wandering like bewildered bums . . .": *WP*, Dec. 19, 1941.

26 "this disgraceful boom . . .": Ibid., Dec. 26, 1941.

26 "pack of semi-communist wolves": Polenberg, p. 7.

26 "We will bargain with . . .": *Time*, March 17, 1941, p. 17.

26 "one split second": *NYT*, March 28, 1941.

27 "I can see we haven't got . . .": *Newsweek*, Sept. 1, 1941, p. 10.

27 "The simple truth is that . . .": *WP*, April 26, 1941.

27 "failure of leadership": Ickes, *Secret Diary*, p. 513.

27 "In every direction I find . . .": Ibid., p. 511.

27 "calculated to scare the daylights . . .": Kennedy, p. 68.

28 "what started as a European war . . .": *NYT*, May 28, 1941.

28 "There was no lack of words . . .": Childs, p. 220.

28 "I wish I knew more than I know . . .": Sandburg, *Memo*, p. 53.

29 "the greatest barbarian . . .": *TRIB*, Sept. 2, 1941.

29 "I would a hundred times . . .": Cole, p. 85.

29 "Of course we are going to give . . .": Klingaman, *1941*, p. 294.

29 "Oh, socks and shoes . . .": Ibid.

30 "no fierce emotional resistance . . .": *Life*, March 3, 1941, p. 41.

30 "reflected the uncertainty in the capital. . . .": Childs, p. 217.

31 "There has never been a summer . . .": Klingaman, p. 332.

31 "two-fifths of our people . . .": W. Johnson, *White*, p. 433.

31 "Too many Americans have not yet . . .": *Life*, Sept. 1, 1941, p. 43.

31 "I can't for the life of me . . .": *NYT*, Dec. 4, 1941.

31 "We grow more like . . .": Klingaman, p. 322.

31 "We are still sitting placid . . .": Sherman, *Sarton*, p. 186.

32 "had put aside their collective worries . . .": *NYT*, Sept. 1, 1941.

33 "in most communities there is . . .": Ibid., Dec. 4, 1941.

34 "extremely ugly" and "tattooing of . . .": *New Yorker*, Sept. 21, 1940, p. 11.

34 "We are physically in a condition . . .": *New Republic*, Dec. 1, 1941, p. 717.

34 "sending masses of troops . . .": *Newsweek*, Oct. 13, 1941, p. 50.

35 "Apparently the men are still . . .": *WP*, Dec. 1, 1941.

35 "The process of weeding out . . .": Ibid.

35 "but the simple fact is you can't perfect units . . .": *NYT*, Dec. 1, 1941.

35 "it is my judgment that, given complete equipment . . .": *SUN*, Dec. 1, 1941.

35 "the wrong war . . .": Goodwin, *No Ordinary*, p. 265.

36 "After that things are . . .": Utley, *Going to War*, p. 174.

36 "It may be that next Thanksgiving . . .": Tully, *My Boss*, p. 250.

36 "this may be the last time . . .": Ibid., p. 251.

36 "the United States does not understand the real situation . . .": *NYT*, Dec. 1, 1941.

36 "We are close to war with Japan . . .": *WP*, Dec. 3, 1941.

36 "The odds, as this is written . . .": Ibid.

36 "for the first time . . .": Ibid., Dec. 4, 1941.

37 "Sane strategists would never permit . . .": *New Republic*, Dec. 8, 1941, p. 751.

37 "our island bases are prepared . . .": *SUN*, Dec. 5, 1941.

37 "Japan is facing international economic . . .": *NYT*, Dec. 4, 1941.

37 "Japan—economically—is living . . .": *WSJ*, Dec. 2, 1941.

37 "threatening movements": *NYT*, Dec. 6, 1941.

37 "A bare chance of peace remained . . .": *Time*, Dec. 8, 1941, p. 15.

37 "polite, mildly affable . . .": *WP*, Dec. 6, 1941.

38 "I am looking forward to my work . . .": *NYT*, Dec. 7, 1941.

38 "oppose further steps to involve us . . .": Ibid.

38 "The old way of life has gone . . .": *BG*, Dec. 6, 1941. Gilmer wrote under the pseudonym of "Dorothy Dix."

38 "capture or destroy": *SUN*, Dec. 4, 1941.

38 "I am proud to report that . . .": *NYT*, Dec. 7, 1941.

38 "an enterprise beyond anything . . .": *Saturday Evening Post*, Dec. 6, 1941, p. 28.

39 "panic low": *Newsweek*, Dec. 8, 1941, p. 46.

39 "Mister Calloway is in the groove . . .": *BG*, Dec. 6, 1941.

39 "immoral and un-Christian": *NYT*, Dec. 7, 1941.

39 "one of the cleverest acts . . .": *WP*, Dec. 8, 1941.

40 "take it easy": Ibid., Dec. 7, 1941.

40 "So ends our reverie . . .": Clapper, p. 276.

## 2: Lights Out

41 "Mr. President . . .": Reiss, *They Were There*, p. 398.

41 "The Japanese have kicked off . . .": *WP*, Dec. 8, 1941.

41 "We don't want to contribute . . .": Ibid.

42    "The Japanese have attacked . . .": *SUN*, Dec. 8, 1941.

42    "WE AIN'T MAD . . .": *Newsweek*, Dec. 15, 1941, p. 18.

42    "Attention, please! . . .": Brown, *The Last Hero*, p. 3.

42    "Japanese bombs have fallen . . .": *New Yorker*, Dec. 23, 1941, p. 21.

42    "It came in slowly . . .": Ibid.

43    "It was a nice, dreamy way . . .": Ibid., p. 24.

43    "taking it easy . . .": Cooke, p. 6.

43    "Listening to the radio I heard the news . . .": A. Lindbergh, pp. 239–41.

43    "All that Sunday was a daze . . .": *BG*, Dec. 19, 1941.

44    "as if they had heard a noise . . .": Cooke, p. 7.

44    "move along . . .": *WP*, Dec. 8, 1941.

45    "the stupid habit . . .": Polenberg, pp. 100–101.

45    "the thugs and gangsters . . .": *SUN*, Dec. 8, 1941.

45    "not to feel entirely secure . . .": Ibid.

45    "Don't it beat hell . . .": *WP*, Dec. 9, 1941.

45    "we'll whip 'em in . . .": *TRIB*, Dec. 8, 1941.

45    "Then I get a call . . .": Klingaman, p. 422.

46    "stayed there for the rest of the day . . .": Houseman, *Run-Through*, p. 485.

46    "Through our (American) laziness . . .": C. Baker, *Hemingway Letters*, p. 532.

46    "I thought the Japanese attack . . .": R. Baker, pp. 206–207.

46    "This Jap tried to invade . . .": *SUN*, Dec. 8, 1941.

46    "but when it comes down to . . .": *Baltimore Afro-American*, Dec. 13, 1941.

46    "an unpleasant necessity . . .": *SUN*, Dec. 9, 1941.

46    "Knock Japan on . . .": *TRIB*, Dec. 8, 1941.

46    "Study hard": *Time*, Dec. 15, 1941, p. 17.

47    "we were safe enough . . .": *New Yorker*, Dec. 20, 1941, p. 9.

47    "some just said . . .": *LAT*, Dec. 9, 1941.

47    "There was silence . . .": *New Republic*, Dec. 15, 1941, p. 863.

47    "Now all doubt is ended . . .": *TRIB*, Dec. 8, 1941.

47    "Everybody is happy . . .": *SUN*, Dec. 8, 1941.

47    "Japan has signed . . .": Ibid.

47    "That's the way those Japs . . .": *WP*, Dec. 8, 1941.

48    "to protect all Japanese nationals . . .": *NYT*, Dec. 8, 1941.

48    "all foreign sailings": Ibid.

48    "dangerous to the peace . . .": *TRIB*, Dec. 8, 1941.

49    "I can't imagine what . . .": *LAT*, Dec. 8, 1941.

49    "now we've got to be . . .": Ibid.

50    "I do not believe . . .": Ibid.

50    "There will be no trouble . . .": Ibid.

50    "if I have to fight . . .": Ibid.

50    "American citizens of Japanese . . .": Ibid.

51    "an elderly florist . . .": Dos Passos, p. 311.

51    "in order to present . . .": *WP*, Dec. 8, 1941.

## 3: An Anxious Trip

53 "I don't remember at all . . .": *BG*, Dec. 19, 1941.
54 "You're in the Army Now": *WP*, Dec. 9, 1941.
54 "a date which will . . .": Ibid.
54 "Republicans will not permit . . .": Ibid., Dec. 11, 1941.
55 "regardless of our attitude . . .": *NYT*, Dec. 9, 1941.
55 "It is well to have a man . . .": *WP*, Dec. 9, 1941.
55 "Everyone thinks . . .": Berle, *Navigating*, p. 384.
55 "The soft talkative times . . .": *WP*, Dec. 11, 1941, p. 19.
55 "I feel as though . . .": A. Lindbergh, p. 242.
56 "the Army is no . . .": *Baltimore Afro-American*, Dec. 13, 1941.
56 "there shall be no discrimination . . .": Kennedy, p. 209.
56 "colored boys": *Baltimore Afro-American*, Dec. 13, 1941.
56 "a flunky": Ibid.
56 "We colored people are . . .": Ibid.
56 "a kind of make-believe . . .": *WP*, Dec. 16, 1941.
56 "Most people thought these . . .": Vorse, *Time*, p. 367.
57 "the Guerrillas": *Time*, Dec. 29, 1941, p. 9.
57 "best shots in West Virginia": *SUN*, Dec. 9, 1941.
57 "those yellow devils": *BG*, Dec. 10, 1941.
57 "we don't want any, either": Ibid., Dec. 12, 1941.
57 "Women are too bossy . . .": Ibid.
57 "we who live on the Atlantic coast . . .": *SUN*, Dec. 9, 1941.
58 "if they're going to bomb Boston . . .": *BG*, Dec. 10, 1941.
58 "one of the sharpest sales . . .": *WP*, Dec. 12, 1941.
58 "consumers' buying wave": Ibid., Dec. 11, 1941.
58 "Not one of our great . . .": *Newsweek*, Dec. 22, 1941, p. 61.
59 "open season on Japs": *NYT*, Dec. 12, 1941.
59 "an American translation": *LAT*, Dec. 9, 1941.
59 "This is the opportunity . . .": Ibid., Dec. 10, 1941.
60 "with a great deal of trepidation": Ibid., Dec. 9, 1941.
60 "were in a state . . .": Ibid.
60 "simply vicious": Ibid.
60 "the children are Americans . . .": Ibid.
60 "when the bombers arrive": Ibid.
61 "S-A-F-E": *Life*, Dec. 22, 1941, p. 20.
61 "Market Street was . . .": Terkel, *Good War*, p. 25.
61 "The Japs are coming! . . .": Ibid.
62 "Don't think this is . . .": *WP*, Dec. 21, 1941.
62 "We've got to show them . . .": *SUN*, Dec. 10, 1941.
62 "Those planes were over . . .": *WP*, Dec. 10, 1941.
62 "criminal, shameful apathy": *NYT*, Dec. 10, 1941.
62 "it might have been better . . .": *WP*, Dec. 10, 1941.
63 "bomb-expectant . . .": *BG*, Dec. 19, 1941.

63 "There is suspense here . . .": Ibid.

63 "them Jap parachutists": Ibid., Dec. 10, 1941.

63 "our inseparable daily drug": Cooke, p. 16.

63 "a sentence more bizarre . . .": Ibid., pp. 16–17.

63 "persistent reports that . . .": *BG*, Dec. 11, 1941.

64 "a sense of terror . . .": Ibid., Dec. 21, 1941.

64 WELCOME TO SAN PEDRO: *WP*, Dec. 25, 1941.

64 "When you swing . . .": *LAT*, Dec. 10, 1941.

64 "verified reports of . . .": *BG*, Dec. 15, 1941.

64 "People were running around . . .": *TRIB*, Dec. 13, 1941.

64 "There were accidents . . .": Ibid.

65 "marauding gangs of . . .": *LAT*, Dec. 18, 1941.

65 "more bewildered than alarmed": *NYT*, Dec. 10, 1941.

65 "the recalcitrant, the blasé . . .": Ibid., Dec. 12, 1941.

66 "What was I to do . . .": Ibid., Dec. 10, 1941.

66 "desirous of being . . .": Beebe, *Snoot*, p. 270.

66 "It was a very pleasant . . .": Ibid., p. 233.

66 "unidentified planes": *Time*, Dec. 22, 1941, p. 71.

66 "people here actually expect . . .": C. Lindbergh, *Journals*, p. 565.

66 "as stripped of motorists . . .": *BG*, Dec. 10, 1941.

67 "calm, rested, cheery [and] buoyant": *Time*, Dec. 22, 1941, p. 9.

67 "so far the news . . .": *WP*, Dec. 10, 1941.

67 "Now, all that I feared . . .": C. Lindbergh, p. 565.

67 "Each man was pretty much . . .": *New Yorker*, Dec. 20, 1941, p. 9.

68 "impertinent": *TRIB*, Dec. 18, 1941.

68 "It has been nothing but war . . .": *WP*, Dec. 21, 1941.

68 "When I did my shopping . . .": Ibid., Dec. 25, 1941.

68 "This is not good for us . . .": *BG*, Dec. 13, 1941.

69 "breaking into routine programs . . .": *WP*, Dec. 21, 1941.

69 "get away from . . .": *TRIB*, Dec. 15, 1941.

69 "report war news calmly . . .": *Time*, Dec. 22, 1941, p. 54.

69 "An open microphone . . .": *TRIB*, Dec. 22, 1941.

69 "The thing doesn't come . . .": *LAT*, Dec. 11, 1941.

70 "To hell with those . . .": *Newsweek*, Dec. 22, 1941, p. 26.

70 "Made in Japan": Ibid.

70 "He seemed a really nice . . .": *NYT*, Dec. 14, 1941.

70 "sly, wily and . . .": *WP*, Dec. 14, 1941.

71 "We even burned up . . .": *WP*, Dec. 11, 1941.

71 "If we can't get . . ." *BG*, Dec. 12, 1941.

71 "We do not want to . . .": *TRIB*, Dec. 12, 1941.

71 "direct action": *NYT*, Dec. 11, 1941.

71 "Japanese who aren't . . .": *LAT*, Dec. 11, 1941.

71 "Free shaves for Japs": Ibid., Dec. 19, 1941.

71 "Don't shoot! . . .": *Seattle Star*, Dec. 17, 1941.

71 "distressing ignorance" and "the delicate question . . .": *Life*, Dec. 22, 1941, p. 81.

71 "virtually all Japanese . . .": *Time*, Dec. 22, 1941, p. 33.
72 "long and delicately boned": *Life*, Dec. 22, 1941, p. 81.
72 "squat, long-torsoed build . . .": Ibid.
72 "more positive, dogmatic . . .": *Time*, Dec. 22, 1941, p. 33.
72 "seldom grow" and "avoid horn-rimmed spectacles": Ibid.
72 "are nervous in . . .": Ibid.
72 "shuffle along more": *BG*, Dec. 14, 1941.
72 "if you forget . . .": *WP*, Dec. 16, 1941.

## 4: Holiday Wishes

73 "the most fateful week . . .": *WP*, Dec. 14, 1941.
73 "It seems like a . . .": Streitmatter, *Empty Without You*, p. 240.
73 "eerie spell": *WP*, Dec. 15, 1941.
74 "The Nazis couldn't . . .": *Life*, Jan. 5, 1942, p. 57.
74 "The expansion of personnel . . .": Ibid., p. 58.
74 "Everyone is up to his ears . . .": Ibid.
74 "The frenzy of wartime Washington . . .": Ibid.
74 "not only a possible . . .": *WP*, Dec. 22, 1941.
74 "an unappealing . . .": Ibid., Dec. 13, 1941.
74 "serve hot soup . . .": Ibid., Dec. 15, 1941.
74 "unnecessary nondefense expenditure": *TRIB*, Dec. 20, 1941.
74 "unless you allow me . . .": Roosevelt, *This I Remember*, p. 237.
75 "after all, these shelters . . .": *SUN*, Dec. 14, 1941.
75 "a swimming pool . . .": *Life*, Dec. 29, 1941, p. 20.
75 "the materials, labor . . .": Ibid.
75 "theoretical target areas": *Newsweek*, Dec. 22, 1941, p. 22.
75 "The Germans can easily . . .": *BG*, Dec. 16, 1941.
75 "our people are in danger": *SUN*, Dec. 17, 1941.
75 "It is only reasonable . . .": Ibid. Dec. 19, 1941.
76 "jittering dramatics . . .": *NYT*, Dec. 24, 1941.
76 "It can happen here . . .": *Tuscaloosa News*, Dec. 14, 1941.
76 "One of the main differences . . .": *SUN*, Dec. 18, 1941.
76 "so much equipment . . .": Roosevelt, p. 237.
76 "For all practical purposes . . .": *SUN*, Dec. 14, 1941.
76 "Enemy bombers . . .": *DFP*, Dec. 15, 1941.
77 "We have rifles . . .": *NYT*, Dec. 18, 1941.
77 "and other aliens" and "highly mobile": Ibid. Dec. 18, 1941.
77 "Unhampered by red tape . . .": Ibid.
77 "Those stiff-necked Vermonters . . .": Ibid. Dec. 10, 1941.
77 "spreading out a welcome mat . . .": *WP*, Dec. 24, 1941.
77 "Logic (and the military experts) . . .": *New Yorker*, Dec. 20, 1941, p. 9.
77 "What To Do In An Air Raid": *NYT*, Dec. 10, 1941; *BG*, Dec. 17, 1941; *BG*, Dec. 12, 1941; *NYT*, Dec. 20, 1941; *BG*, Dec. 16, 1941.
78 "If you see the full . . .": *Life*, Dec. 22, 1941, p. 36.

78 "People are afraid . . .": *NYT*, Dec. 30, 1941.

78 "a special kind" and "a sort of shuffle": *LAT*, Dec. 10, 1941.

78 "You can keep a . . .": Ibid.

78 "practically the reverse . . .": Ibid., Dec. 12, 1941.

79 "Bloomingdale's is prepared . . .": *NYT*, Dec. 12, 1941.

79 "Headquarters for Official . . .": *BG*, Dec. 16, 1941.

79 "necklets and bracelets": Ibid.

79 "the sort of thing . . .": *NYT*, Dec. 24, 1941.

79 "defense-all" and "blackout snatchthiefs": Ibid.

79 "chemically treated": *BG*, Dec. 14, 1941.

79 "blankets, quilts . . .": *WP*, Dec. 16, 1941.

80 "will seriously hinder . . .": Ibid.

80 "If a couple bombs fall . . .": Ibid., Dec. 28, 1941.

80 "They didn't know what . . .": *Life*, Jan. 12, 1942, p. 65.

80 "the California coast . . .": *TRIB*, Dec. 23, 1941.

80 "Let 'em come! . . .": *WP*, Dec. 27, 1941.

80 "We've had much excitement . . .": Karman, *Letters*, p. 168.

80 "It is really very thrilling . . .": Ibid., p. 152.

81 "Heck no . . .": *WP*, Dec. 10, 1941.

81 "brought war home . . .": *LAT*, Dec. 17, 1941.

82 "Uncle Sam will have . . .": *WP*, Dec. 22, 1941.

82 "We used to play . . .": *DFP*, Dec. 23, 1941.

82 "This is going to be . . .": *BG*, Dec. 12, 1941.

82 "the psychology of attack": *WP*, Dec. 23, 1941.

83 "This is a Galento war . . .": Ibid., Dec. 10, 1941.

83 "You may have noticed . . .": *LAT*, Dec. 16, 1941.

83 "You better bring all this stuff . . .": *Time*, Dec. 22, 1941, p. 58.

83 "I saw nothing in it . . .": *SUN*, Dec. 16, 1941.

83 "Phrases, phrases, phrases . . .": *Life*, Jan. 5, 1942, p. 59.

84 "'never before . . .'": Ibid.

84 "nobody knows just who . . .": Ibid.

84 "Enemy Routed . . ." and "Philippines Situation . . .": *LAT*, Dec. 18, 1941.

84 "The newspapers are winning the war . . .": C. Lindbergh, p. 569.

84 "If the government knows what's good . . .": *LAT*, Dec. 10, 1941.

84 "the most effective . . .": *SUN*, Dec. 15, 1941.

84 "The entire country . . .": *LAT*, Dec. 16, 1941.

85 "it is preposterous . . .": Ibid., Dec. 14, 1941.

85 "Can I still . . ." and "Should I fire . . .": Ibid., Dec. 11, 1941.

85 "We are loaded . . .": *BG*, Dec. 12, 1941.

85 "Beware of inquisitive . . .": *WP*, Dec. 25, 1941.

85 "to be on the watch . . .": *NYT*, Dec. 29, 1941.

85 "plant protection rifles" and "Springfield . . .": *WP*, Dec. 10, 1941.

85 "Tear gas pistols . . .": *TRIB*, Dec. 14, 1941.

85 "in constant danger . . .": Ibid., Dec. 20, 1941.

86 "Cloudy and warmer . . .": *DFP*, Dec. 22, 1941.

86 "The pagan enemy . . .": *Eugene Register-Guard*, Dec. 21, 1941.

86 "No one can . . .": *NYT*, Dec. 25, 1941.

86 "increase their vigilance . . .": Ibid., Dec. 24, 1941.

86 "vital points . . .": *WP*, Dec. 26, 1941.

87 "from a very reliable . . .": *NYT*, Dec. 25, 1941.

87 "is being sold . . .": Ibid.

87 "We hear from every . . .": Ibid., Dec. 23, 1941.

87 "You can sell 'em . . .": *SUN*, Dec. 21, 1941.

87 "Everybody appeared . . .": Ibid.

87 "a general look . . .": *DFP*, Dec. 21, 1941.

87 "the hideous world . . .": *NYT*, Dec. 21, 1941.

87 "a happy and . . .": *SUN*, Dec. 23, 1941.

87 "I don't think that it will be . . .": Ibid.

88 "If so, what does . . .": *NYT*, Dec. 14, 1941.

88 "No Christmas tree . . .": *BG*, Dec. 19, 1941.

88 "If you want cameras . . .": *WP*, Dec. 21, 1941.

88 "most prominent feature . . .": *NYT*, Dec. 14, 1941.

88 "Flying Fortress": *SUN*, Dec. 18, 1941.

88 "Turn the crank . . .": *WP*, Dec. 19, 1941.

88 "The time may come . . .": *NYT*, Jan. 4, 1942.

89 "Any way you look at it . . .": *WP*, Dec. 11, 1941.

89 "the most drastic . . .": *Newsweek*, Dec. 29, 1941, p. 32.

89 "Stop unnecessary driving . . .": *NYT*, Dec. 27, 1941

89 "the largest in . . .": *DFP*, Dec. 23, 1941.

90 "we can't fight a war . . .": *Newsweek*, Dec. 29, 1941, p. 32.

90 "the original drive-in town": *LAT*, Jan. 3, 1942.

90 "his pants and socks . . .": *Time*, Jan. 5, 1942, p. 16.

90 "Notice: Because of . . .": *SUN*, Dec. 16, 1941.

90 "nonessential luxury": *WP*, Dec. 21, 1941.

91 "one of the greatest . . .": *NYT*, Dec. 19, 1941.

91 "Anyone buying beyond . . .": Ibid., Dec. 22, 1941.

91 "but it would not do . . .": Ibid., Dec. 26, 1941.

91 "What Americans wanted . . .": Cooke, pp. 19–20.

91 "From the Allied . . .": *WP*, Dec. 26, 1941.

91 "so close . . .": *BG*, Dec. 31, 1941.

92 "There have been . . .": Berle, *Navigating*, p. 386.

92 "the shops were pretty well . . .": Roosevelt, p. 241.

92 "There was little joy . . .": Ibid., p. 243.

93 "The gayety which has . . .": *DFP*, Dec. 25, 1941.

93 "I think it's possible . . .": *WP*, Dec. 14, 1941.

93 "owing to war conditions": Ibid., Dec. 24, 1941.

93 "the Christmas whirl . . .": *LAT*, Dec. 23, 1941.

93 "whose nerves are . . .": *WP*, Dec. 14, 1941.

93 "There is no better . . .": *TRIB*, Dec. 19, 1941.

93 "at which age . . .": *NYT*, Dec. 19, 1941.

94 "Christmas 1941 . . .": *Life*, Dec. 15, 1941, p. 45.

94 "Hitler is to blame . . .": *WP*, Dec. 25, 1941.

94 "What Shall We Teach . . .": *TRIB*, Dec. 21, 1941.

94 "listening to a portable radio . . .": Houseman, *Run-Through*, p. 20.

94 "Spartan simplicity . . .": *SUN*, Dec. 21, 1941.

94 "overestimate our capabilities . . .": *WP*, Dec. 26, 1941.

95 "dangerous enemy aliens": Ibid., Dec. 25, 1941.

95 "under suspicion and . . .": *LAT*, Dec. 23, 1941.

95 "an imperative necessity . . .": Childs, p. 224.

95 "Christmas this year . . .": *New Yorker*, Jan. 3, 1942, p. 9.

95 "The weather today . . .": *WP*, Dec. 27, 1941.

95 "a knockdown fight . . .": *DFP*, Dec. 21, 1941.

95 "constructive criticism": *WP*, Dec. 21, 1941.

95 "Everyone expects the honeymoon . . .": *Life*, Jan. 5, 1942, p. 60.

96 "The country must be . . .": *WP*, Jan. 1, 1942.

96 "the American people must be . . .": Ibid.

96 "dark, grim days" and "The bell will toll . . .": Ibid., Dec. 15, 1941.

96 "so much banal nonsense": *NYT*, Dec. 26, 1941.

96 "an exercise in . . ." and "It's a bit of . . .": *BG*, Dec. 18, 1941.

96 "something of an anti-climax . . .": *New Republic*, Dec. 29, 1941, p. 877.

97 "prevent alarm and hysteria . . .": *SUN*, Dec. 18, 1941.

97 "'Happy New Year' has to be . . .": *LAT*, Dec. 31, 1941.

97 "because we don't know . . .": *DFP*, Dec. 23, 1941.

97 "unnecessary noise": *Newsweek*, Jan. 12, 1942, p. 24.

97 "We scared 'em . . .": Ibid.

97 "It makes you realize . . .": *BG*, Dec. 31, 1942.

97 "bewildering times": Ibid., Dec. 17, 1941.

97 "Remember Pearl Harbor" and "To Hell With Hitler": Ibid., Jan. 1, 1942.

97 "such an outpouring . . .": Aaron, *Inman Diary*, p. 1060.

97 "The superficial celebration . . .": *WP*, Jan. 1, 1942.

98 "In case of an alarm . . .": Ibid.

98 "It seemed that those . . .": *BG*, Jan. 1, 1942.

98 "Knowing that our boys . . .": Berle, p. 392.

## 5: Cloudy, Turning Colder

99 "the backlash of . . .": *WP*, Jan. 7, 1942.

100 "a slow motion circus . . .": Ibid.

100 "General holidays are . . .": Ibid., Dec. 31, 1941.

100 "the worst reverse . . .": Ibid., Jan. 2, 1942.

100 "We have lost . . .": Ibid.

100 "there is not a single ray . . .": Ibid., Jan. 14, 1942.

100 "Every competent person . . .": Ibid., Jan. 2, 1942.

100 "Dark circles ringed . . .": Ibid., Jan. 7, 1942.

100 "a hard war . . .": *NYT*, Jan. 7, 1942.

101 "as our power . . .": Ibid.

101 "taxes and bonds . . .": Ibid.

101 "Let no man say . . .": *WP*, Jan. 7, 1942.

101 "We are not for defense . . .": *SUN*, Jan. 8, 1942.

101 "Where is the Fleet . . .": *Time*, Jan. 12, 1942, p. 9.

101 "The miserable truth . . .": Ibid., p. 12.

101 "The fact is that . . .": *WP*, Jan. 14, 1942.

101 "terrible overlapping . . .": *BG*, Jan. 21, 1942.

101 "The cost of the smugness . . .": *WP*, Jan. 2, 1942.

102 "Nobody ever will be . . .": *DFP*, Jan. 29, 1942.

102 "Demoralization here has . . .": Ibid., Jan. 14, 1942.

102 "shortsighted" and "lackadaisical": *Newsweek*, Jan. 26, 1942, p. 48.

102 "carelessness and inefficiency . . .": *NYT*, Jan. 16, 1942.

102 "Apparently there never has been . . .": Ibid.

102 "we want to know . . .": *SUN*, Jan. 6, 1942.

102 "We want more machine guns . . .": Ibid.

102 "No doubt can now remain . . .": *Time*, Jan. 19, 1942, p. 11.

103 "Business as usual . . .": *DFP*, Jan. 14, 1942.

103 "Get the stuff moving . . .": *NYT*, Jan. 31, 1942.

103 "a belated but nevertheless . . .": Ibid., Jan. 14, 1942.

103 "If the people become . . .": *LAT*, Jan. 8, 1942.

103 "has never known . . .": *WP*, Jan. 20, 1942.

103 "liars" and "swivel-chair scribes" and "some Jap . . .": *NYT*, Jan. 2, 1942.

103 "a pitiful minority . . .": Ibid., Jan. 25, 1942.

104 "glass showcases . . .": Ibid., Jan. 10, 1942.

104 "The only conclusion possible . . .": *DFP*, Jan. 22, 1942.

104 "has been making . . .": *LAT*, Jan. 19, 1942.

104 "viewing posts" and "look in": *NYT*, Jan. 24, 1942.

104 "the worst managed . . .": *DFP*, Jan. 15, 1942.

104 "there was little sign . . .": *Time*, Jan. 19, 1942, p. 61.

104 "mishandling of . . .": *SUN*, Jan. 10, 1942.

105 "to ebb and flow . . .": *BG*, Jan. 1, 1942.

105 "not beyond . . .": *WP*, Jan. 2, 1942.

105 "An effort will . . .": *SUN*, Dec. 22, 1941.

105 "definitely in the cards": *LAT*, Jan. 8, 1942.

105 "more easily than . . .": *BG*, Jan. 15, 1942.

105 "Are they coming over here . . .": *Life*, Jan. 19, 1942, p. 85.

105 "We're pretty well . . .": *DFP*, Dec. 29, 1941.

105 "You might just as well . . .": Ibid.

106 "This war is . . .": Aaron, pp. 1064–65.

106 "People are nervous enough . . .": *DFP*, Dec. 21, 1941.

106 "has planned, and . . .": Ibid., Jan. 13, 1942.

106 "begin at once . . .": *NYT*, Jan. 13, 1942.

106 "No prospect strikes . . .": *WP*, Jan. 15, 1942.

106 "prison housing . . .": *BG*, Dec. 30, 1941.

106 "just in case": *WP*, Jan. 8, 1942.

107 "droning menacingly": *NYT*, Jan. 15, 1942.

107 "Exactly the sort of picture . . .": Ibid.

108 "an acute shortage . . .": *TRIB*, Jan. 3, 1942.

108 "Nobody wants to play a Jap . . .": Ibid.

108 "For Heaven's sake . . .": *WP*, Dec. 27, 1941.

108 "the boys out in Hollywood . . .": *NYT*, Jan. 25, 1942.

108 "screen heroes must . . .": *LAT*, Dec. 12, 1941.

108 "Business in the . . .": *DFP*, Jan. 15, 1942.

109 "Gable's one of the . . .": Harris, *Gable*, p. 242.

109 "The more we whip up . . .": *WP*, Jan. 18, 1942.

109 "the ever-increasing tempo . . .": *DFP*, Jan. 31, 1942.

109 "War urgencies so greatly . . .": *WP*, Jan. 18, 1942.

109 "all up and down . . .": Ibid., Jan. 15, 1942.

109 "increasingly serious": *NYT*, Jan. 17, 1942.

109 "brought the war closer . . .": *BG*, Jan. 17, 1942.

109 "Every sailor I have . . .": *NYT*, Jan. 21, 1942.

110 "closely coordinated . . .": Ibid., Jan. 26, 1942.

110 "a neon shooting gallery": Kennedy, p. 141.

110 "I wouldn't be a bit surprised . . .": *NYT*, Jan. 23, 1942.

110 "Shut Up, America": *Life*, Feb. 9, 1942, p. 36.

110 "Hush-Hush Girl": *TRIB*, Jan. 7, 1942.

110 "Serve with Silence": Ibid.

111 "steer clear of . . .": *WP*, Jan. 17, 1942, p. 5.

111 "appeals for . . .": *DFP*, Jan. 17, 1942, p. 2.

111 "the publication of . . .": *Time*, Jan. 26, 1942, p. 56.

111 "they may get into trouble . . .": *NYT*, Jan. 24, 1942.

111 "The Japs know . . .": *Time*, Jan. 19, 1942, p. 2.

111 "Mr. Roosevelt has . . .": *DFP*, Jan. 29, 1942.

111 "a prolonged artillery duel . . .": *WP*, Jan. 23, 1942.

112 "the public . . . has received . . .": Ibid., Jan. 29, 1942.

112 "For Heaven's sake stop . . .": *LAT*, Jan. 9, 1942.

112 "It is shocking . . .": *TRIB*, Jan. 15, 1942.

112 "The time has come . . .": *SUN*, Jan 15, 1942.

112 "it looks like . . .": *BG*, Jan. 8, 1942.

112 "In Heaven's name . . .": *Newsweek*, Feb. 2, 1942, p. 13.

112 "a greater realization . . .": *DFP*, Dec. 27, 1941.

112 "there is too much . . .": *LAT*, Dec. 31, 1941.

112 "If we were . . .": *Newsweek*, Jan. 26, 1942, p. 68.

113 "we are still complacent . . .": *NYT*, Jan. 3, 1942.

113 "A motor-minded public . . .": *SUN*, Jan. 6, 1942.

113 "everyone seems to want . . .": *DFP*, Jan. 17, 1942.

113 "Since Chicago and vicinity . . .": *TRIB*, Dec. 31, 1941.

113 "hell to pay . . .": *LAT*, Jan. 6, 1942.

113 "the most unreasonable . . .": *Newsweek*, Jan. 12, 1942, p. 32.

113 "to upset our entire . . .": *NYT*, Jan. 14, 1942.

113 "to ask him to intercede . . .": *SUN*, Jan. 6, 1942.

113 "there is no sense . . .": *BG*, Jan. 8, 1942.

114 "already has reached . . .": *NYT*, Jan. 12, 1942.

114 "cannot and will not . . .": *DFP*, Jan. 12, 1942.

114 "The average citizen has . . .": *NYT*, Jan. 10, 1942.

114 "the most magnificent . . .": *TRIB*, Jan. 3, 1942.

114 "complaints alleging violations . . .": *SUN*, Jan. 30, 1942.

114 "accumulating evidence that . . .": *LAT*, Jan. 18, 1942.

114 "who could most frequently drive . . .": Cooke, p. 26.

114 "A bird with . . .": *Life*, Feb. 9, 1942, p. 6.

114 "wave of tire thievery . . .": *WP*, Jan. 3, 1942.

115 "Roses are red . . .": *Time*, Jan. 26, 1942, p. 77.

115 "You will recall . . .": *SUN*, Jan. 17, 1942.

115 "Safti-Brand Service": *NYT*, Feb. 3, 1942.

115 "While the brand . . .": Ibid., Jan. 31, 1942.

115 "He didn't ride . . .": *New Yorker*, Jan. 31, 1942, p. 7.

115 "because if people do . . .": *WP*, Jan. 2, 1942.

115 "We've been living too much apart . . .": *LAT*, Dec. 30, 1941.

116 "Lady with good car . . .": *WP*, Jan. 20, 1942.

116 "We'll be very lucky . . .": Ibid., Jan. 15, 1942.

116 "the former automotive city": *DFP*, Jan. 31, 1942.

116 "designed to create . . .": *NYT*, Jan. 5, 1942.

116 "socialization of industry": *Life*, Jan. 19, 1942, p. 20.

116 "Apparently, no one . . .": *Newsweek*, Jan. 12, 1942, p. 32.

117 "that's a gloomy possibility": *TRIB*, Jan. 3, 1942.

117 "Depends on the Japs": *SUN*, Jan. 3, 1942.

117 "Gas station attendants . . .": *WP*, Jan. 20, 1942.

117 "The 1942 winter season . . .": *DFP*, Jan. 25, 1942.

117 "a bad case of . . .": *WP*, Jan. 19, 1942.

117 "V stands for . . .": *TRIB*, Dec. 31, 1941.

117 "See the Old West . . .": *NYT*, Jan. 21, 1942.

117 "Turn your back on . . .": *Time*, Jan. 19, 1942, p. 66.

117 "travel for mere pleasure . . .": *NYT*, Feb. 5, 1942.

118 "papers, documents, or books . . .": *TRIB*, Jan. 6, 1942.

118 "amateur detectives . . .": *DFP*, Jan. 13, 1942.

118 "misguided patriots . . .": *NYT*, Jan. 5, 1942.

119 "as stupid as . . .": *SUN*, Jan. 3, 1942.

119 "local and patriotic . . .": *NYT*, Jan. 11, 1942.

119 "If one loyal group . . .": *DFP*, Dec. 31, 1941.

119 "the small towns have not changed much . . .": Ibid., Jan. 28, 1942.

119 "There has been very little . . .": *SUN*, Dec. 18, 1941.

119 "I haven't heard a band . . .": *LAT*, Jan. 8, 1942.

119 "Bands and 'Legionnaire' girl . . .": C. Lindbergh, p. 571.

120 "a good five-cent war song" and "The nation is . . .": *NYT*, Jan. 29, 1942.

120 "I've Changed My Penthouse . . .": *NOTP*, Feb. 15, 1942.

120 "most of them . . .": Ibid.

120 "Hi-ho, hi-ho . . .": *LAT*, Jan. 17, 1942.

120 "dribble" and "I wish Tin Pan Alley . . .": *DFP*, Jan. 18, 1942.

120 "It may be the draft . . .": *SUN*, Jan. 1, 1942.

120 "the day of living . . .": *DFP*, Jan. 25, 1942.

121 "in a patriotic fervor . . .": *NYT*, Feb. 2, 1942.

121 "The hysteria of war . . .": *LAT*, Jan 12, 1942.

121 "a peacetime soldier . . .": *Time*, Jan. 12, 1942, p. 57.

121 "We have leaned . . .": *SUN*, Jan. 16, 1942.

121 "an alarming tendency . . .": *NYT*, Jan. 10, 1942.

121 "Dependency is relative": *SUN*, Jan. 16, 1942.

121 "We will not do anything . . .": *WP*, Jan. 10, 1942.

121 "to establish to the . . .": *NYT*, Dec. 30, 1941.

121 "It makes no difference . . .": *TRIB*, Jan. 13, 1942.

122 "We hope this will keep . . .": *LAT*, Jan. 19, 1942.

122 "Members in each city . . .": *DFP*, Jan. 17, 1942.

122 "the most urgent . . .": *Time*, Jan. 26, 1942, p. 31.

122 "one of our most expanded . . .": *NYT*, Jan. 13, 1942.

122 "prophylactic stations": *WP*, Jan. 13, 1942.

122 "ten to fifteen per cent . . .": Warren, *Memoirs*, p. 151.

122 "smoldering incendiaries": *NYT*, Jan. 27, 1942.

122 "Syphilis is Sneaky!": *TRIB*, Jan. 23, 1942.

123 "at very low cost": Ibid., Jan. 19, 1942.

123 "I cannot urge . . .": *NYT*, Jan. 29, 1942.

123 "The medical profession . . .": *Time*, Jan. 12, 1942, p. 57.

## 6: An Unquiet Feeling

125 "The Germans and . . .": *SUN*, Feb. 4, 1942.

125 "to make up for the . . .": *NYT*, Jan. 8, 1942.

125 "save car tires by . . .": Ibid., Jan. 16, 1942.

125 "It's very serious" and "in offices, on subways . . .": *New Yorker*, Jan. 3, 1942, p. 12.

125 "All we want . . .": *LAT*, Jan. 9, 1942.

126 "Rope-skipping is only . . .": *New Yorker*, Jan. 3, 1942, p. 13.

126 "in a total war . . .": *WP*, Feb. 4, 1942.

126 "toughen up everybody . . .": *SUN*, Feb. 13, 1942.

126 "who bend over defense plans . . .": *DFP*, Feb. 6, 1942.

126 "intensify the emphasis . . .": *TRIB*, Jan. 14, 1942.

126 "keep them rolling" and "hit the head-pin . . .": *Time*, March 23, 1942, p. 57.

126 "It's going to be . . .": *WP*, Feb. 14, 1942.

126 "Dawn Patrol" and "midnight wives": *LAT*, Jan. 9, 1942.

126 "to lure the man . . .": *NYT*, Dec. 28, 1941.

126 "training and toughening": Ibid., Feb. 16, 1942.

127 "teach men how to . . .": *WP*, Feb. 16, 1942.

127 "too much emphasis . . .": *SUN*, Feb. 19, 1942.

127 "a little dumber . . .": Ibid. Feb. 8, 1942.

127 "Could we be dumber . . .": *NYT*, Feb. 28, 1942.

127 "grotesquely naive" and "By all means . . .": *SUN*, Feb. 9, 1942.

127 "Never before in the . . .": *WP*, Jan. 16, 1942.

127 "nutritional intelligence": *NYT*, Jan. 10, 1942.

127 "make you fit for defense": Ibid. Dec. 20, 1941.

127 "fortify the family": Ibid. Jan. 31, 1942.

127 "wartime vitality": *WP*, Jan. 24, 1942.

128 "Dining is Defense . . .": *NYT*, Jan. 29, 1942.

128 "Uncle Sam says . . .": *Time*, Jan. 26, 1942, p. 25.

128 "'plenty to eat' . . .": Ibid., Feb. 23, 1942, p. 33.

128 "nutritional defense": *WP*, Jan. 16, 1942.

128 "to aid the average citizen . . .": *NYT*, Feb. 17, 1942.

128 "You can't take people . . .": *SUN*, Feb. 6, 1942.

128 "DO NOT HOARD . . .": *NYT*, Dec. 18, 1941.

128 "she who hoards . . .": *LAT*, Dec. 19, 1941.

129 "cousins, daughters . . .": *NYT*, Dec. 25, 1941.

129 "We don't have any sugar . . .": *WP*, Jan. 20, 1942.

129 "souvenirs": *NYT*, Jan. 23, 1942.

129 "Go easy on the sugar . . .": *NOTP*, Feb. 4, 1942.

129 "How to use . . .": *NYT*, Jan. 27, 1942.

130 "Corn Sugar is . . .": Cooke, p. 136.

130 "there just won't be . . .": *WP*, Jan. 19, 1942.

130 "We'd better prepare . . .": Ibid.

130 "there has been a . . .": *SUN*, Feb. 7, 1942.

130 "traitorous": *BG*, Feb. 20, 1942.

131 "relatively few cases . . .": *SUN*, Feb. 7, 1942.

131 "A house to house search . . .": *TRIB*, Feb. 3, 1942.

131 "sell some of it . . .": *NYT*, Feb. 20, 1942.

131 "only a negligible . . .": Ibid., Feb. 27, 1942.

131 "Winning back the Far East . . .": *DFP*, Feb. 5, 1942.

132 "If there has been . . .": *NYT*, Feb. 11, 1942.

132 "There was a melancholy tune . . .": Cooke, p. 20.

132 "large vessels": *NYT*, Feb. 15, 1942.

132 "Lunching by one's self . . .": Ibid.

132 "This world is bitched proper . . .": Blotner, *Faulkner*, p. 148.

133 "I have a chance . . .": Ibid.

133 "We do not fully appreciate . . .": *Time*, Feb. 16, 1942, p. 11.

133 "Reports from the country . . .": *NYT*, Feb. 8, 1942.

133 "the unawareness . . .": *WP*, Feb. 7, 1942.

133 "I find all around me . . .": *SUN*, Feb. 7, 1942.

133 "It is no secret, that . . .": *WP*, Feb. 9, 1942.

133 "Pearl Harbor was a jolt . . .": *New Republic*, Feb. 2, 1942, p. 135.

134 "The general public . . .": *Time*, Feb. 16, 1942, p. 11.

134 "I do not see yet . . .": Ibid., Feb. 23, 1942, p. 14.

134 "general smugness . . .": Ibid., Feb. 16, 1942, p. 11.

134 "armchair complacency": *SUN*, Feb. 14, 1942.

134 "We in America must . . .": Ibid.

134 "face the facts . . .": *NYT*, Feb. 13, 1942.

134 "The fact that . . .": R. Dallek, *Lone Star*, p. 232.

134 "dangerously complacent": *NYT*, Feb. 18, 1942. The phrase is Herbert Lehman's.

134 "blind, stupid or arrogant": Ibid., Feb. 15, 1942.

134 "The war is unreal and remote . . .": Ibid., Feb. 21, 1942.

135 "The people's emotions . . .": Ibid., Feb. 19, 1942.

135 "one of the most . . .": Ibid., Feb. 15, 1942.

135 "sporadic triumphs here and there . . .": D. Lawrence, *Diary*, p. 305.

135 "They persist in this . . .": *DFP*, Feb. 15, 1942.

135 "one American can lick . . .": Ibid.

135 "lethargic" and "We've been too . . .": *NYT*, Feb. 13, 1942.

135 "the American people are . . .": *LAT*, Feb. 5, 1942.

135 "the sumptuous publicity . . .": Cooke, p. 21.

136 "The truth is that we have . . .": *NYT*, Feb. 22, 1942.

136 "complacency has no . . ." and "the critical year . . .": *DFP*, Feb. 14, 1942.

136 "stop thinking about . . .": *NYT*, Feb. 16, 1942.

137 "We must have every . . .": Ibid., Feb. 15, 1942.

137 "it would not be necessary . . .": Ibid., Feb. 20, 1942.

137 "a rush of . . .": *LAT*, Jan. 10, 1942.

137 "We have been having . . .": *TRIB*, Jan. 9, 1942.

137 "Department store counters . . .": *Time*, Jan. 26, 1942, p. 67.

138 "but it's respectable . . .": *LAT*, Jan. 5, 1942.

138 "we haven't even had . . .": *NYT*, Feb. 3, 1942.

138 "It's coming in without . . .": Ibid., Feb. 1, 1942.

138 "stocking up": *WP*, Feb. 14, 1942.

138 "The major portion . . .": *DFP*, Feb. 14, 1942.

138 "Americans are on a . . .": *LAT*, Jan. 25, 1942.

138 "Foolish Spending . . .": *NYT*, Feb. 27, 1942.

138 "It is no part of . . .": *LAT*, Dec. 30, 1941.

138 "You cannot buy victory . . .": *NYT*, Jan. 28, 1942.

138 "some citizens are pitifully slow . . .": *WP*, Jan. 23, 1942.

139 "some of our people . . .": *TRIB*, Jan. 28, 1942.

139 "tended to regard . . .": *WP*, Jan. 31, 1942.

139 "They don't want a riot . . .": *NYT*, Jan. 28, 1942.

139 "For Distinguished Service . . .": Ibid., Feb. 13, 1942.

139 "if a certain furbearing animal . . .": *BG*, Feb. 1, 1942.

139 "servicemen's valentines" and "It's O.K. . . .": *NYT*, Feb. 11, 1942.

139 "I wish I had . . .": Ibid.

140 "I'm sending you my . . .": *BG*, Feb. 14, 1942.

140 "would not be consistent . . .": *NYT*, Dec. 13, 1941.

140 "Unquestionably New Orleans . . .": *NOTP*, Jan. 4, 1942.

140  "Louisiana is not . . .": Ibid., Feb. 2, 1942.

140  "splendid objectives for saboteurs": Ibid., Feb. 17, 1942.

140  "sniff out spies . . .": *Time*, Jan. 12, 1942, p. 58.

141  "In some portions . . .": *NYT*, Feb. 4, 1942.

141  "infested with politics": Ibid., Feb. 25, 1942.

141  "Civilian defense has failed . . .": *DFP*, Feb. 17, 1942.

141  "We haven't any protection . . .": *NYT*, Feb. 18, 1942.

141  "we are totally unprepared": *NOTP*, Feb. 14, 1942.

141  "It is an open secret . . .": Ibid.

141  "Don't let anyone . . .": *TRIB*, Jan. 31, 1942.

142  "mercilessly" and "I believe we are . . .": *WP*, Feb. 21, 1942.

142  "the United States Army . . .": *NYT*, Feb. 20, 1942.

142  "tries hard enough . . .": Ibid.

142  "We've got an awful lot . . .": Ibid.

142  "provided, of course . . .": *BG*, Jan. 18, 1942.

142  "prepare smaller quantities . . .": *NYT*, Jan. 8, 1942.

142  "honest but panicky guests": *Newsweek*, Jan. 19, 1942, p. 48.

143  "service might be discreetly arranged . . .": *NYT*, Jan. 8, 1942.

143  "It lights the way . . .": *WP*, Jan. 21, 1942.

143  "Instead, people are . . .": *New Yorker*, Feb. 21, 1942, p. 55.

143  "The typical sight . . .": *NYT*, March 2, 1942.

143  "There is waiting . . .": Ibid.

143  "We have the most . . .": *WP*, Jan. 17, 1942.

144  "The ugly fact that no one . . .": Ibid., Jan. 27, 1942.

144  "House and room overcrowding . . .": Ibid., Jan. 14, 1942.

144  "a problem almost . . .": *BG*, Jan. 18, 1942.

144  "all rapidly deteriorating . . .": Ibid.

144  "Slum conditions in many spots . . .": *WP*, Jan. 21, 1942.

145  "Syphilis and tuberculosis . . .": Ibid., Jan. 6, 1942.

145  "decent living accommodations": Ibid., Jan. 10, 1942.

145  "men only": Ibid., Jan. 30, 1942.

145  "In contrast to . . .": Ibid., Feb. 10, 1942.

145  "It's downright unpatriotic . . .": Ibid., Jan. 30, 1942.

145  "There isn't enough . . .": Ibid., Feb. 7, 1942.

145  "peptic ulcers . . .": *Life*, Jan. 5, 1942, p. 63.

145  "high-strung, frail . . .": *Time*, March 16, 1942, p. 15. The quote is *Time*'s.

145  "A visitor would stake . . .": *Life*, Jan. 5, 1942, p. 63.

146  "tempos": *WP*, Dec. 21, 1941.

146  "temporary shelters" and "seriously overtax . . .": *SUN*, Jan. 30, 1942.

146  "the dark age": *Newsweek*, Feb. 2, 1942, p. 26.

146  "for people here merely . . .": *WP*, Jan. 31, 1942.

146  "ARE YOU A PARASITE?": *Time*, Feb. 9, 1942, p. 12.

146  "get-out-of-here": *WP*, Jan. 31, 1942.

146  "I've lived here . . .": Ibid., Feb. 1, 1942.

147  "parasite": *TRIB*, Feb. 1, 1942.

147 "Everybody in Washington . . .": *WP*, Jan. 31, 1942.

147 "send in names . . .": Ibid.

147 "non-production residents": Ibid., Feb. 2, 1942.

147 "Move to Miami . . .": Ibid., Feb. 13, 1942.

147 "If the President had spent . . .": Ibid., Feb. 10, 1942.

147 "to strip the government . . .": *NYT*, Feb. 13, 1942.

148 "amply demonstrated . . .": *SUN*, Feb. 5, 1942.

148 "boondoggling": Ibid., Feb. 7, 1942.

148 "Billions for defense . . .": *Newsweek*, Feb. 23, 1942, p. 30.

148 "a social reformatory": *SUN*, Feb. 14, 1942.

148 "pink tea party": *TRIB*, Feb. 5, 1942.

148 "trying to take over . . .": *SUN*, Feb. 9, 1942.

148 "lighter aspects of bolstering morale": Ibid., Feb. 8, 1942.

148 "Know Your Government": *DFP*, Feb. 19, 1942.

148 "parasites and leeches": *SUN*, Feb. 7, 1942.

148 "pointed to a . . .": Ibid., Feb. 8, 1942.

148 "Will change name . . .": *NYT*, Feb. 10, 1942.

148 "instruction in physical fitness . . .": *SUN*, Feb. 7, 1942.

148 "it is urgently necessary that . . .": *DFP*, Feb. 19, 1942.

149 "It is the poor example . . .": *WP*, Feb, 10, 1942.

149 "carelessness, waste and favoritism . . .": *NYT*, Feb. 8, 1942.

149 "a kind of personal . . .": *DFP*, Feb. 7, 1942.

149 "purely political . . .": Cook, *Eleanor Roosevelt*, p. 415.

149 "To know me . . .": *Newsweek*, Feb. 23, 1942, p. 30.

149 "a small but very vocal . . .": *NYT*, Feb. 23, 1942.

149 "It was a symptom . . .": Ibid. Feb. 12, 1942.

149 "basically and bitterly . . .": *New Republic*, Feb. 16, 1942, p. 224.

149 "still get the creeps . . .": *SUN*, Feb. 8, 1942.

150 "not absolutely sure . . .": *WP*, Feb. 7, 1942.

150 "incompetent and unskillful leadership": *SUN*, Feb. 12, 1942.

150 "the colossal dislocation . . .": *NYT*, Feb. 12, 1942.

150 "a totalitarian collectivism": Ibid.

150 "The war has been taken . . .": *TRIB*, Feb. 9, 1942.

150 "Those in Washington . . .": Ibid., Jan. 5, 1942.

150 "This campaign of . . .": *NYT*, Feb. 28, 1942.

150 "destroy and disunite . . .": *DFP*, Feb. 3, 1942.

150 "it is now plain . . .": *Time*, Feb. 16, 1942, p. 16, and *DFP*, Feb. 3, 1942.

## 7: The Golden West

151 "I am not one . . .": N. Roberts and A. Roberts, *"As Ever, Gene,"* p. 215.

151 "Much work to be done . . .": Bogard and Bryer, *Letters*, p. 526.

151 "even if I were . . .": N. Roberts and A. Roberts, p. 215.

152 "We were caught short . . .": Karman, p. 184.

152 "danger, attack and terror": *NYT*, March 18, 1942.

152 "actually believed that . . .": *LAT*, Feb. 16, 1942.

152 "are on the alert . . .": *TRIB*, Feb. 4, 1942.

152 "to cluster in the . . .": Murray, *Historical Memories*, p. 32.

153 "a menace to . . .": *LAT*, Jan. 23, 1942.

153 "Chinese Operated . . .": *American Magazine*, March 1942, p. 102.

153 "We just felt that . . .": *NYT*, Jan. 29, 1942.

153 "Achilles' heel . . .": Ibid., Jan. 31, 1942.

154 "the movement of all . . .": *LAT*, Jan. 22, 1942.

154 "it is not asking too much . . .": Ibid.

154 "the Japanese" and "feel that they are living . . .": Robinson, *Order*, p. 96.

154 "It is scarcely believable . . .": *LAT*, Jan. 26, 1942.

154 "A great deal of damage . . .": Ibid., Jan. 30, 1942.

155 "public hysteria" and "the comments of . . .": Murray, p. 34.

155 "taking every precaution . . .": *SUN*, Feb. 2, 1942.

155 "profoundly unwise" and "profoundly un-American": *LAT*, Feb. 6, 1942.

155 "Francis Biddle's measures . . .": *Time*, Feb. 16, 1942, p. 15.

155 "to meet a man . . .": *DFP*, Feb. 7, 1942.

155 "looking at the Japanese situation . . .": *LAT*, Feb. 8, 1942.

155 "a mounting undercover feeling . . .": *DFP*, Jan. 31, 1942.

155 "maudlin attitude toward . . .": *LAT*, Jan. 29, 1942.

155 "there will occur . . .": *SUN*, Jan. 29, 1942.

155 "America's Nipponese": *NYT*, Feb. 8, 1942.

155 "certainly not as fantastic . . .": *WP*, Feb. 2, 1942.

156 "serious consideration": *LAT*, Feb. 6, 1942.

156 "productive agricultural labor" and "be invited to . . .": Ibid. Feb. 12, 1942.

156 "all persons of . . .": *NYT*, Feb. 5, 1942.

156 "the temper of the people of . . .": *LAT*, Feb. 4, 1942.

156 "the more serious aspects . . .": *NYT*, Feb. 6, 1942.

157 "I think apart from . . .": Ibid. Jan. 4, 1942.

157 "war colleges of . . .": *DFP*, Jan. 31, 1942.

157 "We have stood for . . .": *TRIB*, Jan. 8, 1942.

157 "ivory tower" and "puerile pacifism": *SUN*, Jan. 4, 1942.

157 "Whether you like it or not . . .": *WP*, Dec. 24, 1941.

158 "Hurrying boys and girls . . .": *LAT*, Feb. 18, 1942.

158 "sing for defense" and "in time of . . .": *SUN*, March 3, 1942.

158 "the desire to destroy . . .": *DFP*, March 15, 1942.

158 "the most health-adequate . . .": *Time*, April 13, 1942, p. 48.

158 "We're not depriving . . .": Ibid., p. 50.

159 "We are faced, therefore . . .": *SUN*, Jan. 4, 1942.

159 "the sudden acquisition . . .": *NYT*, Feb. 16, 1942.

159 "In many . . .": Ibid., March 17, 1942.

159 "the swamp which . . .": *WP*, Feb. 4, 1942.

159 "Packing-box shanties . . .": Ibid.

160 "the impact of defense conditions . . .": *NYT*, March 17, 1942.

160 "the blighting of . . .": Elias, *Dreiser*, p. 953.

160 "There are one million children . . .": Ibid., p. 955.

160 "it has always been true . . .": Ibid., p. 952.

160 "utility houses": SUN, Jan. 19, 1942.

160 "When I begin to grumble . . .": Ibid.

161 "seeing couples move in and out . . .": Ibid.

161 "for fear of running . . .": Ibid.

161 "filthy poor whites . . .": Hobson, Mencken, p. 450.

161 "The Negroes are much more civilized": Ibid., p. 457.

162 "It also will be . . .": SUN, Jan. 25, 1942.

162 "A great defense plant . . .": BG, Jan. 7, 1942.

162 "a tragedy . . .": Ibid.

162 "a boom town . . .": Ibid.

162 "is beginning to hit close, now . . .": BG, March 2, 1942.

162 "If Lincoln were alive . . .": LAT, Feb. 13, 1942.

162 "the nerve center": Sitton, Los Angeles Transformed, p. 64.

162 "hundreds of letters . . .": Ibid.

162 "Those little men . . .": LAT, Feb. 13, 1942.

163 "just nuts": Murray, p. 35.

163 "the immediate evacuation . . .": Ibid., p. 27.

163 "It is impossible to know . . .": LAT, Feb. 21, 1942.

163 "We're splitting hairs and . . .": Ibid., Feb. 13, 1942.

163 "there has been no substantial evidence . . .": NYT, Feb. 6, 1942.

163 "very absence of sabotage . . .": Ibid., Feb. 22, 1942.

163 "The Pacific Coast is in imminent danger . . .": WP, Feb. 12, 1942.

164 "secret documents and uniforms": NYT, Feb. 17, 1942.

164 "signaling devices": Ibid., Feb. 15, 1942.

164 "a sinister reminder . . .": Time, Feb. 23, 1942, p. 14.

164 "This is one of those moments . . .": DFP, Feb. 12, 1942.

164 "Japan controls now . . .": Ibid., Feb. 18, 1942.

164 "the second 'Jap Sunday'": WP, Feb. 17, 1942.

164 "This was the worst week . . .": Time, Feb. 23, 1942, p. 14.

164 "The considered judgment . . .": NYT, Feb. 16, 1942.

165 "the battle front will move . . .": Newsweek, Feb. 23, 1942, p. 30.

165 "Perhaps it is good for us . . .": DFP, Feb. 18, 1942.

165 "to imprison all Japanese Americans . . .": Robinson, p. 106.

165 "If we don't move . . .": SUN, Feb. 19, 1942.

165 "all the Japs out . . .": Ibid., Jan. 21, 1942.

165 "Once a Jap . . .": WP, Feb. 19, 1942.

165 "will make a tremendous . . .": Robinson, p. 105.

165 "do anything you think necessary . . .": Murray, p. 33.

165 "to prescribe military areas . . .": NYT, Feb. 21, 1942.

166 "the move has been taken . . .": Ibid.

166 "a step in the right direction": LAT, Feb. 21, 1942.

166 "We know we are loyal . . .": Ibid., Feb. 20, 1942.

166 "We have advised . . .": NYT, Feb. 21, 1942.

166 "After Singapore . . .": *LAT*, Feb. 15, 1942.

166 "The big dance bands . . .": *New Yorker*, March 14, 1942, p. 76.

166 "panty-waist numbers" and "Add a crooner . . .": *TRIB*, March 1, 1942.

167 "We must pay . . .": *NYT*, Jan. 26, 1942.

167 "for whose maintenance . . .": Ibid. Jan. 23, 1942.

167 "we don't want to . . .": *TRIB*, Jan. 23, 1942.

167 "taxes to beat the Axis!": *Time*, Feb. 9, 1942, p. 36.

167 "They were being uprooted . . .": Capra, p. 326. Capra was paraphrasing Marshall.

167 "explain to a great many . . .": Guth, p. 214.

168 "no pretty writing" and "It is dangerous . . .": Ibid.

168 "The swiftest and simplest . . .": *NYT*, Feb. 10, 1942.

168 "The people wanted to hear . . .": *Time*, March 2, 1942, p. 10.

168 "Preach hell to us . . .": *SUN*, Feb. 19, 1942.

168 "Now we take you . . .": *NYT*, March 1, 1942.

168 "unusually grave": Ibid.

168 "We Americans have been compelled . . .": *WP*, Feb. 24, 1942.

168 "great geography lesson": *New Yorker*, March 7, 1942, p. 7.

168 "turtle policy" and "We prefer to retain . . .": *NYT*, Feb. 24, 1942.

169 "we shall not stop work . . .": Ibid.

169 "It will be sort of . . .": *New Yorker*, March 14, 1942, p. 13.

169 "We still find a tendency . . .": *NYT*, Feb. 24, 1942.

169 "a hurried and nervous . . .": *LAT*, Feb. 25, 1942.

169 "execrable marksmanship": Ibid.

169 "There is reason to believe . . .": Ibid.

169 "I think there'll be a lot more . . .": Ibid.

169 "Any day now . . .": G. Marx, pp. 29–30.

170 "On the one hand . . .": *SUN*, Feb. 11, 1942.

170 "Such films seem a bit . . .": *New Yorker*, Feb. 21, 1942, p. 49.

170 "This contempt for the Nazis . . .": *NYT*, Feb. 22, 1942.

170 "concise and comforting commentary": *WP*, Feb. 25, 1942.

170 "a strange blending . . .": Crowther, *Letters*, p. 43.

170 "Public Illness Number One": *American Magazine*, Jan. 1942, p. 29.

170 "One of the minor difficulties . . .": *New Yorker*, Jan. 10, 1942, p. 9.

170 "how in thunder . . .": *American Magazine*, Jan. 1942, p. 29.

170 "Almost always somewhere . . .": *TRIB*, Jan. 5, 1942.

171 "professional listeners": *American Magazine*, Jan. 1942, p. 29.

171 "the prevailing mood . . .": *WP*, Feb. 23, 1942.

171 "radio fatigue" and "uses up the energy . . .": *LAT*, Feb. 26, 1942.

171 "We're jumpy enough . . .": *New Republic*, Jan. 12, 1942, p. 47.

171 "in perfectly awful trouble": Ibid.

171 "I started this war . . .": *Time*, March 2, 1942, p. 6.

171 "Haven't the American people . . .": *DFP*, April 25, 1942.

171 "something quiet and nostalgic . . .": *SUN*, March 29, 1942.

171 "dancing is the best tonic . . .": *NYT*, Jan. 29, 1942.

172 "People must mix . . .": *SUN*, March 10, 1942.

172 *"How to Avoid and . . .*": *WP*, April 21, 1942.

172 "the nervous strain . . .": *NYT*, Feb. 13, 1942.

172 "all day in the warm sunshine . . .": *WP*, Feb. 22, 1942.

172 "the first real show . . .": *NYT*, Feb. 26, 1942.

172 "screeching like . . ." and "come backta bed": *LAT*, Feb. 27, 1942.

173 "They came in great dark clouds": Ibid., Feb. 26, 1942.

173 "there were seven planes . . .": Ibid.

173 "Roaring out of a brilliant . . .": *Time*, March 9, 1942, p. 14.

173 "I was having a . . .": Davies, *Times*, p. 313.

173 "You never heard . . .": Ibid.

173 "Airplanes, particularly enemy airplanes . . .": *LAT*, Feb. 26, 1942.

174 "just a false alarm": *Time*, March 9, 1942, p. 15.

174 "operated by enemy agents": *NYT*, Feb. 27, 1942.

174 "Conflicting statements . . .": *WP*, Feb. 27, 1942.

174 "fake reports" and "they are beginning to believe . . .": *NYT*, Feb. 27, 1942.

174 "This incident is a cause . . .": Ibid., Feb. 28, 1942.

174 "The Negro people . . .": *BG*, Feb. 9, 1942.

175 "whole-heartedly, unselfishly, all-out": *NYT*, Jan. 11, 1942.

175 "radical, nationwide change . . .": *Life*, March 23, 1942, p. 65.

175 "We have no written . . .": *Baltimore Afro-American*, Jan. 31, 1942.

176 "that our records show . . .": *NYT*, March 18, 1942.

176 "We have loads of discrimination": Ibid. Feb. 17, 1942.

176 "To deprive America's . . .": *Baltimore Afro-American*, Jan. 17, 1942.

176 "they would walk out . . .": *NYT*, Feb. 18, 1942.

176 "I'll guarantee that . . .": *Baltimore Afro-American*, Feb. 28, 1942.

176 "qualified and needed . . .": *LAT*, Jan. 19, 1942.

176 "a good many years": *Time*, April 6, 1942, p. 4.

177 "This is no longer . . .": *DFP*, Feb. 28, 1942.

177 "We want White Neighbors": *Time*, March 9, 1942, p. 14.

178 "There is no use . . .": Ibid.

178 "The Army is about to . . .": Ibid.

## 8: Dark Tidings, Straight, No Sugar

179 "to see what the war . . .": Cooke, p. 24.

179 "I drove almost a dozen miles . . .": Ibid., p. 29.

179 "the town was . . .": Ibid., p. 30.

180 "a town doing business . . .": Ibid., p. 33.

180 "You smell around the town . . .": Ibid.

180 "A distrust has been building . . .": Ibid.

180 "in the interests of . . .": Ibid., p. 36.

180 "To an eskimo . . .": Ibid., p. 35.

180 "The thing that startles . . .": *NYT*, March 10, 1942.

181 "The docile maid-of-all-work . . .": *LAT*, Dec. 19, 1942.

181 "I now have . . .": G. Marx, p. 30.

181 "It is practically impossible . . .": Bogard, pp. 215–16.

182 "Your duty is to . . .": *SUN*, March 4, 1942.

182 "victory army": *Newsweek*, May 18, 1942, p. 42.

182 "tractorettes": *DFP*, March 13, 1942.

182 "In effect, the United States . . .": *Time*, March 16, 1942, p. 14.

182 "the complete conversion . . .": Ibid. April 20, 1942, p. 77.

182 "most, if not all . . .": *NYT*, Jan. 30, 1942.

182 "This means a cut in . . .": *Time*, April 27, 1942, p. 16.

182 "despite all the wars . . .": Cleator, *Letters from Baltimore*, p. 123.

182 "Never announce to the . . .": *New Yorker*, June 27, 1942, p. 9.

182 "crowds of typical . . .": *NYT*, March 31, 1942.

182 "They knew that . . .": *Time*, March 23, 1942, p. 16.

184 "It's not flashy . . .": *WP*, Jan. 28, 1942.

184 "the only way . . .": *DFP*, March 11, 1942.

184 "freeze the existing . . .": *NYT*, March 10, 1942.

184 "radical changes in fashion . . .": Ibid.

184 "Taste without waste": *Newsweek*, April 20, 1942, p. 46.

184 "The overdressed woman . . .": *Time*, April 20, 1942, p. 17.

185 "We're going to be . . .": *LAT*, Feb. 18, 1942.

185 "Suddenly, nothing suits you . . .": *NYT*, March 8, 1942.

185 "a new kind of living . . .": *WP*, Feb. 20, 1942.

185 "an affectation which is . . .": *New Yorker*, May 2, 1942, p. 54.

185 "this emphatically must stop . . .": Ibid.

185 "Rule 1—Don't wear . . .": *BG*, March 15, 1942.

185 "the simplification of . . .": Ibid., March 28, 1942.

185 "I don't think slacks . . .": Ibid., May 15, 1942.

185 "At night, when we . . .": Crowther, p. 45.

186 "so terrible discouraging": Symonette and Kowalke, *Speak Low*, p. 296.

186 "the most serious . . .": *NYT*, March 15, 1942.

186 "And Australia is in peril": *Time*, March 9, 1942, p. 16.

186 "We have been pounded . . .": *NYT*, March 9, 1942.

186 "at present we are . . .": C. Lindbergh, p. 604.

186 "the ban on new radios . . .": *New Yorker*, March 14, 1942, p. 51.

186 "We are discouraged . . .": Ibid., p. 13.

186 "unnecessary suspense . . .": *NYT*, March 12, 1942.

186 "an unfortunate implication . . .": Avery, *Dramatist*, pp. 120–21.

187 "Ballyhoo doesn't win . . .": Lawrence, *Diary*, p. 328.

187 "Let's go to Tokio": *DFP*, March 9, 1942.

187 "We're in it . . .": Ibid.

187 "The feeling that it is . . .": *Newsweek*, April 13, 1942, p. 32.

187 "of doubletalk . . . of those phony . . .": *Time*, March 9, 1942, pp. 2, 4.

187 "Here on the East Coast . . .": Riggio, *Dreiser-Mencken*, p. 673.

187 "that we're in for a short war . . .": *LAT*, Feb. 27, 1942.

187 "Things are not good . . .": *NOTP*, Feb. 24, 1942.

187 "despite submarine shelling . . .": *DFP*, March 11, 1942.

187 "It is good to be alive in the spring . . .": Ibid., March 7, 1942.

187 "For too long this war . . .": *NYT*, March 9, 1942.

188 "I wonder why we are . . .": *Time*, March 23, 1942, p. 15.

188 "lack of leadership and information": Ibid., March 9, 1942, pp. 2, 4.

188 "bewildered, distrustful despair": *WP*, Feb. 18, 1942.

188 "People are not . . .": *Time*, March 9, 1942, p. 2.

188 "hasn't the whole picture . . .": *NYT*, Feb. 17, 1942.

189 "Hoarded dollars are . . .": *SUN*, April 15, 1942.

189 "Some bankers . . .": *Time*, March 9, 1942, p. 78.

189 "with more unpainted barns . . .": Cooke, p. 36.

189 "what the radio commentators . . .": Ibid., p. 39.

189 "The young ones know . . .": Ibid.

189 "It is the first town we have seen . . .": Ibid.

189 "Early every morning . . .": Ibid., pp. 42–43.

189 "the sort of town . . .": Ibid., p. 43.

190 "till every muddy patch . . .": Ibid., p. 47.

190 "fifteen dollars a week . . .": Ibid.

190 "This prospect . . .": Ibid., p. 50.

190 "the greatest single job ever tackled . . .": *SUN*, Feb. 18, 1942.

190 "ordinary lumps": Ibid. April 18, 1942.

190 "instinctively resent . . .": *WSJ*, May 5, 1942.

191 "household hoard": *SUN*, April 23, 1942.

191 "the country is in no mood . . .": Ibid.

191 "remarkable how many . . .": Ibid., May 5, 1942.

191 "thinking of going into . . .": *NYT*, May 7, 1942.

191 "sugar girls": *New Yorker,* March 28, 1942, pp. 14–15.

191 "kindly report persons . . .": *Time*, April 27, 1942, p. 89.

191 "Our volume has . . .": *NYT*, Feb. 9, 1942.

192 "Oil is ammunition . . .": Ibid. Feb. 25, 1942.

192 "Maybe you *can't* . . .": *WP*, Feb. 20, 1942.

192 "tourists bent on . . .": *Time*, March 16, 1942, p. 16.

192 "If you're careless today . . .": Ibid., May 4, 1942, p. 9.

193 "reasonable, prudent driving": *NYT*, March 15, 1942.

193 "frantic and purposeless . . .": *WP*, Feb. 17, 1942.

193 "Conservation of tires . . .": *DFP*, March 22, 1942.

193 "quickly, cheaply . . .": *WP*, April 10, 1942.

193 "if the people become . . .": Ibid.

193 "Everyone of us . . .": Ibid., Feb. 15, 1942.

193 "essential vehicles": *NYT*, March 6, 1942.

194 "beyond all argument . . .": Ibid., March 15, 1942.

194 "Real conservation requires . . .": Ibid., March 9, 1942.

194 "anything from a beach wagon . . .": *BG*, Feb. 6, 1942.

195 "We had to travel . . .": A. Lawrence, *Duke Ellington*, p. 310.

195 "The bicycle situation . . .": *DFP*, March 9, 1942.

195 "It's no use rushing around . . .": *SUN*, March 7, 1942.

195 "The order was issued . . .": *WP*, April 3, 1942.

195 "The worst possible [censorship] policy . . .": *NYT*, April 11, 1942.

196 "Yanks Smash Bataan Attacks . . .": *WP*, April 3, 1942.

196 "Americans did not yet believe . . .": *Time*, April 20, 1942, p. 18.

196 "Perhaps we are now fully awake . . .": *WP*, April 12, 1942.

196 "We should honestly face . . .": *DFP*, April 20, 1942.

197 "Perelman, Perel-Man . . .": Crowther, p. 43.

197 "men who had been just old enough . . .": *Time*, June 15, 1942, p. 59.

197 "We are the tough old . . .": Ibid.

197 "The attitude now seems to be . . .": *NYT*, Feb. 6, 1942.

197 "Labor dislocations . . .": *WP*, April 20, 1942.

197 "the man-power situation . . .": *Newsweek*, May 4, 1942, p. 31.

198 "As a rule, there is no one . . .": D. Lawrence, p. 346.

198 "women have shown . . .": *WP*, May 23, 1942.

198 "The bars are down . . .": Ibid., Jan. 19, 1942.

198 "if I can get . . .": Ibid., Jan. 31, 1942.

198 "I honestly feel that . . .": *NYT*, Jan. 17, 1942.

198 "There are owners . . .": *WP*, Feb. 6, 1942.

198 "We cordially invite you . . .": *DFP*, March 7, 1942.

200 "This is a daytime game . . .": *WP*, May 12, 1942.

200 "Play will be enlivened . . .": Ibid., April 10, 1942.

200 "It is probably . . .": Ibid.

200 "because of circumstances . . .": *DFP*, March 13, 1942.

200 "The ball players will be . . .": *NYT*, April 11, 1942.

201 "The attitude of the interior states . . .": Department of War, *Final Report*, p. 43.

201 "We don't want them . . .": Murray, p. 59.

201 "The Japs live like . . .": Reeves, *Infamy*, p. xvi.

201 "send them all back . . .": Murray, p. 59.

201 "a dumping ground": *NYT*, March 2, 1942.

201 "if you bring . . .": Reeves, p. xvi.

201 "For Rent": *NYT*, March 6, 1942.

201 "Evacuation Sale . . .": *Time*, April 6, 1942, p. 12.

202 "Now they have to . . .": *DFP*, Feb. 23, 1942.

202 "Unfortunately, in a war . . .": Ibid., March 23, 1942.

202 "Most of us understand . . .": *Time*, April 6, 1942, pp. 12–13.

202 "Why should we support . . .": Ibid.

202 "sick of the job": Murray, p. 57.

202 "we as Americans are . . .": Ibid.

## 9: Games of Chance

203 "disastrous": *New Yorker*, April 25, 1942, p. 30.

203 "sadly disappointing": *WP*, April 26, 1942.

203 "The war is a . . .": *NYT*, March 1, 1942.

203 "more like idle . . .": *SUN*, Feb. 22, 1942.

203 "a slightly paralyzing effect . . .": *Time*, Feb. 16, 1942, p. 63.

204 "to put some personal . . .": *DFP*, Feb. 7, 1942.

204 "unquestionably the best . . .": *New Yorker*, May 2, 1942, p. 31.

204 "Vaudeville never died . . .": *BG*, June 28, 1942.

204 "There still seems to be . . .": Ibid., April 25, 1942.

204 "The gloomy implications . . .": Ibid.

204 "where, for a little bit . . .": Ibid.

204 "well-meant, sometimes . . .": *Time*, April 13, 1942, p. 43.

204 "what we say tonight . . .": Ibid., Feb. 23, 1942, p. 61.

205 "Hawthorne would hardly know . . .": Hendrick, *Selected Letters*, p. 152.

205 "decent, catchy song": *New Yorker*, June 20, 1942, p. 9.

205 "For some reason . . .": *SUN*, May 11, 1942.

205 "One of the difficulties . . .": *New Yorker*, June 20, 1942, p. 9.

205 "the natural fellowship . . .": Kaufman, *American Radical*, p. 92.

205 "If a blackout comes . . .": Ibid., p. 94.

206 "about fifty ships behind in announcing . . .": Winnick, *MacLeish*, p. 312.

206 "the ghastly and humiliating things . . .": *DFP*, June 1, 1942.

206 "There's no use . . .": *Time*, June 15, 1942, p. 24.

206 "He confesses that . . .": Cooke, p. 76.

206 "By the time I git to . . .": Ibid.

206 "Might just as well . . .": Ibid., p. 77.

206 "all potentially dangerous lighting": *WP*, March 22, 1942.

206 "the lights were like . . .": *Time*, March 30, 1942, p. 25.

206 "the glare from the city lights . . .": *SUN*, April 21, 1942.

206 "like a gigantic furnace": Ibid., April 29, 1942.

207 "murderous mound of light": Ibid., May 22, 1942.

207 "We are suffering a major defeat . . .": *DFP*, May 23, 1942.

207 "The time may be close at hand . . .": *Time*, June 1, 1942, p. 12.

207 "German submarines have been . . .": *NYT*, June 6, 1942.

207 "flagrant violations": Ibid., June 1, 1942.

207 "Boston still hasn't . . .": *BG*, June 19, 1942.

207 "at least four or five times . . .": *SUN*, June 10, 1942.

207 "good for Hitler": *BG*, July 19, 1942.

207 "whole communities . . .": *NYT*, June 1, 1942.

207 "a good many violations": *SUN*, July 5, 1942.

208 "it is unthinkable . . .": *Newsweek*, May 4, 1942, p. 47.

208 "getting a damn sight more . . .": *SUN*, May 9, 1942.

208 "the American public . . .": *BG*, May 10, 1942.

208 "the truth about total war . . .": *Time*, May 18, 1942, p. 11.

208 "This is a test . . .": *NYT*, May 9, 1942.

209 "The public immorality . . .": *Time*, May 25, 1942, p. 16.

209 "The demand for X cards . . .": *WSJ*, May 16, 1942.

209 "only about 25 per cent . . .": *Newsweek*, May 25, 1942, p. 28.

209 "If we are unwilling . . .": *NYT*, May 16, 1942.

209 "By far the majority . . .": *SUN*, May 14, 1942.

209 "because of the disorderly . . .": Ibid.

209 "scandalized at the number . . .": *NYT*, May 14, 1942.

209 "unwarranted demand": Ibid.

209 "the most disgraceful thing . . .": Ibid.; May 14, May 17, 1942.

209 "100 per cent": *NOTP*, May 14, 1942.

209 "rationing is producing . . .": *NYT*, May 14, 1942.

209 "Apparently there wasn't . . .": Ibid.

209 "increasing indications of . . .": Ibid.

210 "Congress has bungled . . .": *WP*, May 16, 1942.

210 "very wrong, very foolish . . .": *NOTP*, May 28, 1942.

210 "a stupidity that is . . .": *DFP*, May 15, 1942.

210 "selfish and destructive conduct": Ibid., May 16, 1942.

210 "This war can't be won . . .": *WP*, May 14, 1942.

210 ""I am going to take . . .": *DFP*, May 16, 1942.

210 "we're not going to take . . .": Ibid.

210 "As an example of . . .": Ibid., Feb. 5, 1942.

211 "war-stricken": Ibid., Feb. 6, 1942.

211 "Don't worry about . . .": *NYT*, Feb. 4, 1942.

211 "the bitterest criticism . . .": *WP*, Feb. 14, 1942.

211 "a studied effort to destroy . . .": Ibid. May 31, 1942.

211 "our whole system of government . . .": *DFP*, May 15, 1942.

211 "taking cracks such as this . . .": Ibid., May 14, 1942.

211 "seditious conduct": *Time*, May 25, 1942, p. 12.

211 "newspaper columnists and . . .": *DFP*, May 15, 1942.

211 "As a force in our Government . . .": Ibid., May 18, 1942.

211 "none had ever been . . .": *Time*, Feb. 16, 1942, p. 14.

212 "through a mistake . . .": *WSJ*, May 16, 1942.

212 "Gestapo": *NYT*, May 17, 1942.

212 "The privileged ones . . .": *DFP*, May 20, 1942.

213 "as though the war . . .": *WP*, April 6, 1942.

213 "sentimental slush": Ibid., April 10, 1942.

213 "The People's War" and other suggestions: Ibid., April 7, April 10, 1942; *Time*, April 13, 1942, p. 15; May 4, 1942, p. 2.

213 "it comes pretty close . . .": *NYT*, April 15, 1942.

213 "met a frosty silence": Ibid., June 28, 1942.

213 "'survival' is a negative term . . .": *WSJ*, May 8, 1942.

213 "Slogans are not enough . . .": *New Yorker*, March 7, 1942, pp. 60–61.

213 "The time has now come . . .": *Time*, March 9, 1942, p. 10.

213 "We should begin to think . . .": Ibid., p. 9.

214 "Morally and psychologically . . .": *NYT*, April 20, 1942.

214 "If we can do it . . .": Ibid.

214 "Air attacks of greater power . . .": *BG*, April 21, 1942.

214 "wars are not won . . .": *SUN*, May 16, 1942.

214 "The war in the Pacific . . .": Ibid., May 6, 1942.

215 "With the Americans the . . .": *Newsweek*, May 25, 1942, p. 26.

215 "the Jap had taken . . .": *Time*, May 18, 1942, p. 20.

215 "Throughout the land . . .": Ibid., June 15, 1942, p. 10.

215 "As America approaches . . .": *WP*, May 31, 1942.

215 "In the name of . . .": *Time*, June 1, 1942, p. 54.

215 "The effect of such . . .": *WP*, May 31, 1942.

215 "apathy that hangs like . . .": *NYT*, June 28, 1942.

215 "it is hard to get . . .": Ibid.

215 "I am afraid that too many . . .": *Time*, June 29, 1942, p. 14.

216 "Everywhere the story . . .": *Newsweek*, May 25, 1942, p. 42.

216 "over the hump . . .": *SUN*, April 20, 1942.

216 "more war materiel . . .": *WP*, April 19, 1942 (*Post* paraphrase of speech).

216 "near-miracle": *NYT*, May 23, 1942.

216 "we have found that . . .": *WP*, June 20, 1942.

216 "chocolate-covered facts": *NYT*, August 10, 1942.

217 "these trials and errors . . .": Baruch, *Public Years*, p. 294.

217 "blanket priorities" and "unbalanced and . . .": *WP*, June 11, 1942.

217 "dangerous proportions": *NYT*, Aug. 19, 1942.

217 "There's too damned much . . .": *SUN*, April 15, 1942.

217 "ships could be built . . .": *DFP*, Feb. 20, 1942.

217 "Money seems to be . . .": *Time*, May 4, 1942, p. 14.

218 "One thing that . . .": Guth and White, p. 222.

218 "traitors [who] should be . . .": *NYT*, March 9, 1942.

218 "The local will have to . . .": *SUN*, June 3, 1942.

219 "disloyal": *WP*, June 19, 1942.

219 "wouldn't gain one . . .": *NYT*, April 8, 1942.

219 "a good thing that . . .": *Time*, March 30, 1942, p. 9.

219 "pampering" and "to produce cheap . . .": *WSJ*, May 18, 1942.

219 "special presentments" and "a betrayal of . . .": *TRIB*, April 17, 1942.

220 "shanghaiing of ships' crews . . .": *WP*, May 31, 1942.

220 "work-while-you-eat": *NYT*, April 1, 1942.

220 "It makes a good meal . . .": *New Yorker*, March 7, 1942, p. 26.

220 "The Man Who Relaxes . . .": *WP*, Jan. 28, 1942.

220 "the Tokio Kid": *Time*, June 15, 1942, p. 36.

220 "Workers in munitions factories . . .": *New Yorker*, May 23, 1942, p. 23.

221 "No nation, fighting with . . .": *NYT*, July 24, 1942.

221 "There is no excuse . . .": Ibid., July 27, 1942.

221 "the pernicious red-light districts . . .": Ibid., June 29, 1942.

221 "a huge increase in prostitution": Ibid., August 11, 1942.

221 "whose morals had . . .": Cooke, p. 68.

221 "total physical and moral fitness": *WP*, June 18, 1942.

222 "have more of everything . . .": *Time*, July 20, 1942, p. 13.

222 "a real boom town" and "every night . . .": *SUN*, April 26, 1942.

222 "Never so much money . . .": *New Yorker*, May 30, 1942, p. 42.

223 "more than ever . . .": *WP*, May 28, 1942.

223 "we are woefully...": *SUN*, May 14, 1942.

223 "it is not only discouraging...": *WP*, June 17, 1942.

223 "far behind schedule...": *SUN*, April 30, 1942.

223 "acute" and "Every room...": *NYT*, June 9, 1942.

223 "boats, trailers...": *SUN*, May 20, 1942.

223 "tenement barracks" and "as badly as...": *New Yorker*, May 23, 1942, p. 57.

223 "it's a crime the way...": *WP*, June 17, 1942.

223 "housing is not a problem...": *SUN*, Aug. 17, 1942.

223 "because they can find...": *WP*, April 4, 1942.

223 "vicious and insanitary...": *DFP*, April 18, 1942.

223 "Every day more and more workers...": *NYT*, March 31, 1942.

224 "There is hardly a day...": Ibid., Dec. 5, 1942.

224 "They're talking about...": *WP*, April 29, 1942.

224 "It is exceedingly urgent...": Shogan and Craig, *Detroit Race Riot*, p. 31.

224 "hell is going to be...": Ibid.

224 "People seem to be...": *DFP*, Feb. 22, 1942.

224 "You'd be surprised...": Ibid., March 17, 1942.

225 "the golden era": *WSJ*, June 30, 1942.

225 "Nothing takes a man's mind...": *New Yorker*, Jan. 10, 1942, p. 34.

225 "Taking a quick whirl...": *SUN*, May 18, 1942.

225 "wide-eyed as at...": *Time*, May 11, 1942, p. 71.

225 "the most successful...": *NYT*, May 10, 1942.

225 "the gaudiest betting day...": *WP*, May 31, 1942.

225 "New York has gone...": Ibid., May 26, 1942.

226 "motor traffic had...": *New Yorker*, May 30, 1942, pp. 55–58.

226 "practically abandoned": *BG*, May 25, 1942.

226 "Swim at uncrowded beaches": *New Yorker*, Aug. 22, 1942, p. 34.

226 "A survey of the...": *WSJ*, July 2, 1942.

226 "a $100,000,000 tourist business": *NYT*, June 30, 1942.

226 "fighting for their existence...": *Time*, June 29, 1942, p. 10.

227 "absolutely unfounded": Ibid., p. 8.

227 "We are bathing as usual...": Ibid., p. 10.

227 "there can be no...": *New Yorker*, May 30, 1942, p. 38.

227 "And you won't want to miss...": *NYT*, May 1, 1942.

227 "we can't sell our stuff...": *SUN*, May 27, 1942.

227 "the customary tourist...": *WP*, April 2, 1942.

## 10: Borrowed Time

230 "a momentous victory": *NYT*, June 7, 1942.

230 "vivid accounts of...": Ibid., Aug. 1, 1942.

230 "I've been buoyed up...": Ibid., June 21, 1942.

230 "Plainly, the war in the Pacific...": Ibid., June 14, 1942.

230 "Japanese marauders masquerading...": Ibid., June 7, 1942.

231 "All it takes...": Cooke, p. 170.

231 "a civilian's manual . . .": *Time*, March 16, 1942, p. 54.

231 "a wire cable . . .": Ibid.

231 "If the Japanese try to land . . .": Tillamookheadlightherald.com, April 7, 2010.

231 "We in San Francisco are . . .": *Time*, July 6, 1942, p. 2.

232 "Why worry . . .": Ibid., June 15, 1942, p. 59.

232 "The trouble seemed to lie . . .": Ibid., Aug. 10, 1942, p. 71.

232 "It's a lot more . . .": *TRIB*, June 5, 1942.

232 "If the public is confused . . .": *WP*, June 21, 1942.

232 "positively alarming . . .": Ibid., June 24, 1942.

232 "The Japs are headed . . .": Ibid., July 23, 1942.

232 "gloom and dejection . . .": *NYT*, June 28, 1942.

233 "the remarkable delay . . .": Ibid., July 22, 1942.

233 "That's 10,000 too many": *WP*, August 2, 1942.

233 "if we needed Kiska . . .": Ibid., August 15, 1942.

233 "I am scared . . .": *Newsweek*, July 13, 1942, p. 22.

233 "The public continued to be fed . . .": *WP*, August 26, 1942.

233 "bloody and terrible . . .": E. B. White, *One Man's*, p. 332.

233 "This second war . . .": Ibid., pp. 332–33.

233 "These are no times . . .": *Time*, May 4, 1942, p. 32.

234 "Guns, guns, guns! . . .": Ibid., May 18, 1942, p. 58.

234 "No careless toleration now . . .": Ibid., Sept. 14, 1942, p. 96.

234 "Reveille for America . . .": *Life*, March 30, 1942, p. 6.

234 "In the tempo we live today . . .": *New Yorker*, July 25, 1942, p. 37.

234 "For the duration . . .": *WP*, July 19, 1942.

234 "an evident tendency . . .": *NYT*, March 8, 1942.

234 "This year we will . . .": *WSJ*, May 6, 1942.

234 "In the wartime United States . . .": *Time*, May 4, 1942, p. 16.

234 "the economic group . . .": *WP*, April 30, 1942.

234 "Nothing in the economic field . . .": *NYT*, March 5, 1942.

234 "a little inflation . . ." and "a fellow who took . . .": Polenberg, p. 23.

235 "There had been war booms before . . .": Dos Passos, *The Theme*, p. 164.

235 "the greatest possible volume . . .": *NYT*, March 4, 1942.

235 "The adjustment will be . . .": Ibid., March 5, 1942.

235 "At present my principal . . .": C. Baker, *Hemingway Letters*, pp. 535–36.

236 "No American citizen . . .": *NYT*, June 17, 1942.

236 "prevent anybody . . .": *BG*, April 28, 1942.

236 "morale-building": *NYT*, June 17, 1942.

236 "more cheerfully" and "that rich and poor alike . . .": *WP*, June 16, 1942.

236 "destructive of American . . .": *LAT*, April 30, 1942.

236 "unblushingly borrowed from . . .": *NYT*, Dec. 3, 1942.

236 "an almost irrelevant . . .": *WSJ*, May 3, 1942.

236 "novel and capricious . . .": *NYT*, June 17, 1942.

236 "a permanent sleeping partner": *DFP*, May 3, 1942.

236 "something very fundamental . . .": Ibid.

237 "health and decency": *WSJ*, May 11, 1942.

237 "Either we must . . .": *NYT*, May 18, 1942.

237 "Until there is a tax bill . . .": *Time*, May 11, 1942, p. 15.

237 "175 Ways to Prepare Soups": *NYT*, March 2, 1942.

237 "Victory Meals . . .": *Time*, May 18, 1942, p. 94.

237 "The American farmer . . .": *WSJ*, May 6, 1942.

238 "Everyone admits that . . .": Polenberg, p. 24.

238 "After seven months . . .": *NYT*, July 5, 1942.

238 "clearly fumbling its responsibility . . .": *WP*, July 5, 1942.

238 "a mood of angry irritation . . .": Ibid.

238 "This is the summer . . .": *New Yorker*, August 22, 1942, p. 7.

238 "an almost ominous silence": *WP*, July 5, 1942.

238 "not to waste . . .": Ibid.

238 "breach of the peace": *NYT*, July 4, 1942.

238 "as quiet as a cornfield": Ibid. July 5, 1942.

238 "super-siren": Ibid. July 4, 1942.

238 "the loudest sustained . . .": *New Yorker*, Aug. 1, 1942, p. 11.

238 "Coney Island is . . .": *Time*, June 8, 1942, p. 74.

238 "the best show . . .": *NYT*, July 5, 1942.

240 "on borrowed time": *TRIB*, July 5, 1942.

240 "popcorn being poured . . .": *DFP*, July 5, 1942.

240 "I'm awfully tired . . .": *TRIB*, July 5, 1942.

240 "down in the dumps . . .": Ibid.

241 "give the war some glamor": *Newsweek*, July 13, 1942, p. 32.

241 "it's been bad physically . . .": *Time*, July 13, 1942, p. 18.

241 "disappointed by what . . .": Ibid.

241 "the greatest military spectacle . . .": *LAT*, July 5, 1942.

241 "a state of mind . . .": *BG*, Sept. 19, 1942.

241 "All routes and services . . .": *SUN*, May 15, 1942.

241 "it seems to be part . . .": *BG*, May 16, 1942.

242 "Every train is really . . .": Bayley, *Porter*, p. 242.

242 "People, this year . . .": *BG*, July 12, 1942.

242 "People who were . . .": *New Yorker*, Aug. 8, 1942, p. 52.

242 "Pictures of our . . .": *NYT*, June 17, 1942.

242 "I'm not at all sure . . .": *Time*, June 15, 1942, p. 10.

242 "purely personal": *BG*, July 18, 1942.

243 "War Calls Come First": *New Yorker*, September 19, 1942, p. 1.

243 "Don't say 'Hello.' . . .": *NYT*, Feb. 18, 1942.

243 "widespread evidence": *SUN*, June 8, 1942.

243 "With a little trouble . . .": *WSJ*, May 28, 1942.

243 "a dozen hoaxes . . .": *NYT*, May 29, 1942.

243 NO GAS HERE . . .: Ibid., June 22, 1942.

243 "Like rats after . . .": *Time*, July 6, 1942, p. 16.

243 "Hell had seen no furies . . .": Ibid.

244 "I can live with . . .": *WP*, June 18, 1942.

244 "constant public scrutiny": *NYT*, June 20, 1942.

245 "Our reserve petroleum stocks . . .": *WP*, July 19, 1942.

245 "farce" and "there were more tickets sold . . .": Ibid., June 29, 1942.

245 "When the rubber is gone . . .": *SUN*, May 13, 1942.

245 "if normal driving habits . . .": Ibid., June 1, 1942.

245 "The Rubber Shortage Is More . . .": *Time*, June 22, 1942, pp. 2–3.

245 "The Administration has done a . . .": *DFP*, June 9, 1942.

245 "the rubber-gas rationing question . . .": Baruch, p. 302.

245 "that this is all the bunk . . .": *DFP*, June 8, 1942.

246 "Rubber Shortage A Myth": *Time*, July 27, 1942, p. 66.

246 "The resident of the midlands . . .": *SUN*, June 7, 1942.

246 "The Washington dreamers have stated . . .": Ibid.

246 "an unwarranted invasion . . .": *LAT*, June 3, 1942.

246 "it is a violation of the spirit of . . .": Ibid., June 10, 1942.

246 "is getting sick and tired . . .": *SUN*, June 7, 1942.

246 "would actually cripple the war effort . . .": *NYT*, June 6, 1942.

246 "I can see no reason for it . . .": Ibid., May 29, 1942.

246 "uncalled for . . .": Ibid., June 5, 1942.

246 "disastrous": *LAT*, June 3, 1942.

247 "a dictator": *NYT*, June 6, 1942.

247 "Maybe I was wrong . . .": *DFP*, June 8, 1942.

247 "a short, quick and snappy campaign": *WP*, June 10, 1942.

247 "get in the scrap . . ." and "scrap rubber will . . .": *NYT*, June 28, 1942.

247 "We suspect that people are . . .": Ibid., June 30, 1942.

248 "disappointing": Ibid.

248 "President Roosevelt knows . . .": *DFP*, Aug. 13, 1942.

248 "procrastinations, indecisions . . .": *NYT*, Sept. 11, 1942.

248 "discomfort and defeat": Ibid.

248 "We find the existing situation . . .": *Time*, Sept. 21, 1942, p. 15.

248 "no rubber in the fourth quarter . . .": *NYT*, Sept. 11, 1942.

248 "there would be an all but complete collapse . . .": Ibid. Nov. 25, 1942.

248 "the only way to save rubber": Baruch, p. 305.

249 "I think it buffaloes . . .": Kunkel, *Ross*, p. 179.

249 "The war tends to make me . . .": Guth and White, p. 222.

249 "all that comes forth I drop without regret . . .": E. B. White, pp. 312–13.

249 "I suppose it is . . .": *New Yorker*, March 7, 1942, p. 59.

249 "The one issue we must all . . .": Bogard and Bryer, p. 529.

250 "A personal hate . . .": Kaufman, pp. 96–97.

250 "Evil and predatory forces . . .": *Time*, April 6, 1942, p. 63.

250 "Anger is what the people want . . .": Ibid., May 18, 1942, p. 54.

250 "Our greatest danger is . . .": Ibid., May 4, 1942, pp. 5–6.

250 "we must not permit ourselves . . .": Ibid. May 18, 1942, p. 54.

250 "some day . . . it will spread . . .": Ibid., June 15, 1942, p. 37.

251 "both unnecessary and unwise": *WSJ*, May 19, 1942.

251 "wretched little films . . .": *NYT*, June 28, 1942.

251 "well might have been . . .": *Time*, Aug. 17, 1942, p. 44.

251 "conventional claptrap adventure": *New Yorker*, June 13, 1942, p. 58.

251 "who insist on having . . .": *LAT*, July 6, 1942.


## 11: Last Call

253 "people in the by-ways . . .": *NYT*, Aug. 16, 1942.

253 "In case a farmer . . .": Ibid.

253 "a green football team . . .": *WP*, Nov. 2, 1942.

254 "operations are continuing . . .": Ibid., Aug. 14, 1942.

254 "a minor affair . . .": *DFP*, Sept. 1, 1942.

254 "Day by day . . .": *Time*, Sept. 7, 1942, p. 71.

255 "Alerts were blown . . .": *NYT*, Sept. 8, 1942.

255 "the blackout organization . . .": Ibid.

255 "Our city fathers were . . .": Elias, p. 948.

255 "Apparently we look upon . . .": *NYT*, Aug. 16, 1942.

257 "five or six": *Newsweek*, July 27, 1942, p. 33.

257 "the great air marker hoax": *NYT*, Aug. 12, 1942.

258 "We are deep in . . .": *Time*, Aug. 17, 1942, p. 14.

258 "we have done pretty well . . .": *NYT*, Aug. 8, 1942.

258 "Never have ships been built . . .": *DFP*, Aug. 13, 1942.

258 "We have never . . . : *NYT*, Aug. 8, 1942.

258 "America thinks it has . . .": Ibid., Aug. 9, 1942.

258 "the news from Detroit . . .": Elson, *Time*, p. 41.

258 "so many things are wrong . . .": *DFP*, Aug. 13, 1942.

259 "It just takes too damned long . . .": *Time*, Sept. 7, 1942, p. 24.

259 "There'll be no more . . .": *DFP*, Aug. 21, 1942.

259 "The performance . . .": *Time*, Oct. 12, 1942, p. 16.

259 "everything, from battleships": Ibid., Aug. 31, 1942, p. 19.

259 "the inevitable mess": Ibid., July 27, 1942, p. 13.

259 "operating from day to day . . .": *NYT*, July 21, 1942.

259 "Junk Needed For War": Ibid.

259 "with a fine tooth comb": Ibid.

259 "If we, as a nation . . .": *WP*, Sept. 5, 1942.

260 "ineptitude all down the line": Ibid.

260 "fourth and fifth rate statues": *NYT*, Nov. 1, 1942.

260 "a double service . . .": Ibid.

260 "It isn't supplying us . . .": *SUN*, Oct. 29, 1942.

261 "staggering": *WP*, Sept. 6, 1942.

261 "There just isn't . . .": Ibid., Aug. 9, 1942.

261 "we have reached . . .": Ibid.

261 "by this time . . .": *Time*, Sept. 7, 1942, p. 26.

262 "mass exodus": Ibid.

262 "We must stop inducting . . .": *NYT*, Nov. 15, 1942.

262 "turnover in West Coast war plants . . .": *SUN*, Oct. 22, 1942.

262 "gravely concerned" and "can make greater . . .": *Time*, Sept. 14, 1942, pp. 21–22.

263 "Monday morning sickness" and "Pay-day richness": *DFP*, Sept. 14, 1942.

263 "the business section . . .": Dos Passos, *State*, pp. 12–13.

263 "People buy whatever . . .": Ibid., pp. 13–14.

263 "This is something like . . .": *TRIB*, Sept. 24, 1942.

263 "The extent to which . . .": *SUN*, Sept. 30, 1942.

263 "work skipping": *Newsweek*, Oct. 19, 1942, p. 18.

263 "Any man who practices absenteeism . . .": *SUN*, Sept. 30, 1942.

264 "We tried flimsy uniforms . . .": *NYT*, March 4, 1942.

264 "This year fashion decrees . . .": *BG*, June 14, 1942.

264 "They no longer regard them . . .": Ibid., Dec. 6, 1942.

265 "it looks as though women . . .": *LAT*, Jan. 28, 1942.

266 "You know how men are": *Time*, May 11, 1942, p. 63.

266 "We are trying to bring . . .": *NYT*, March 30, 1942.

266 "will try to run . . .": Ibid., Dec. 3, 1942.

266 "There are no surplus materials . . .": *SUN*, Sept. 30, 1942.

266 "In some communities . . .": *NYT*, Oct. 13, 1942.

267 "on the level with . . .": Ibid., Sept. 1, 1942.

267 "rushing them almost literally . . .": Ibid., Nov. 8, 1942.

267 "The women which the . . .": *SUN*, Oct. 29, 1942.

268 "Absenteeism is prevalent . . .": *NYT*, Dec. 16, 1942.

268 "Mothers who have a job to do . . .": Ibid., Dec. 11, 1942.

269 "thousands of children . . .": *Time*, Aug. 2, 1942, pp. 1, 7.

269 "sometimes the mother . . .": Ibid., p. 7.

269 "In the cases of war working mothers . . .": *BG*, April 16, 1943.

269 "just one more move . . .": *WP*, Nov. 25, 1942.

269 "every child welfare and . . .": *NYT*, Dec. 15, 1942.

270 "High school courses should be . . .": Ibid., Nov. 5, 1942.

270 "I don't want to hurt . . .": *WP*, Sept. 30, 1942.

270 "unprecedentedly high wages . . .": *NYT*, Sept. 23, 1942.

270 "unprecedented": Ibid., April 2, 1942.

270 "are now earning . . .": *BG*, July 12, 1942.

270 "High wages for young people . . .": *NYT*, Nov 20, 1942.

271 "we do not get all the children . . .": Ibid., Nov. 5, 1942.

271 "an alarming rise in juvenile delinquency . . .": *WP*, Dec. 24, 1942.

271 "Crimes of violence among boys . . .": *LAT*, Sept. 13, 1942.

272 "Since this war is greater . . .": *WP*, Feb. 22, 1943.

272 "commercialized vice": Ibid., Feb. 20, 1943.

272 "to look eighteen or twenty": *NYT*, Nov. 19, 1942.

272 "They think that the boys . . .": Ibid.

272 "There are thousands of . . .": *Time*, Oct. 5, 1942, p. 24.

272 "have more money to spend . . .": *BG*, April 12, 1942.

272 "To their families . . .": Cooke, p. 102.

272 "most of them are just . . .": *WP*, Nov. 6, 1942.

272 "Games seem dull . . .": Ibid., Dec. 3, 1942.

273 "war babies": *NYT*, Nov. 19, 1942.

273 "If we win the war . . .": Ibid., Dec. 16, 1942.

273 "I hardly need to . . .": Ibid., Oct. 7, 1942.

273 "The war was taking . . .": Clark, p. 362.

273 "I have felt . . .": Ibid., p. 391.

273 "Their response to . . .": *NYT*, Oct. 14, 1942.

273 "the realistic but ugly fact": *Time*, July 6, 1942, p. 12.

274 "The time has come . . .": *DFP*, Sept. 2, 1942.

274 "For several months past . . .": Ibid., Sept. 8, 1942.

274 "I believe that it will be . . .": *WP*, Oct. 13, 1942.

274 "Has Congress decided . . .": Ibid., Oct. 18, 1942.

274 "I ask the House . . .": Ibid.

275 "Remember, these are . . .": Ibid., Oct. 23, 1942.

275 "almost impossible . . .": Ibid., Oct. 18, 1942.

275 "There is a good solid kind . . .": Bayley, p. 242.

## 12: End of the Beginning

277 "As a nation we are . . .": *New Yorker*, Aug. 22, 1942, p. 43.

277 "If everybody will be sensible . . .": *NYT*, Oct. 23, 1942.

278 "acute shortages": *WP*, Oct. 3, 1942.

278 "Sorry, no coffee . . .": *NYT*, Oct. 23, 1942.

278 "Please don't be silly . . .": Ibid., Nov. 2, 1942.

278 "unfit for human consumption": Ibid., Oct. 23, 1942.

278 "an after-dinner demi tasse": *WP*, Oct. 27, 1942.

278 "considerable stimulation and . . .": Ibid.

278 "might as well have advised . . .": *NYT*, Nov. 3, 1942.

278 "Coffee is coffee . . .": *WP*, Oct. 27, 1942.

279 "With nearly everybody working . . .": *NYT*, Aug. 18, 1942.

279 "carnivorous adults": Ibid., Sept. 25, 1942.

279 "This is not privation": Ibid., Sept. 26, 1942.

280 "My cook tells me . . .": Cleator, pp. 136–37.

280 "Popular ballad . . .": *Time*, Aug. 10, 1942, p. 98.

280 "awfully short for . . .": *WSJ*, Nov. 21, 1942.

280 "chaos, chiseling and black markets": *NYT*, Dec. 5, 1942.

280 "Changing times . . .": Ibid., June 26, 1942.

281 "This winter New York's going to . . .": *New Yorker*, Aug. 15, 1942, p. 30.

281 "standsit": *Time*, Sept. 21, 1942, p. 84.

281 "There was not yet . . .": Cooke, pp. 98–99.

281 "a figure which can only be . . .": *NYT*, Nov. 4, 1942.

282 "the profligate use of . . .": *SUN*, Oct. 30, 1942.

282 "Most of my titles . . .": *Time*, Oct. 12, 1942, p. 72.

282 "being crammed down the throats . . .": *SUN*, Nov. 26, 1942.

282 "this idea of having somebody . . .": Ibid.

283 "sowing seeds of . . .": Ibid., Nov. 28, 1942.

283 "ignorant" and "intentionally traitorous": Ibid.

283 "almost universal" and "the selfish . . .": Ibid., Nov. 21, 1942.

283 "an organized opposition . . ." Ibid.

283 "we can not and will not . . .": *NYT*, Dec. 1, 1942.

283 "increasingly grave petroleum . . .": *BG*, Aug. 2, 1942.

283 "Every user of fuel and heating oil . . .": Ibid.

284 "Such reports are worse than mischievous": *SUN*, Sept. 26, 1942.

284 "Another bout with the blanks": *BG*, Oct. 11, 1942.

284 "The great majority of the consumers . . .": *SUN*, Nov. 29, 1942.

284 "We've never been able . . .": Ibid., Nov. 25, 1942.

285 "*Every* girl's a sweater girl now": *NYT*, Dec. 4, 1942.

285 "far more serious than . . .": Ibid., Dec. 3, 1942.

285 "There is no use trying to conceal . . .": *BG*, Nov. 20, 1942.

285 "no one should have to . . .": *SUN*, Nov. 21, 1942.

285 "these bureaucrats in their big cars . . .": *NYT*, Dec. 2, 1942.

285 "The effects of the war are beginning . . .": Felcher, *Mencken Diary*, Dec. 27, 1942.

286 "What he was doing . . .": *Time*, Aug. 24, 1942, p. 11.

286 "His manner becomes abrupt . . .": Dos Passos, *The Theme*, pp. 168–69.

286 "The tide of war . . .": *Time*, Oct. 12, 1942, p. 16.

286 "How about, for a change . . .": Ibid.

286 "The Allies have taken a terrific . . .": Ibid.

286 "There has never been . . .": *DFP*, Oct. 12, 1942.

287 "The Republican drift . . .": *Newsweek*, Oct. 19, 1942, p. 88.

287 "lack of confidence in the accuracy . . .": *NYT*, Nov. 2, 1942.

287 "The job isn't exactly . . .": *SUN*, June 3, 1942.

287 "Gentlemen, it is open season . . .": *WP*, Oct. 22, 1942.

287 "Without a substantial number . . .": *NYT*, June 16, 1942.

287 "virtual serfs, who . . .": Cooke, p. 137.

288 "Labor leaders must learn . . .": *Time*, July 27, 1942, p. 12.

288 "The eternal right-hand man": Ibid., Nov. 30, 1942, p. 21.

288 "the steepest tax bill . . .": *WP*, Oct. 21, 1942.

288 "It's all right . . .": Ibid., Oct. 18, 1942.

289 "Nearly every adult American . . .": *NYT*, Oct. 25, 1942.

289 "There is no 'shopping' . . .": Ibid., Oct. 24, 1942.

289 "Liquor buyers must be hoarding it . . .": *TRIB*, Oct. 31, 1942.

289 "an intense lack of excitement": *DFP*, Oct. 21, 1942.

290 "the great majority of . . .": *NYT*, Nov. 5, 1942.

290 "All the boys who . . .": R. Dallek, p. 245.

290 "There was surely no precedent . . .": *WP*, Nov. 5, 1942.

290 "Voters felt the war was not . . .": Ibid., Nov. 6, 1942.

290 "an important reverse for the Administration": *NYT*, Nov. 4, 1942.

290 "the clearly demonstrated delays . . .": Ibid., Nov. 5, 1942.

290 "speeding war information . . .": *WP*, Nov. 6, 1942.

290 "It was a bad election . . .": *Newsweek*, Dec. 14, 1942, p. 52.

291 "reaction is now in the saddle . . .": R. Dallek, p. 245.

291 "Under the circumstances of this election . . .": *WP*, Nov. 6, 1942.

291 "People are affected by this war . . .": Clapper, *Watching*, pp. 99–100.

291 "You must not talk to . . .": *SUN*, Nov. 10, 1942.

292 "a powerful American force . . .": *NYT*, Nov. 8, 1942.

292 "This must be the second front . . .": *BG*, Nov. 9, 1942.

292 "anarchy and success": Atkinson, *Army at Dawn*, p. 85.

292 "The radio is full of blasts . . .": Stuhlmann, *Miller Letters*, p. 311.

292 "the start of the real American war . . .": *WP*, Nov. 8, 1942.

292 "It is itself only a first step . . .": *BG*, Nov. 9, 1942.

292 "Hazardous as these operations may be . . .": *NYT*, Nov. 9, 1942.

## Epilogue: December 7, 1942

293 "in remembrance of a day . . .": *LAT*, Dec. 7, 1942.

293 "for victory and peace": *NYT*, Dec. 8, 1942.

293 "It ought to be a day . . .": *WP*, Dec. 8, 1942.

294 "In 1942 we were . . .": *NYT*, Dec. 6, 1942.

294 "the damnedest fight . . .": Berle, p. 425.

294 "To land an expedition . . .": *NYT*, Dec. 7, 1942.

294 "The authorities in London . . .": Atkinson, p. 198.

295 "uneasy and suspicious": *NYT*, Nov. 5, 1942.

295 "not in a position . . .": *WP*, Oct. 27, 1942.

295 "In all governmental affairs . . .": Ibid.

296 "The people who are . . .": Bogard and Bryer, p. 539.

296 "over-staffed, over-stuffed government": R. Dallek, p. 253.

296 "acting chief . . .": Black, *Nixon*, p. 55.

296 "were obsessed with . . .": Ibid., p. 56.

296 "non-essential government employees": *TRIB*, Dec. 2, 1942.

296 "will not work" and "It had better . . .": Ibid., Dec. 1, 1942.

296 "New Deal tormentors": Ibid., Dec. 3, 1942.

297 "spread the suffering campaign": Ibid.

297 "The public thinks that rationing . . .": *LAT*, Dec. 3, 1942.

297 "Our ability to meet the extraordinary . . .": *SUN*, Nov. 11, 1942.

297 "Unless tankship deliveries . . .": *BG*, Dec. 9, 1942.

297 "If it ever came to a choice . . .": *SUN*, Nov. 20, 1942.

297 "it is quite evident . . .": *Time*, Dec. 7, 1942, p. 24.

297 "virtually dictatorial powers": *NYT*, Dec. 7, 1942.

298 "more power over more men . . .": Ibid.

298 "a slap in the face" and "Before American labor . . .": *DFP*, Dec. 7, 1942.

298 "nineteen forty-three . . .": *NYT*, Dec. 13, 1942.

299 "a medley of . . .": *Time*, Oct. 26, 1942, p. 50.

299 "thus far the thing . . .": *WP*, Oct. 27, 1942.

299 "Rule for a Wartime Yule . . .": *NYT*, Nov. 8, 1942.

299 "Practical gifts are . . .": *WP*, Nov. 9, 1942.

299 "A good sweater . . .": *NYT*, Nov. 10, 1942.

300 "automatically grow warmer . . .": Ibid., Nov. 8, 1942.

300 "can learn the basic facts . . .": *SUN*, Nov. 8, 1942.

300 "Before the sun sets . . .": *BG*, Dec. 13, 1942.

300 "There can be no doubt . . .": *WP*, Dec. 8, 1942.

300 "It has been a year . . .": *NYT*, Dec. 7, 1942.

301 "Americans temperamentally . . .": Cooke, p. 309.

301 "There's one thing . . .": *NYT*, Dec. 4, 1942.

# Bibliography

Newspapers and Periodicals, 1939–1942

*American Magazine*

*Baltimore Afro-American*

*Baltimore Sun*

*Boston Globe*

*Chicago Tribune*

*Detroit Free Press*

*Eugene (OR) Register-Guard*

*Life*

*Los Angeles Times*

*New Orleans Times-Picayune*

*New Republic*

*Newsweek*

*New Yorker*

*New York Times*

*Seattle Star*

*Time*

*Tuscaloosa News*

*Wall Street Journal*

*Washington Post*

## Books

Aaron, Daniel, ed. *The Inman Diary: A Public and Private Confession*. Cambridge, Mass.: Harvard University Press, 1985.

Adams, Henry. *Thomas Hart Benton: Discoveries and Interpretations*. Columbia: University of Missouri Press, 2015.

Adams, Phelps, et al. *Reporting World War II: American Journalism, 1938–1946*. New York: Library of America, 2001.

Affront, Charles. *Lillian Gish: Her Legend, Her Life*. New York: Scribner, 2001.

Agar, Herbert. *A Time for Greatness*. Boston: Little, Brown, 1943.

Ahearn, Barry, ed. *The Correspondence of William Carlos Williams & Louis Zukofsky*. Middletown, Conn.: Wesleyan University Press, 2003.

Anderson, William, ed. *The Selected Letters of Laura Ingalls Wilder*. New York: HarperCollins, 2016.

Andrews, Clarence A., ed. *Growing Up in the Midwest*. Ames: Iowa State University Press, 1981.

Aptheker, Herbert, ed. *The Correspondence of W. E. B. Du Bois*. Vol. 2, *Selections, 1934–1944*. Amherst: University of Massachusetts Press, 1976.

Arce, Hector. *Groucho*. New York: G. P. Putnam's Sons, 1979.

Asimov, Isaac. *I, Asimov*. New York: Doubleday, 1994.

Atkinson, Rick. *An Army at Dawn: The War in North Africa, 1942–1943*. New York: Henry Holt, 2002.

Avery, Laurence G., ed. *Dramatist in America: Letters of Maxwell Anderson, 1912–1958*. Chapel Hill: University of North Carolina Press, 1977.

Baker, Carlos, ed. *Ernest Hemingway: Selected Letters, 1917–1961*. New York: Charles Scribner's Sons, 1981.

Baker, Russell. *Growing Up*. New York: Congdon & Weed, 1982.

Baker, William J. *Jesse Owens: An American Life*. New York: Free Press, 1986.

Bakish, David. *Jimmy Durante: His Show Business Career*. Jefferson, N.C.: McFarland, 1995.

Banfield, Stephen. *Jerome Kern*. New Haven, Conn.: Yale University Press, 2006.

Banner, Lois. *Marilyn: The Passion and the Paradox*. New York: Bloomsbury, 2012.

Baruch, Bernard. *Baruch: The Public Years*. New York: Holt, Rinehart & Winston, 1960.

Bayley, Isabel, ed. *Letters of Katherine Anne Porter*. New York: Atlantic Monthly Press, 1990.

Beebe, Lucius. *Snoot If You Must*. New York: D. Appleton-Century, 1943.

Berg, Herbert. *Elijah Muhammad*. London: Oneworld Publications, 2013.

Berle, Adolf A. *Navigating the Rapids, 1918–1971*. New York: Harcourt Brace Jovanovich, 1973.

Bernard, Emily, ed. *Remember Me to Harlem: The Letters of Langston Hughes and Carl Van Vechten, 1925–1964*. New York: Alfred A. Knopf, 2001.

Beschloss, Michael R. *Kennedy and Roosevelt: The Uneasy Alliance*. New York: Harper & Row, 1980.

Biddle, Francis. *In Brief Authority*. Garden City, N.Y.: Doubleday, 1962.

Bigsby, Christopher. *Arthur Miller: 1915–1962*. Cambridge, Mass.: Harvard University Press, 2009.

Black, Conrad. *Richard M. Nixon: A Life in Full*. New York: Public Affairs, 2007.

Blotner, Joseph, ed. *Selected Letters of William Faulkner*. New York: Random House, 1977.

Blum, John Morton, ed. *Public Philosopher: Selected Letters of Walter Lippmann*. New York: Ticknor & Fields, 1985.

Bogard, Travis, and Jackson R. Bryer, eds. *Selected Letters of Eugene O'Neill*. New Haven, Conn.: Yale University Press, 1988.

Bradlee, Ben, Jr. *The Kid: The Immortal Life of Ted Williams*. New York: Little, Brown, 2013.

Bradley, Omar, and Clay Blair. *A General's Life: An Autobiography*. New York: Simon & Schuster, 1983.

Brinkley, Alan. *The Publisher: Henry Luce and His American Century*. New York: Alfred A. Knopf, 2010.

Brinkley, David. *Washington Goes to War*. New York: Alfred A. Knopf, 1988.

Brinkley, Douglas. *Cronkite*. New York: HarperCollins, 2012.

Brown, Anthony Cave. *The Last Hero: Wild Bill Donovan*. New York: Times Books, 1982.

Bullitt, Orville H., ed. *For the President: Personal and Secret: Correspondence Between Franklin D. Roosevelt and William C. Bullitt*. Boston: Houghton Mifflin, 1972.

Burns, Edward, ed. *The Letters of Gertrude Stein and Carl Van Vechten, 1913–1946*. Vol. 2. New York: Columbia University Press, 1986.

Burns, James MacGregor. *Roosevelt: The Soldier of Freedom*. New York: Harcourt Brace Jovanovich, 1970.

Calloway, Cab, and Bryant Rollins. *Of Minnie the Moocher & Me*. New York: Thomas Y. Crowell, 1976.

Campbell, D'Ann. *Women at War with America: Private Lives in a Patriotic Era*. Cambridge, Mass.: Harvard University Press, 1984.

Campbell, Louise, ed. *Letters to Louise: Theodore Dreiser's Letters to Louise Campbell*. Philadelphia: University of Pennsylvania Press, 1959.

Capra, Frank. *The Name Above the Title: An Autobiography*. New York: Da Capo Press, 1997.

Caro, Robert A. *The Years of Lyndon Johnson: The Path to Power*. New York: Alfred A. Knopf, 1982.

Carr, Virginia. *Dos Passos: A Life*. Garden City, N.Y.: Doubleday, 1984.

Caughey, John, and LaRee Caughey. *Los Angeles: Biography of a City*. Oakland: University of California Press, 1976.

Cerf, Bennett. *At Random: The Reminiscences of Bennett Cerf*. New York: Random House, 1977.

Chandler, Charlotte. *Marlene*. New York: Simon & Schuster, 2011.

Childs, Marquis W. *I Write from Washington*. New York: Harper & Brothers, 1942.

Christie, Jean, and Leonard Dinnerstein, eds. *Decisions and Revisions: Interpretations of Twentieth-Century American History*. New York: Praeger Publishers, 1975.

Clapper, Raymond. *Watching the World*. New York: McGraw-Hill, 1944.

Clark, William Bedford. *Selected Letters of Robert Penn Warren*. Vol. 2, *The "Southern Review" Years, 1935–1942*. Baton Rouge: Louisiana State University Press, 2001.

Cleator, P. E., ed. *Letters from Baltimore: The Mencken-Cleator Correspondence*. Rutherford N. J.: Fairleigh Dickinson University Press, 1982.

Clegg, Claude Andrew, III. *An Original Man: The Life and Times of Elijah Muhammad*. New York: St. Martin's Press, 1997.

Cohen, Harvey G. *Duke Ellington's America*. Chicago: University of Chicago Press, 2010.

Cole, Wayne S. *America First*. Madison: University of Wisconsin Press, 1953.

Commins, Dorothy, ed. *"Love and Admiration and Respect": The O'Neill-Commins Correspondence*. Durham, N.C.: Duke University Press, 1986.

Conant, James B. *My Several Lives: Memoirs of a Social Inventor*. New York: Harper & Row, 1970.

Cook, Blanche Wiesen. *Eleanor Roosevelt*. Vol. 3, *The War Years and After, 1939–1962*. New York: Viking, 2016.

Cooke, Alistair. *The American Home Front, 1941–1942*. New York: Atlantic Monthly Press, 2006.

Cramer, Richard Ben. *Joe DiMaggio: The Hero's Life*. New York: Simon & Schuster, 2000.

Crawford, Evelyn Louise, and Mary Louise Patterson, eds. *Letters from Langston: From the Harlem Renaissance to the Red Scare and Beyond*. Berkeley: University of California Press, 2016.

Crowther, Prudence, ed. *Don't Tread on Me: The Selected Letters of S. J. Perelman*. New York: Viking, 1987.

Curtis, Brian. *Fields of Battle: Pearl Harbor, the Rose Bowl, and the Boys Who Went to War*. New York: Flatiron Books, 2016.

Dallek, Matthew. *Defenseless Under the Night: the Roosevelt Years and the Origins of Homeland Security*. New York: Oxford University Press, 2016.

Dallek, Robert. *Lone Star Rising: Lyndon Johnson and His Times, 1908–1960*. New York: Oxford University Press, 1991.

Davies, Marion. *The Times We Had*. Indianapolis: Bobbs-Merrill, 1975.

Day, Barry. *Dorothy Parker: In Her Own Words*. Lanham, Md.: Taylor Trade Publishing, 2004.

Demény, Janos, ed. *Béla Bartok Letters*. New York: St. Martin's Press, 1971.

Department of War, United States. *World War II Japanese American Internment Reports: Final Report of Army General DeWitt on Japanese Evacuation from the West Coast 1942, Rationale and Details of Relocation Process, Nisei and Issei*. Washington, D.C.: Government Printing Office, 1943.

Devlin, Albert J., and Nancy M. Tischler, eds. *Selected Letters of Tennessee Williams*. Vol. 1, *1920–1945*. New York: New Directions, 2000.

Diehl, Lorraine B. *Over Here! New York City During World War II*. New York: HarperCollins, 2010.

Dixon, Willie with Don Snowden. *I Am the Blues: The Willie Dixon Story*. New York: Da Capo, 1989.

Donaldson, Scott. *Archibald MacLeish: An American Life*. Boston: Houghton Mifflin, 1992.

Dos Passos, John. *State of the Nation*. Boston: Houghton Mifflin, 1944.

———. *The Theme Is Freedom*. New York: Dodd, Mead, 1956.

Dunn, Susan. *1940: FDR, Willkie, Lindbergh, Hitler—The Election amid the Storm*. New Haven Conn.: Yale University Press, 2013.

Edel, Leon, ed. *Edmund Wilson: The Forties, from Notebooks and Diaries of the Period*. New York: Farrar, Straus & Giroux, 1983.

Elias, Robert H., ed. *Letters of Theodore Dreiser: A Selection*. Vol. 3. Philadelphia: University of Pennsylvania Press, 1959.

Ellis, Edward Robb, ed. *A Diary of the Century: Tales from America's Greatest Diarist*. New York: Kodansha International, 1995.

Elson, Robert T. *The World of Time Inc.: The Intimate History of a Publishing Enterprise*, Vol. 2, *1941–1960*. New York: Atheneum, 1973.

Escobedo, Elizabeth R. *From Coveralls to Zoot Suits: The Lives of Mexican American Women on the World War II Home Front*. Chapel Hill: University of North Carolina Press, 2013.

Evans, Peter, and Ava Gardner. *Ava Gardner: The Secret Conversations*. New York: Simon & Schuster, 2013.

Evanzz, Karl. *The Messenger: The Rise and Fall of Elijah Muhammad*. New York: Pantheon Books, 1999.

Felcher, Charles, ed. *The Diary of H. L. Mencken*. New York: Alfred A. Knopf, 1989.

Fenton, Charles A., ed. *Selected Letters of Stephen Vincent Benét*. New Haven, Conn.: Yale University Press, 1960.

Ferrell, Robert H., ed. *Dear Bess: The Letters from Harry to Bess Truman, 1910–1959*. New York: Dutton, 1983.

Flynt, Wayne. *Alabama in the Twentieth Century*. Tuscaloosa: University of Alabama Press, 2004.

Forgue, Guy J., ed. *Letters of H. L. Mencken*. New York: Alfred A. Knopf, 1961.

Fussell, Paul. *Wartime: Understanding and Behavior in the Second World War*. New York: Oxford University Press, 1989.

Gallagher, Tag. *John Ford: The Man and His Films*. Berkeley: University of California Press, 1986.

Garrison, Dee. *Mary Heaton Vorse: The Life of an American Insurgent*. Philadelphia: Temple University Press, 1989.

———, ed. *Rebel Pen: The Writings of Mary Heaton Vorse*. New York: Monthly Review Press, 1985.

Gillon, Steven M. *Pearl Harbor: FDR Leads the Nation into War*. New York: Basic Books, 2011.

Glynn, Gary. *Montana's Home Front During World War II*. Missoula, Mont.: Pictorial Histories Publishing, 1994.

Goodwin, Doris Kearns. *No Ordinary Time*. New York: Simon & Schuster, 1994.

Grade, Arnold, ed. *Family Letters of Robert and Elinor Frost*. Albany: State University of New York Press, 1972.

Grafton, Samuel. *An American Diary*. Garden City, N. Y.: Doubleday, 1943.

Groom, Winston. *1942: The Year That Tried Men's Souls*. New York: Grove Press, 2005.

Guth, Dorothy Lobrano, and Martha White, eds. *Letters of E. B. White*. New York: HarperCollins, 2006.

Guthrie, Woody. *Bound for Glory*. New York: Dutton, 1976.

Hamilton, Charles V. *Adam Clayton Powell, Jr.: The Political Biography of an American Dilemma*. New York: Atheneum, 1991.

Harris, Warren G. *Clark Gable: A Biography*. New York: Harmony Books, 2002.

Havoc, June. *More Havoc*. New York: Harper & Row, 1980.

Hayes, Helen, with Katherine Hatch. *My Life in Three Acts*. New York: Harcourt Brace Jovanovich, 1990.

Haygood, Wil. *King of the Cats: The Life and Times of Adam Clayton Powell, Jr.* Boston: Houghton Mifflin, 1993.

Hecht, Benjamin. *A Child of the Century*. New York: Simon & Schuster, 1954.

Hendrick, George, ed. *The Selected Letters of Mark Van Doren*. Baton Rouge: Louisiana State University Press, 1987.

Herrmann, Dorothy. *S. J. Perelman: A Life*. New York: G. P. Putnam's Sons, 1986.

Hobson, Fred. *Mencken: A Life*. New York: Random House, 1994.

Hogan, William, and William German, eds. *The San Francisco Chronicle Reader*. New York: McGraw-Hill, 1962.

Hosokawa, Bill. *Nisei: The Quiet Americans*. New York: William Morrow, 1969.

Houseman, John. *Front and Center*. New York: Simon & Schuster, 1979.

———. *Run-Through: A Memoir*. New York: Simon & Schuster, 1972.

Hunt, Tim, ed. *The Collected Poetry of Robinson Jeffers*: Vol. 3, *1938–1962*. Stanford, Calif.: Stanford University Press, 1991.

Hyams, Joseph. *Bogie: The Biography of Humphrey Bogart*. New York: New American Library, 1966.

Ickes, Harold. *The Secret Diary of Harold L. Ickes*, Vol. 2. New York: Simon & Schuster, 1954.

Isaacson, Walter. *Einstein: His Life and Universe*. New York: Simon & Schuster, 2007.

Jackson, Harvey H. III. *Inside Alabama: A Personal History of My State*. Tuscaloosa: University of Alabama Press, 2004.

Jackson, Mark Allan. *Prophet Singer: The Voice and Vision of Woody Guthrie*. Jackson: University Press of Mississippi, 2007.

Jarrell, Mary, ed. *Randall Jarrell's Letters: An Autobiographical and Literary Selection*. Boston: Houghton Mifflin, 1985.

Jeffries, John W. *Wartime America: The World War II Home Front*. Chicago: Ivan R. Dee, 1996.

Johnson, Walter, ed. *Selected Letters of William Allen White: 1899–1943*. New York: Henry Holt, 1947.

Jones, Jesse H., with Edward Angly. *Fifty Billion Dollars: My Thirteen Years with the RFC (1932–1945)*. New York: Macmillan, 1951.

Kaplan, Fred. *Gore Vidal: A Biography*. New York: Doubleday, 1999.

Kaplan, James. *Frank: The Voice*. New York: Doubleday, 2010.

Karman, James, ed. *The Collected Letters of Robinson Jeffers, with Selected Letters of Una Jeffers*, Vol. 3, *1940–1962*. Stanford, Calif.: Stanford University Press, 2015.

Katcher, Leo. *Earl Warren: A Political Biography*. New York: McGraw-Hill, 1967.

Katz, Esther, ed. *The Selected Papers of Margaret Sanger*. Vol. 3, *The Politics of Planned Parenthood, 1939–1966*. Urbana: University of Illinois Press, 2010.

Kaufman, Will. *Woody Guthrie, American Radical*. Urbana: University of Illinois Press, 2011.

Kelley, Robin D. G. *Thelonious Monk: The Life and Times of an American Original*. New York: Free Press, 2009.

Kellner, Bruce. *Letters of Carl Van Vechten*. New Haven, Conn.: Yale University Press, 1987.

Kendrick, Alexander. *Prime Time: The Life of Edward R. Murrow*. Boston: Little, Brown, 1969.

Kennedy, David M. *The American People in World War II. Freedom from Fear: Part II.* New York: Oxford University Press, 1999.

Kersten, Andrew E. *Labor's Home Front: The American Federation of Labor During World War II.* New York: New York University Press, 2006.

Kessler-Harris, Alice. *Out to Work: A History of Wage-Earning Women in the United States.* New York: Oxford University Press, 1982.

Killorin, Joseph, ed. *Selected Letters of Conrad Aiken.* New Haven, Conn.: Yale University Press, 2013.

Kinney, Harrison, ed. *The Thurber Letters: The Wit, Wisdom, and Surprising Life of James Thurber.* New York: Simon & Schuster, 2002.

Klingaman, William. *1941: Our Lives in a World on the Edge.* New York: Harper & Row, 1988.

Krock, Arthur. *Memoirs: Sixty Years on the Firing Line.* New York: Funk & Wagnalls, 1968.

Kunkel, Thomas, ed. *Letters from the Editor: The* New Yorker's *Harold Ross.* New York: Modern Library, 2000.

Lawrence, A. H. *Duke Ellington and His World: A Biography.* New York: Routledge, 2001.

Lawrence, David. *Diary of a Washington Correspondent.* New York: H. C. Kinsey, 1942.

Lerner, Max. *Public Journal: Marginal Notes on Wartime America.* New York: Viking Press, 1945.

Lertzmann, Richard A., and William J. Birnes. *The Life and Times of Mickey Rooney.* New York: Simon & Schuster, 2015.

Levine, Lawrence W., and Cornelia R. Levine. *The People and the President: America's Conversation with FDR.* Boston: Beacon Press, 2002.

Limmer, Ruth, ed. *What the Woman Lived: Selected Letters of Louise Bogan, 1920–1970.* New York: Harcourt Brace Jovanovich, 1973.

Lindbergh, Anne Morrow. *War Within and Without: Diaries and Letters of Anne Morrow Lindbergh, 1939–1944.* New York: Harcourt Brace Jovanovich, 1980.

Lindbergh, Charles. *The Wartime Journals of Charles Lindbergh.* New York: Harcourt Brace Jovanovich, 1970.

Litoff, Judy Barrett, and David C. Smith, eds. *Since You Went Away: World War Two Letters from American Women on the Home Front.* New York: Oxford University Press, 1991.

Lopach, James. J., and Jean A. Lukowski. *Jeannette Rankin: A Political Woman.* Boulder: University Press of Colorado, 2005.

Loving, Jerome. *The Last Titan: A Life of Theodore Dreiser.* Berkeley: University of California Press, 2005.

Lowenstein, Roger. *Buffett: The Making of an American Capitalist.* New York: Random House, 1995.

Lowery, Robert G. and Patricia Angelin, eds. *My Very Dear Sean: George Jean Nathan to Sean O'Casey, Letters and Articles.* Rutherford, N.J.: Farleigh Dickinson University Press, 1985.

Lutz, Catherine. *Homefront: A Military City and the American Twentieth Century.* Boston: Beacon Press, 2001.

MacDougall, Allan Ross, ed. *Letters of Edna St. Vincent Millay.* New York: Grosset & Dunlap, 1952.

Manfull, Helen. *Additional Dialogue: Letters of Dalton Trumbo, 1942–1962.* New York: M. Evans, 1970.

Maraniss, David. *When Pride Still Mattered: A Life of Vince Lombardi.* New York: Simon & Schuster, 2007.

Marrs, Suzanne. *Eudora Welty: A Biography.* Orlando: Harcourt, 2005.

Marsh, Dave, and Harold Leventhal, eds. *Pastures of Plenty: A Self Portrait, Woody Guthrie.* New York: HarperCollins, 1990.

Marx, Arthur. *My Life with Groucho: A Son's Eye View.* New York: Robson Books, 1988.

Marx, Groucho. *The Groucho Letters: Letters from and to Groucho Marx.* New York: Simon & Schuster, 1967.

Marx, Harpo, with Rowland Barber. *Harpo Speaks!* New York: Limelight Editions, 1988.

McAdams, Frank. *The American War Film: History and Hollywood.* Westport, Conn.: Praeger, 2002.

McAleer, John. *Rex Stout: A Biography.* Boston: Little, Brown, 1977.

McBrien, William. *Cole Porter: A Biography.* New York: Alfred A. Knopf, 1998.

Mitgang, Herbert, ed. *The Letters of Carl Sandburg.* New York: Harcourt, Brace & World, 1968.

Morgan, Bill, ed. *The Letters of Allen Ginsberg.* New York: Da Capo Press, 2008.

Murray, Alice Yang. *Historical Memories of the Japanese American Internment and the Struggle for Redress.* Stanford, Calif.: Stanford University Press, 2008.

Nasaw, David. *The Chief: The Life of William Randolph Hearst.* Boston: Houghton Mifflin, 2000.

Nelson, Donald. *Arsenal of Democracy: The Story of American War Production.* New York: Harcourt, Brace, 1946.

Nicholas, H. G., ed. *Washington Despatches, 1941–1945: Weekly Political Reports from the British Embassy.* Chicago: University of Chicago Press, 1981.

Nicholson, Stuart. *Reminiscing in Tempo: A Portrait of Duke Ellington.* Boston: Northeastern University Press, 1999.

Niven, Penelope. *Carl Sandburg: A Biography.* New York: Charles Scribner's Sons, 1991.

Nott, Robert. *He Ran All the Way: The Life of John Garfield.* New York: Limelight Editions, 2003.

Olson, Lynne. *Those Angry Days: Roosevelt, Lindbergh, and America's Fight over World War II, 1939–1941.* New York: Random House, 2013.

O'Neill, William L. *A Democracy at War: America's Fight at Home & Abroad in World War II.* Cambridge, Mass.: Harvard University Press, 1993.

Pagan, Eduardo Obregon. *Murder at the Sleepy Lagoon: Zoot Suits, Race, and Riot in Wartime L.A.* Chapel Hill: University of North Carolina Press, 2003.

Parini, Jay. *John Steinbeck: A Biography.* London: Heinemann, 1964.

Pepper, Claude Denson, with Hays Gorey. *Pepper: Eyewitness to a Century.* San Diego: Harcourt Brace Jovanovich, 1987.

Poen, Monte M., ed. *Letters Home by Harry Truman.* New York: G. P. Putnam's Sons, 1984.

Polenberg, Richard. *War and Society: The United States, 1941–1945.* Philadelphia: J. B. Lippincott, 1972.

Pyron, Darden Asbury. *Liberace: An American Boy.* Chicago: University of Chicago Press, 2000.

Rampersad, Arnold, and David Roessel, eds. *Selected Letters of Langston Hughes.* New York: Alfred A. Knopf, 2015.

Reeves, Richard. *Infamy: The Shocking Story of the Japanese American Internment in World War II.* New York: Macmillan, 2015.

Reiss, Curt, ed. *They Were Three: The Story of World War II and How It Came About.* New York: G. P. Putnam's Sons, 1944.

Riggio, Thomas P., ed. *Dreiser-Mencken Letters: The Correspondence of Theodore Dreiser and H. L. Mencken, 1907–1945.* Philadelphia: University of Pennsylvania Press, 1986.

Roberts, Jerry, ed. *Mitchum in His Own Words.* New York: Limelight Editions, 2000.

Roberts, Nancy L., and Arthur W. Roberts, eds. *"As Ever, Gene": The Letters of Eugene O'Neill to George Jean Nathan.* Rutherford, N.J.: Fairleigh Dickinson University Press, 1987.

Robeson, Paul, Jr. *The Undiscovered Paul Robeson: Quest for Freedom, 1939–1976.* Hoboken, N.J.: John Wiley & Sons, 2010.

Robinson, Greg. *By Order of the President: FDR and the Internment of Japanese Americans.* Cambridge, Mass.: Harvard University Press, 2001.

Rollyson, Carl. *Marilyn Monroe Day by Day.* Lanham, Md.: Rowman & Littlefield, 2014.

Roosevelt, Eleanor. *This I Remember.* New York: Harper & Brothers, 1949.

Roper, Robert. *Nabokov in America: On the Road to "Lolita."* New York: Bloomsbury, 2015.

Rosebery, Mercedes. *This Day's Madness: A Story of the American People Against the Background of the War Effort.* New York: Macmillan, 1944.

Rosenman, Samuel I., ed. *The Public Papers and Addresses of Franklin Delano Roosevelt.* Vol. 10, *The Call to Battle Stations, 1941.* New York: Russell & Russell, 1969.

Sandburg, Carl. *Home Front Memo.* New York: Harcourt, Brace, 1942.

Sanders, Ronald. *The Days Grow Short: The Life and Music of Kurt Weill.* New York: Holt, Rinehart & Winston, 1980.

Sandler, Gilbert. *Home Front Baltimore: An Album of Stories from World War II.* Baltimore: Johns Hopkins University Press, 2011.

Sanson, Jerry Purvis. *Louisiana During World War II: Politics and Society, 1939–1945.* Baton Rouge: Louisiana State University Press, 1999.

Santelli, Robert, and Emily Davidson, eds. *Hard Travelin': The Life and Legacy of Woody Guthrie.* Hanover, N.H.: Wesleyan University Press, 1999.

Schary, Dore. *Heyday: An Autobiography.* Boston: Little, Brown, 1979.

Schwartz, Charles. *Cole Porter: A Biography.* New York: Dial Press, 1977.

Sheehan, Marion Turner, ed. *The World at Home: Selections from the Writings of Anne O'Hare McCormick.* New York: Alfred A. Knopf, 1956.

Sherman, Susan, ed. *Dear Juliette: Letters of May Sarton to Juliette Huxley.* New York: W. W. Norton, 1999.

———. *May Sarton: Selected Letters, 1916–1954.* New York: W. W. Norton, 1997.

Shipton, Alyn. *Hi-De-Ho: The Life of Cab Calloway.* New York: Oxford University Press, 2010.

Shogan, Robert, and Tom Craig. *The Detroit Race Riot: A Study in Violence.* Philadelphia: Chilton Books, 1964.

Simeone, Nigel, ed. *The Leonard Bernstein Letters.* New Haven, Conn.: Yale University Press, 2013.

Sinclair, Andrew. *John Ford.* New York: Dial Press, 1979.

Sitton, Tom. *Los Angeles Transformed: Fletcher Bowron's Urban Reform Revival, 1938–1953.* Albuquerque: University of New Mexico Press, 2005.

Smith, Richard Norton. *Thomas E. Dewey and His Times.* New York: Simon & Schuster, 1982.

Sparrow, James T. *Warfare State: World War II Americans and the Age of Big Government.* New York: Oxford University Press, 2011.

Sperber, A. M., and Eric Lax. *Bogart.* New York: William Morrow, 1997.

Spinney, Robert G. *World War II in Nashville: Transformation of the Homefront.* Knoxville: University of Tennessee Press, 1998.

Stevens, Holly, ed. *Letters of Wallace Stevens.* Berkeley: University of California Press, 1996.

Stravinsky, Vera, and Robert Craft. *Stravinsky in Pictures and Documents.* New York: Simon & Schuster, 1978.

Streitmatter, Rodger, ed. *Empty Without You: The Intimate Letters of Eleanor Roosevelt and Lorena Hickok.* New York: Free Press, 1998.

Strout, Richard L. *TRB: Views and Perspectives on the Presidency.* New York: Macmillan, 1979.

Stuhlmann, Gunther, ed. *Henry Miller Letters to Anaïs Nin.* New York: Paragon House, 1988.

Sudhalter, Richard M. *Stardust Melody: The Life and Music of Hoagy Carmichael.* New York: Oxford University Press, 2002.

Swanson, Gloria. *Swanson on Swanson.* New York: Random House, 1980.

Symonette, Lys, and Kim H. Kowalke, eds. *Speak Low (When You Speak Love): The Letters of Kurt Weill and Lotte Lenya.* Berkeley: University of California Press, 1996.

Taylor, Benjamin. *Saul Bellow: Letters.* New York: Viking, 2010.

Teachout, Terry. *Pops: A Life of Louis Armstrong.* Boston: Houghton Mifflin Harcourt, 2009.

Terkel, Studs. *"The Good War": An Oral History of World War Two.* New York: Pantheon Books, 1984.

Thompson, Lawrence, ed. *Selected Letters of Robert Frost.* New York: Holt, Rinehart & Winston, 1964.

Townsend, Charles R. *San Antonio Rose: The Life and Music of Bob Wills*. Urbana: University of Illinois Press, 1976.

Troyan, Michael. *A Rose for Mrs. Miniver: The Life of Greer Garson*. Lexington: University Press of Kentucky, 1999.

Tully, Grace. *FDR: My Boss*. New York: Charles Scribner's Sons, 1949.

Utley, Jonathan G. *Going to War with Japan, 1937–1941*. Knoxville: University of Tennessee Press, 1985.

Veeck, Bill, with Ed Linn. *Veeck—As in Wreck*. Chicago: University of Chicago Press, 1962.

Vorse, Mary Heaton. *Time and the Town: A Provincetown Chronicle*. New Brunswick, N.J.: Rutgers University Press, 1991.

Wainwright, Loudon. *The Great American Magazine: An Inside History of "Life."* New York: Alfred A. Knopf, 1986.

Walsh, Stephen. *Stravinsky: The Second Exile, France and America, 1934–1971*. New York: Alfred A. Knopf, 2006.

Wapshott, Nicholas. *The Sphinx: Franklin Roosevelt, the Isolationists, and the Road to World War II*. New York: W. W. Norton, 2015.

Warren, Earl. *The Memoirs of Earl Warren*. Garden City, N.Y.: Doubleday, 1977.

Watkins T. H. *Righteous Pilgrim: The Life and Times of Harold L. Ickes, 1874–1952*. New York: Henry Holt, 1990.

Watts, Steven. *The People's Tycoon: Henry Ford and the American Century*. New York: Alfred A. Knopf, 2005.

Weber, Karl, ed. *The Best of I. F. Stone*. New York: Public Affairs, 2006.

Wells, Donald R. *Baseball's Western Front: The Pacific Coast League During World War II*. Jefferson, N.C.: McFarland, 2004.

White, E. B. *One Man's Meat*. New York: Harper & Row, 1944.

White, G. Edward. *Earl Warren: A Public Life*. New York: Oxford University Press, 1982.

Wilder, Robin G., and Jackson R. Bryer, eds. *The Selected Letters of Thornton Wilder*. New York: HarperCollins, 2008.

Williams, Mason B. *City of Ambition: FDR, La Guardia, and the Making of Modern New York*. New York: W. W. Norton, 2013.

Williams, Tom. *A Mysterious Something in the Light: The Life of Raymond Chandler*. Chicago: Chicago Review Press, 2013.

Wilson, Elena, ed. *Edmund Wilson: Letters on Literature and Politics, 1912–1972*. New York: Farrar, Straus & Giroux, 1977.

Winnick, R. H. *Letters of Archibald MacLeish, 1907 to 1982*. Boston: Houghton Mifflin, 1983.

Wyatt, Wilson W., Sr. *Whistle Stops: Adventures in Public Life*. Lexington: University Press of Kentucky, 1985.

# Index